Multi–Objective Stochastic Programming in Fuzzy Environments

Animesh Biswas
University of Kalyani, India

Arnab Kumar De
Government College of Engineering and Textile Technology Serampore, India

A volume in the Advances
in Computer and Electrical
Engineering (ACEE) Book Series

Published in the United States of America by
    IGI Global
    Engineering Science Reference (an imprint of IGI Global)
    701 E. Chocolate Avenue
    Hershey PA, USA 17033
    Tel: 717-533-8845
    Fax: 717-533-8661
    E-mail: cust@igi-global.com
    Web site: http://www.igi-global.com

Library of Congress Cataloging-in-Publication Data

Names: Biswas, Animesh, author.
Title: Multi-objective stochastic programming in fuzzy environments / by
  Animesh Biswas and Arnab Kumar De.
Description: Hershey, PA : Engineering Science Reference, an imprint of IGI
  Global, [2019] | Includes bibliographical references.
Identifiers: LCCN 2018050681| ISBN 9781522583011 (hardcover) | ISBN
  9781522583028 (ebook)
Subjects: LCSH: Multiple criteria decision making. | Fuzzy decision making.
Classification: LCC T57.95 .B58 2019 | DDC 519.5/42--dc23 LC record available at https://lccn.
loc.gov/2018050681

This book is published in the IGI Global book series Advances in Computer and Electrical Engineering (ACEE) (ISSN: 2327-039X; eISSN: 2327-0403)

British Cataloguing in Publication Data
A Cataloguing in Publication record for this book is available from the British Library.

All work contributed to this book is new, previously-unpublished material.
The views expressed in this book are those of the authors, but not necessarily of the publisher.

For electronic access to this publication, please contact: eresources@igi-global.com.

Advances in Computer and Electrical Engineering (ACEE) Book Series

ISSN:2327-039X
EISSN:2327-0403

Editor-in-Chief: Srikanta Patnaik, SOA University, India

MISSION

The fields of computer engineering and electrical engineering encompass a broad range of interdisciplinary topics allowing for expansive research developments across multiple fields. Research in these areas continues to develop and become increasingly important as computer and electrical systems have become an integral part of everyday life.

The **Advances in Computer and Electrical Engineering (ACEE) Book Series** aims to publish research on diverse topics pertaining to computer engineering and electrical engineering. **ACEE** encourages scholarly discourse on the latest applications, tools, and methodologies being implemented in the field for the design and development of computer and electrical systems.

COVERAGE

- Optical Electronics
- Chip Design
- Computer Architecture
- Microprocessor Design
- Qualitative Methods
- Analog Electronics
- Programming
- VLSI Design
- Computer Hardware
- Computer Science

IGI Global is currently accepting manuscripts for publication within this series. To submit a proposal for a volume in this series, please contact our Acquisition Editors at Acquisitions@igi-global.com or visit: http://www.igi-global.com/publish/.

Titles in this Series

For a list of additional titles in this series, please visit:
https://www.igi-global.com/book-series/advances-computer-electrical-engineering/73675

Code Generation, Analysis Tools, and Testing for Quality
Ricardo Alexandre Peixoto de Queirós (Polytechnic Institute of Porto, Portugal) Alberto Simões (Polytechnic Institute of Cávado and Ave, Portugal) and Mário Teixeira Pinto (Polytechnic Institute of Porto, Portugal)
Engineering Science Reference • ©2019 • 288pp • H/C (ISBN: 9781522574552) • US $205.00

Global Virtual Enterprises in Cloud Computing Environments
N. Raghavendra Rao (FINAIT Consultancy Services, India)
Engineering Science Reference • ©2019 • 281pp • H/C (ISBN: 9781522531821) • US $215.00

Advancing Consumer-Centric Fog Computing Architectures
Kashif Munir (University of Hafr Al-Batin, Saudi Arabia)
Engineering Science Reference • ©2019 • 217pp • H/C (ISBN: 9781522571490) • US $210.00

New Perspectives on Information Systems Modeling and Design
António Miguel Rosado da Cruz (Polytechnic Institute of Viana do Castelo, Portugal) and Maria Estrela Ferreira da Cruz (Polytechnic Institute of Viana do Castelo, Portugal)
Engineering Science Reference • ©2019 • 332pp • H/C (ISBN: 9781522572718) • US $235.00

Advanced Methodologies and Technologies in Network Architecture, Mobile Computing, ...
Mehdi Khosrow-Pour, D.B.A. (Information Resources Management Association, USA)
Engineering Science Reference • ©2019 • 1857pp • H/C (ISBN: 9781522575986) • US $595.00

Emerging Innovations in Microwave and Antenna Engineering
Jamal Zbitou (University of Hassan 1st, Morocco) and Ahmed Errkik (University of Hassan 1st, Morocco)
Engineering Science Reference • ©2019 • 437pp • H/C (ISBN: 9781522575399) • US $245.00

Advanced Methodologies and Technologies in Artificial Intelligence, Computer Simulation, ...
Mehdi Khosrow-Pour, D.B.A. (Information Resources Management Association, USA)
Engineering Science Reference • ©2019 • 1221pp • H/C (ISBN: 9781522573685) • US $545.00

For an entire list of titles in this series, please visit:
https://www.igi-global.com/book-series/advances-computer-electrical-engineering/73675

701 East Chocolate Avenue, Hershey, PA 17033, USA
Tel: 717-533-8845 x100 • Fax: 717-533-8661
E-Mail: cust@igi-global.com • www.igi-global.com

This Book is dedicated to:
Sri Saroj Kumar Biswas (Uncle of Dr. Animesh Biswas)
Late Asim Kumar De (Uncle of Dr. Arnab Kumar De)
For their devotions in the way of our lives

Table of Contents

Section 2
Applications

Preface

The purpose of this book is to demonstrate comprehensively and constructively the methodological developments of multi-objective programming models in probabilistically as well as possibilistically uncertain decision making environments. Due to increasing complexities in modern society (considering social, environmental and economic conditions), it is necessary to develop multi-objective optimization tools rather than considering single objective only. A class of optimization problems, identified as multi-objective optimization problems, is associated with several objectives subject to the conditions that those satisfy some set of system constraints whose parameters are generally described precisely on the basis of decision makers' understanding of the nature of the problems. There are several techniques to solve these kinds of optimization problems and also there are number of real-life decision-making applications that happen in our daily life.

In most of the decision-making models, it is frequently observed that the decision makers fail to gather enough information about the parameters associated with the model. Thus the parameters associated with the decision making processes are articulated imprecisely, i.e., optimization problems involved with some kinds of imprecision and uncertainty. As a consequence, the traditional classical tools that are used to solve classical optimization problems become inefficient to provide satisfactory solutions in imprecise decision-making situations.

The multi-objective optimization problems under uncertainties can be handled efficiently using probability theory and fuzzy set theory. Optimization problems including multiple objectives, with parameters involving probabilistic uncertainties are termed as multi-objective stochastic programming problems, where as if those involve fuzzy or possibilistic uncertainties are known as multi-objective fuzzy programming problems.

In multi-objective stochastic programming models some or all the parameters associated with the problems are expressed in terms of random variables rather than by deterministic quantities to capture the probabilistic uncertainties as much as possible. The main concepts of stochastic programming are to convert the probabilistic nature of the problem into an equivalent deterministic state through some methodologies.

Again, in multi-objective fuzzy programming imprecision or vagueness inherently involved with the parameters associated with the problems. In this situation the uncertain parameters of the problems are expressed in terms of fuzzy sets, more specifically, fuzzy numbers, instead of crisp numbers.

In real-world decision-making situations it is significantly observed that there are various practical decision making situations where both type of uncertainties i.e., probabilistic and possibilistic uncertainties occurs simultaneously. As a consequence, it is necessary to capture both type uncertainties at the same time. This type of hybrid uncertain situation can be tackled successfully by introducing the concept of multi-objective fuzzy stochastic programming models. In multi-objective fuzzy stochastic programming the notion of fuzzy random variables are introduced through which both uncertainties can be captured proficiently.

The main objective of this book is to explore some emerging concepts on decision making models with simultaneous consideration of fuzzy as well as stochastic uncertainties in a simpler and systematic manner so that it can easily be understandable to the readers. The readers will also be highly benefited to learn these emerging areas which in turn motivate them to apply these developed methodologies in their own research fields. The methodologies conferred in this book are very much innovative and relevant with the current decision-making scenario. These methodologies are explained elaborately, and the models are validated by providing various numerical examples which will grow interests to the readers to apply the methodology in related areas. Different types of probability distributions are considered in this book so that the method is easily comprehensible to the readers. Also, different types of fuzzy numbers and different defuzzification techniques are used in this book. Several theories relating to fuzzy stochastic fractional programming, fuzzy stochastic multi-objective programming and fuzzy stochastic non-linear programming which are emerging topics for future researchers are discussed in this book elaborately. Priority based fuzzy goal programming or weighted fuzzy goal programming techniques are applied to obtain best optimal values of the multiple objectives which are unique contributions in this book.

The content of this book is consisting of 10 chapters which are divided into two parts, viz., methodological developments and applications. Chapter 1 is introductory in nature and consists of historical backgrounds and literature review of the allied areas of the book. In the subsequent six chapters, contained in Section 1 of the book, methodologies for solving mathematical programming problems in the context of multi-objective decision making in fuzzy stochastic environments are discussed elaborately. Section 2 consists of three chapters presenting some real life applications. In these chapters the innovative methodologies developed in part I of this book are used for solving several real-world decision-making problems.

The contents of the 10 chapters of the book are presented here briefly. Starting from historical development on multi-objective decision making in probabilistic and possibilistic environments, some fundamental concepts which are essential for the readers for better understanding of the book are briefly discussed in the first two chapters of the book. A concise discussions on the existing optimization tools, viz., chance constrained programming, goal programming, fuzzy goal programming, fuzzy chance constrained programming, etc. are presented. The basic concepts of probability theory, fuzzy set theory, fuzzy random variables which are used for the development of various mathematical models are briefly recapitulated for the readers. The basic operations on fuzzy sets, different types of fuzzy numbers are further elaborated. Different defuzzification processes of fuzzy numbers and mathematical formulation of different defuzzification techniques are also discussed in detail in Chapter 2.

The main contribution of this book starts from Chapter 3. Different forms of multi-objective linear stochastic programming models considering various probability distributions in fuzzy uncertain environment are discussed in this chapter. The authors demonstrate the variation that occurs in stochastic mathematical programming models with the change of different forms of continuous probability distributions. Different defuzzification processes those are presented in the preceding chapter are taken into consideration to develop various multi-objective linear programming models in crisp environment. Fuzzy goal programming methodologies are used to find the compromise solution in multi-objective decision-making context. Some numerical examples are illustrated in this chapter to make the developed methodologies easily understandable to the readers.

Chapter 4 deals with multi-objective fractional programming models in fuzzy stochastic environment. The authors present two different forms of fractional programming in this chapter, in which some uncertain parameters are expressed either in terms of fuzzy numbers or in terms of fuzzy random variables. Different fuzzy approaches are used in this chapter to find the compromise solution of the objectives. Numerical examples are provided and solved using the methodologies developed in this chapter. Finally, the compromise solutions obtained by these methodologies are compared to the solutions obtained by some existing methodologies to establish the superiority of the presented methodologies over some predefined methodologies proposed by other renowned researchers.

In the fifth chapter the authors try to develop two stochastic quadratic programming models in fuzzy uncertain environment involving multiple objectives. In the first model based on the $\alpha -$ cut of fuzzy numbers the model involving fuzzy parameters are converted into interval parameter quadratic programming model. Then the concepts of fuzzy partial order relations are implemented to form an equivalent deterministic model. Defuzzification procedure of FNs is employed in the second model to form the multi-objective quadratic programming in crisp environment. Two linearization techniques are incorporated to the non-linear programming models to form an equivalent linear programming model. Numerical examples are provided to demonstrate the methodologies presented in this chapter.

In Chapter 6 the authors propose the methodological development of fully fuzzified linear programming model in which not only the parameters but also the variables are expressed in terms of fuzzy numbers. The expectation and variance model of the objectives are developed in this chapter. In the expectation model the objectives, with expected value of the parameters, are maximized, whereas in case of variance model the objectives, involving variance value of the parameters, are minimized. To form the corresponding deterministic model a ranking function of fuzzy numbers is considered in this chapter and finally weighted fuzzy goal programming methodology is fired to find the most acceptable solution of all the objectives.

The authors in Chapter 7 suggest a methodology through which a multi-objective stochastic programming following joint probability distribution in fuzzy uncertain environment can be solved proficiently. At first the chance constrained programming methodology is applied in joint probabilistic decision-making environment and then a defuzzification process of fuzzy numbers is employed to each fuzzy parameters of the fuzzy programming model to form an optimization model in crisp environment. Finally, in the concluding part of this chapter numerical examples are provided for the readers for their better understanding of the methodology highlighted in this chapter.

In the second part of this book three chapters are provided in which the methodologies described in the earlier chapters are applied to solve real-life decision-making problems in the field of solid waste management, transportation problem and the allocation of lands in agricultural sectors.

Chapter 8 presents an application of the multi-objective fuzzy stochastic linear programming models; those were discussed in chapter 3, in the context of municipal solid waste management. In this chapter the authors explain the necessity of considering uncertain parameters of the waste management models and how these parameters are expressed in the form of either fuzzy numbers or fuzzy random variables following continuous probability distribution. The deterministic model of the solid waste management model involving uncertain parameters is constructed on the basis of the tolerance of the fuzzy numbers. In the final section of this chapter a modified form of hypothetical case example, studied earlier, is considered and solved using the developed methodology to exemplify the validity of the presented methodology.

Chapter 9 presents an unbalanced multi-choice, multi-objective stochastic transportation problem in fuzzy uncertain environment. In this chapter the authors present how the uncertainties concerning supplies and demands of the products at the origins and destinations, respectively, and the capacity of the conveyances can be resolved using either fuzzy numbers or fuzzy random variables with some known continuous fuzzy probability distributions. A multi-objective fuzzy stochastic linear programming model is developed in this chapter to express the transportation model. The chance constrained programming methodology and defuzzification process of fuzzy numbers are used step by step to form an equivalent multi-objective transportation model in crisp environment. In the last part of this chapter numerical examples representing hypothetical transportation problems are provided for the sake of illustrate the methodology presented in this chapter.

Finally, in Chapter 10, a fuzzy multi-objective stochastic programming model is applied for planning of proper allocation of lands in agricultural sectors. A weighted fuzzy goal programming methodology is implemented in this chapter to develop a model, from which a suitable solution is obtained, i.e., the authors present a solution technique that provides the solution for proper utilization of agricultural lands considering several uncertain parameters associated with the model. The potential use of this methodology is illustrated through a case study of the Nadia District, West Bengal, India, in the context of land allocation problems. Finally, the achieved solution is compared to the existing land allocation to demonstrate the acceptance of the methodology presented in this chapter.

It is expected that this book may become useful for the following groups based on their specific objectives. Primarily, the graduate, post graduate students, research scholars and research practitioners, academicians will be highly benefited from this book. Again, from the view point of potential applications of the methodologies of this proposed book, several architects or application developers may prepare different software to apply those techniques in some relevant fields. From the unique real-world applications which are discussed in this book may attract different project managers, government agencies, NGOs to adopt the methodologies in their own arena. After learning the methodologies based on different uncertain situations, the readers must be interested to apply them in various decision-making situations where the probabilistic and imprecise uncertainties occur, simultaneously. The presented case studies may also help different project managers, government agencies, NGOs for better utilization of resources.

Thus, it is hoped that the proposed publication may open up new vistas into the way of making decision in a stochastically defined fuzzily uncertain decision-making arena.

The authors remain grateful to Prof. Bijay Baran Pal, Ex-Professor, Department of Mathematics, University of Kalyani, Dr. Nilkanta Modak and Dr. Bhola Nath Moitra, Past Research Students of the Department of Mathematics, University of Kalyani, India for their active support in different research phases of the development of this book. Finally, the authors are very much thankful to the editorial team of IGI Global, especially the development editors Ms. Jordan Tepper, Ms. Jan Travers and Ms. Courtney Tychinski, for providing truly professional assistance, expert advice, and continuous encouragement during the realization of this project.

Animesh Biswas
University of Kalyani, India

Arnab Kumar De
Government College of Engineering and Textile Technology Serampore, India

Section 1
Methodological Developments

Chapter 1
Introduction and Historical Background

ABSTRACT

This chapter describes the evolution of different multi-objective decision-making (MODM) models with their historical backgrounds. Starting from MODM models in deterministic environments along with various solution techniques, the chapter presents how different kinds of uncertainties may be associated with such decision-making models. Among several types of uncertainties, it has been found that probabilistic and possibilistic uncertainties are of special interests. A brief literature survey on different existing methods to solve those types of uncertainties, independently, is discussed and focuses on the need of considering simultaneous occurrence of those types of uncertainties in MODM contexts. Finally, a bibliographic survey on several approaches for MODM under hybrid fuzzy environments has been presented. Through this chapter the readers can be able to get some concepts about the historical development of MODM models in hybrid fuzzy environments and their importance in solving various real-life problems in the current complex decision-making arena.

1.1 INTRODUCTION TO MULTI-OBJECTIVE DECISION MAKING

In every aspect of daily life human beings are taking decisions to make their surroundings more comfortable for living and to fulfill their needs and desires so that the world becomes more compatible for the future inhabitants. To tackle complex situations, most of the times it becomes inevitable to use some

DOI: 10.4018/978-1-5225-8301-1.ch001

decision making tools for taking proper resolutions. Optimization theory may be regarded as one such decision making tool for taking successful decisions. In real life it is frequently observed that most of the decision making problems involve several objectives and the aim of the decision makers is to find best decisions by fulfilling aspiration levels of all the objectives. Optimization problems involving several conflicting objectives are termed as multi-objective programming (MOP) problems or multi-objective decision making (MODM). MOP is also treated as an area of multiple criteria decision making that concerned with mathematical optimization problems involving more than one objective. MODM is especially suitable for the design and planning steps and allows a decision maker to achieve the optimal or aspired goals by considering the various interactions of the given constraints.

Mathematically, a multi-objective optimization problem can be formulated as

Optimize

$$f(x) = (f_1(x), f_2(x), ..., f_K(x))$$

satisfying the conditions

$$g_i(x) \leq or = or \geq b_i \, ; \ i = 1, 2, ..., m$$

where x is an n dimensional vector and $K \geq 2$.

In the following section historical backgrounds on MODM problems with its various solution procedures are discussed.

1.2 HISTORICAL DEVELOPMENTS OF MULTI-OBJECTIVE DECISION MAKING

The concept of optimization theory in MODM was introduced by Kuhn and Tucker (1951). Thereafter, Charnes (1952) extended the concept and developed a methodology for solving optimization problems with several conflicting objectives. Subsequently, several researchers (Arrow et al., 1958; Charnes and Cooper, 1961; Briskin, 1966; Cochrane and Zeleny, 1973; Steuer 1977; Leitmann, 1976; Keeney and Raiffa 1976) made a significant impact in the field of MODM. Hwang and Masud (1979), Naccache (1979), Corley (1981) and other researchers scientifically classified and discussed the methodologies for solving MODM problems. Other methodological development in the field of optimization problems were presented in the books and monographs written by Goicoechea et al. (1982), Sawaragi et al. (1985), Yu (1985) and others. Due to the significant contribution of the pioneer researchers (Chiang and Tzeng, 2000; Chiou and Tzeng, 2003; Yu et al., 2004; Tzeng et al., 2007; Faulkenberg, 2009; Baky, 2010; Huang et al., 2012) MODM problems were applied to various real life decision making problems. Recently, Qu et al. (2018) developed an efficient multi-objective evolutionary algorithm as an effective tool to solve highly constrained complex bi-objective optimization problems.

In mathematical programming with multiple objectives it is not always possible to attain the best value of all the objectives simultaneously because of their conflicting nature. Therefore, some computational procedures are needed for achieving the solutions by negotiation of the objectives as much as possible. These solutions are termed as compromise solution in MODM context. There are several computational techniques available in optimization theory for finding compromise solutions of MODM problems. Some of the methods are highlighted in this chapter as follows:

1. Weighted Sum Method
2. Compromise Programming
3. Interactive Method
4. Goal Programming (GP)

1.2.1 Weighted Sum Method

The weighted sum method (Belaïd and Martel, 2005; Stacey, 2009) is the simplest approach and probably the most widely used classical method in the context of MODM. In weighted sum method the weighting coefficients corresponding to the objectives are to be selected and then the set of objectives are converted into a single objective by multiplying each objective with the weighted coefficient.

1.2.2 Compromise Programming

The concept of compromise programming method or global criterion method was introduced by Zeleny (1973). Thereafter, Yu and Leitmann (1974), Gearhart (1979), and other researchers studied and extended the methodology in an intensive manner. The basic idea of compromise programming is to find a point in the feasible set for which objective values is close to some ideal point for a given distance (Voorneveld et al., 2008). Rao (1996) describing the global criterion method as an interesting strategy. According to Rao (1996) the global criterion method can be characterized as a strategy in which the optimal solution is found by minimizing a pre-selected global criterion.

1.2.3 Interactive Method

In many MODM problems it is observed that the decision makers do not have a complete idea about the desired performance level over a set of objectives. In this situation it is suitable to rely on the progressive definition of the decision makers' preferences along with the exploration of the criterion space. Interactive method is an iterative method. In this method decision makers continuously interact while searching for the most preferred solution. Like other iterative processes, interactive methods contain some basic steps. At first the initial solution is guessed by the decision makers. After that an improved solution is evaluated based on the iterative process. If the decision maker is satisfied, then the process stops. Otherwise, another improved solution is needed and the process continues.

Several interactive methods exist in the literature out of which the sequential proxy optimization technique introduced by Sakawa (2009) and the reference point method (Wierzbicki, 1998) are most commonly used.

1.2.4 Goal Programming Method

GP method is the mostly used tool in solving multi-objective optimization problems. In GP, target level of each objective and relative importance of achieving that target level are assigned. GP aims to find an optimal solution that comes as close as possible to the target values. One significant difference between GP methodology and other methodologies is that it uses goal constraints in addition to system constraints. Generally, in GP the following three types of analysis are performed:

1. Determine the required resources to achieve a desired set of objective values.
2. Determine the degree of attainment of the goals with the available resources.

3.   Providing the best satisfying solution under a varying amount of resources and priorities of the goals.

The concept of GP was first introduced by Charnes, Cooper and Ferguson (1955), although the actual name GP was first appeared in a text by Charnes and Cooper (1961). The most famous and important reviews of GP approach are found in the works of Charnes, Cooper and Ijiri (1963), Lee (1973), Ignizio (1978), Zanakis and Gupta (1985), Romero (1985), Ignizio and Cavalier (1994), Schniederjans (1995), Saber and Ravindran (1996), Tamiz et. al. (1999). After successful development of GP methodology, several researchers (Charnes and Storbeck, 1980; Kvanli, 1980; Dobbins and Mapp, 1982; Taylor et al., 1982; Dryzan, 1985; Rehman and Romero, 1987) applied this concept in solving different real life MODM problems.

In the next section optimization theories are discussed systematically under various uncertain environments.

1.3 UNCERTAINTY ARISES IN MULTI-OBJECTIVE DECISION MAKING

Due to the presence of linguistic information and vague data set, and also due to lack of sufficient knowledge of the decision makers about the parameters, almost every real life decision making problems involve some amount of uncertainties. Although, numerous computational techniques exist in the literature for solving optimization problems in crisp environments, but these solution methodologies fail to handle properly such types of optimization problems under various uncertainties. Therefore, it is a challenging task to the researchers to develop several scientific techniques through which mathematical programming models under uncertainties can be solved efficiently. Optimization under uncertainty refers to a new branch of optimization due to its huge application in real life decision making problems. Uncertainty can be described in several ways based on the availability of information. Generally, probability theory and fuzzy set theory are the most common and efficient tools through which various uncertainties in MODM problems are resolved properly. Dubois and Prade (1980) pointed out the importance of pondering uncertain quantification in complex systems. With the development of different computational approaches and scientific computing techniques, optimization models involving uncertainties (Zhou et al., 1996; Arnuautu et al., 2005; Pachter and Sturmfels, 2007) can be solved efficiently. Accessible accounts of these tools may be found in the works of Shafer (1976), Sakawa (1993), Shiryaer (1996), Liu (2007) and others. A group of MODM problems with uncertainty can be solved using stochastic programming methodology. In contrast, imprecision in decision making problems can be handled through fuzzy programming methodology. Researchers in the past decades showed their greater interests and the research progressed in the fields of stochastic optimization (Vajda, 1972; Kall, 1976; Kall and Wallace, 1994; Schultz and Tiedemann, 2006; Wagner, 2008) and fuzzy mathematical techniques (Zimmermann, 1976; Luhandjula, 1989; Lai and Hwang, 1992; Bhaskar et al., 2004) at a rapid speed.

1.3.1 Probabilistic Uncertainty in Decision Making

It is already known to us that the parameters in mathematical programming models of the objectives as well as the constraints are not always precise in nature. Some level of uncertainty about the layout of the problem components or about the values to be assigned to various parameters exists in most of the practical decision making problems. For example in the context of managing working capital of a firm, it is realistic to express the level of sales parameters in terms of random variables. Again, in solid waste management (SWM) model due to its uncertain nature, the parameters representing waste generation rate, landfilling capacity are better to express in terms of random variables (discussed in chapter 8). If the parameters of the mathematical programming models are represented in terms of random variables, then the mathematical programming problems are termed as stochastic programming and the concepts of probability theory are employed there. Probabilistic programming is considered as one of the most efficient and challenging development of mathematical programming. To handle randomness in decision making, Dantzig (1955) introduced stochastic programming using the concept of probability theory. Afterwards several researchers (Ferguson and Dantzig, 1956; Kataoka, 1963; Walkup and Wets, 1967; Wets, 1974; Beale et al., 1980; Bereanu, 1980) used probability theory to capture the uncertainty in linear programming. With the assistance of probability theory, Ziemba (1971), Thompson et al. (1974) and Bereanu (1980) enriched optimization theory under uncertain environments.

Two main methodologies for solving stochastic programming problems are as follows:

1.   Two Stage Programming
2.   Chance Constrained Programming (CCP)

   A brief discussion on them is presented below.

1.3.1.1 Two Stage Programming

Beale (1955) and Dantzig (1955) introduced the concept of two stage programming for stochastic programming. Thereafter, several distinguished researchers (Madansky, 1963; Wets, 1966; Wets, 1966[a]; Sengupta, 1972; Kall, 1976) extended the methodologies of two stage programming for handling stochastic programming problems more competently.

   In two stage programming technique the stochastic programming problems are converted into its equivalent deterministic one without allowing any constraints to be violated. In this method at the initial stage, a decision has to be taken by assumption by the decision makers without knowing the values of the random variables, exactly; and then in the next stage, after the random events took place and knowing the values, a second or better decision is generated in order to minimize the penalties that may appear due to any kind of infeasibility. In 2018, Hsu et al., (2018) developed a two-stage stochastic programming model for capturing all possible demand variations on a construction site. This model is evaluated using a case study from the residential construction sector. Fathollahi-Fard and Hajiaghaei-Keshteli (2018) developed a two-stage stochastic MOP model for a closed-loop supply chain by considering the environmental aspects and downside risk, simultaneously.

1.3.1.2 Chance Constrained Programming Methodology

It is frequently observed by the decision makers that in model formulation process the occurrences of some system constraints as well as their parameters are uncertain due to lack of information about those parameters. One of the major approaches for solving these types of optimization problems is the CCP methodology. Charnes and Cooper (1959) first introduced the CCP technique to deal with uncertainties in stochastic programming models. Three models involving different objective functions and probabilistic types of constraints are suggested by Charnes and Cooper (1959). Those are presented as follows:

1.   Model that maximizes the expected value of the objective function (i.e., the E-model)

2. Model that minimizes the generalized mean square of the objective function (i.e., the V-model)
3. Model that maximizes the probability of exceeding an aspiration level of the objective function (i.e., the P-model).

Thereafter, different aspects of CCP were further investigated by Kataoka (1963), Prekopa (1970) and other researchers. The goal of CCP methodology is to convert the probabilistic nature of the stochastic programming problems into an equivalent deterministic model depending on the specified confidence levels and the nature of the distribution followed by the random variables. Contini (1978) developed a solution algorithm for stochastic programming where the random variables follow normal distribution with known mean and variances. After the successful methodological development of CCP, it had been applied to solve various real life decision making problems in which the parameters are expressed by random variables. Sharafali et al. (2004) considered a model for production scheduling in a flexible manufacturing system with stochastic demand. Wu and Ierapetritou (2007) presented a production planning and scheduling model through a hierarchical framework. A multi-objective production planning model with probabilistic constraints was developed by Sahoo and Biswal (2009). An interval-parameter dynamic CCP approach for capacity planning under uncertainty was developed by Dai et al. (2012). In a recent paper, an efficient dynamic model for solving a portfolio selection with uncertain chance constraint models is developed by Omidi et al. (2017). To implement mechanical load requirements in wind turbine controller design procedures, Cao et al. (2018) proposed stochastic programming model. In this approach the parameter representing extreme loads follows a generalized extreme value distribution.

1.3.2 Possibilistic Uncertainty in Decision Making

It has already mentioned that in formulating real life decision making problems, it is very much difficult by the experts to obtain the parameters of the model in a precise manner. Therefore, some efficient tools are to be developed to express uncertainties involved with these types of problems. Under this context, the concept of fuzzy set theory establishes its potentiality for modeling mathematical programming problems in an efficient manner. Especially, if the parameters of the mathematical programming models are not precise, only some vague or imprecise information about the parameters are given, fuzzy set theory plays a remarkable role to capture these uncertain parameters. In almost every real life examples it is observed that the parameters cannot be expressed by a definite real number, rather the observed values of the parameters are close to that real number. Thus, it is very much convenient to express these uncertain model parameters using fuzzy sets or fuzzy numbers (FNs) (this explanation is presented in chapter 2). For example, in manufacturing industry the real observations of continuous quantities are expressed in terms of FNs. Also, in agricultural land allocation problem the parameters representing the production of crops, expenditure, total machine hours etc., are expressed in terms of FNs (discussed in chapter 10). The concept of decision making in fuzzy uncertain environment was introduced first by Bellman and Zadeh (1970). Then, Tanaka et al. (1973) extended this concept for solving mathematical programming problems. After that Zimmermann (1978, 1983) presented a revolutionary work in the field of decision making with possibilistic uncertainties. Usually, the following two methodological tools are available in the literature to solve mathematical programming problems in possibilistic uncertain environments.

1. Interactive Fuzzy Satisficing Method
2. Fuzzy Programming (FP) Methodology

1.3.2.1 Interactive Fuzzy Satisficing Method

Interactive fuzzy satisficing method is an effective tool for solving MOP problems involving fuzzy uncertain parameters. In this process it is necessary to develop membership function for each objective and reference membership values and/or degrees are assigned by the decision makers. Sakawa et al. (1997) proposed an interactive fuzzy programming methodology for solving multi-objective 0-1 programming problems. Thereafter, an interactive fuzzy programming scheme for multilevel linear programming problems by eliminating the fuzzy goals of the decision variables is suggested by Sakawa et al. (1998). Also, Chakraborty et al. (2001) developed an interactive method for multi-objective linear programming problems with FNs as parameters. From an interactive MOP perspective, Sakawa (2001) formulated a solution algorithm based on genetic algorithms to derive satisficing solutions to multi-objective optimization problems with discrete decision variables. Thereafter, Biswas and Pal (2004) established a methodology for fuzzy multilevel programming problems in hierarchical decision making context.

Afterwards, for solving fuzzy MOP problems some methodologies were developed by several researchers (Perkgoz et al., 2004; Perkgoz et al., 2005; Kato et al., 2009). In recent years Ren et al. (2016) proposed an interactive programming approach for solving the fully fuzzy bilevel linear programming problem. Also, Alavidoost et al. (2016) applied interactive approach for solving bi-objective straight and U-shaped assembly line balancing problems in intuitionistic fuzzy environment. Recently, Zhao et al. (2017) developed a methodology for solving multilevel programming problems with intuitionistic fuzzy parameters using interactive fuzzy satisfying method.

1.3.2.2 Fuzzy Programming Methodology

In an optimization problem possibilistic uncertainty occurs when some sort of ambiguous data remain present in that problem and if decision makers have insufficient understanding about the nature of parameters of the problem. In fuzzy programming methodology the imprecise parameters of the optimization problem are expressed in terms of FNs to capture the uncertain situation as much as possible. Zimmermann (1978) first introduced FP methodology based on fuzzy set theory (Zadeh, 1968). Thereafter, Leberling (1980), Sakawa (1993) and other researchers took the responsibility to extend the methodological development of fuzzy programming methodology. Delgado et al. (1989) presented a solution procedure for solving fuzzy linear programming problems in which constraints involve with fuzzy inequality and the parameters are represented in terms of FNs. After that Rommelfanger (1996) proposed a model that is capable for solving fuzzy linear programming models. In 1996 Lai and Hwang (1996) introduced the concept of fuzzy sets in a hierarchical decision making context. In order to solve fuzzy linear programming problems without converting it to crisp linear programming problems, Ganesan and Veeramani (2006) proposed a new method for solving fuzzy linear programming problems. There after a plenty of work has been done from the view point of its potential application in different real life planning problems (Pal and Basu, 1996; Biswas and Pal, 2005). Ren et al., (2017) developed a multi-objective fuzzy programming model for simultaneous optimization of the use of water and land resources for irrigation under fuzzy uncertainty. Lu and Liu (2018) developed a non-linear fuzzy programming model to calculate the fuzzy signal-to-noise ratio for the assessment of the manufacturing processes with fuzzy observations.

1.3.3 Decision Making Under Hybrid Uncertainty

In the previous two subsections of this chapter the importance of considering possibilistic and probabilistic uncertainties in the field of optimization theory have been explained and a brief literature review on them has been performed. In those subsections it is highlighted that the research works were progressed by considering two specific types of uncertainties, independently. However, the researchers felt the importance of amalgamating both the uncertainties, simultaneously, under a common framework for its modeling aspects and enormous applicability in solving different real life planning problems. Mathematical programming problems with joint occurrence of possibilistic and probabilistic uncertainties are known as decision making under hybrid uncertainty. Methodological development for solving optimization problems under fuzzy stochastic uncertainties has attracted more attention in recent years to the researchers. The hybrid approaches of stochastic programming and fuzzy programming was proposed by Hulsurkar et al. (1997). Sinha et al. (1998) developed fuzzy programming approach for solving multi-objective probabilistic linear programming problems (where only right side parameters of system constraints are random variables) on the basis of Lai and Hwang's (1994) max-min approach. The methodological development were further studied and extended by Liu (2001), Luhandjula (2006), and others. A brief survey on the developments of stochastic programming models including fuzzy random variables (FRVs) is found in the work of Luhandjula (2004). Sakawa et al. (2004) suggested an interactive method for solving fuzzy multi-objective linear programming problems with parameters as random variables. Buckley (2003, 2004ᵃ, 2004ᵇ) defined fuzzy probability using FNs as parameters in probability density function and probability mass function. This approach of fuzzy probability theory is dissimilar from his predecessors and also comfortable for computational point of view. In fuzzy probability approach the fuzzy parameters are obtained from the set of confidence intervals. Like Sakawa et al., (2004), Katagiri et al. (2008) proposed an interactive method through which multi-objective linear programming problems with FRV parameters can be solved effectively. Sakawa et al., (2011) proposed computational procedure for solving fuzzy stochastic MOP problems. Das and Maiti (2013) developed a fuzzy stochastic model for solving production inventory model via optimal control method. Biswas and De (2014) proposed a methodology for solving multi-objective quadratic programming problems in fuzzy probabilistic environment. Again Modak and Biswas (2014) proposed a fuzzy programming methodology for bilevel stochastic programming problems. Biswas and De (2016) presented a fuzzy stochastic programming methodology for municipal SWM under multiple uncertainties. Recently, Suo et al. (2017) developed a fuzzy CCP methodology for planning Shanghai's energy systems. Li et al., (2018) developed a multi-stage fuzzy stochastic programming model for water resource management in which uncertainties are expressed through fuzzy sets and probability distributions. Farrokh et al., (2018) proposed a closed loop supply chain network design problem under fuzzy stochastic uncertainties. Tsao et al. (2018) developed a multi-objective stochastic programming and fuzzy programming model for use in the design of a sustainable supply chain network under uncertain conditions. Babbar and Amin (2018) proposed a multi-objective stochastic programming model for supplier selection and order allocation based on fuzzy QFD in beverages industry.

The authors in the last part of this book present the above fact by considering three real life applications in the fields of municipal SWM, land allocation in agricultural sector and transportation problems, and also discussed how various parameters of the problems comprise with uncertainties.

Now, in the last section of this chapter, a brief description of the contents of all the remaining chapters of this book has been presented.

1.4 DESCRIPTION OF CONTENTS

In this book, the authors tried to introduce and explain the latest advancements in the niche of multi-objective fuzzy stochastic optimization. After going through this chapter, Chapter 1, thoroughly, the readers can grasp the idea that the authors discussed about the historical background of multi-objective optimization, mathematical programming under probabilistic and possibilistic uncertainties and fuzzy stochastic optimization models. In the second chapter the basic definitions and preliminary ideas on probability theory and fuzzy set theory are discussed. Other chapters are constructed on the basis of the authors continuing research works. There are two parts in this book. Starting from Chapter 2 to Chapter 7, methodological development of MOP models in hybrid uncertain environments are discussed. In Chapter 8, 9, and 10, three real life applications in the field of waste management, transportation and agriculture planning are presented, respectively. Organization of each chapter (stating from Chapter 3) is briefly summarized as follows.

Chapter 3 deals with modeling multi-objective linear programming problems in fuzzy stochastic uncertain environments. In this chapter, parameters of the various models follow FRVs following different probability distributions. Different defuzzification methodologies those are presented in chapter 1 are used to develop multi-objective linear programming models in crisp environment. To illustrate the developed methodologies numerical examples are given in this chapter.

In Chapter 4 two multi-objective fractional programming models are presented in hybrid uncertain environment. The right sided parameters of the chance constraints are taken as exponentially distributed FRVs. Different fuzzy approaches are used in this chapter to find the compromise solution of the objectives.

Chapter 5 presents two fuzzy multi-objective quadratic programming models in probabilistic environment. In the first model fuzzy partial order relations are implemented to form quadratic programming model with interval parameters. Defuzzification techniques of FNs are used in the second model to form the multi-objective quadratic programming problem in crisp environment. Two linearization techniques are executed to linearize both the models presented in this chapter.

In Chapter 6 methodological developments of fully fuzzified linear programming model are discussed. The expectation and variance model are developed. Ranking function of FNs is used in this chapter and finally, weighted fuzzy goal programming (FGP) methodology is employed to find the compromise solution of the multiple objectives.

Chapter 7 demonstrates a methodology for solving fuzzy stochastic programming following joint probability distribution. At first the CCP technique and then a defuzzification technique of FNs are applied to form optimization model in crisp environment. In the concluding section of the chapter two numerical examples are presented to explain the methodology highlighted in this chapter.

In the next three chapters the above developed methodologies are applied to solve several real-life decision-making problems.

In Chapter 8 fuzzy stochastic linear programming problems that was discussed in chapter 3, are applied to municipal SWM. The associated parameters are considered as either FNs or FRVs following continuous probability distributions. On the basis of the tolerance ranges the deterministic model of the SWM model is constructed. In the final section a hypothetical case study is presented and solved to illustrate the developed methodology.

Chapter 9 presents an unbalanced multi-objective, multi-choice transportation problem in hybrid uncertain environment. The supplies of the products, demands of the products at the destinations and capacity of the conveyances are expressed as either FNs or FRVs with some known continuous fuzzy probability distributions. In the last part of the chapter numerical examples are provided for the sake of illustrating the proposed methodology presented in this chapter.

In Chapter 10 a fuzzy MOP is applied to land allocation problems in agricultural sector. Solving the FGP model presented in this chapter, a compromise solution is obtained. The potential use of this methodology is illustrated by a case example in the context of land allocation problems. Finally, the achieved solution is compared with the existing land allocation to demonstrate the acceptance of the methodology presented in this chapter.

REFERENCES

Alavidoost, M. H., Babazadeh, H., & Sayyari, S. T. (2016). An interactive fuzzy programming approach for bi-objective straight and U-shaped assembly line balancing problem. *Applied Soft Computing*, *40*, 221–235. doi:10.1016/j.asoc.2015.11.025

Arnuautu, V., Sprekels, J., & Tiba, D. (2005). Optimization problems for curved mechanical structures. *SIAM Journal on Control and Optimization*, *44*(2), 743–775. doi:10.1137/S0363012903426252

Arrow, K. J., Hurwicz, L., & Uzawa, H. (1958). *Studies in Linear and Non-Linear Programming*. Stanford, CA: Stanford University Press.

Babbar, C., & Amin, S. H. (2018). A multi-objective mathematical model integrating environmental concerns for supplier selection and order allocation based on fuzzy QFD in beverages industry. *Expert Systems with Applications*, *92*, 27–38. doi:10.1016/j.eswa.2017.09.041

Baky, I. A. (2010). Solving multi-level multi-objective linear programming problems through fuzzy goal programming approach. *Applied Mathematical Modelling*, *34*(9), 2377–2387. doi:10.1016/j.apm.2009.11.004

Beale, E. M. L. (1955). On minimizing a convex function subject to linear inequalities. *Journal of the Royal Statistical Society. Series B. Methodological*, *17*, 173–184.

Beale, E. M. L., Forrest, J. J. H., & Taylor, C. J. (1980). Multi-time-period stochastic programming. Academic Press. In M. Dempster (Ed.), *Stochastic Programming* (pp. 387–402). New York: Academic Press.

Belaïd, A., & Martel, J. M. (2005). Goal programming: Theory and applications. Information Systems and Operational Research, 42(4).

Bellman, R. E., & Zadeh, L. A. (1970). Decision making in a fuzzy environment. *Management Science, 17*(4), 141–164. doi:10.1287/mnsc.17.4.B141

Bereanu, B. (1980). Some numerical methods in stochastic linear programming under risk and uncertainty. In Stochastic programming. Academic Press.

Bhaskar, T., Sundararajan, R., & Krishnan, P. G. (2004). A fuzzy mathematical Programming approach for cross-sell optimization in retail banking. *The Journal of the Operational Research Society, 60*(5), 717–727. doi:10.1057/palgrave.jors.2602609

Biswas, A., & De, A. K. (2014). On Solving Multiobjective Quadratic Programming Problems in a Probabilistic Fuzzy Environment. *Advances in Intelligent Systems and Computing, 335*, 543–557. doi:10.1007/978-81-322-2217-0_44

Biswas, A., & De, A. K. (2016). A Fuzzy Goal Programming Approach for Solid Waste Management under Multiple Uncertainties. *Procedia Environmental Sciences, 35*, 245–256. doi:10.1016/j.proenv.2016.07.090

Biswas, A., & Pal, B. B. (2004). A Fuzzy Multilevel Programming Method for Hierarchical Decision Making. *Lecture Notes in Computer Science, 3316*, 904–911. doi:10.1007/978-3-540-30499-9_139

Biswas, A., & Pal, B. B. (2005). Application of fuzzy goal programming technique to land use planning in agricultural system. *Omega, 33*(5), 391–398. doi:10.1016/j.omega.2004.07.003

Briskin, L. E. (1966). A Method of Unifying Multiple Objective Functions. *Management Science, 12*(10), 406–416. doi:10.1287/mnsc.12.10.B406

Buckley, J. J. (2003). *New Approach and Applications, Fuzzy Probabilities.* Physica Verlag Heidelberg. doi:10.1007/978-3-642-86786-6

Buckley, J. J., & Eslami, E. (2004). Uncertain Probabilities – II. *Soft Computing, 8*(3), 193–199. doi:10.100700500-003-0263-5

Buckley, J. J., & Eslami, E. (2004). Uncertain Probabilities – III. *Soft Computing, 8*(3), 200–206. doi:10.100700500-003-0263-5

Cao, Y., Zavala, V. M., & D'Amato, F. (2018). Using stochastic programming and statistical extrapolation to mitigate long-term extreme loads in wind turbines. *Applied Energy, 230*, 1230–1241. doi:10.1016/j.apenergy.2018.09.062

Chakraborty, S., Erlebach, T., & Thiele, L. (2001). Lecture Notes in Computer Science: Vol. 2125. *On the complexity of scheduling conditional real-time code*. Springer. doi:10.1007/3-540-44634-6_5

Charnes, A. (1952). Optimality and degeneracy in linear programming. *Econometrica, 20*, 135–159. doi:10.2307/1907844

Charnes, A., & Cooper, W. W. (1959). Chance Constrained Programming. *Management Science, 6*(1), 73–79. doi:10.1287/mnsc.6.1.73

Charnes, A., & Cooper, W. W. (1961). *Management Models and Industrial Applications of Linear Programming*. New York: Wiley.

Charnes, A., Cooper, W. W., & Ferguson, R. (1955). Optimal estimation of executive compensation by linear programming. *Management Science, 1*(2), 138–151. doi:10.1287/mnsc.1.2.138

Charnes, A., Cooper, W. W., & Ijiri, Y. (1963). Break-Even Budgeting and Programming to Goals. *Journal of Accounting Research, 1*(1), 16–41. doi:10.2307/2489841

Charnes, A., & Storbeck, J. (1980). A Goal Programming Model for the Sitting of Multilevel EMS Systems. *Socio-Economic Planning Sciences, 14*(4), 155–161. doi:10.1016/0038-0121(80)90029-4 PMID:10248423

Chiang, C. I., & Tzeng, G. H. (2000). A New Efficiency Measure for DEA: Efficiency Achievement Measure Established on Fuzzy Multiple Objectives Programming. *Journal of Management, 17*(2), 369–388.

Chiou, H. K., & Tzeng, G. H. (2003). *An Extended Approach of Multicriteria Optimization for MODM Problems*. Springer. doi:10.1007/978-3-540-36510-5_13

Cochrane, J. L., & Zeleny, M. (1973). *Multiple Criteria Decision Making*. Columbia, SC: University of South Carolina Press.

Contini, B. (1978). A stochastic approach to goal programming. *Operations Research, 16*(3), 576–586. doi:10.1287/opre.16.3.576

Corley, H. W. (1981). Duality for maximizations with respect to cones. *Journal of Mathematical Analysis and Applications, 84*(2), 560–568. doi:10.1016/0022-247X(81)90188-8

Dai, C., Li, Y. P., & Huang, G. H. (2012). An interval-parameter chance-constrained dynamic programming approach for capacity planning under uncertainty. *Resources, Conservation and Recycling, 62*, 37–50. doi:10.1016/j.resconrec.2012.02.010

Dantzig, G. B. (1955). Linear programming under uncertainty. *Management Science, 1*(3-4), 197–206. doi:10.1287/mnsc.1.3-4.197

Das, B., & Maiti, M. (2013). Fuzzy stochastic inequality and equality possibility constraints and their application in a production-inventory model via optimal control method. *Journal of Computational Science, 4*(5), 360–369. doi:10.1016/j.jocs.2012.03.005

Delgado, M., Verdegay, J. L., & Vila, M. A. (1989). A general model for fuzzy linear programming. *Fuzzy Sets and Systems, 29*(1), 21–29. doi:10.1016/0165-0114(89)90133-4

Dobbins, C. L., & Mapp, H. P. (1982). A Comparison of Objective Function Structures Used in a Recursive Goal Programming Simulation Model of Farm Growth. *Southern Journal of Agricultural Economics, 14*(02), 9–16. doi:10.1017/S0081305200024766

Dryzan, R. G. (1985). Goal Programming and Multiple Criteria Decision Making in Farm Planning: An Expository Analysis – A comment. *Journal of Agricultural Economics, 36*(3), 421–424. doi:10.1111/j.1477-9552.1985.tb00189.x

Dubois, D., & Prade, H. (1980). *Fuzzy sets and systems: Theory and Applications.* Academic Press.

Farrokh, M., Azar, A., Jandaghi, G., & Ahmadi, E. (2018). A novel robust fuzzy stochastic programming for closed loop supply chain network design under hybrid uncertainty. *Fuzzy Sets and Systems, 341*, 69–91. doi:10.1016/j.fss.2017.03.019

Fathollahi-Fard, A. M., & Hajiaghaei-Keshteli, M. (2018). A stochastic multi-objective model for a closed-loop supply chain with environmental considerations. *Applied Soft Computing, 69*, 232–249. doi:10.1016/j.asoc.2018.04.055

Faulkenberg, S. L. (2009). *Quality representation in multiobjective programming*. Clemson University.

Ferguson, A. R., & Dantzig, G. B. (1956). The allocation of aircraft to routes-an example of linear programming under uncertain demand. *Management Science, 3*(1), 45–73. doi:10.1287/mnsc.3.1.45

Ganesan, K., & Veeramani, P. (2006). Fuzzy linear programs with trapezoidal fuzzy numbers. *Annals of Operations Research, 143*(1), 305–315. doi:10.100710479-006-7390-1

Gearhart, W. B. (1979). Compromise Solutions and Estimation of the Non-Inferior Set. *Journal of Optimization Theory and Applications, 28*(1), 29–47. doi:10.1007/BF00933599

Goicoechea, A., Hansen, D. R., & Duckstein, L. (1982). *Multiobjective Decision Analysis with Engineering and Business Applications*. New York: Wiley.

Hsu, P. Y., Angeloudis, P., & Aurisicchio, M. (2018). Optimal logistics planning for modular construction using two-stage stochastic programming. *Automation in Construction, 94*, 47–61. doi:10.1016/j.autcon.2018.05.029

Huang, C. Y., Tzeng, G. H., Chen, Y. T., & Chen, H. (2012). Performance Evaluation of Leading Fabless Integrated Circuit Design Houses by Using a Multiple Objective Programming Based Data Envelopment Analysis Approach. *International Journal of Innovative Computing, Information, & Control, 8*(8), 5899–5916.

Hulsurkar, S., Biswal, M. P., & Shinha, S. B. (1997). Fuzzy Programming Approach to Multi-Objective Stochastic Linear Programming Problems. *Fuzzy Sets and Systems, 88*(2), 173–181. doi:10.1016/S0165-0114(96)00056-5

Hwang, L., & Masud, A. S. M. (1979). *Multiple Objective Decision Making – Methods and Applications*. Berlin: Springer-Verlag. doi:10.1007/978-3-642-45511-7

Ignizio, J. P. (1978). A Review of Goal Programming: A Tool for Multiobjective Analysis. *The Journal of the Operational Research Society, 29*(11), 1109–1119. doi:10.1057/jors.1978.243

Ignizio, J. P., & Cavalier, T. M. (1994). *Linear programming*. Prentice Hall.

Kall, P. (1976). *Stochastic linear programming. In Econometrices and Operations Research.* Berlin: Springer.

Kall, P., & Wallace, S. W. (1994). *Stochastic Programming.* Chichester, UK: John Wiley & Sons.

Katagiri, H., Sakawa, M., Kato, K., & Nishizaki, I. (2008). Interactive Multiobjective Fuzzy Random Linear Programming: Maximization of Possibility and Probability. *European Journal of Operational Research, 188*(2), 530–539. doi:10.1016/j.ejor.2007.02.050

Kataoka, S. (1963). A stochastic programming model. *Econometrica, 31*(1/2), 181–196. doi:10.2307/1910956

Kato, K., Sakawa, M., & Katagiri, H. (2009). Interactive fuzzy programming based on expectation optimization and variance minimization for two level stochastic linear programming problems. *KES Journal, 13*, 111–118. doi:10.3233/KES-2009-0179

Keeney, R. L., & Raiffa, H. (1976). *Decisions with Multiple Objectives.* New York: Wiley.

Kuhn, H. W., & Tucker, A. W. (1951). Nonlinear programming. *Proceedings of the Second Berkeley Symposium on Mathematical Statistics and Probability*, 481-492.

Kvanli, A. H. (1980). Financial planning using goal programming. *Omega, 8*(2), 207–218. doi:10.1016/0305-0483(80)90025-0

Lai, Y. J., & Hwang, C. L. (1992). *Fuzzy mathematical programming.* Berlin: Springer. doi:10.1007/978-3-642-48753-8

Lai, Y. J., & Hwang, C. L. (1994). *Fuzzy Multiple Objective Decision Making: Methods and Applications.* Berlin: Springer Verlag. doi:10.1007/978-3-642-57949-3

Lai, Y. J., & Hwang, C. L. (1996). *Fuzzy Mathematical Programming Methods and Applications.* Springer.

Leberling, H. (1980). On finding compromise solution in multicriteria problems using the fuzzy min-operator. *Fuzzy Sets and Systems, 6*(2), 105–118. doi:10.1016/0165-0114(81)90019-1

Lee, S. M. (1973). Goal programming for decision analysis of multiple objectives. *Sloan Management Review, 14*, 11–24.

Leitmann, G. (1976). *Multicriteria Decision Making and Differential Games*. New York: Plenum. doi:10.1007/978-1-4615-8768-2

Li, C., Cai, Y., & Qian, J. (2018). A multi-stage fuzzy stochastic programming method for water resources management with the consideration of ecological water demand. *Ecological Indicators*, *95*, 930–938. doi:10.1016/j.ecolind.2018.07.029

Liu, B. (2001). Fuzzy random chance-constrained programming. *IEEE Transactions on Fuzzy Systems*, *9*(5), 713–720. doi:10.1109/91.963757

Liu, B. (2007). *Uncertain Theory* (2nd ed.). Berlin: Springer-Verlag.

Lu, T., & Liu, S. T. (2018). Fuzzy nonlinear programming approach to the evaluation of manufacturing processes. *Engineering Applications of Artificial Intelligence*, *72*, 183–189. doi:10.1016/j.engappai.2018.04.003

Luhandjula, M. K. (1989). Fuzzy Optimization: An appraisal. *Fuzzy Sets and Systems*, *30*(3), 257–282. doi:10.1016/0165-0114(89)90019-5

Luhandjula, M. K. (2004). Optimization under Hybrid Uncertainty. *Fuzzy Sets and Systems*, *146*(2), 187–203. doi:10.1016/j.fss.2004.01.002

Luhandjula, M. K. (2006). Fuzzy Stochastic linear programming: Survey and future research directions. *European Journal of Operational Research*, *174*(3), 1353–1367. doi:10.1016/j.ejor.2005.07.019

Madansky, A. (1963). Tests of homogeneity for correlated samples. *Journal of the American Statistical Association*, *58*(301), 97–119. doi:10.1080/01621459.1963.10500835

Modak, N., & Biswas, A. (2014). A Fuzzy Programming Approach for Bilevel Stochastic Programming. *Advances in Intelligent Systems and Computing*, *236*, 125–136. doi:10.1007/978-81-322-1602-5_14

Naccache, P. H. (1979). Stability in multicriteria optimization. *Journal of Mathematical Analysis and Applications*, *68*(2), 441–453. doi:10.1016/0022-247X(79)90128-8

Omidi, F., Abbasi, B., & Nazemi, A. (2017). An efficient dynamic model for solving a portfolio selection with uncertain chance constraint models. *Journal of Computational and Applied Mathematics*, *319*, 43–55. doi:10.1016/j.cam.2016.12.020

Pachter, L., & Sturmfels, B. (2007). The mathematics of phylogenomics. *SIAM Review*, *49*(1), 3–31. doi:10.1137/050632634

Pal, B. B., & Basu, I. (1996). Selection of appropriate priority structure for optimal land allocation in agricultural planning through goal programming. *Indian Journal of Agricultural Economics*, *51*, 342–354.

Pekgoz, C., Sakawa, M., Kato, K., & Katagiri, H. (2005). "An interactive fuzzy satisficing method for multiobjective stochastic integer programming problems through a probability maximization model", Asia Pacific Management review. *International Journal (Toronto, Ont.)*, *10*, 29–35.

Perkgoz, C., Kato, K., Katagiri, H., & Sakawa, M. (2004). An interactive fuzzy satisficing method for multiobjective stochastic integer programming problems through variance minimization model. Scientiae Mathematicae Japonicae online, 10, 99-107.

Prekopa, A. (1970). On probabilistic constrained programming. *Mathematical Programming Study*, *28*, 113-138.

Qu, B. Y., Zhu, Y. S., Jiao, Y. C., Wu, M. Y., Suganthan, P. N., & Liang, J. J. (2018). A survey on multi-objective evolutionary algorithms for the solution of the environmental/economic dispatch problems. *Swarm and Evolutionary Computation*, *38*, 1–11. doi:10.1016/j.swevo.2017.06.002

Rao, S. S. (1996). *Engineering optimization: theory and practice* (3rd ed.). John Wiley & Sons.

Rehman, T., & Romeo, C. (1987). Goal Programming with Penalty Functions and Livestock Ration Formulation. *Agricultural Systems*, *23*(2), 117–132. doi:10.1016/0308-521X(87)90090-4

Ren, A., Wang, Y., & Xue, X. (2016). Interactive programming approach for solving the fully fuzzy bilevel linear programming problem. *Knowledge-Based Systems*, *99*, 103–111. doi:10.1016/j.knosys.2016.01.044

Ren, C., Guo, P., Tan, Q., & Zhang, L. (2017). A multi-objective fuzzy programming model for optimal use of irrigation water and land resources under uncertainty in Gansu Province, China. *Journal of Cleaner Production*, *164*, 85–94. doi:10.1016/j.jclepro.2017.06.185

Romero, C. (1985). Multiobjective and Goal-Programming approaches as a Distance Function Model. *The Journal of the Operational Research Society*, *36*(3), 249–251. doi:10.1057/jors.1985.43

Rommelfanger, H. (1996). Fuzzy linear programming and applications. *European Journal of Operational Research, 92*(3), 512–527. doi:10.1016/0377-2217(95)00008-9

Saber, H. M., & Ravindran, A. (1996). A Partitioning Gradient Based algorithm for solving nonlinear goal programming problems. *Computers & Operations Research, 23*(2), 141–152. doi:10.1016/0305-0548(95)00011-A

Sahoo, N. P., & Biswal, M. P. (2009). Computation of a multi-objective production planning model with probabilistic constraints. *International Journal of Computer Mathematics, 86*(1), 185–198. doi:10.1080/00207160701734207

Sakawa, M. (1993). *Fuzzy sets and interactive multiobjective optimization.* New York: Plenum Press. doi:10.1007/978-1-4899-1633-4

Sakawa, M. (2001). *Genetic algorithms and fuzzy multiobjective optimization.* Boston: Kluwer Academic Publishers.

Sakawa, M. (2009). *Interactive Multiobjective by Sequential Proxy Optimization Technique.* Kobe University.

Sakawa, M., Kato, K., & Katagiri, H. (2004). An Interactive Fuzzy Satisfying Method for Multiobjective Linear Programming Problems with Random Variable Coefficients through a Probability Maximization Model. *Fuzzy Sets and Systems, 146*(2), 205–220. doi:10.1016/j.fss.2004.04.003

Sakawa, M., Kato, K., Sunada, H., & Shibano, T. (1997). Fuzzy programming for multiobjective 0-1 programming problems through revised genetic algorithms. *European Journal of Operational Research, 97*(1), 149–158. doi:10.1016/S0377-2217(96)00023-9

Sakawa, M., Nishizaki, I., & Katagiri, H. (2011). *Fuzzy Stochastic Multiobjective Programming.* Springer. doi:10.1007/978-1-4419-8402-9

Sakawa, M., Nishizaki, I., & Uemura, Y. (1998). Interactive fuzzy programming for multilevel linear programming problems. *Computers & Mathematics with Applications (Oxford, England), 36*(2), 71–86. doi:10.1016/S0898-1221(98)00118-7

Sawaragi, Y., Nakayama, H., & Tanino, T. (1985). *Theory of Multiobjective Optimization.* Orlando, FL: Academic.

Schniederjans, M. J. (1995). *Goal programming methodology and applications.* Boston: Kluwer publishers. doi:10.1007/978-1-4615-2229-4

Schultz, R., & Tiedemann, S. (2006). Conditional value-at-risk in stochastic programs with mixed-integer recourse. *Mathematical Programming*, *105*(2-3), 365–386. doi:10.100710107-005-0658-4

Sengupta, J. K. (1972). Stochastic Programming: Methods and Applications. North-Holland Publishing Company.

Shafer, G. (1976). *A Mathematical Theory of Evidence*. Princeton University Press.

Sharafali, M., Co, H. C., & Goh, M. (2004). Production scheduling in a flexible manufacturing system under random demand. *European Journal of Operational Research*, *158*(1), 89–102. doi:10.1016/S0377-2217(03)00300-X

Shiryaer, A. (1996). *Probability* (2nd ed.). Springer-Verlag. doi:10.1007/978-1-4757-2539-1

Sinha, S. B., Biswal, M. P., & Hulsurkar, S. (1998). Fuzzy programming approach to multiobjective probabilistic linear programming problems where only bi's are probabilistic. *The Journal of Fuzzy Mathematics*, *6*(1), 63–73.

Stacey, L. F. (2009). *Quality representation in multiobjective programming*. Clemson University.

Steuer, R. E. (1977). An Interactive Multiple Objective Linear Programming Procedure. In TIMS Studies in the Management Sciences, 6, 225–239.

Suo, C., Li, Y. P., Wang, C. X., & Yu, L. (2017). A type-2 fuzzy chance-constrained programming method for planning Shanghai's energy system. *International Journal of Electrical Power & Energy Systems*, *90*, 37–53. doi:10.1016/j.ijepes.2017.01.007

Tamiz, M., Mirrazavi, S. K., & Jones, D. F. (1999). Extensions of Pareto efficiency analysis to integer goal programming. *Omega*, *27*(2), 179–188. doi:10.1016/S0305-0483(98)00038-3

Tanaka, H., Okuda, T., & Asai, K. (1973). On fuzzy mathematical programming. *Journal of Cybernetics and Systems*, *3*(4), 37–46. doi:10.1080/01969727308545912

Taylor, B. W. III, Moore, L. J., & Clayton, E. R. (1982). R & D Project Selection and Manpower Allocation with Integer Nonlinear Goal Programming. *Management Science*, *28*(10), 1149–1158. doi:10.1287/mnsc.28.10.1149

Thompson, H. E., Matthews, J. P., & Li, B. C. (1974). Insurance exposure and investment risks: An analysis using chance-constrained programming. *Operations Research, 22*(5), 991–1007. doi:10.1287/opre.22.5.991

Tsao, Y. C., Thanh, V. V., Lu, J. C., & Yu, V. (2018). Designing sustainable supply chain networks under uncertain environments: Fuzzy multi-objective programming. *Journal of Cleaner Production, 174*, 1550–1565. doi:10.1016/j.jclepro.2017.10.272

Tzeng, G. H., Cheng, H. J., & Huang, T. D. (2007). Multi-objective Optimal Planning for Designing Relief Delivery Systems. *Transportation Research Part E, Logistics and Transportation Review, 43*(6), 673–686. doi:10.1016/j.tre.2006.10.012

Vajda, S. (1972). *Probabilistic programming.* New York: Academic press.

Voorneveld, M., van den Nouweland, A., & McLean, R. (2008). *An axiomatization of the Euclidean compromise solution.* Working Paper Series in Economics and Finance 703. Stockholm School of Economics.

Wagner, M. R. (2008). Stochastic 0-1 linear programming under limited distributional information. *Operations Research Letters, 36*(2), 150–156. doi:10.1016/j.orl.2007.07.003

Walkup, D. W., & Wets, R. (1967). Stochastic programming with recourse. *SIAM Journal on Applied Mathematics, 15*(5), 139–162. doi:10.1137/0115113

Wets, R. (1974). Stochastic programming with fixed recourse: The equivalent deterministic program. *SIAM Review, 16*(3), 309–339. doi:10.1137/1016053

Wets, R. J. B. (1966a). Programming under uncertainty: The equivalent convex program. *SIAM Journal on Applied Mathematics, 14*(1), 89–105. doi:10.1137/0114008

Wets, R. J. B. (1966b). Programming under uncertainty: The complete problem. *Zeitschriftfür Wahrscheinlichkeitstheorie und Verwandte Gebiete, 4*(4), 316–339. doi:10.1007/BF00539117

Wierzbicki, A. P. (1998). *Reference Point Methods in Vector Optimization and Decision Support. In International Institute for Applied Systems Analysis Interim Report* (pp. IR-98–IR-017). Laxenburg, Austria.

Wu, D., & Ierapetritou, M. (2007). Hierarchical approach for production planning and scheduling under uncertainty. *Chemical Engineering and Processing: Process Intensification*, *46*(11), 1129–1140. doi:10.1016/j. cep.2007.02.021

Yu, J. R., Tzeng, Y. C., Tzeng, G. H., Yu, T. Y., & Sheu, H. J. (2004). Fuzzy Multiple Objective Programming Approach to DEA with Imprecise Data. *International Journal of Uncertainty, Fuzziness and Knowledge-based Systems*, *12*(05), 591–600. doi:10.1142/S0218488504003090

Yu, P. L. (1985). *Multiple Criteria Decision Making: Concepts, Techniques and Extensions*. New York: Plenum Press. doi:10.1007/978-1-4684-8395-6

Yu, P. L., & Leitmann, G. (1974). Compromise Solutions, Dominations Structures and Salukvadze's Solution. *Journal of Optimization Theory and Applications*, *13*(3), 362–378. doi:10.1007/BF00934871

Zadeh, L. A. (1968). Probability Measures of Fuzzy Events. *Journal of Mathematical Analysis and Applications*, *23*(2), 421–427. doi:10.1016/0022-247X(68)90078-4

Zanakis, S. H., & Gupta, S. K. (1985). A categorized bibliographic survey of goal programming. *Omega*, *13*(3), 211–222. doi:10.1016/0305-0483(85)90059-3

Zeleny, M. (1973). Compromise Programming. In *Multiple Criteria Decision Making* (pp. 262–301). Columbia, SC: University of South Carolina Press.

Zhao, X., Zheng, Y., & Wan, Z. (2017). Interactive intuitionistic fuzzy methods for multilevel programming problems. *Expert Systems with Applications*, *72*, 258–268. doi:10.1016/j.eswa.2016.10.063

Zhou, K., Doyle, J., & Glover, K. (1996). *Robust and Optimal Control*. Prentice-Hall.

Ziemba, W. T. (1971). Transforming stochastic dynamic programming problems into nonlinear programs. *Management Science*, *17*(7), 450–462. doi:10.1287/mnsc.17.7.450

Zimmermann, H. J. (1976). Description and optimization of fuzzy systems. *International Journal of General Systems*, *2*(4), 209–215. doi:10.1080/03081077608547470

Zimmermann, H. J. (1978). Fuzzy programming and linear programming with several objective functions. *Fuzzy Sets and Systems*, *1*(1), 45–55. doi:10.1016/0165-0114(78)90031-3

Zimmermann, H. J. (1983). Fuzzy Mathematical Programming. *Computers & Operations Research*, *10*(4), 291–298. doi:10.1016/0305-0548(83)90004-7

Chapter 2
Fundamental Concepts

ABSTRACT

In this chapter, the authors discuss some basic concepts of probability theory and possibility theory that are useful when reading the subsequent chapters of this book. The multi-objective fuzzy stochastic programming models developed in this book are based on the concepts of advanced topics in fuzzy set theory and fuzzy random variables (FRVs). Therefore, for better understanding of these advanced areas, the authors at first presented some basic ideas of probability theory and probability density functions of different continuous probability distributions. Afterwards, the necessity of the introduction of the concept of fuzzy set theory, some important terms related to fuzzy set theory are discussed. Different defuzzification methodologies of fuzzy numbers (FNs) that are useful in solving the mathematical models in imprecisely defined decision-making environments are explored. The concept of using FRVs in decision-making contexts is defined. Finally, the development of different forms of fuzzy goal programming (FGP) techniques for solving multi-objective decision-making (MODM) problems is underlined.

2.1 ELEMENTARY IDEA ON PROBABILITY THEORY

FRVs play an important role in developing multi-objective fuzzy stochastic programming models. To get a brief concept on FRVs, the concept of random variables is highly needed by the readers. From that view point a short discussion on basic probability theory with various types of probability distributions are briefly highlighted at first in this section, so that the readers

DOI: 10.4018/978-1-5225-8301-1.ch002

can easily capture the idea of FRVs and can distinguish the difference between random variables and FRVs.

- **Definition 2.1.1: (σ – Algebra):** Let E be a random experiment and S be its sample space. A non-empty collection Δ of subsets of S is said to form an σ – algebra, if the following conditions are satisfied

  ○   if $A_1, A_2, A_3, \ldots \in \Delta$, then $\bigcup\limits_{i=1}^{\infty} A_i \in \Delta$.

  ○   if $A \in \Delta$, then $A^c \in \Delta$.

- **Definition 2.1.2: (Probability Space):** Let Δ be a σ – algebra. A mapping $P : \Delta \to \mathbb{R}$ that maps each element of $A \in \Delta$ to a real number $P(A)$, is called probability measure. If S is a sample space, then the triple (S, Δ, P) is called a probability space.

- **Definition 2.1.3: (Random Variables):** Let E be a random experiment and S be its sample space. If for each event point U of the sample space S, there is a real number $X(U)$ by a given rule, i.e., if X is a mapping from the sample space S to the set of real numbers $\mathbb{R}$, i.e., $X : S \to \mathbb{R}$, such that $\{\omega \in S : X(\omega) \leq x\} \in \Delta$ for all $x \in \mathbb{R}$, then X is called a random variable or a stochastic variable.

The range of the mapping X is called the spectrum of the random variable. The spectrum may be discrete or continuous and based on the nature of spectrum; the random variable can be categorized into discrete and continuous random variable.

- **Definition 2.1.4: (Distribution Function):** Let E be a random experiment and S be its sample space. Also let X be a random variable defined on the sample space S. Then a distribution function F of the random variable X with respect to the probability space (S, Δ, P) is defined as a real valued function of a real variable x, such that $F_X(x) = P(-\infty < X \leq x)$, $x \in \mathbb{R}$.

- **Definition 2.1.5: (Probability Density Function):** Let X be a continuous random variable. Then a probability density function of the random variable X is a function $f(x)$ such that for any two numbers a and b with $a \leq b$, $P(a \leq X \leq b) = \int\limits_a^b f(x)\, dx$.

i.e., the probability that X takes on a value in the interval $[a,b]$ is the area within this interval and inscribed by the graph of the density function. The graph of $f(x)$ is often referred to as the probability density curve.

2.1.1 Probability Distributions

The probability density functions are defined based on different types of probability distributions. In this subsection different types of probability distributions with their probability density function and probability density curve are described as follows.

The continuous probability distributions, *viz.*, normal distributions, log-normal distributions, Cauchy distributions, extreme value distributions, exponential distribution, Bur-XII distribution, Pareto distribution, Frechet distribution, Weibull distribution which are used in this book under fuzzily described environment are presented in crisp environment.

2.1.1.1 Random Variable Following Normal Distribution

Let X be a continuous random variable following normal distribution. Then its probability density function takes the form

$$f\left(x \; ; m \; , \sigma\right) = \frac{1}{\sqrt{2\pi}\sigma} e^{-\frac{(x-m)^2}{2\sigma^2}} \; , \quad -\infty < x < \infty$$

The parameter m is called as mean and the other parameter $\sigma \; (> 0)$ is the standard deviation of normal distribution.

Graphically, the density function of normal distribution is expressed as shown in Figure 1.

2.1.1.2 Random Variable Following Log-Normal Distribution

Let X be a log-normal variate. The probability density function of log-normally distributed random variable X is written as

$$f\left(x \; ; m \; , \sigma\right) = \frac{1}{x\sigma\sqrt{2\pi}} e^{\left(-\frac{1}{2\sigma^2}\left(\log(x)-m\right)^2\right)} \; , \quad x > 0$$

Figure 1. Density curve of normal distribution

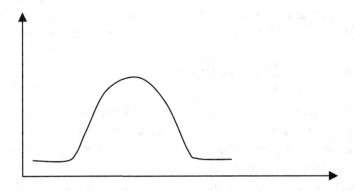

The parameter m is the location parameter and other parameter σ (> 0) is called the scale parameter of the lognormal distribution. The mean and variance of the log-normal distribution is given by $e^{\left(m+\frac{\sigma^2}{2}\right)}$ and $e^{\left(2m+\sigma^2\right)}\left(e^{\sigma^2}-1\right)$, respectively.

The density curve of log-normal distribution is expressed as shown in Figure 2.

2.1.1.3 Probability Density Function for Cauchy Distribution

Let X be a Cauchy distributed random variable. Then the probability density function of the random variable X is given by

Figure 2. Density curve of log-normal distribution

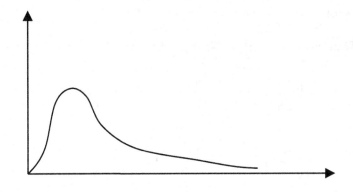

$$f\left(x;\ r,s\right)=\frac{r}{\pi\left[r^2+\left(x-s\right)^2\right]}\ ;\ -\infty<x<\infty$$

The parameter s is known as location parameter and the other parameter r is called scale parameter.

The graph of the probability density function of Cauchy distribution is shown in Figure 3.

2.1.1.4 Probability Density Function for Extreme Value Distribution

If X be a random variable following extreme value distribution, then its probability density function $f(x;c,h)$ is given by

$$f\left(x\ ;c,h\right)=\frac{1}{c}e^{-\frac{\left(x-h\right)}{c}}\ e^{-e^{-\frac{\left(x-h\right)}{c}}}\ ;\ -\infty<x<\infty$$

The parameter $c\left(>0\right)$ is known as scale parameter and the parameter h is called location parameter of the extreme value distribution.

Graphically the density function of extreme value distribution are expressed as shown in Figure 4.

Figure 3. Density curve of Cauchy distribution

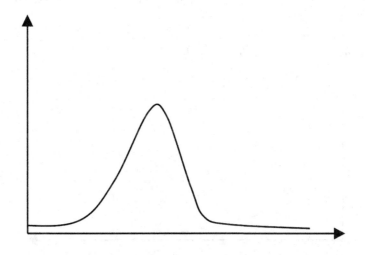

Figure 4. Density curve of extreme value distribution

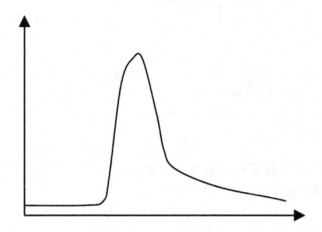

2.1.1.5 Random Variable Following Weibull Distribution

Let X be a Weibull distributed continuous random variable. Its probability density function is written as

$$f\left(x\ ;s\ ,p\right)=\left(\frac{p}{s}\right)\left(\frac{x}{s}\right)^{p-1}e^{-\left(\frac{x}{s}\right)^{p}},\ x\geq 0$$

The parameter $p\left(>0\right)$ is called the shape parameter and the other parameter $s\ (>0)$ is known as scale parameter of the distribution.

The density curve of Weibull distribution is expressed as shown in Figure 5.

Figure 5. Density curve of Weibull distribution

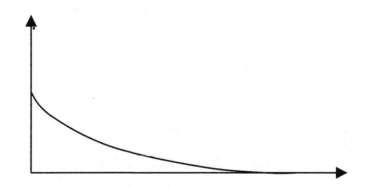

2.1.1.6 Probability Density Function for Exponential Distribution

Let X be a continuous random variable following exponential distribution. Its probability density function is of the form

$$f\left(x\ ;s\right)=s.exp\left(-sx\right);\ 0<x<\infty$$

The parameter $s\ (>0)$ is called the rate parameter of the distribution. Geometrically its density function is expressed as shown in Figure 6.

2.1.1.7 Probability Density Function for Bur-XII Distribution

Let X be Bur-XII distributed random variable. Then the density function of the Bur-XII distributed random variable X with shape parameters $s\ (>0)$ and $t\ (>0)$ is written in the following form as

$$f\left(x;s,t\right)=stx^{t-1}\left(1+x^{t}\right)^{-(s+1)};\ 0<x<\infty$$

The density curve of Bur-XII distribution is shown in Figure 7.

Figure 6. Density curve of exponential distribution

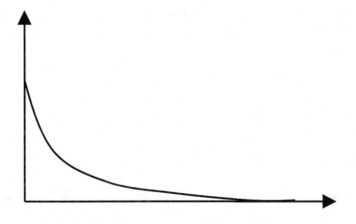

Figure 7. Density curve of Bur-XII distribution

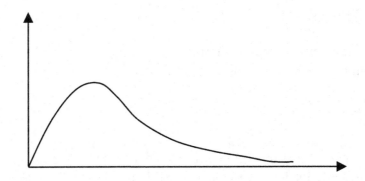

2.1.1.8 Probability Density Function for Frechet Distribution

Let X be a Frechet distributed random variable, its probability density function is written as

$$f\left(x \; ;r \; ,q,d\right) = \frac{r}{q}\left(\frac{x-d}{q}\right)^{-1-r} e^{-\left(\frac{x-d}{q}\right)^{-r}}, \; x \geq d \, .$$

The parameter r (> 0) is the shape parameter, parameter s (> 0) is the scale parameter and the parameter m is the location parameter of the Frechet distribution.

The density curve of Frechet distribution takes the form shown in Figure 8.

Figure 8. Density curve of Frechet distribution

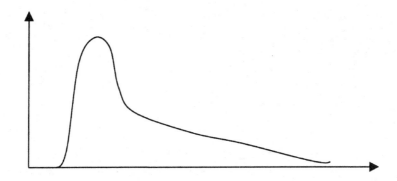

2.1.1.9 Probability Density Function for Pareto Distribution

Let X be a Pareto distributed random variable. Its probability density function is written as

$$f\left(x\ ;v\ ,u\right)=\frac{uv^{u}}{x^{u+1}}\ ;\ x>v$$

The parameter $u\ (>0)$ is called the shape parameter and other parameter $v\ (>0)$ is known as scale parameter of Pareto distribution.

The density curve of Pareto distribution is expressed as shown in Figure 9.

In the next part of this chapter preliminary idea of fuzzy set are discussed briefly.

2.2 BASIC CONCEPTS OF FUZZY SET THEORY

In this subsection basic definitions of some important terms in the context of fuzzy set theory are presented for the better understanding of the readers.

In classical set theory, a crisp set or a set A defined on a universal set X is presented in terms of a function χ_A, called the characteristic function of A, that helps to identify which elements belongs to the set A and which are not in A. Mathematically, the characteristic function of A is defined as

$$\chi_A:X\to\left\{0,1\right\}\text{by }\chi_A\left(x\right)=\begin{cases}1 & if\quad x\in A\\ 0 & if\quad x\notin A\end{cases},$$

Figure 9. Density curve of Pareto distribution

i.e., if an element x belongs to the set A, then the characteristic value of the element x is 1 and if x does not belongs to the set A, then the function χ_A assigns 0 corresponding to the element x.

For example if $A = \{1, 2, 3, \ldots, 10\}$ be a subset of $\mathbb{Z}$, then

$$\chi_A(1) = \chi_A(2) = \ldots = \chi_A(10) = 1$$

and $\chi_A(x) = 0$ for other integer values of x. Graphically, it can be represented as shown in Figure 10.

Thus, in classical set theory, the characteristic value of elements in a set is assessed using binary terms according to a bivalent condition- an element either belongs or does not belong to the set. Sometimes, this concept fails to represent every set or this concept is inadequate when describing human reasoning. For example, if A be a set "close to 5", then it is not clear whether 4 is in the set or not. To resolve this difficulty, Zadeh (1965) generalized the concept and the notion of fuzzy set. In general, fuzzy set uses the whole interval between 0 and 1 rather than only 0 and 1 to describe human reasoning more perfectly. Fuzzy set theory is an extension of classical set theory where the image of each element x is a number between 0 and 1, called the membership grade of x. The higher membership value increases the occurrence possibility of the element x. Thus fuzzy set can be defined as follows:

- **Definition 2.2.1: (Fuzzy Set):** Let X be a universe of discourse. A fuzzy set $\tilde{A}$ on X is characterized by its membership function

Figure 10. Crisp set

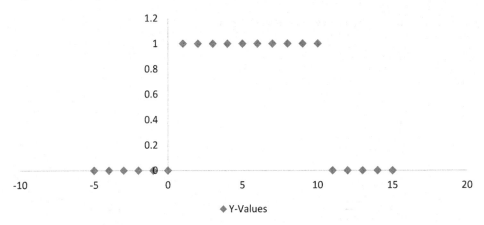

$\mu_{\tilde{A}} : X \to [0,1]$ and $\mu_{\tilde{A}}(x)$ is interpreted as the degree of membership of the element x in the fuzzy set $\tilde{A}$ for each $x \in X$. Thus the fuzzy set $\tilde{A}$ is completely determined by the set of ordered pairs

$$\tilde{A} = \left\{ \left(x, \mu_{\tilde{A}}(x) \right) : x \in X \right\}.$$

The set of all fuzzy set on X is denoted by $\mathcal{F}(X)$.

If $X = \{x_1, x_2, \ldots, x_n\}$ be a finite discrete set, then the fuzzy set $\tilde{A}$ is expressed as

$$\tilde{A} = \mu_1 / x_1 + \mu_2 / x_2 + \ldots + \mu_n / x_n = \sum_{i=1}^{n} \mu_i / x_i,$$

where the term μ_i / x_i indicates that μ_i has the grade of membership of x_i in the fuzzy set $\tilde{A}$ and the '+' sign represents the union.

If the universe of discourse X be continuous, then the fuzzy set $\tilde{A}$ on X is expressed as

$$\tilde{A} = \int_X \mu_{\tilde{A}}(x) / x$$

For example, the fuzzy set $\tilde{A}$ "close to 5", can be represented graphically as shown in Figure 11.

From this figure it is clear that the membership value at 5 is 1, and for the elements away from 5 the membership value diminishes. Also, from this diagram it can be stated that elements less than 4 and greater than 6.5 are not in the fuzzy set $\tilde{A}$.

- **Definition 2.2.2: (Level Set of a Fuzzy Set):** The range of the membership function $\mu_{\tilde{A}} : X \to [0,1]$ is called the level set of the fuzzy set $\tilde{A}$. Thus level set of a fuzzy set $\tilde{A}$ is a subset of $[0,1]$.
- **Definition 2.2.3: (Support of a Fuzzy Set):** Let $\tilde{A}$ be a fuzzy set defined on a universal set X. The support of $\tilde{A}$, denoted by $\text{Supp}(\tilde{A})$,

Figure 11. Fuzzy set

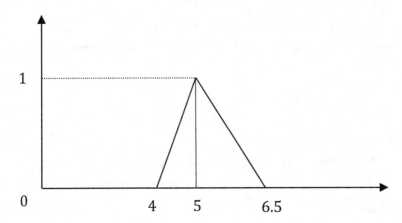

is the crisp subset of X whose elements all have nonzero membership grades in $\tilde{A}$. Thus support of a fuzzy set can be expressed as

$$\text{Supp}(\tilde{A}) = \{x \in X : \mu_{\tilde{A}}(x) > 0\}.$$

- **Definition 2.2.4: (Normal Fuzzy Set):** A fuzzy subset $\tilde{A}$ of a universal set X is called normal if there exists at least one $x \in X$ such that $\mu_{\tilde{A}}(x) = 1$. Otherwise the fuzzy set $\tilde{A}$ is subnormal.
- **Definition 2.2.5: (α – Cut of a Fuzzy Set):** An α – cut of a fuzzy set $\tilde{A}$ on X is a crisp set denoted by $\tilde{A}[\alpha]$ or $^{\alpha}A$ and is defined by

Figure 12. Support of a fuzzy set supp($\tilde{A}$)

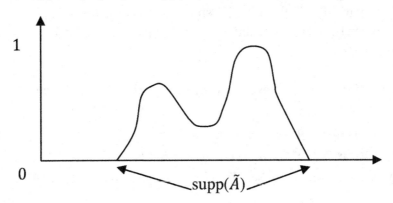

Figure 13. Normal fuzzy set

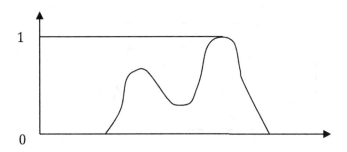

$$\tilde{A}[\alpha] = \left\{x : x \in X \ \&\mu_{\tilde{A}}(x) \geq \alpha\right\}.$$

- **Definition 2.2.6: (Strong α – Cut of a Fuzzy Set):** The strong α – cut of a fuzzy set $\tilde{A}$ is denoted by $\tilde{A}[\alpha +]$ or $^{\alpha +}A$ and is defined by

$$\tilde{A}[\alpha +] = \{x : x \in X \ \&\mu_{\tilde{A}}(x) > \alpha\}.$$

- **Definition 2.2.7: (Height of a Fuzzy Set):** The height of a fuzzy set $\tilde{A}$ is denoted by $h\left(\tilde{A}\right)$ and defined as the maximum membership grade of x in the fuzzy set $\tilde{A}$, for all $x \in X$, i.e.

$$h\left(\tilde{A}\right) = \sup_{x \in X} \mu_{\tilde{A}}(x)$$

Figure 14. α – cut of a fuzzy set

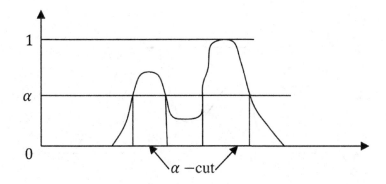

Figure 15. Height of a Fuzzy Set

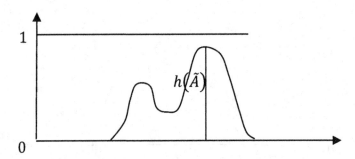

- **Definition 2.2.8: (Core of a Fuzzy Set):** The core of a fuzzy set $\tilde{A}$, denoted by $\text{Core}(\tilde{A})$, is the crisp subset of X which contains those elements of X whose membership value is 1. Thus Core of a fuzzy set can be expressed as

$$\text{Core}(\tilde{A}) = \left\{ x : x \in X \ \& \mu_{\tilde{A}}(x) = 1 \right\}$$

- **Definition 2.2.9: (Convex Fuzzy Set):** A fuzzy set $\tilde{A}$ on X is said to be a convex fuzzy set if $\tilde{A}[\alpha]$ is a convex set of X for all $\alpha \in [0,1]$.

Again, an fuzzy set $\tilde{A}$ defined on X is said to be a convex fuzzy set if and only if the condition

$$\mu_{\tilde{A}}\left(\lambda x + (1-\lambda)y\right) \geq \min\left[\mu_{\tilde{A}}(x), \mu_{\tilde{A}}(y)\right], \ \lambda \in [0,1] \ \forall x, y \in X,$$

Figure 16. Core of a fuzzy set

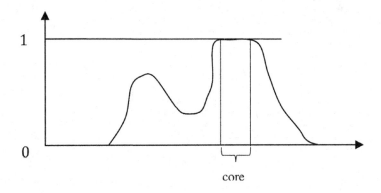

is satisfied.

- **Definition 2.2.10: (Cardinality of a Fuzzy Set):** The cardinality or scalar cardinality of a finite fuzzy set $\tilde{A}$ on X is denoted by $|\tilde{A}|$ and is defined as the sum of membership values of all the elements of X. Thus the cardinality of $\tilde{A}$ is defined as

$$|\tilde{A}| = \sum_{x \in X} \mu_{\tilde{A}}(x).$$

For example, if

$$\tilde{A} = 0.13 / 10 + 0.56 / 11 + 0.93 / 12 + 1 / 13 + 0.87 / 14 + 0.5 / 15 + 0.15 / 16,$$

then $|\tilde{A}| = 4.14$.

- **Definition 2.2.11: (Fuzzy Cardinality of a Fuzzy Set):** The fuzzy cardinality of a fuzzy set $\tilde{A}$ is defined as the number of elements of the universal set X that maps to each element of the level set of the fuzzy set $\tilde{A}$. Thus, fuzzy cardinality of a fuzzy set $\tilde{A}$ is a fuzzy set defined on the set of natural numbers $\mathbb{N}$.

2.2.1 Operations on Fuzzy Sets

The three basic operations on crisp sets i.e. the complement, intersection and union can be generalized on fuzzy sets in more than one way. In this book one particular generalization is discussed which is referred as standard fuzzy set operations.

- **Definition 2.2.12: (Intersection of Fuzzy Sets):** The intersection of two fuzzy sets $\tilde{A}$ and $\tilde{B}$ defined on X is denoted by $\tilde{A} \cap \tilde{B}$ whose membership function is defined as

$$\mu_{\tilde{A} \cap \tilde{B}}(x) = \min\left\{\mu_{\tilde{A}}(x), \mu_{\tilde{B}}(x)\right\} = \mu_{\tilde{A}}(x) \wedge \mu_{\tilde{B}}(x),$$

Figure 17. Intersection of fuzzy sets

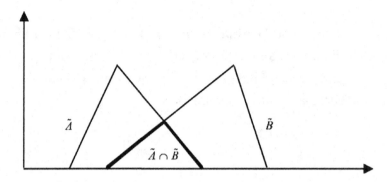

for all $x \in X$.

- **Definition 2.2.13: (Union of Fuzzy Sets):** The union of two fuzzy sets $\tilde{A}$ and $\tilde{B}$ defined on X is denoted by $\tilde{A} \cup \tilde{B}$ whose membership function is defined as

$$\mu_{\tilde{A} \cup \tilde{B}}\left(x\right) = \max\left\{\mu_{\tilde{A}}\left(x\right), \mu_{\tilde{B}}\left(x\right)\right\} = \mu_{\tilde{A}}\left(x\right) \vee \mu_{\tilde{B}}\left(x\right),$$

for all $x \in X$.

- **Definition 2.2.14: (Complement of a Fuzzy Set):** The complement of a fuzzy set $\tilde{A}$ defined on X is denoted by $\overline{\tilde{A}}$ whose membership function is defined as

Figure 18. Union of fuzzy sets

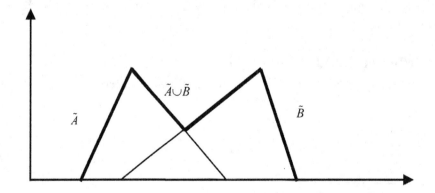

Figure 19. Complement of a fuzzy set

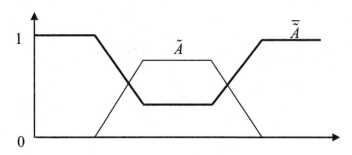

$$\mu_{\bar{\tilde{A}}}\left(x\right) = 1 - \mu_{\tilde{A}}\left(x\right), \text{ for all } x \in X.$$

There is one-to-one relationship between a fuzzy set and it's $\alpha-$ cuts. The following theorem establishes that relationship.

2.2.2 First Decomposition Theorem (Klir and Yuan, 1994)

Let X be a universal set and $\tilde{A}$ be a fuzzy set defined on X. Now, in this theorem it is shown that the fuzzy set $\tilde{A}$ can also be expressed as the standard union of a new fuzzy set $_\alpha\tilde{A}$ which is the product of α and the $\alpha-$ cut $\tilde{A}[\alpha]$, i.e., $_\alpha\tilde{A} = \alpha.\tilde{A}[\alpha]$. Thus, it can be stated as follows,

Let $\tilde{A}$ be any fuzzy set defined on X. Then the fuzzy set $\tilde{A}$ can be expressed as $\tilde{A} = \bigcup_{\alpha \in [0,1]} {}_\alpha A$.

Proof: Let x be a fixed element of the universe of discourse X. Then the membership value $\mu_{\tilde{A}}(x)$ lies in $[0,1]$. Let $\mu_{\tilde{A}}(x) = a$.

Now,

$$\mu_{\left(\bigcup_{\alpha \in [0,1]} {}_\alpha A\right)}(x) = \sup_{\alpha \in [0,1]} \mu_{\alpha A}(x) = \max\left[\sup_{\alpha \in [0,a]} \mu_{\alpha A}(x), \sup_{\alpha \in (a,1]} \mu_{\alpha A}(x)\right]$$

Again if $\alpha \in (a,1]$, then $\mu_{\tilde{A}}(x) = a < \alpha$. Hence $\mu_{\alpha A}(x) = 0.$ But for each $\alpha \in [0,a]$, the corresponding membership value is $\mu_{\tilde{A}}(x) = a \geq \alpha$, therefore the membership value of new fuzzy set $\mu_{\alpha A}(x) = \alpha.$

Thus,

$$\mu_{\left(\underset{\alpha\in[0,1]}{\cup}\alpha A\right)}(x) = \sup_{\alpha\in[0,1]}\mu_{\alpha A}(x) = \max\left[\sup_{\alpha\in[0,a]}\mu_{\alpha A}(x), \sup_{\alpha\in(a,1]}\mu_{\alpha A}(x)\right] = \sup_{\alpha\in[0,a]}\alpha =$$

$$a = \mu_{\tilde{A}}(x)$$

This is true for all $x \in X$. Thus $\tilde{A} = \underset{\alpha\in[0,1]}{\cup}\alpha A$.

This theorem is now explained through the following example.

Let $X = \{x_1, x_2, x_3, x_4, x_5, x_6\}$ be a universal set. A fuzzy set $\tilde{A}$ on X is defined as

$$\tilde{A} = 0.15 / x_1 + 0.3 / x_2 + 0.5 / x_3 + 0.65 / x_4 + 0.8 / x_5 + 1 / x_6.$$

The α – cut of the fuzzy set $\tilde{A}$ is expressed as

$$\tilde{A}[0.15] = 1 / x_1 + 1 / x_2 + 1 / x_3 + 1 / x_4 + 1 / x_5 + 1 / x_6$$

$$\tilde{A}[0.3] = 0 / x_1 + 1 / x_2 + 1 / x_3 + 1 / x_4 + 1 / x_5 + 1 / x_6$$

$$\tilde{A}[0.5] = 0 / x_1 + 0 / x_2 + 1 / x_3 + 1 / x_4 + 1 / x_5 + 1 / x_6$$

$$\tilde{A}[0.65] = 0 / x_1 + 0 / x_2 + 0 / x_3 + 1 / x_4 + 1 / x_5 + 1 / x_6$$

$$\tilde{A}[0.8] = 0 / x_1 + 0 / x_2 + 0 / x_3 + 0 / x_4 + 1 / x_5 + 1 / x_6$$

$$\tilde{A}[1] = 0 / x_1 + 0 / x_2 + 0 / x_3 + 0 / x_4 + 0 / x_5 + 1 / x_6$$

Thus the special fuzzy set $_\alpha\tilde{A} = \alpha.\tilde{A}[\alpha]$ is expressed as

$$_{0.15}A = 0.15\tilde{A}[0.15] = 0.15 / x_1 + 0.15 / x_2 + 0.15 / x_3 + 0.15 / x_4 + 0.15 / x_5 + 0.15 / x_6$$

$$_{0.3}A = 0.3\tilde{A}\big[0.3\big] = 0\,/\,x_1 + 0.3\,/\,x_2 + 0.3\,/\,x_3 + 0.3\,/\,x_4 + 0.3\,/\,x_5 + 0.3\,/\,x_6$$

$$_{0.5}A = 0.5\tilde{A}\big[0.5\big] = 0\,/\,x_1 + 0\,/\,x_2 + 0.5\,/\,x_3 + 0.5\,/\,x_4 + 0.5\,/\,x_5 + 0.5\,/\,x_6$$

$$_{0.65}A = 0.65\tilde{A}\big[0.65\big] = 0\,/\,x_1 + 0\,/\,x_2 + 0\,/\,x_3 + 0.65\,/\,x_4 + 0.65\,/\,x_5 + 0.65\,/\,x_6$$

$$_{0.8}A = 0.8\tilde{A}\big[0.8\big] = 0\,/\,x_1 + 0\,/\,x_2 + 0\,/\,x_3 + 0\,/\,x_4 + 0.8\,/\,x_5 + 0.8\,/\,x_6$$

$$_{1}A = 1\tilde{A}\big[1\big] = 0\,/\,x_1 + 0\,/\,x_2 + 0\,/\,x_3 + 0\,/\,x_4 + 0\,/\,x_5 + 1\,/\,x_6$$

Thus the fuzzy set can be expressed as
$\tilde{A} = {}_{0.15}A \cup {}_{0.3}A \cup {}_{0.5}A \cup {}_{0.65}A \cup {}_{0.8}A \cup {}_{1}A$.

- **Definition 2.2.15: (Interval Valued Fuzzy Set):** The concept of an fuzzy set is generalized based on the fact that the membership functions of an fuzzy set are often too precise. This situation is overcome by assigning a subinterval of $[0,1]$ for each x instead of a real number between 0 and 1.

Let X be the universe of discourse. An interval valued fuzzy set $\tilde{A}$ on X is characterized by the membership function $\mu_{\tilde{A}} : X \to \varepsilon\big([0,1]\big)$ such that each $a \in X$ assign a subinterval in $[0,1]$ instead of a point in $[0,1]$. Thus $\mu_{\tilde{A}}(a) = [x_1, x_2]$, where $[x_1, x_2] \subset [0,1]$ and $\varepsilon\big([0,1]\big)$ is the set of all subsets of $[0,1]$.

- **Definition 2.2.16: (Type-II Fuzzy Set):** Interval valued fuzzy set are now generalized by allowing the interval to be fuzzy, i.e., for each x an fuzzy set can be assigned instead of assigning a subinterval in $[0,1]$. This concept can be implemented when boundaries of the intervals are not definite.

A Type-II fuzzy set is an fuzzy set whose membership values are expressed in terms of fuzzy sets defined on $[0,1]$. Thus the membership function of a

Figure 20. Interval valued fuzzy set

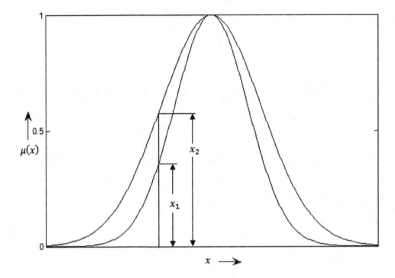

Type-II fuzzy set is of the form $\mu_{\tilde{A}} : X \rightarrow \chi\big(\big[0,1\big]\big)$, where $\chi\big(\big[0,1\big]\big)$ denotes the set of all fuzzy sets defined on $\big[0,1\big]$.

- **Definition 2.2.17:** (L – **Fuzzy Set**): In fuzzy sets the membership values are restricted to a number between 0 and 1. If the restriction be omitted and allowing the membership value to be elements of any arbitrary set L, i.e., if the membership function $\mu_{\tilde{A}}$ is a mapping from X to L, then the fuzzy set is termed as L – Fuzzy set.

Figure 21. Type-II fuzzy set

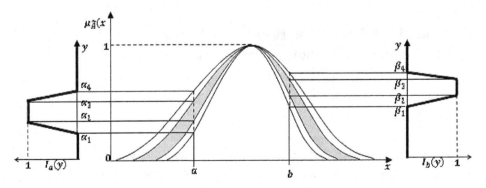

- **Definition 2.2.18: (Level-2 Fuzzy Set):** The interval valued fuzzy set, type-II fuzzy set, $L -$ Fuzzy set are all generalized form of fuzzy sets, but in all these cases fuzzy sets are defined on an universal set X, i.e., generalization are made by extending the codomain set. Now, if the domain set X be extended to the set $\mathcal{F}(X)$ of all fuzzy sets defined on X, i.e., if the membership function $\mu_{\tilde{A}}$ is a mapping $\mu_{\tilde{A}}: \mathcal{F}(X) \to [0,1]$. This concept can be implemented when the elements of the universal set are not specified precisely.

- **Definition 2.2.19: (Intuitionistic Fuzzy Set):** The concept of fuzzy set is developed based on the membership values of each element of the universal set X to deal with the possibilistic uncertainties. However, the fuzzy sets are not always capable of dealing with lack of knowledge with respect to degrees of membership. Realizing the fact Atanassov (1986) introduced the concept of intuitionistic fuzzy sets by implementing a non- membership degree which can handle the drawback of fuzzy sets and express more abundant and flexible information than the fuzzy sets.

Let X be a universal set. An intuitionistic fuzzy set $\tilde{A}$ in X assigns to each element x of X a membership degree $\mu_{\tilde{A}}(x) \in [0,1]$ and a non-membership degree $\nu_{\tilde{A}}(x) \in [0,1]$ such that $\mu_{\tilde{A}}(x) + \nu_{\tilde{A}}(x) \leq 1$. An intuitionistic fuzzy set $\tilde{A}$ is mathematically represented as $\{\langle x, \mu_{\tilde{A}}(x), \nu_{\tilde{A}}(x)\rangle : x \in X\}$.

- **Definition 2.2.20: (Fuzzy Number):** A fuzzy set $\tilde{A}$ on $\mathbb{R}$ is said to be a FN if
  - $\tilde{A}$ is a normal F.
  - The $\alpha -$ cut $\tilde{A}[\alpha]$ is a closed interval for all $\alpha \in (0,1]$.
  - The support of $\tilde{A}$, i.e., $\tilde{A}[0 +]$ is bounded.

Alternatively, an FN can also be expressed in the following form
A fuzzy set $\tilde{A}$ defined on the set of real numbers, $\mathbb{R}$, is said to be an FN if its membership function $\mu_{\tilde{A}}(x)$ satisfies the following characteristics:

1. $\mu_{\tilde{A}}: \mathbb{R} \to [0,1]$ is continuous.
2. $\mu_{\tilde{A}}(x) = 0$ for all $x \in (-\infty, a] \cup [d, \infty)$.
3. $\mu_{\tilde{A}}(x)$ is strictly increasing on $[a,b]$ and strictly decreasing on $[c,d]$.

4. $\mu_{\tilde{A}}(x) = 1$ for all $x \in [b,c]$ where $a \le b \le c \le d$.

The concept of an FN is illustrated by Figure 22.

- **Definition 2.2.21: (L-R Type Fuzzy Number):** An FN $\tilde{A} = (a,b,c,d;1)$ is said to be a L-R type FN if its membership function is expressed in the form

$$\mu_{\tilde{A}}(x) = \begin{cases} L\left(\dfrac{x-a}{b-a}\right) & if \quad a \le x \le b \\ 1 & if \quad b \le x \le c \\ R\left(\dfrac{d-x}{d-c}\right) & if \quad c \le x \le d \\ 0 & otherwise \end{cases}$$

Here L and R are reference functions.

- **Definition 2.2.22: (Trapezoidal Fuzzy Number):** A $L-R$ type FN $\tilde{A} = (a,b,c,d;1)$ is called a trapezoidal FN if its membership function takes the form

Figure 22. FN

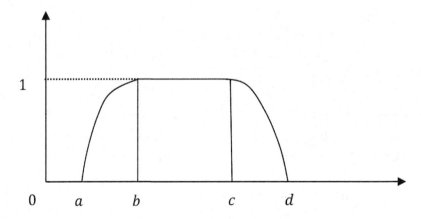

$$\mu_{\tilde{A}}(x) = \begin{cases} \dfrac{x-a}{b-a} & if \quad a \le x \le b \\ 1 & if \quad b \le x \le c \\ \dfrac{d-x}{d-c} & if \quad c \le x \le d \\ 0 & otherwise \end{cases}$$

Diagrammatically, a trapezoidal FN is represented by Figure 23.

- **Definition 2.2.23: (Triangular Fuzzy Number):** A trapezoidal FN $\tilde{A} = (a, b, c, d; 1)$ is said to be a triangular FN if $b = c$. Thus the membership function of a triangular FN $\tilde{A} = (a, b, d; 1)$ is

$$\mu_{\tilde{A}}(x) = \begin{cases} \dfrac{x-a}{b-a} & if \quad a \le x \le b \\ \dfrac{d-x}{d-b} & if \quad b \le x \le d \\ 0 & otherwise \end{cases}$$

It is expressed by Figure 24.

Figure 23. Trapezoidal FN

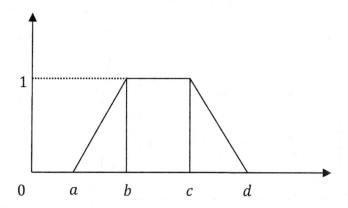

Figure 24. Triangular FN

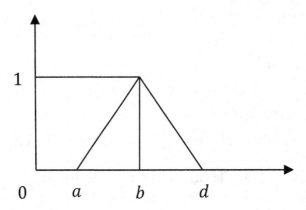

- **Definition 2.2.24: (Generalized Fuzzy Number):** A fuzzy set $\tilde{A} = \left(a, b, c, d; w\right)$ defined on the set of real numbers, $\mathbb{R}$, is said to be a generalized FN if its membership function $\mu_{\tilde{A}}\left(x\right)$ has the following characteristics:
  - $\mu_{\tilde{A}} : \mathbb{R} \to \left[0, w\right]$ is continuous.
  - $\mu_{\tilde{A}}\left(x\right) = 0$ for all $x \in \left(-\infty, a\right] \cup \left[d, \infty\right)$.
  - $\mu_{\tilde{A}}\left(x\right)$ is strictly increasing on $\left[a, b\right]$ and strictly decreasing on $\left[c, d\right]$.
  - $\mu_{\tilde{A}}\left(x\right) = w$ for all $x \in \left[b, c\right]$ where $a \leq b \leq c \leq d$ and $0 < w \leq 1$.

Figure 25. Comparison between generalized FN and FN

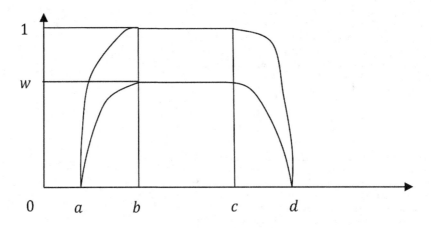

Thus it is observed that in case of generalized FN the height of the corresponding fuzzy set may not be equal to one. When the height of a generalized FN is equals to one then it becomes an FN. The generalized FN can also be classified into generalized L-R type FN, generalized trapezoidal FN, generalized triangular FN, etc., based on their membership functions.

A generalized FN $\tilde{A} = (a, b, c, d; w)$ will be a generalized L-R type FN if its membership function is expressed in the form

$$
\mu_{\tilde{A}}(x) = \begin{cases}
wL\left(\dfrac{x-a}{b-a}\right) & if \quad a \leq x \leq b \\
w & if \quad b \leq x \leq c \\
wR\left(\dfrac{d-x}{d-c}\right) & if \quad c \leq x \leq d \\
0 & otherwise
\end{cases}
$$

Again, the generalized L-R type FN $\tilde{A} = (a, b, c, d; w)$ is a generalized trapezoidal FN if its membership function takes the form

$$
\mu_{\tilde{A}}(x) = \begin{cases}
w\dfrac{x-a}{b-a} & if \quad a \leq x \leq b \\
w & if \quad b \leq x \leq c \\
w\dfrac{d-x}{d-c} & if \quad c \leq x \leq d \\
0 & otherwise
\end{cases}
$$

Figure 26. Comparison between generalized trapezoidal FN and trapezoidal FN

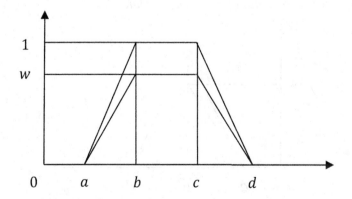

From the above diagram it is clear that the height of a trapezoidal FN is one, whereas the height of the generalized trapezoidal FN may not be equal to one.

Similarly, a generalized trapezoidal FN $\tilde{A} = \left(a, b, c, d; w\right)$ will to be a generalized triangular FN if $b = c$. Thus the membership function of a generalized triangular FN $\tilde{A} = \left(a, b, d; w\right)$ is

$$\mu_{\tilde{A}}\left(x\right) = \begin{cases} w\dfrac{x - a}{b - a} & if \quad a \leq x \leq b \\ w\dfrac{d - x}{d - b} & if \quad b \leq x \leq d \\ 0 & otherwise \end{cases}$$

- **Definition 2.2.25: (Fuzzy Inequality):** Let $F\left(\mathbb{R}\right)$ be the set of all FNs defined on $\mathbb{R}$. On $F\left(\mathbb{R}\right)$ different types of partial order relations may be defined. In this book a fuzzy partial order relation is presented due to Kaufmann and Gupta (1985). A fuzzy partial order relation $'\succsim'$ between two FNs $\tilde{A}$ and $\tilde{B}$ is denoted by $\tilde{A} \succsim \tilde{B}$, and defined as "$\tilde{A} \succsim \tilde{B}$ if and only if $a^L \geq b^L$ and $a^R \geq b^R$", where $\tilde{A}\left[\alpha\right] = \left[a^L, a^R\right]$ and $\tilde{B}\left[\alpha\right] = \left[b^L, b^R\right]$. The advantage of using this type of partial order relation is that it reduces mathematical computation, significantly.

In the next subsection some well-known defuzzification techniques of FNs and generalized FNs are discussed.

Figure 27. Comparison between generalized triangular FN and triangular FN

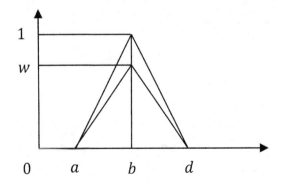

2.2.3 Defuzzification of a Fuzzy Number

To convert fuzzy programming model into its equivalent deterministic model different defuzzification methodologies of FNs are used. Defuzzification of FN is a mapping from the set of all FNs to the set of real numbers and that real value is known as the defuzzified value of the corresponding FN. The idea of defuzzification was first proposed by Jain (1976). Later on Yager (1981) proposed four indices which are used for the purpose of ordering fuzzy quantities in $[0,1]$. In 1998 Cheng (1998) proposed a defuzzification technique for finding equivalent crisp value of an FNs using distance method. A defuzzification method based on the $\alpha-$ cut of the FNs was presented by Delgado et al. (1998). For ranking generalized trapezoidal FNs, Chen and Chen (2007) proposed a defuzzification method in the context of fuzzy risk analysis. Kumar et al. (2011) suggested a defuzzification technique for L-R FNs and further based on the defuzzified value ranking of L-R FNs are also presented. Different defuzzification techniques have been studied and were applied to fuzzy control and fuzzy expert system (Filev and Yager, 1991; Yager and Filev, 1993) by several researchers in the past. The major idea behind these methods was to obtain a typical value from a given fuzzy set according to some specified characters, such as central gravity, median etc. A technique for defuzzification of FN using Mellin's transform was developed by Saneifard and Saneifard (2011). A defuzzification method of FNs using the distance between two FNs was developed by Ma et al. (2000). Another defuzzification method of FNs by centroid method was presented by Wang *et al.* (2006). Abbasbandy and Asady (2006) developed a method of ranking FN based on sign distance between FNs. Different defuzzification techniques were further developed by Yoon (1996), Asady (2010), Brandas (2011) and others. Recently, a defuzzification technique based on possibility theory is proposed by Qiupeng and Zuxing (2016) for ranking generalized FNs.

Let $F(\mathbb{R})$ be the set of all FNs. A defuzzification of FN is a mapping from the set $F(\mathbb{R})$ to the set of real number $\mathbb{R}$. Thus, if V be a mapping, $V:F(\mathbb{R}) \rightarrow \mathbb{R}$, then the real number $V(\tilde{A})$ is called the defuzzified value of the FN $\tilde{A}$.

Now some well-known defuzzification methods are presented in this section to provide a clear concept to the readers. Using the first five methodologies as described below, defuzzified value of FNs is calculated and the last methodology helps to find the defuzzified value of generalized FNs.

2.2.3.1 Different Defuzzification Techniques

1. Canonical form of an FN.
2. Defuzzification of an FN using $\alpha-$ cuts.
3. Defuzzification of an FN using probability density function.
4. Centroid of an FN.
5. Nearest symmetric triangular defuzzification.
6. Ranking of FN based on possibility theory.

2.2.3.1.1 Canonical Form of an Fuzzy Number

This defuzzification technique was developed by Delgado *et al.* (1998). Let $\tilde{A}$ be an FN. In this chapter it is discussed that $\alpha-$ cut of FN is a closed interval. Therefore $\alpha-$ cut of the FN $\tilde{A}$ is $\tilde{A}[\alpha] = \left[L_{\tilde{A}}(\alpha), \ R_{\tilde{A}}(\alpha) \right]$. According to Delgado et al. (1998) the defuzzified value of the FN $\tilde{A}$ is evaluated by using the following formula

$$V\left(\tilde{A}\right) = \int_0^1 \left(L_{\tilde{A}}(\alpha) + R_{\tilde{A}}(\alpha) \right) s(\alpha) \, d\alpha$$

where $s : [0,1] \to [0,1]$ is known as reducing function.

If $\tilde{A} = \left(a^L, a, a^R \right)$ be any triangular FN, then the defuzzified value of $\tilde{A}$ is evaluated by applying Delgado's defuzzification technique. The membership function $\mu_{\tilde{A}}(x)$ of the triangular FN $\tilde{A} = \left(a^L, a, a^R \right)$ is expressed as

$$\mu_{\tilde{A}}(x) = \begin{cases} \dfrac{\left(x - a^L \right)}{\left(a - a^L \right)} & if \quad a^L \le x \le a \\[2mm] \dfrac{\left(a^R - x \right)}{\left(a^R - a \right)} & if \quad a \le x \le a^R \\[2mm] 0 & otherwise \end{cases}.$$

Then the $\alpha-$ cut of the triangular FN $\tilde{A} = \left(a^L, a, a^R \right)$ is written as

$$\tilde{A}[\alpha] = \left[a^L + \left(a - a^L \right)\alpha, a^R - \left(a^R - a \right)\alpha \right].$$

Now the defuzzified value of the triangular FN $\tilde{A}$ is calculated according to the formula

$$V\left(\tilde{A}\right) = \int\limits_0^1 \left(a^L + \left(a - a^L \right)\alpha \right)\alpha d\alpha + \int\limits_0^1 \left(a^R - \left(a^R - a \right)\alpha \right)\alpha d\alpha$$

$$= \left[\frac{a^L}{2} + \frac{\left(a - a^L \right)}{3} + \frac{a^R}{2} - \frac{\left(a^R - a \right)}{3} \right] = \frac{\left(a^L + 4a + a^R \right)}{6}.$$

Here the reducing function is taken as $s(\alpha) = \alpha$.

Instead of taking triangular FN if the FN $\tilde{A}$ is considered as trapezoidal FN of the form $\tilde{A} = (a,b,c,d)$ then the $\alpha -$ cut of the FN $\tilde{A}$ is $\tilde{A}[\alpha] = \left[a + \left(b - a \right)\alpha, d - \left(d - c \right)\alpha \right]$. Thus, the defuzzified value of $\tilde{A}$ is

$$V\left(\tilde{A}\right) = \int\limits_0^1 \left(a + \left(b - a \right)\alpha \right)\alpha d\alpha + \int\limits_0^1 \left(d - \left(d - c \right)\alpha \right)\alpha d\alpha$$

$$= \left[\frac{a}{2} + \frac{\left(b - a \right)}{3} + \frac{d}{2} - \frac{\left(d - c \right)}{3} \right]$$

$$= \frac{\left[a + 2b + 2c + d \right]}{6}.$$

2.2.3.1.2 Defuzzification of a Fuzzy Number Using $\alpha -$ Cuts

In 2011 Kumar *et al.* (2011) developed an approach of defuzzification of FNs using $\alpha -$ cuts of FNs.

Let $\tilde{A}$ be an FN. Then, its $\alpha -$ cut is a closed interval of the form $\tilde{A}[\alpha] = \left[L_{\tilde{A}}(\alpha), R_{\tilde{A}}(\alpha) \right]$. The defuzzified value of the FN $\tilde{A}$ in this method is evaluated by the expression as

$$V\left(\tilde{A}\right) = \lambda \int_0^1 L_{\tilde{A}}\left(\alpha\right) d\alpha + \left(1 - \lambda\right) \int_0^1 R_{\tilde{A}}\left(\alpha\right) d\alpha, \ 0 < \lambda < 1$$

From the above it is clear that the formula is based on the convex combination of the integrals $\int_0^1 L_{\tilde{A}}\left(\alpha\right) d\alpha$ and $\int_0^1 R_{\tilde{A}}\left(\alpha\right) d\alpha$.

For example, if $\tilde{A} = \left(a^L, a, a^R\right)$ be any triangular FN, then the defuzzified value of $\tilde{A}$ is obtained using the following process.

The $\alpha-$ cut of the FN $\tilde{A}$ is given by
$$\tilde{A}[\alpha] = \left[a^L + \left(a - a^L\right)\alpha, \ a^R - \left(a^R - a\right)\alpha\right].$$

So, the defuzzified value of $\tilde{A}$ (according to Kumar et al. (2011)) is formulated as

$$V\left(\tilde{A}\right) = \lambda \int_0^1 (a^L + \left(a - a^L\right)\alpha \ ) d\alpha + \left(1 - \lambda\right) \int_0^1 (a^R - \left(a^R - a\right)\alpha \ ) d\alpha$$

$$= \frac{\lambda}{2}\left(a + a^L\right) + \frac{\left(1 - \lambda\right)}{2}\left(a + a^R\right),$$

Again if $\tilde{A}$ is considered as trapezoidal FN of the form $\tilde{A} = \left(a,b,c,d\right)$ then the defuzzified value of $\tilde{A}$ is calculated as

$$V\left(\tilde{A}\right) = \lambda \int_0^1 \left(a + \left(b - a\right)\alpha\right) d\alpha + \left(1 - \lambda\right) \int_0^1 \left(d - \left(d - c\right)\alpha\right) d\alpha$$

$$= \frac{\lambda}{2}\left(a + b\right) + \frac{\left(1 - \lambda\right)}{2}\left(c + d\right).$$

2.2.3.1.3 Defuzzification of a Fuzzy Number Using Proportional Probability Density Function

This methodology is based on proportional probability density function of every FN.

Let $\tilde{A}$ be any FN and let $\mu_{\tilde{A}}(x)$ be its membership function. Then a probability density function for the FN $\tilde{A}$ can be constructed by defining $f_{\tilde{A}}(x) = c\mu_{\tilde{A}}(x)$, called the proportional probability density function associated with the FN $\tilde{A}$. Here c is a constant obtained by using the property of probability density function $\int\limits_{-\infty}^{\infty} f_{\tilde{A}}(x)\,dx = 1$, i.e. $\int\limits_{-\infty}^{\infty} c\mu_{\tilde{A}}(x)\,dx = 1$

After that, the Mellin transform is used to calculate the defuzzified or expected value of an FN. Now, the Mellin transform $M_X(t)$ of a probability density function $f_{\tilde{A}}(x)$ is written as $M_X(t) = \int\limits_{0}^{\infty} x^{t-1} f_{\tilde{A}}(x)\,dx$

Also the expected value of the function x^{t-1} is given by $E\left(X^{t-1}\right) = \int\limits_{-\infty}^{\infty} x^{t-1} f_{\tilde{A}}(x)\,dx$.

As x is positive, therefore $E\left(X^{t-1}\right) = \int\limits_{0}^{\infty} x^{t-1} f_{\tilde{A}}(x)\,dx = M_X(t)$.

Thus the expected value of the FN is $E(X) = M_X(2)$ (put $t = 2$). This defuzzification technique was developed by Saneifard and Saneifard (2011). Like the other defuzzification techniques this methodology is also explained through triangular and trapezoidal FNs.

Let $\tilde{A}$ be a triangular FN. Then $\tilde{A}$ is of the form $\tilde{A} = \left(a^L, a, a^R\right)$ and whose membership function is given by

$$\mu_{\tilde{A}}(x) = \begin{cases} \dfrac{x - a^L}{a - a^L} & a^L \leq x \leq a \\ \dfrac{a^R - x}{a^R - a} & a \leq x \leq a^R, \\ 0 & \text{otherwise} \end{cases}$$

The proportional probability density function is calculated as presented in the development section $f_{\tilde{A}}(x) = c\mu_{\tilde{A}}(x)$, where c is calculated as $\int\limits_{-\infty}^{\infty} f_{\tilde{A}}(x)\,dx = 1$.

i.e., $c \int\limits_{a^L}^{a} \dfrac{x - a^L}{a - a^L} \, dx + c \int\limits_{a}^{a^R} \dfrac{a^R - x}{a^R - a} \, dx = 1$

i.e., $c = \dfrac{2}{\left(a^R - a^L\right)}$

Thus the proportional probability density function corresponding to the triangular FN $\tilde{A}$ is given by

$$f_{X_{\tilde{A}}}(x) = \begin{cases} \dfrac{2\left(x - a^L\right)}{\left(a - a^L\right)\left(a^R - a^L\right)} & a^L \leq x \leq a \\[4mm] \dfrac{2\left(a^R - x\right)}{\left(a^R - a\right)\left(a^R - a^L\right)} & a \leq x \leq a^R \;. \\[4mm] 0 & \text{otherwise} \end{cases}$$

Again by using Mellin transform,

$$M_{X_{\tilde{A}}}(t) = \int\limits_{0}^{\infty} x^{t-1} f_{X_{\tilde{A}}}(x) \, dx$$

$$= \int\limits_{a^L}^{a} x^{t-1} \dfrac{2\left(x - a^L\right)}{\left(a - a^L\right)\left(a^R - a^L\right)} \, dx + \int\limits_{a}^{a^R} x^{t-1} \dfrac{2\left(a^R - x\right)}{\left(a^R - a\right)\left(a^R - a^L\right)} \, dx$$

$$M_{X_{\tilde{A}}}(t) = \dfrac{2}{\left(a^R - a^L\right)(t+1)} \left[\dfrac{a^R\left(\left(a^R\right)^t - a^t\right)}{a^R - a} - \dfrac{a^L\left(a^t - \left(a^L\right)^t\right)}{a - a^L} \right]$$

Thus the mean of the random variable $X_{\tilde{A}}$ can be obtained as

$$E\left(X_{\tilde{A}}\right) = M_{X_{\tilde{A}}}\left(2\right) = \frac{a^{L} + a + a^{R}}{3}.$$

Instead of taking triangular FN if $\tilde{A}$ be considered as trapezoidal FN of the form $\tilde{A} = \left(a,b,c,d\right)$, then the value of the constant c is evaluated as $c = \dfrac{2}{c + d - a - b}$. Thus the proportional probability density function of the random variable corresponding to a trapezoidal FN $\tilde{A} = \left(a,b,c,d\right)$ is

$$f_{X_{\tilde{A}}}\left(x\right) = \begin{cases} \dfrac{2\left(x - a\right)}{\left(b - a\right)\left(c + d - a - b\right)} & a \le x \le b \\[2ex] \dfrac{2\left(d - x\right)}{\left(d - c\right)\left(c + d - a - b\right)} & c \le x \le d \\[2ex] 0 & \text{otherwise} \end{cases}$$

Then using the Mellin's transform the defuzzified value of the trapezoidal FN is obtained as

$$E\left(X_{\tilde{A}}\right) = M_{X_{\tilde{A}}}\left(2\right) = \frac{1}{3}\left(a + b + c + d + \frac{\left(ab - cd\right)}{\left(c + d - a - b\right)}\right).$$

2.2.3.1.4 Centroid of a Fuzzy Number

This defuzzification technique was developed by Wang *et al.* (2006). This methodology is based on the distance between the centroid point and the origin.

Let $\tilde{A}$ be an FN and $\mu_{\tilde{A}}\left(x\right)$ be its membership function which is expressed as

$$\mu_{\tilde{A}}\left(x\right) = \begin{cases} f_{\tilde{A}}^{L}\left(x\right) & a \le x \le b \\ 1 & b \le x \le c, \\ f_{\tilde{A}}^{R}\left(x\right) & c \le x \le d \end{cases}$$

where $f_{\tilde{A}}^L : [a,b] \to [0,1]$ and $f_{\tilde{A}}^R : [c,d] \to [0,1]$ are two strictly monotonic and continuous mappings from $\mathbb{R}$ to the closed interval $[0,1]$.

Since $f_{\tilde{A}}^L$ and $f_{\tilde{A}}^R$ are both strictly monotonic and continuous functions, their inverse functions exist and should also be continuous and strictly monotonic.

Let $g_{\tilde{A}}^L : [0,1] \to [a,b]$ and $g_{\tilde{A}}^R : [0,1] \to [c,d]$ be the inverse functions of $f_{\tilde{A}}^L(x)$ and $f_{\tilde{A}}^R(x)$, respectively. Then $g_{\tilde{A}}^L(y)$ and $g_{\tilde{A}}^R(y)$ are integrable on the closed interval $[0,1]$.

The centroid point of the FN $\tilde{A}$ is calculated as

$$x_0(\tilde{A}) = \frac{\int_{-\infty}^{\infty} x\mu_{\tilde{A}}(x)\,dx}{\int_{-\infty}^{\infty} \mu_{\tilde{A}}(x)\,dx} = \frac{\int_a^b xf_{\tilde{A}}^L(x)\,dx + \int_b^c x\,dx + \int_c^d xf_{\tilde{A}}^R(x)\,dx}{\int_a^b f_{\tilde{A}}^L(x)\,dx + \int_b^c dx + \int_c^d f_{\tilde{A}}^R(x)\,dx}$$

$$y_0(\tilde{A}) = \frac{\int_0^1 y\,(g_{\tilde{A}}^R(y) - g_{\tilde{A}}^L(y))\,dy}{\int_0^1 (g_{\tilde{A}}^R(y) - g_{\tilde{A}}^L(y))\,dy}$$

Thus the centroid point is evaluated as $\left(x_0(\tilde{A}), y_0(\tilde{A})\right)$ and the defuzzified value is obtained by calculating the distance of the point from the origin.

Hence the defuzzified value of $\tilde{A}$ is $V(\tilde{A}) = \sqrt{\left(x_0(\tilde{A})\right)^2 + \left(y_0(\tilde{A})\right)^2}$.

Let $\tilde{A} = \left(a^L, a, a^R\right)$ be a triangular FN, then the Centroid point of the triangular region is calculated by the equations defined above as

$$x_0(\tilde{A}) = \frac{1}{3}\left(a^L + a + a^R\right) \text{ and } y_0(\tilde{A}) = \frac{1}{3},$$

i.e., the centroid point is $\left(x_0(\tilde{A}), y_0(\tilde{A})\right) = \left[\frac{1}{3}\left(a^L + a + a^R\right), \frac{1}{3}\right]$.

Thus the defuzzified value of $\tilde{A}$ is $V(\tilde{A}) = \frac{1}{3}\sqrt{\left(\left(a^L + a + a^R\right)\right)^2 + 1}$.

Again, if $\tilde{A} = (a,b,c,d)$ be a trapezoidal FN, then the centroid point of the trapezoidal region is evaluated as

$$x_0\left(\tilde{A}\right) = \frac{1}{3}\left(a + b + c + d + \frac{\left(ab - cd\right)}{\left(c + d - a - b\right)}\right)$$

and $y_0\left(\tilde{A}\right) = \frac{1}{3}\left(1 + \frac{c - b}{\left(c + d - a - b\right)}\right)$,

i.e., the centroid point is computed as

$$\left(x_0\left(\tilde{A}\right), y_0\left(\tilde{A}\right)\right) = \left(\frac{1}{3}\left(a + b + c + d + \frac{\left(ab - cd\right)}{\left(c + d - a - b\right)}\right), \frac{1}{3}\left(1 + \frac{c - b}{\left(c + d - a - b\right)}\right)\right).$$

Hence the defuzzified value is described as

$$V\left(\tilde{A}\right) = \frac{1}{3}\sqrt{\left(\left(a + b + c + d + \frac{\left(ab - cd\right)}{\left(c + d - a - b\right)}\right)\right)^2 + \left(\left(1 + \frac{c - b}{\left(c + d - a - b\right)}\right)\right)^2}.$$

2.2.3.1.5 Nearest Symmetric Triangular Defuzzification

This defuzzification procedure was proposed by Ma *et al.* (2000). In this defuzzification approach at first each FNs are expressed in parametric form and then a symmetric triangular FN is generated to every FN. Finally minimizing the distance between these two FNs a defuzzified value of the former is obtained.

Let $\tilde{u}$ be a FN which is expressed in the parametric form as $\left(\underline{u}\left(r\right), \bar{u}\left(r\right)\right)$, $\left(0 \leq r \leq 1\right)$ and which satisfies the relation

1. $\underline{u}\left(r\right)$ is bounded monotonic increasing left continuous function.
2. $\bar{u}\left(r\right)$ is bounded monotonic decreasing left continuous function.
3. $\underline{u}\left(r\right) \leq \bar{u}\left(r\right)$, $0 \leq r \leq 1$

A popular FN which is the symmetric triangular FN $S[x_0,\sigma]$ centered at x_0 with basis σ is expressed as

$$S[x_0,\sigma] = \begin{cases} \dfrac{x - x_0 + \sigma}{\sigma} & x_0 - \sigma \leq x \leq x_0 \\ \dfrac{x_0 + \sigma - x}{\sigma} & x_0 \leq x \leq x_0 + \sigma \\ 0 & \text{otherwise} \end{cases}$$

Its parametric form is $\underline{u}(r) = x_0 - \sigma + \sigma r$ and $\overline{u}(r) = x_0 + \sigma - \sigma r$.

Now a distance between two FNs is defined as follows.

Let $\tilde{u} = (\underline{u},\overline{u})$ and $\tilde{v} = (\underline{v},\overline{v})$ be two FNs. The distance between $\tilde{u}$ and $\tilde{v}$ is defined as

$$D(\tilde{u},\tilde{v}) = \int_0^1 \left(\underline{u}(r) - \underline{v}(r)\right)^2 dr + \int_0^1 \left(\overline{u}(r) - \overline{v}(r)\right)^2 dr$$

Thus the distance between the above defined FNs $\tilde{u} = (\underline{u},\overline{u})$ and $S[x_0,\sigma]$ is calculated as

$$D(\tilde{u},S[x_0,\sigma]) = \int_0^1 \left(\underline{u}(r) - \underline{S[x_0,\sigma]}(r)\right)^2 dr + \int_0^1 \left(\overline{u}(r) - \overline{S[x_0,\sigma]}(r)\right)^2 dr$$

To minimize the distance $D(\tilde{u},S[x_0,\sigma])$, it is necessary to evaluate the first order partial derivatives $\dfrac{\partial D(\tilde{u},S[x_0,\sigma])}{\partial \sigma}$, $\dfrac{\partial D(\tilde{u},S[x_0,\sigma])}{\partial x_0}$ and equate those with zero, i.e., $\dfrac{\partial D(\tilde{u},S[x_0,\sigma])}{\partial \sigma} = 0$ and $\dfrac{\partial D(\tilde{u},S[x_0,\sigma])}{\partial x_0} = 0$.

Now $\dfrac{\partial D(\tilde{u},S[x_0,\sigma])}{\partial \sigma} = 0$ provides

$$2\int_0^1 \left(\underline{u}(r) - \sigma r - x_0 + \sigma\right)\left(1 - r\right)dr + 2\int_0^1 \left(\overline{u}(r) + \sigma r - x_0 - \sigma\right)\left(r - 1\right)dr = 0$$

i.e.,

$$-2\int_0^1 \left[\overline{u}(r) - \underline{u}(r)\right]\left(1 - r\right)dr + 4\int_0^1 \sigma\left(1 - r\right)^2 dr = 0$$

Again $\dfrac{\partial D\left(\tilde{u}, S\left[x_0, \sigma\right]\right)}{\partial x_0} = 0$ provides

$$-2\int_0^1 \left(\underline{u}(r) - \sigma r - x_0 + \sigma\right)dr - 2\int_0^1 \left(\overline{u}(r) + \sigma r - x_0 - \sigma\right)dr = 0.$$

The solution is obtained as $x_0 = \dfrac{1}{2}\int_0^1 \left[\underline{u}(r) + \overline{u}(r)\right]dr$ and

$$\sigma = \dfrac{3}{2}\int_0^1 \left[\overline{u}(r) - \underline{u}(r)\right]\left(1 - r\right)dr.$$

Thus the defuzzified value of $\tilde{u}$ is found as $V\left(\tilde{u}\right) = \dfrac{1}{2}\int_0^1 \left[\underline{u}(r) + \overline{u}(r)\right]dr$.

According to the procedure the defuzzified value of the triangular FN $\tilde{A} = \left(a^L, a, a^R\right)$ is given by $V\left(\tilde{A}\right) = \dfrac{\left(a^L + 2a + a^R\right)}{4}$. Again by applying the above defuzzification methodology the defuzzified value of the trapezoidal FN $\tilde{A} = \left(a, b, c, d\right)$ is determined as $V\left(\tilde{A}\right) = \dfrac{\left(a + b + c + d\right)}{4}$.

2.2.3.1.6 Ranking of Fuzzy Number Based on Possibility Theory

In this process a defuzzified value of generalized FNs are calculated based on possibilistic mean and possibilistic standard deviation. This concept of defuzzification was proposed by Qiupeng and Zuxing (2016). It is already stated that FNs is a normal fuzzy set, whereas, in the case of generalized FN, the height of the fuzzy set may not be equals to 1. Let $\tilde{A}$ be a generalized FN. Then its membership function $\mu_{\tilde{A}}(x)$ can be expressed as

$$\mu_{\tilde{A}}(x) = \begin{cases} wf_{\tilde{A}}^{L}(x) & a \leq x \leq b \\ w & b \leq x \leq c, \\ wf_{\tilde{A}}^{R}(x) & c \leq x \leq d \end{cases}$$

where $wf_{\tilde{A}}^{L} : [a,b] \rightarrow [0,w]$ and $wf_{\tilde{A}}^{R} : [c,d] \rightarrow [0,w]$ are two strictly monotonic and continuous mappings from R to the closed interval $[0,w]$, $(0 < w \leq 1)$.

The possibilistic mean value of the generalized FN is calculated on the basis of $\alpha-$ cut of the FN $\tilde{A}$. Let the $\alpha-$ cut of the FN $\tilde{A}$ be $\tilde{A}[\alpha] = [a_1(\alpha), a_2(\alpha)]$. Thus the possibilistic mean value of $\tilde{A}$ is evaluated as

$$M(\tilde{A}) = \frac{\int_0^w \left(\frac{\alpha\left(a_1(\alpha) + a_2(\alpha)\right)}{2} \right) d\alpha}{\int_0^w \alpha \, d\alpha} = \frac{1}{w^2} \int_0^w \left(\alpha\left(a_1(\alpha) + a_2(\alpha)\right) \right) d\alpha.$$

Now the possibilistic standard deviation of the generalized FN $\tilde{A}$ is calculated as

$$\sigma(\tilde{A}) = \sqrt{\frac{1}{2}\left[\int_0^w \alpha\left(a_2(\alpha) - a_1(\alpha)\right)^2 d\alpha\right]}.$$

According to Qiupeng and Zuxing (2016) the magnitude or the defuzzified value of the generalized FN $\tilde{A}$ is $Mag(\tilde{A}) = M(\tilde{A}) + \sigma(\tilde{A})$.

This defuzzification process is explained through generalized triangular and trapezoidal FNs.

If $\tilde{A} = \left(a^L, a, a^R; w\right)$ be a generalized triangular FN, then its $\alpha-$ cut is

$$\tilde{A}[\alpha] = \left[a^L + \left(a - a^L\right)\frac{\alpha}{w}, a^R - \left(a^R - a\right)\frac{\alpha}{w}\right].$$

Therefore, the possibilistic mean and possibilistic standard deviation is calculated as

$$M\left(\tilde{A}\right) = \frac{1}{w^2} \int_0^w \left[\alpha\left(a^L + \left(a - a^L\right)\frac{\alpha}{w} + a^R - \left(a^R - a\right)\frac{\alpha}{w}\right)\right] d\alpha = \frac{\left(a^L + 4a + a^R\right)}{6}$$

and

$$\sigma\left(\tilde{A}\right) = \sqrt{\frac{1}{2}\left[\int_0^w \alpha\left(a^R - \left(a^R - a\right)\frac{\alpha}{w} - a^L - \left(a - a^L\right)\frac{\alpha}{w}\right)^2 d\alpha\right]} = \frac{\left(a^R - a^L\right)w}{2\sqrt{6}} .$$

Therefore, the magnitude of the FN is given by

$$Mag\left(\tilde{A}\right) = \frac{\left(a^L + 4a + a^R\right)}{6} + \frac{\left(a^R - a^L\right)w}{2\sqrt{6}} .$$

Similarly, a generalized trapezoidal FN $\tilde{A} = \left(a,b,c,d;w\right)$ is taken into consideration. Then it's $\alpha -$ cut is expressed as

$$\tilde{A}[\alpha] = \left[a + \left(b - a\right)\frac{\alpha}{w}, d - \left(d - c\right)\frac{\alpha}{w}\right] .$$

Thus the possibilistic mean and possibilistic standard deviation in this case is calculated as

$$M\left(\tilde{A}\right) = \frac{1}{w^2} \int_0^w \left[\alpha\left(a + \left(b - a\right)\frac{\alpha}{w} + d - \left(d - c\right)\frac{\alpha}{w}\right)\right] d\alpha = \frac{\left(a + 2b + 2c + d\right)}{6}$$

and

$$\sigma\left(\tilde{A}\right) = \sqrt{\frac{1}{2}\left[\int_0^w \alpha\left(d - \left(d - c\right)\frac{\alpha}{w} - a - \left(b - a\right)\frac{\alpha}{w}\right)^2 d\alpha\right]}$$

$$= \frac{w}{\sqrt{2}} \sqrt{\frac{\left(d - a\right)^2}{2} + \left(d - c + b - a\right)^2 - \frac{2}{3}\left(d - a\right)\left(d - c + b - a\right)} .$$

Hence the magnitude of the FN is found as

$$Mag\left(\tilde{A}\right) = \frac{\left(a + 2b + 2c + d\right)}{6} + \frac{w}{\sqrt{2}} \sqrt{\left[\frac{\left(d - a\right)^2}{2} + \left(d - c + b - a\right)^2 - \frac{2}{3}\left(d - a\right)\left(d - c + b - a\right)\right]} \cdot$$

Using different defuzzification techniques as mentioned above, the defuzzified value of each FNs of various forms is calculated and based on those defuzzified value of the FNs the fuzzy programming models are converted into equivalent deterministic models and then solved to achieve the best compromise solution in the probabilistically uncertain fuzzily defined decision making environments.

In the next subsection the background of FRVs with its definition are discussed concisely.

2.3 FUZZY RANDOM VARIABLE

The concept of FRVs were introduced in the literature to analyze vaguely defined measurable functions related to the sample space of a random experiment, where the imprecision or roughness in values of these functions is expressed in terms of fuzzy sets. It is well known fact to the readers that in the case of random variables the parameters of the probability distribution are precise. Thus, if the parameters are imprecise in nature, the concept of random variables fails to represent them properly. From that view point the concept of FRVs were introduced. In the literature the concept of FRVs are presented in different approaches. Among those, the approach introduced by Kwakernaak (1978, 1979), approach presented by Kruse and Meyer (1987), and approach proposed by Puri and Ralescu (1986) and Klement et al. (1986) are widely used. Luhandjula (1996) introduced the concept of FRVs in optimization theory. It is already stated that FRV is an efficient tool through which hybrid uncertain situation in optimization theory can be handle successfully. A brief survey on the developments of fuzzy stochastic programming models including FRVs are found in the work of Luhandjula (2006). Several research studies dealing with FRVs were carried out especially in the last two decades. Most of these research work concern probabilistic aspects and results like, for instance, integration and differentiation of FRVs in probabilistic settings (Gil et al., 1998; Roman-Flores and Rojas-Medar, 1998; Gong, 2002; Rodriguez-Muniz et al., 2003) fuzzy martingales, sub- and super-martingales (Feng, 2000; Li et al., 2001; Li and Ogura, 2003), etc.

The formal definition of FRV is presented below.

- **Definition 2.3.1:** Let S be a sample space connecting to a random experiment E and P be a probability measure. A FRV on a probability space (S, Δ, P) is a fuzzy valued function $X : S \to \Phi_0(\mathbb{R})$, $\omega \to X_\omega$ such that for every Borel set B of $\mathbb{R}$ and for every $\alpha \in (0,1]$, $(X[\alpha])^{-1}(B) \in \Delta$, where $\Phi_0(\mathbb{R})$ and $X[\alpha]$ are the set of FNs and the set valued function, respectively. The set valued function or the α – cut of the FN X, $X[\alpha]$, has the form $X[\alpha] : S \to 2^{\mathbb{R}}$, $\omega \to X_\omega[\alpha] = \{x \in \mathbb{R} : X_\omega(x) \geq \alpha\}$.

By using decomposition theorem of FNs, the FRVs can be expressed as

$$X = \bigcup_{\alpha \in (0,1]} \alpha X.$$

In this book all FRVs are considered as continuous FRVs. A continuous FRV can be defined as follows:

Let X be a continuous random variable with probability density function $f(x,\theta)$, where θ is the parameter of the probability density function. If θ is uncertain in nature then θ can be represented in terms of an FN $\tilde{\theta}$. Then the continuous random variable with parameter as FN $\tilde{\theta}$ is termed as continuous FRV $\tilde{X}$. The probability density function of the continuous FRV $\tilde{X}$ is denoted by $f(x,\tilde{\theta})$ with the property $\int_{-\infty}^{\infty} f(x,\theta)\,dx = 1$; $\theta \in \tilde{\theta}[\alpha]$, where $\tilde{\theta}[\alpha]$ is the α – cut of the FN $\tilde{\theta}$.

As an efficient tool for solving MODM problems in hybrid decision making environments, FGP is widely used. In the last subsection of this chapter FGP methodology is discussed briefly. It is used for finding most suitable compromise solution of the objectives in an efficient manner.

2.4 FUZZY GOAL PROGRAMMING

In the context of MODM, goal programming appeared as an competent tool for finding compromise solution considering all the objectives. In goal programming, it is necessary to set definite aspiration level for each objective. But in actual practice it is not always possible to provide definite aspiration values of each objective. From that view point the concept of FGP was developed by Narasimhan (1980) as an extension of goal programming technique. Thereafter, Yang et al., (1991), Rao et al. (1992), Roy and Maiti (1998) were extended the concept of FGP in nonlinear programming problems. A method to solve FGP problems with preemptive priority structure via utilizing a penalty cost was proposed by Wang and Fu (1997). Arora and Gupta (2009) presented a FGP approach for bilevel programming problems with the characteristics of dynamic programming. An efficient methodology for solving CCP problems by using FGP technique were studied by Biswas and Modak (2011, 2012, 2013), Biswas and Bose (2011), etc.

In modeling real world decision problems (Chen et al., 2017), FGP appeared as a prominent tool for resolving uncertainties in a systematic manner. In FGP model formulation process, the membership functions (constructed on the basis of fuzzy goals) are first transformed into flexible membership goals by introducing under- and over- deviational variables to each of them and after that assigning the highest membership value (unity) as the aspiration level to each of them. Also it is obvious that in multi-objective decision making context full achievement of all the membership goals is not possible simultaneously. For that reason, to achieve the goal values of objectives as much as possible, the under-deviational variables are minimized in the decision making context.

In this book, two mostly used FGP methodologies are taken into consideration for solving multi-objective decision making problems in hybrid uncertain environment. They are

1.   Weighted FGP
2.   Priority based FGP

2.4.1 Weighted Fuzzy Goal Programming

Kim and Whang (1998) provided an approach to solve a weighted FGP problem with unequal weight unbalanced triangular membership functions. Iskander (2004) proposed a fuzzy weighted additive approach for solving FGP problems. Biswas and Bose (2013) suggested a weighted FGP approach for solving quadratic multi-objective multilevel programming problems.

The mathematical formulation of weighted FGP is expressed as follows

An optimization problem with K objectives can be presented in a fuzzy environment as

Find $X\left(x_1, x_2, \ldots, x_n\right)$

So as to satisfy

$$Z_k\left(X\right)\begin{pmatrix} \lesssim \\ \gtrsim \end{pmatrix} g_k, \ k = 1, 2, \ldots, K$$

subject to

$$\tilde{A}X\begin{pmatrix} \lesssim \\ \cong \\ \gtrsim \end{pmatrix}\tilde{b}$$

$$X \geq 0$$

where X is the vector of decision variables, and $\cong$, $\gtrsim$, $\lesssim$ indicates the equality, greater than or equal and less than or equal in fuzzy sense. The parameters $\tilde{A}$ and $\tilde{b}$ of the constraints are matrices with fuzzy entries. Let g_k^l and g_k^u be the lower and upper tolerance limits, respectively, for achievement of the aspired level g_k of the k – th fuzzy objective goal. Then the membership function of the fuzzy goal $Z_k\left(X\right)$ is characterized as follows:

For $\lesssim$ type restriction,

$$\mu_{Z_k}\left(X\right) = \begin{cases} 1 & if \quad Z_k\left(X\right) \leq g_k \\ \dfrac{g_k^u - Z_k\left(X\right)}{g_k^u - g_k} & if \quad g_k \leq Z_k\left(X\right) \leq g_k^u \\ 0 & if \quad Z_k\left(X\right) \geq g_k^u \end{cases}$$

For $\gtrsim$ type restriction,

$$\mu_{Z_k}(X) = \begin{cases} 1 & if & Z_k(X) \geq g_k \\ \dfrac{Z_k(X) - g_k^l}{g_k - g_k^l} & if & g_k^l \leq Z_k(X) \leq g_k \\ 0 & if & Z_k(X) \leq g_k^l \end{cases}$$

Thus the mathematical formulation of weighted FGP model is expressed as Find $X(x_1, x_2, \ldots, x_n)$ so as to

$$\text{Min } D = \sum_{k=1}^{K} w_k d_k^-$$

and satisfy

$$\mu_{Z_k}(X) + d_k^- - d_k^+ = 1 \text{ for } k = 1, 2, \ldots, K$$

Subject to

$$\tilde{A} X \begin{pmatrix} \lesssim \\ \cong \\ \gtrsim \end{pmatrix} \tilde{b}$$

$X \geq 0$ and $d_k^-, d_k^+ \geq 0$ with $d_k^- . d_k^+ = 0$, $k = 1, 2, \ldots, K$

where $w_k > 0$ represents the numerical weights of the goals which are determined as:

$$w_k = \frac{1}{\left(g_k^u - g_k\right)} \text{ for } \lesssim \text{type restriction and } w_k = \frac{1}{\left(g_k - g_k^l\right)} \text{ for } \gtrsim \text{type}$$

restriction.

2.4.2 Priority Based Fuzzy Goal Programming

The methodology based on the use of a nested hierarchy of priorities for each goal was proposed by Rubin and Narasimhan (1984). Tiwari et al. (1986) demonstrated a computational algorithm for solving an FGP problem with symmetrical triangular membership functions of fuzzy goals and preemptive priority structure. Pal and Moitra (2003) introduced an alternative idea, a multi-stage dynamic programming model, in order to solve GP problems with preemptive priority for achieving of the highest degree of each of the membership function. Biswas and Dewan (2012) and Biswas and De (2013) used the concept of priority based FGP technique for solving fractional programming problems.

Mathematical formulation of priority based FGP model is expressed as

Find $X\left(x_1, x_2, \ldots, x_n\right)$ so as to

$$\text{Min } D = \left[P_1\left(d^-\right), P_2\left(d^-\right), \ldots, P_n\left(d^-\right), \ldots, P_N\left(d^-\right)\right]$$

and satisfy

$$\mu_{Z_k}\left(X\right) + d_k^- - d_k^+ = 1$$

Subject to

$$\tilde{A}X \begin{pmatrix} \lesssim \\ \cong \\ \gtrsim \end{pmatrix} \tilde{b}$$

$X \geq 0$ and $d_k^-, d_k^+ \geq 0$ with $d_k^- . d_k^+ = 0$, $k = 1, 2, \ldots, K$.

where the $n-$th priority factor $\left(P_n\right)$ is assigned to the set of commensurable goals that are grouped together in the problem formulation and the priority factors have the relationship

$$P_1 >>> P_2 >>> \ldots >>> P_n >>> \ldots >>> P_N.$$

where ' $>>>$ ' implies much greater than i.e., the membership goals at the highest priority level $\left(P_1\right)$ are achieved to the extent possible before the set of membership goals at the next priority level $\left(P_2\right)$ is considered, and so forth.

REFERENCES

Abbasbandy, S., & Asady, B. (2006). Ranking of fuzzy numbers by sign distance. *Information Sciences*, *176*(16), 2405–2416. doi:10.1016/j. ins.2005.03.013

Arora, S. R., & Gupta, R. (2009). Interactive fuzzy goal programming approach for bilevel programming problem. *European Journal of Operational Research*, *194*(2), 368–376. doi:10.1016/j.ejor.2007.12.019

Asady, B. (2010). The revised method of ranking LR fuzzy number based on deviation degree. *Expert Systems with Applications*, *37*(7), 5056–5060. doi:10.1016/j.eswa.2009.12.005

Atanassov, K. T. (1986). Intuitionistic Fuzzy Sets. *Fuzzy Sets and Systems*, *20*(1), 87–96. doi:10.1016/S0165-0114(86)80034-3

Biswas, A., & Bose, K. (2011). A Fuzzy Programming Approach for Solving Quadratic Bilevel Programming Problems with Fuzzy Resource Constraints. *International Journal of Operational Research*, *12*(2), 142–156. doi:10.1504/IJOR.2011.042503

Biswas, A., & Bose, K. (2013). A Fuzzy Goal Programming Technique for Quadratic Multi-objective Multilevel Programming. *Proceedings of the 2013 IEEE International Conference on Fuzzy Systems (FUZZ IEEE 2013)*, 1 – 8.

Biswas, A., & De, A. K. (2013). A Priority based Fuzzy Programming Approach for Multi-objective Probabilistic Linear Fractional Programming. *Proceedings of the 2013 IEEE International Conference on Fuzzy Systems (FUZZ IEEE 2013)*, 1 – 6.

Biswas, A., & Dewan, S. (2012). Priority based Fuzzy Goal Programming Technique for Solving Fractional Fuzzy Goals by using Dynamic Programming. *Fuzzy Information and Engineering*, *4*(2), 165–180. doi:10.100712543-012-0109-x

Biswas, A., & Modak, N. (2011). A fuzzy goal programming method for solving chance constrained programming with fuzzy parameters. *Communications in Computer and Information Science, 140*, 187–196. doi:10.1007/978-3-642-19263-0_23

Biswas, A., & Modak, N. (2011). A Fuzzy Goal Programming Method for Solving Chance Constrained Programming with Fuzzy Parameters. *Communications in Computer and Information Science, 140*, 187–196. doi:10.1007/978-3-642-19263-0_23

Biswas, A., & Modak, N. (2012). A Fuzzy Goal Programming Approach for Fuzzy Multi-objective Stochastic Programming through Expectation Model. *Communications in Computer and Information Science, 283*, 124–135. doi:10.1007/978-3-642-28926-2_14

Biswas, A., & Modak, N. (2013). A Fuzzy Goal Programming Technique for Multi-objective Chance Constrained Programming with Normally Distributed Fuzzy Random Variables and Fuzzy Numbers. *International Journal of Mathematics in Operational Research, 5*(5), 551–570. doi:10.1504/IJMOR.2013.056116

Brandas, A. (2011). Approximation of fuzzy numbers by trapezoidal fuzzy numbers preserving the core the ambiguity and the value. Stud. Univ. *Babȩs-Bolyai Math., 56*(2), 247–259.

Chen, L. H., Ko, W. C., & Yeh, F. T. (2017). Approach based on fuzzy goal programing and quality function deployment for new product planning. *European Journal of Operational Research, 259*(2), 654–663. doi:10.1016/j.ejor.2016.10.028

Chen, S. J., & Chen, S. M. (2007). Fuzzy risk analysis based on the ranking of generalized trapezoidal fuzzy numbers. *Applied Intelligence, 26*(1), 1–11. doi:10.100710489-006-0003-5

Cheng, C. H. (1998). A new approach for ranking fuzzy numbers by distance method. *Fuzzy Sets and Systems, 95*(3), 307–317. doi:10.1016/S0165-0114(96)00272-2

Delgado, M., Vila, M. A., & Voxman, W. (1998). On a canonical representation of fuzzy number. *Fuzzy Sets and Systems, 93*(1), 125–135. doi:10.1016/S0165-0114(96)00144-3

Feng, Y. (2000). Decomposition theorems for fuzzy super martingales and sub martingales. *Fuzzy Sets and Systems*, *116*(2), 225–235. doi:10.1016/S0165-0114(98)00065-7

Filev, D. P., & Yager, R. R. (1991). A generalized defuzzification method via Bad Distribution. *International Journal of Intelligent Systems*, *6*(7), 687–697. doi:10.1002/int.4550060702

Gil, M. A., López-Díaz, M., & López-García, H. (1998). The fuzzy hyperbolic inequality index associated with fuzzy random variables. *European Journal of Operational Research*, *110*(2), 377–391. doi:10.1016/S0377-2217(97)00252-X

Gong, Z., Wu, C., & Li, B. (2002). On the problem of characterizing derivatives for the fuzzy-valued functions. *Fuzzy Sets and Systems*, *127*(3), 315–322. doi:10.1016/S0165-0114(01)00109-9

Iskander, M. G. (2004). A Fuzzy Weighted Additive Approach for Stochastic Fuzzy Goal Programming. *Applied Mathematics and Computation*, *154*(2), 543–553. doi:10.1016/S0096-3003(03)00734-3

Jain, R. (1976). Decision-making in the presence of fuzzy variables. *IEEE Transactions on Systems, Man, and Cybernetics*, *6*(10), 698–703. doi:10.1109/TSMC.1976.4309421

Kaufmann, A., & Gupta, M. M. (1985). *Introduction to fuzzy arithmetic: Theory and applications*. New York: Van Nostrand Reinhold.

Kim, J. S., & Whang, K. S. (1998). A Tolerance Approach to the Fuzzy Goal Programming Problems with Unbalanced Triangular Membership Function. *European Journal of Operational Research*, *107*(3), 614–624. doi:10.1016/S0377-2217(96)00363-3

Klement, E. P., Puri, M. L., & Ralescu, D. A. (1986). Limit theorems for fuzzy random variables. *Proceedings of the Royal Society of London A: Mathematical, Physical and Engineering Sciences*, *407*, 171–182. 10.1098/rspa.1986.0091

Klir, G. J., & Yuan, B. (1994). *Fuzzy Sets and Fuzzy Logic: Theory and Applications*. Prentice Hall of India.

Kruse, R., & Meyer, K. D. (1987). *Statistics with Vague Data*. Dordrecht: Reidel Publication Company. doi:10.1007/978-94-009-3943-1

Kumar, A., Singh, P., Kaur, P., & Kaur, A. (2011). A new approach for ranking of L-R type generalized fuzzy numbers. *Expert Systems with Applications, 38*(9), 10906–10910. doi:10.1016/j.eswa.2011.02.131

Kwakernaak, H. (1978). Fuzzy random variable –I. Definitions and theorems. *Information Sciences, 15*(1), 1–29. doi:10.1016/0020-0255(78)90019-1

Kwakernaak, H. (1979). Fuzzy Random variable-II. Algorithms and examples for the discrete case. *Information Sciences, 17*(3), 253–278. doi:10.1016/0020-0255(79)90020-3

Li, S., & Ogura, Y. (2003). A convergence theorem of fuzzy-valued martingales in the extended Hausdorff metric H-∞. *Fuzzy Sets and Systems, 135*(3), 391–399. doi:10.1016/S0165-0114(02)00145-8

Li, S., Ogura, Y., & Nguyen, H. T. (2001). Gaussian processes and martingales for fuzzy valued random variables with continuous parameter. *Information Sciences, 133*(1-2), 7–21. doi:10.1016/S0020-0255(01)00074-3

Luhandjula, M. K. (1996). Fuzziness and randomness in an optimization framework. *Fuzzy Sets and Systems, 77*(3), 291–297. doi:10.1016/0165-0114(95)00043-7

Luhandjula, M. K. (2006). Fuzzy Stochastic linear programming: Survey and future research directions. *European Journal of Operational Research, 174*(3), 1353–1367. doi:10.1016/j.ejor.2005.07.019

Ma, M., Kandel, A., & Friedman, M. (2000). A new approach for defuzzification. *Fuzzy Sets and Systems, 111*(3), 351–356. doi:10.1016/S0165-0114(98)00176-6

Narasimhan, R. (1980). On fuzzy goal programming–Some comments. *Decision Sciences, 11*, 532–538. doi:10.1111/j.1540-5915.1980.tb01142.x

Pal, B. B., & Moitra, B. N. (2003). A Goal Programming Procedure for Solving Problems with Multiple Fuzzy Goals Using Dynamic Programming. *European Journal of Operational Research, 144*(3), 480–491. doi:10.1016/S0377-2217(01)00384-8

Puri, M. L., & Ralescu, D. A. (1986). Fuzzy random variables. *Journal of Mathematical Analysis and Applications, 114*(2), 409–422. doi:10.1016/0022-247X(86)90093-4

Qiupeng, G., & Zuxing, X. (2016). A new approach for ranking fuzzy numbers based on possibility theory. *Journal of Computational and Applied Mathematics*. doi:10.1016/j.cam.2016.05.017

Rao, S., Sundararaju, K., Prakash, B. G., & Balakrishna, C. (1992). Fuzzy Goal Programming Approach for Structural Optimization. *AIAA Journal*, *30*(5), 1425–1432. doi:10.2514/3.11079

Rodríguez-Muñiz, L., López-Díaz, M., & Gil, M. A. (2003). Differentiating random upper semi continuous functions under the integral sign. *Test*, *12*(1), 241–258. doi:10.1007/BF02595821

Román-Flores, H., & Rojas-Medar, M. A. (1998). Differentiability of fuzzy-valued mapping. *Revista de Matemática e Estatística*, *16*, 223–239.

Roy, T. K., & Maiti, M. (1998). Multi-Objective Inventory Models of Deteriorating Items with Some Constraints in a Fuzzy Environment. *Computers & Operations Research*, *25*(12), 1085–1095. doi:10.1016/S0305-0548(98)00029-X

Rubin, P. A., & Narasimhan, R. (1984). Fuzzy goal programming with nested priorities. *Fuzzy Sets and Systems*, *14*(2), 115–129. doi:10.1016/0165-0114(84)90095-2

Saneifard, R., & Saneifard, R. (2011). A modified method for defuzzification by probability density function. *Journal of Applied Sciences Research*, *7*(2), 102–110.

Tiwari, R. N., Dharmar, S., & Rao, J. R. (1986). Priority structure in fuzzy goal programming. *Fuzzy Sets and Systems*, *19*(3), 251–259. doi:10.1016/0165-0114(86)90054-0

Wang, H. F., & Fu, C. C. (1997). A Generalization of Fuzzy Goal Programming with Preemptive Structure. *Computers & Operations Research*, *24*(9), 819–828. doi:10.1016/S0305-0548(96)00096-2

Wang, Y. M., Yang, J. B., Xu, D. L., & Chin, K. S. (2006). On the centroids of fuzzy numbers. *Fuzzy Sets and Systems*, *157*(7), 919–926. doi:10.1016/j.fss.2005.11.006

Yager, R. R. (1981). A procedure for ordering fuzzy subsets of the unit interval. *Information Sciences*, *24*(2), 143–161. doi:10.1016/0020-0255(81)90017-7

Yager, R. R., & Filev, D. P. (1993). A simple adaptive defuzzification method. *IEEE Transactions on Fuzzy Systems*, *1*(1), 69–78. doi:10.1109/TFUZZ.1993.390286

Yang, T., Ignizio, J. P., & Kim, H. J. (1991). Fuzzy programming with nonlinear membership functions: Piecewise linear approximation. *Fuzzy Sets and Systems*, *41*(1), 39–53. doi:10.1016/0165-0114(91)90156-K

Yoon, K. P. (1996). A probabilistic approach to rank complex fuzzy numbers. *Fuzzy Sets and Systems*, *80*(2), 167–176. doi:10.1016/0165-0114(95)00193-X

Zadeh, L. A. (1965). Fuzzy sets. *Information and Control*, *8*(3), 338–353. doi:10.1016/S0019-9958(65)90241-X

Chapter 3
Fuzzy Linear Multi-Objective Stochastic Programming Models

ABSTRACT

In this chapter, fuzzy goal programming (FGP) technique is presented to solve fuzzy multi-objective chance constrained programming (CCP) problems having parameters associated with the system constrains following different continuous probability distributions. Also, the parameters of the models are presented in the form of crisp numbers or fuzzy numbers (FNs) or fuzzy random variables (FRVs). In model formulation process, the imprecise probabilistic problem is converted into an equivalent fuzzy programming model by applying CCP methodology and the concept of α – cuts of FNs, successively. If the parameters of the objectives are in the form of FRVs then expectation model of the objectives are employed to remove the probabilistic nature from multiple objectives. Afterwards, considering the fuzzy nature of the parameters involved with the problem, the model is converted into an equivalent crisp model using two different approaches. The problem can either be decomposed on the basis of tolerance values of the parameters; alternatively, an equivalent deterministic model can be obtained by applying different defuzzification techniques of FNs. In the solution process, the individual optimal value of each objective is found in isolation to construct the fuzzy goals of the objectives. Then the fuzzy goals are transformed into membership goals on the basis of optimum values of each objective. Then priority-based FGP under different priority structures or weighted FGP is used for achievement of the highest membership degree to the extent possible to achieve the ideal point dependent solution in the decision-making context. Finally, several numerical examples considering different types of probability distributions and different forms of FNs are considered to illustrate the developed methodologies elaborately.

DOI: 10.4018/978-1-5225-8301-1.ch003

3.1 FUZZY CHANCE CONSTRAINED PROGRAMMING MODEL

In previous chapters, it is already mentioned that CCP methodology is used to solve stochastic programming problems in which the associated parameters are in the form of random variables following some known probability distribution. In 1959, Charnes and Cooper (1959) first introduced the concept of CCP as a tool to solve optimization problems with probabilistic uncertainties. In CCP (Kataoka, 1963; Prekopa, 1973; Sinha et al., 1998) if the problem contains several numbers of conflicting objectives, it is known as multi-objective CCP. Methodological aspects of CCP problems were further studied (Mohammed, 2000) and applied to solve different real life decision making problems by several researchers in the field of watershed nutrient load reduction (Dong et al., 2014), vehicle routine problem (ZareMehrjerdi, 1986), urban land-use planning and land use policy analysis (Zhou, 2015), etc.

Again, in modeling real life problems, a decision may have to be taken on the basis of some data which are not only probabilistic but also possibilistic or a combination of both. This situation occurs due to the lack of decision makers' sufficient knowledge about the occurrence as well as value of the parameters involved with the process concerned. So the concept of FRVs (Kwakernaak, 1978) was introduced in hybrid decision making environments. Different researchers (Sakawa et al., 2003; Luhandjula and Robert 2010) developed various techniques using FRVs (Lai and Hwang, 1994; Luhandjula, 1996) to solve CCP problems in fuzzy stochastic environment. In 2001, Liu (2001) proposed a simple expected value model with FRVs. An FGP technique for solving CCP with FRVs associated with the system constraints was presented by Biswas and Modak (2011, 2012). A new method for solving multi-objective linear programming models with FRVs is developed by Nematian (2012). Yano and Sakawa (2012) proposed an interactive method for solving multi-objective fuzzy random linear programming problem through fractile criteria. In 2017 Katagiri et al. (2017) developed a necessity measure based probabilistic expectation models for linear programming problems with discrete FRVs. Recently, De et al. (2018), formulated a methodology for solving multi-objective fuzzy stochastic programming problems with Cauchy and extreme value distributed FRVs.

It has been found that most of the parameters of probabilistic models assume normal distribution (Hock and Schittkowski, 1981) and some of them follow exponential distribution (Biswal et al, 1998) also. During the last decade stochastic linear programming with Cauchy distribution and extreme value distribution was investigated by Sahoo and Biswal (2005). In their method two multi-objective linear programming models are considered with right side parameters of the constraints of one model as Cauchy distributed random variables and another as extreme value distributed random variables. Finally, to find the compromise solution goal programming methodology is used for both the models. Like various probability distributions Cauchy distribution provides distribution of ratio of two independent standardized normal variates whereas extreme value distribution presents a limiting model for the distribution of the maximum or minimum of finite number of values selected from an exponential type distribution such as normal, gamma, exponential. Also log-normal distribution plays an important role for its wide applications in the fields of engineering, earth sciences, medicines, radioactivity and other decision making arena. The genesis of log normal distribution is found during nineteenth century in the work of Galton (1879), Weber (1834), Fechner (1897) and others.

In the present chapter FGP process is adopted for solving two types of fuzzy multi-objective CCP models where the parameter of the objectives is either crisp numbers or FNs or FRVs following various continuous probability distributions. The parameters of the system constraints are also considered as either FNs or FRVs. Based on the nature of the parameters of the fuzzy stochastic linear programming model various situations are discussed in this chapter. In the model formulation process the fuzzy multi-objective CCP problem is converted into FP problem with the help of CCP methodology, $\alpha -$ cut of FNs and first decomposition theorem on fuzzy set theory. Then considering either the tolerance of the FNs, the problem is decomposed on the basis of their tolerance ranges of fuzzy parameters, or the problem is converted into a deterministic problem by using different methods of defuzzification. Based on the imprecise aspiration level of each of the individual objective, the membership functions are defined to measure the degree of achievements of the goal levels of the objectives. Finally, an FGP model is developed for the achievement of highest degree of each of the defined membership goals to the extent possible by minimizing group regrets in the decision making context.

3.2 MODEL DESCRIPTION

In this chapter it is assumed that the objective functions of the mathematical programming model are linear in nature and its parameters may appear in different forms, *viz.*, crisp numbers or FNs with various types or FRVs following different continuous probability distributions. Also, all the parameters (left sided as well as right sided) of the system constraints are considered as either crisp numbers or FNs or FRVs with some known continuous probability distributions. The decision variables of the problem can also be taken as fuzzy variables (the concept of fuzzy decision variables are discussed in chapter 6). Thus the general form of linear multi-objective fuzzy probabilistic mathematical programming models is expressed as:

Find $X\left(x_1, x_2, \ldots x_n\right)$ so as to

Maximize $Z_k = \sum_{j=1}^{n} c_{kj} x_j$; $k = 1, 2, \ldots\ldots, K$

subject to

$$\Pr\left(\sum_{j=1}^{n} a_{ij} x_j \lesssim b_i\right) \geq 1 - \alpha_i \; ; \; i = 1, 2, \ldots\ldots, m \tag{1}$$

$x_j \geq 0 \, ; j = 1, 2, \ldots\ldots, n$

Here α_i denotes any real number lies in $\left[0,1\right]$ and "$\lesssim$" denotes less than or equal in fuzzy sense.

Depending on the nature of the parameters c_{kj}, a_{ij}, b_i

$\left(k = 1, 2, \ldots\ldots, K; \quad i = 1, 2, \ldots\ldots, m; j = 1, 2, \ldots\ldots, n\right)$,

the following cases may arise:

I. c_{kj} are crisp numbers, a_{ij} are FNs and b_i are FRVs.
II. c_{kj} are crisp numbers, a_{ij} are FRVs and b_i are FNs.

III. c_{kj} are crisp numbers, a_{ij} and b_i are FRVs.

IV. c_{kj} are FNs, a_{ij} are FNs and b_i are FRVs.

V. c_{kj} are FNs, a_{ij} are FRVs and b_i are FNs.

VI. c_{kj} are FNs, a_{ij} and b_i are FRVs.

VII. c_{kj} and b_i are FRVs, a_{ij} are FNs.

VIII. c_{kj} and a_{ij} are FRVs and b_i are FNs.

IX. All the parameters c_{kj}, a_{ij}, b_i are FRVs.

Only the cases I, V and IX are discussed elaborately from the above nine cases as those are the basic forms of the proposed model. Similarly, the other cases can be obtained by combining these three cases.

Case I: c_{kj} are crisp numbers, a_{ij} are FNs and b_i are FRVs:

In this case the model (1) can be reformulated as
Find $X\left(x_1, x_2, \ldots x_n\right)$ so as to

$$\text{Maximize } Z_k = \sum_{j=1}^{n} c_{kj} x_j \, ; \; k = 1, 2, \ldots\ldots, K$$

subject to

$$\Pr\left(\sum_{j=1}^{n} \tilde{a}_{ij} x_j \lesssim \tilde{b}_i\right) \geq 1 - \alpha_i \, ; i = 1, 2, \ldots\ldots, m \tag{2}$$

$$x_j \geq 0 \, ; \; j = 1, 2, \ldots\ldots, n$$

Here, c_{kj} are crisp numbers, $\tilde{a}_{ij}$ are FNs and $\tilde{b}_i$ are FRVs following different continuous probability distributions. Throughout this chapter it is assumed that the FNs are in linear forms.

Case V: c_{kj} are FNs, a_{ij} are FRVs and b_i are FNs:

The model (1) in this case can be expressed as
Find $X\left(x_1, x_2, \ldots x_n\right)$ so as to

Maximize $\tilde{Z}_k \cong \sum_{j=1}^{n} \tilde{c}_{kj} x_j$; $k = 1, 2, \ldots\ldots, K$

subject to

$$\text{Pr}\left(\sum_{j=1}^{n} \tilde{a}_{ij} x_j \lesssim \tilde{b}_i\right) \geq 1 - \alpha_i ; i = 1, 2, \ldots\ldots, m \qquad (3)$$

$x_j \geq 0$; $j = 1, 2, \ldots\ldots, n$

Here, $\tilde{c}_{kj}$ and $\tilde{b}_i$ are either triangular or trapezoidal FNs and $\tilde{a}_{ij}$ are FRVs following different continuous probability distributions.

Case IX: c_{kj}, a_{ij}, b_i are FRVs:

As all the parameters associated with the model (1) are FRVs, therefore the model (1) can be described as
Find $X\left(x_1, x_2, \ldots x_n\right)$ so as to

Maximize $\tilde{Z}_k \cong \sum_{j=1}^{n} \tilde{c}_{kj} x_j$; $k = 1, 2, \ldots\ldots, K$

subject to

$$\text{Pr}\left(\sum_{j=1}^{n} \tilde{a}_{ij} x_j \lesssim \tilde{b}_i\right) \geq 1 - \alpha_i ; i = 1, 2, \ldots\ldots, m \qquad (4)$$

$x_j \geq 0$; $j = 1, 2, \ldots\ldots, n$

Here, all the parameters c_{kj}, $\tilde{a}_{ij}$ and $\tilde{b}_i$ are FRVs following different continuous probability distributions.

3.3 CONVERSION OF FUZZY PROBABILISTIC CONSTRAINTS INTO FUZZY CONSTRAINTS

In this section the methodology for converting the fuzzy stochastic models considering some well-known continuous probability distributions into fuzzy programming models is described. It has already been mentioned that the cases I, V and IX are the basic forms of the proposed model, so, the conversion technique for those cases are discussed in details. The remaining cases can easily be derived by the readers using those three cases.

3.3.1 When Right Side Parameters ($\tilde{b}_i$) of the Chance Constraints Are Fuzzy Random Variables

At first the model described in Case I under hybrid uncertain environment are converted into fuzzy programming model through CCP methodology. If $\tilde{b}_i$ is a FRV with probability density function $f\left(b_i ; \tilde{\beta}_i\right)$, where $\tilde{\beta}_i$ is the fuzzy parameter of the distribution, then chance constraints $\Pr\left(\sum_{j=1}^{n}\tilde{a}_{ij}x_j \precsim \tilde{b}_i\right) \geq 1 - \alpha_i$ in fuzzy uncertain environment are modified using CCP methodology as

$$\Pr\left(\tilde{A}_i \precsim \tilde{b}_i\right) \geq 1 - \alpha_i ,$$

where $\tilde{A}_i \cong \sum_{j=1}^{n}\tilde{a}_{ij}x_j$ i.e.,

$$\left[\int_{u_i}^{\infty}f\left(b_i ; \beta_i\right)db_i; u_i \in \tilde{A}_i[\alpha], \beta_i \in \tilde{\beta}_i[\alpha]\right] \geq 1 - \alpha_i \tag{5}$$

After integration and using first decomposition theorem, the constraint with fuzzy parameters is developed.

This procedure is explicitly explained by considering the following continuous probability distributions for the right side parameters of the fuzzy probabilistic constraints:

1. Weibull distribution
2. Cauchy distribution
3. Extreme value distribution

3.3.1.1 The Parameter $\tilde{b}_i$ Follows Weibull Distributed Fuzzy Random Variables

At first it is assumed that the parameters $\tilde{b}_i$ $\left(i = 1, 2, \ldots\ldots, m\right)$ of the chance constraints are FRVs following weibull distribution. The probability density function of weibull distribution is given by

$$f\left(b_i \; ; \tilde{\beta}_i \;, \tilde{\lambda}_i\right) = \left(\frac{p_i}{s_i}\right)\left(\frac{b_i}{s_i}\right)^{p_i - 1} e^{-\left(\frac{b_i}{s_i}\right)^{p_i}} \;, \; p_i \in \tilde{\lambda}_i\left[\alpha\right], s_i \in \tilde{\beta}_i\left[\alpha\right]$$

where the support of $\tilde{b}_i$ is the set of non-negative real numbers. Here $\tilde{\lambda}_i\left[\alpha\right], \tilde{\beta}_i\left[\alpha\right]$ are the α − cut of FNs $\tilde{\lambda}_i, \tilde{\beta}_i$ whose support are the set of positive real numbers.

The CCP methodology is employed to the chance constraints

$$\Pr\left(\sum_{j=1}^{n} \tilde{a}_{ij} x_j \leq \tilde{b}_i\right) \geq 1 - \alpha_i \; ; i = 1, 2, \ldots, m \,,$$

to convert the fuzzy stochastic model into fuzzy programming model. This conversion is developed as follows:

Considering $\tilde{A}_i \cong \sum_{j=1}^{n} \tilde{a}_{ij} x_j$ as in the previous situation, the above constraints become $\Pr\left(\tilde{A}_i \leq \tilde{b}_i\right) \geq 1 - \alpha_i$ i.e.,

$$\int_{u_i}^{\infty} \left(\frac{p_i}{s_i}\right)\left(\frac{b_i}{s_i}\right)^{p_i - 1} e^{-\left(\frac{b_i}{s_i}\right)^{p_i}} db_i \geq 1 - \alpha_i \,,$$

where

$$\left(s_i \in \tilde{\beta}_i\left[\alpha\right], p_i \in \tilde{\lambda}_i\left[\alpha\right], u_i \in \tilde{A}_i\left[\alpha\right]\right)$$

i.e., $u_i \leq s_i \left[\ln\left(\dfrac{1}{1-\alpha_i}\right) \right]^{\frac{1}{p_i}}$; $i = 1, 2, \ldots, m$ (6)

Since this inequality is true for all $\alpha \in (0,1]$, the expression can be written in terms of $\alpha -$ cut as

$$\tilde{A}_i[\alpha] \leq \tilde{\beta}_i[\alpha] \left(\ln\left(\dfrac{1}{1-\alpha_i}\right) \right)^{\frac{1}{\bar{\lambda}_i[\alpha]}},$$

i.e., $\displaystyle\sum_{j=1}^{n} \tilde{a}_{ij}[\alpha] x_j \leq \tilde{\beta}_i[\alpha] \left(\ln\left(\dfrac{1}{1-\alpha_i}\right) \right)^{\frac{1}{\bar{\lambda}_i[\alpha]}}$; $i = 1, 2, \ldots, m$

Now using first decomposition theorem, the above equation is reduced to the following form as

$$\sum_{j=1}^{n} \tilde{a}_{ij} x_j \leq \tilde{\beta}_i \left(\ln\left(\dfrac{1}{1-\alpha_i}\right) \right)^{\frac{1}{\bar{\lambda}_i}} ; \quad i = 1, 2, \ldots, m \qquad (7)$$

Thus the fuzzy programming model takes the form
Find $X\left(x_1, x_2, \ldots x_n\right)$ so as to

Maximize $Z_k = \displaystyle\sum_{j=1}^{n} c_{kj} x_j$; $k = 1, 2, \ldots, K$

subject to

$$\sum_{j=1}^{n} \tilde{a}_{ij} x_j \leq \tilde{\beta}_i \left(\ln\left(\dfrac{1}{1-\alpha_i}\right) \right)^{\frac{1}{\bar{\lambda}_i}} ; \quad i = 1, 2, \ldots, m$$

$$x_j \geq 0 \,;\; j = 1, 2, \ldots\ldots, n \tag{8}$$

where c_{kj} are crisp numbers and $\tilde{a}_{ij}$, $\tilde{\lambda}_i$ and $\tilde{\beta}_i$ are either triangular or trapezoidal FNs.

3.3.1.2 The Parameter $\tilde{b}_i$ Is Cauchy Distributed Fuzzy Random Variables

In this case the right side parameters $\tilde{b}_i$ $\left(i = 1, 2, \ldots\ldots, m\right)$ of the constraints are represented through Cauchy distributed FRVs. The probability density function of $\tilde{b}_i$ is given as

$$f\left(b_i;\, \tilde{\beta}_i,\, \tilde{\lambda}_i\right) = \frac{r}{\pi\left[r^2 + \left(b_i - s\right)^2\right]}$$

where the support of $\tilde{b}_i$ is defined on the set of real numbers; $r \in \tilde{\beta}\left[\alpha\right], s \in \tilde{\lambda}\left[\alpha\right]$; $\tilde{\beta}\left[\alpha\right], \tilde{\lambda}\left[\alpha\right]$ being the $\alpha-$ cut of the FNs $\tilde{\beta}$, $\tilde{\lambda}$, respectively. The fuzzy parameter $\tilde{\lambda}_i$ is the median of the random variable $\tilde{b}_i$ and $\tilde{\beta}_i$ is the scale parameters of the random variable $\tilde{b}_i$.

Now the conversions of fuzzy stochastic constraint involving Cauchy distribution to fuzzy constraints through CCP methodology are as follows:

$$\Pr\left(\sum_{j=1}^{n} \tilde{a}_{ij} x_j \lesssim \tilde{b}_i\right) \geq 1 - \alpha_i \,;\, i = 1, 2, \ldots., m\,.$$

Considering $\tilde{A}_i = \sum_{j=1}^{n} \tilde{a}_{ij} x_j$ as in the previous situation, the above constraints become $\Pr\left(\tilde{A}_i \lesssim \tilde{b}_i\right) \geq 1 - \alpha_i$;

$$i.e. \left\{ \int_{u_i}^{\infty} \frac{r}{\pi\left[t^2 + \left(b_i - s\right)^2\right]}\, db_i : r \in \tilde{\beta}_i\left[\alpha\right], s \in \tilde{\lambda}_i\left[\alpha\right], u_i \in \tilde{A}_i\left[\alpha\right] \right\} \geq 1 - \alpha_i$$

$$i.e. \ \frac{\pi}{2} - \tan^{-1} \frac{(u_i - s)}{r} \geq \pi \left(1 - \alpha_i\right) \Rightarrow u_i \leq s + r \ \tan\left[\pi\alpha_i - \frac{\pi}{2}\right]$$

$$i = 1, 2, ..., m.$$
; (9)

Since this inequality is true for all $\alpha \in (0,1]$, the expression is written in terms of $\alpha -$ cut as

$$\tilde{A}_i[\alpha] \leq \tilde{\lambda}_i[\alpha] + \tilde{\beta}_i[\alpha] \tan\left[\pi\alpha_i - \frac{\pi}{2}\right].$$

i.e.,
$$\sum_{j=1}^{n} \tilde{a}_{ij}[\alpha] x_j \leq \tilde{\lambda}_i[\alpha] + \tilde{\beta}_i[\alpha] \tan\left[\pi\alpha_i - \frac{\pi}{2}\right]; \ i = 1, 2, ..., m$$
(10)

Now using first decomposition theorem, the above equation is reduced to the following form as

$$\sum_{j=1}^{n} \tilde{a}_{ij} x_j \leq \tilde{\lambda}_i + \tilde{\beta}_i \tan\left[\pi\alpha_i - \frac{\pi}{2}\right]; \ i = 1, 2, ..., m$$
(11)

Therefore, the fuzzy stochastic mathematical programming model with Cauchy distributed FRVs as right sided parameter is modified in the following fuzzy mathematical model as:

Find $X\left(x_1, x_2, ... x_n\right)$ so as to

Maximize $Z_k = \sum_{j=1}^{n} c_{kj} x_j; \ k = 1, 2, ..., K$

subject to

$$\sum_{j=1}^{n} \tilde{a}_{ij} x_j \leq \tilde{\lambda}_i + \tilde{\beta}_i \tan\left[\pi\alpha_i - \frac{\pi}{2}\right]; \ i = 1, 2, ..., m$$

$$x_j \geq 0; \ j = 1, 2, ..., n$$
(12)

where c_{kj} are crisp numbers and $\tilde{a}_{ij}$, $\tilde{\lambda}_i$ and $\tilde{\beta}_i$ are either triangular or trapezoidal FNs.

3.3.1.3 The Parameter $\tilde{b}_i$ Is Extreme Value Distributed Fuzzy Random Variables

In this situation the right hand side parameters $\tilde{b}_i \left(i = 1, 2, \ldots\ldots, m \right)$ of the constraints are taken as extreme value distributed FRVs. Then the probability density function of $\tilde{b}_i$ is written as

$$f\left(b_i \; ; \tilde{\mu}_i \, , \tilde{\nu}_i \right) = \frac{1}{c} e^{-\frac{(b_i - h)}{c}} e^{-e^{-\frac{(b_i - h)}{c}}} \, ,$$

where the support of $\tilde{b}_i$ is defined on the set of real numbers;

$$c \in \tilde{\mu}_i\left[\alpha\right], h \in \tilde{\nu}_i\left[\alpha\right] \; ; \tilde{\mu}_i\left[\alpha\right], \, \tilde{\nu}_i\left[\alpha\right]$$

are the $\alpha - $ cut of the FNs $\tilde{\mu}_i \, , \tilde{\nu}_i$. The fuzzy parameter $\tilde{\nu}_i$ is the median of the random variable $\tilde{b}_i$ and $\tilde{\beta}_i$ is the scale parameters of the random variable $\tilde{b}_i$.

Thus the chance constraints involving extreme value distributed FRVs are presented as

$$\Pr\left(\sum_{j=1}^{n} \tilde{a}_{ij} x_j \lesssim \tilde{b}_i \right) \geq 1 - \alpha_i ; \; \left(i = 1, 2, \ldots, \; \mathrm{m} \right)$$

i.e., $\Pr\left(\tilde{A}_i \lesssim \tilde{b}_i \right) \geq 1 - \alpha_i ; \left(i = 1, 2, \ldots, \; \mathrm{m} \right),$

where

$$\tilde{A}_i \cong \sum_{j=1}^{n} \tilde{a}_{ij} x_j$$

$$i.e. \left\{ \int_{u_i}^{\infty} \frac{1}{c} e^{-\frac{(b_i-h)}{c}} e^{-e^{-\frac{(b_i-h)}{c}}} db_i \right\} \geq 1 - \alpha_i \; : c \in \tilde{\mu}_i [\alpha], \; h \in \tilde{\nu}_i [\alpha], u_i \in \tilde{A}_i [\alpha] \qquad (13)$$

$$i.e. u_i \leq h - c \ln \left(- \ln \left(\alpha_i \right) \right)$$

where

$$u_i \in \tilde{A}_i [\alpha], c \in \tilde{\mu}_i [\alpha], h \in \tilde{\nu}_i [\alpha].; \; (i = 1, 2, ..., \; m)$$

This inequality is true for all $\alpha \in (0,1]$, the expression can be written in terms of $\alpha - $ cut as

$$\tilde{A}_i [\alpha] \leq \tilde{\nu}_i [\alpha] - \tilde{\mu}_i [\alpha] \ln \left(- \ln \left(\alpha_i \right) \right)$$

$$i.e., \sum_{j=1}^{n} \tilde{a}_{ij} [\alpha] x_j \leq \tilde{\nu}_i [\alpha] - \tilde{\mu}_i [\alpha] \ln \left(- \ln \left(\alpha_i \right) \right) \qquad (14)$$

Using first decomposition theorem, the above equation is reduced to the following form as

$$\sum_{j=1}^{n} \tilde{a}_{ij} x_j \leq \tilde{\nu}_i - \tilde{\mu}_i \ln \left(- \ln \left(\alpha_i \right) \right); \; (i = 1, 2, ..., m) \qquad (15)$$

Therefore, the fuzzy stochastic mathematical programming model presented above is converted in the following fuzzy mathematical model as:

Find $X \left(x_1, x_2, ..., x_n \right)$ so as to

$$\text{Maximize } Z_k = \sum_{j=1}^{n} c_{kj} x_j \; ; \; k = 1, 2, ..., K$$

subject to

$$\sum_{j=1}^{n} \tilde{a}_{ij} x_j \leq \tilde{\nu}_i - \tilde{\mu}_i ln\left(-\ln\left(\alpha_i\right)\right); \left(i = 1, 2, ..., m\right)$$

$$x_j \geq 0; \, j = 1, 2, ..., n \tag{16}$$

where c_{kj} are crisp numbers and $\tilde{a}_{ij}$, $\tilde{\lambda}_i$ and $\tilde{\beta}_i$ are either triangular or trapezoidal FNs.

3.3.2 When Left Side Parameters Are Fuzzy Random Variables

In this subsection the hybrid model described in Case V are converted into fuzzy programming model using CCP methodology as in the previous subsection. This methodology is discussed by considering the following continuous probability distributions as the left hand side parameter of the fuzzy probabilistic constraints.

1. Exponential distribution
2. Log-normal distribution

3.3.2.1 The Parameter $\tilde{a}_{ij}$ Is Exponentially Distributed Fuzzy Random Variables

In this situation it is assumed that n left sided parameters of each constraint are exponentially distributed FRVs. Now the conversion of fuzzy stochastic constraints to fuzzy constraint through CCP methodology is done by considering at first $n = 2$.

Therefore, the probabilistic constraints become

$$\Pr\left(\tilde{a}_{i1} x_1 + \tilde{a}_{i2} x_2 \leq \tilde{b}_i\right) \geq 1 - \alpha_i; \left(i = 1, 2, ..., m\right)$$

Here the parameters $\tilde{a}_{i1}$, $\tilde{a}_{i2}$ are mutually independent FRVs following exponential distribution. Thus the joint density function of $\tilde{a}_{i1}$, $\tilde{a}_{i2}$ is given by

$$f\left(a_{i1}, a_{i2} \; ; \tilde{\lambda}_{i1}, \; \tilde{\lambda}_{i2}\right) = f\left(a_{i1} ; \tilde{\lambda}_{i1}\right) f\left(a_{i2} ; \tilde{\lambda}_{i2}\right) = \lambda_{i1} \lambda_{i2} e^{-\lambda_{i1} a_{i1}} e^{-\lambda_{i2} a_{i2}},$$

where $\lambda_{i1} \in \tilde{\lambda}_{i1}\left[\alpha\right]$ and $\lambda_{i2} \in \tilde{\lambda}_{i2}\left[\alpha\right]$

Let $\tilde{Y}_i = \tilde{a}_{i1} x_1 + \tilde{a}_{i2} x_2$. Then the probability distribution function of $\tilde{Y}_i$ is calculated as

$$G_i\left(y_i\right) = \int_0^{y_i / x_2} \int_0^{\left(y_i - a_{i2} x_2\right) / x_1} \lambda_{i1} \lambda_{i2} e^{-\lambda_{i1} a_{i1}} e^{-\lambda_{i2} a_{i2}} da_{i1} da_{i2}$$

After integration and simplification, it reduces to

$$G_i\left(y_i\right) = 1 - e^{-y_i \lambda_{i2} / x_2} + \frac{x_1 \lambda_{i2} e^{-y_i \lambda_{i1} / x_1}}{x_2 \lambda_{i1} - x_1 \lambda_{i2}} - \frac{x_1 \lambda_{i2} e^{-y_i \lambda_{i2} / x_2}}{x_2 \lambda_{i1} - x_1 \lambda_{i2}} \tag{17}$$

The probability density function $g_i\left(y_i\right)$ of $\tilde{Y}_i$ is obtained by differentiating $G_i\left(y_i\right)$ with respect to y_i as

$$g_i\left(y_i\right) = \frac{\lambda_{i1} \lambda_{i2} e^{-y_i \lambda_{i1} / x_1}}{x_1 \lambda_{i2} - x_2 \lambda_{i1}} + \frac{\lambda_{i1} \lambda_{i2} e^{-y_i \lambda_{i2} / x_2}}{x_2 \lambda_{i1} - x_1 \lambda_{i2}} , y_i > 0$$

Hence the i – th chance constraint $\Pr\left(\tilde{a}_{i1} x_1 + \tilde{a}_{i2} x_2 \leq \tilde{b}_i\right) \geq 1 - \alpha_i$ becomes

$$\Pr\left(\tilde{Y}_i \leq \tilde{b}_i\right) \geq 1 - \alpha_i$$

i.e., $\displaystyle\int_0^{b_i} \left[\frac{\lambda_{i1} \lambda_{i2} e^{-y_i \lambda_{i1} / x_1}}{x_1 \lambda_{i2} - x_2 \lambda_{i1}} + \frac{\lambda_{i1} \lambda_{i2} e^{-y_i \lambda_{i2} / x_2}}{x_2 \lambda_{i1} - x_1 \lambda_{i2}}\right] dy_i \geq 1 - \alpha_i,$

where

$$b_i \in \tilde{b}_i\left[\alpha\right], \lambda_{i1} \in \tilde{\lambda}_{i1}\left[\alpha\right], \lambda_{i2} \in \tilde{\lambda}_{i2}\left[\alpha\right]$$

i.e., $\lambda_{i1}\lambda_{i2}\left[\dfrac{x_1 e^{-b_i\lambda_{i1}/x_1}}{\lambda_{i1}\left(x_1\lambda_{i2}-x_2\lambda_{i1}\right)}+\dfrac{x_2 e^{-b_i\lambda_{i2}/x_2}}{\lambda_{i2}\left(x_2\lambda_{i1}-x_1\lambda_{i2}\right)}\right]\leq\alpha_i,$

where

$b_i\in\tilde{b}_i\left[\alpha\right],\lambda_{i1}\in\tilde{\lambda}_{i1}\left[\alpha\right],\lambda_{i2}\in\tilde{\lambda}_{i2}\left[\alpha\right]$

As this inequality is valid for every elements of $\alpha-$ cut, the expression can be written in terms of $\alpha-$ cut as

$$\tilde{\lambda}_{i1}\left[\alpha\right]\tilde{\lambda}_{i2}\left[\alpha\right]\left[\dfrac{x_1 e^{-\tilde{b}_i[\alpha]\tilde{\lambda}_{i1}[\alpha]/x_1}}{\tilde{\lambda}_{i1}\left[\alpha\right]\left(x_1\tilde{\lambda}_{i2}\left[\alpha\right]-x_2\tilde{\lambda}_{i1}\left[\alpha\right]\right)}+\dfrac{x_2 e^{-\tilde{b}_i[\alpha]\tilde{\lambda}_{i2}[\alpha]/x_2}}{\tilde{\lambda}_{i2}\left[\alpha\right]\left(x_2\tilde{\lambda}_{i1}\left[\alpha\right]-x_1\tilde{\lambda}_{i2}\left[\alpha\right]\right)}\right]\leq\alpha_i$$

$\left(i=1,2,....,m\right)$ (18)

Now, using the first decomposition theorem, the above expression modifies to the following form

$$\tilde{\lambda}_{i1}\tilde{\lambda}_{i2}\left[\dfrac{x_1 e^{-\tilde{b}_i\tilde{\lambda}_{i1}/x_1}}{\tilde{\lambda}_{i1}\left(x_1\tilde{\lambda}_{i2}-x_2\tilde{\lambda}_{i1}\right)}+\dfrac{x_2 e^{-\tilde{b}_i\tilde{\lambda}_{i2}/x_2}}{\tilde{\lambda}_{i2}\left(x_2\tilde{\lambda}_{i1}-x_1\tilde{\lambda}_{i2}\right)}\right]\leq\alpha_i\left(i=1,2,....,m\right).$$

The same approach is now applied to the fuzzy probabilistic constraints having n decision variables. Then the chance constraints

$$\Pr\left(\tilde{a}_{i1}x_1+\tilde{a}_{i2}x_2+...+\tilde{a}_{in}x_n\leq\tilde{b}_i\right)\geq 1-\alpha_i;\ i=1,2,....,\mathrm{m}$$

in fuzzy uncertain environment are converted into the following form

$$\prod_{p=1}^{n}\tilde{\lambda}_{ip}\left[\sum_{j=1}^{n}\dfrac{x_j^{n-1}e^{-\tilde{b}_i\tilde{\lambda}_{ij}/x_j}}{\tilde{\lambda}_{ij}\prod_{\substack{l=1\\l\neq j}}^{n}\left(x_j\tilde{\lambda}_{il}-x_l\tilde{\lambda}_{ij}\right)}\right]\leq\alpha_i\left(i=1,2,....,m\right)$$ (19)

Thus the fuzzy stochastic model presented in Case V are modified to non-linear fuzzy programming model as

Find $X\left(x_1, x_2, \ldots x_n\right)$ so as to

Maximize $\tilde{Z}_k \cong \sum_{j=1}^{n} \tilde{c}_{kj} x_j$; $k = 1, 2, \ldots\ldots, K$

subject to

$$\prod_{p=1}^{n} \tilde{\lambda}_{ip} \left[\sum_{j=1}^{n} \frac{x_j^{n-1} e^{-\tilde{b}_i \tilde{\lambda}_{ij}/x_j}}{\tilde{\lambda}_{ij} \prod_{\substack{l=1 \\ l \neq j}}^{n} \left(x_j \tilde{\lambda}_{il} - x_l \tilde{\lambda}_{ij}\right)} \right] \leq \alpha_i \; ; \; i = 1, 2, \ldots\ldots, m$$

$x_j \geq 0 \, ; \; j = 1, 2, \ldots\ldots, n$ \hfill (20)

Here, $\tilde{c}_{kj}$, $\tilde{b}_i$ and $\tilde{\lambda}_{ij}$ are either triangular or trapezoidal FNs.

3.3.2.2 The Parameter $\tilde{a}_{ij}$ Is Log-Normally Distributed Fuzzy Random Variables

In this case n left sided parameters $\tilde{a}_{i1}$, $\tilde{a}_{i2}$, $\ldots$, $\tilde{a}_{in}$ of $i-$ th constraint $\left(i = 1, 2, \ldots, m\right)$ are considered as log-normally distributed FRVs. As $\tilde{a}_{ij}$ is log-normally distributed FRVs, then $ln\left(\tilde{a}_{ij}\right) = \tilde{d}_i$ is normally distributed FRVs with mean $E\left(\tilde{d}_i\right) = E\left(ln\left(\tilde{a}_{ij}\right)\right) = m_{\tilde{d}_i}$ and variance

$$Var\left(\tilde{d}_i\right) = Var\left(ln\left(\tilde{a}_{ij}\right)\right) = \sigma_{\tilde{d}_i}^2 \, .$$

Hence the mean and variance of the log-normal variates $\tilde{a}_{ij}$ can be obtained as

$$E\left(\tilde{a}_{ij}\right) = \exp\left(m_{\tilde{d}_i} + \frac{\sigma_{\tilde{d}_i}^2}{2}\right)$$

and

$$Var\left(\tilde{a}_{ij}\right) = \exp\left(2m_{\tilde{a}_i} + \sigma_{\tilde{a}_i}^2\right)\left(\exp\left(\sigma_{\tilde{a}_i}^2\right) - 1\right).$$

Now the chance constraint in fuzzy uncertain environment can be transformed into fuzzy constraint as follows

$$\Pr\left(\sum_{j=1}^{n}\tilde{a}_{ij}x_j \lesssim \tilde{b}_i\right) \geq 1 - \alpha_i \; ; \; i = 1, 2, \ldots\ldots, m$$

i.e., $\Pr\left(\tilde{A}_i \lesssim \tilde{b}_i\right) \geq 1 - \alpha_i \; ; \; i = 1, 2, \ldots\ldots, m$,

where

$$\tilde{A}_i \cong \sum_{j=1}^{n}\tilde{a}_{ij}x_j$$

i.e., $\Pr\left(\dfrac{\ln\left(\tilde{A}_i\right) - E\left(\ln\left(\tilde{A}_i\right)\right)}{\sqrt{Var\left(\ln\left(\tilde{A}_i\right)\right)}} \lesssim \dfrac{\ln\left(\tilde{b}_i\right) - E\left(\ln\left(\tilde{A}_i\right)\right)}{\sqrt{Var\left(\ln\left(\tilde{A}_i\right)\right)}}\right) \geq 1 - \alpha_i \; ; \; i = 1, 2, \ldots, m$

i.e., $\Phi\left(\dfrac{\ln\left(\tilde{b}_i\right) - E\left(\ln\left(\tilde{A}_i\right)\right)}{\sqrt{Var\left(\ln\left(\tilde{A}_i\right)\right)}}\right) \geq 1 - \alpha_i \; ; \; i = 1, 2, \ldots, m$

i.e., $\dfrac{\ln\left(\tilde{b}_i\right) - E\left(\ln\left(\tilde{A}_i\right)\right)}{\sqrt{Var\left(\ln\left(\tilde{A}_i\right)\right)}} \geq \Phi^{-1}\left(1 - \alpha_i\right) \; ; \; i = 1, 2, \ldots, m$

i.e., $E\left(\ln\left(\tilde{A}_i\right)\right) \leq \ln\left(\tilde{b}_i\right) - \sqrt{Var\left(\ln\left(\tilde{A}_i\right)\right)}\,\Phi^{-1}\left(1 - \alpha_i\right) \; ; \; i = 1, 2, \ldots, m$

i.e.,
$$E\left[\ln\left(\sum_{j=1}^{n}\tilde{a}_{ij}x_j\right)\right] \leq \ln\left(\tilde{b}_i\right) - \sqrt{Var\left(\ln\left(\sum_{j=1}^{n}\tilde{a}_{ij}x_j\right)\right)}\,\Phi^{-1}\left(1-\alpha_i\right), \quad i=1,2,\ldots,m$$

$$(21)$$

Thus the fuzzy stochastic model presented in Case V are modified into fuzzy programming model as

Find $X\left(x_1,x_2,\ldots.x_n\right)$ so as to

$$\text{Maximize } \tilde{Z}_k \cong \sum_{j=1}^{n}\tilde{c}_{kj}x_j\,; \quad k=1,2,\ldots\ldots,K$$

subject to

$$E\left[\ln\left(\sum_{j=1}^{n}\tilde{a}_{ij}x_j\right)\right] \leq \ln\left(\tilde{b}_i\right) - \sqrt{Var\left(\ln\left(\sum_{j=1}^{n}\tilde{a}_{ij}x_j\right)\right)}\,\Phi^{-1}\left(1-\alpha_i\right)\,; \quad i=1,2,\ldots,m$$

$$x_j \geq 0\,; \quad j=1,2,\ldots\ldots,n \qquad\qquad (22)$$

Here, $\tilde{c}_{kj}$, $\tilde{b}_i$, $E\left(ln\left(\tilde{a}_{ij}\right)\right)$ and $Var\left(ln\left(\tilde{a}_{ij}\right)\right)$ are either triangular or trapezoidal FNs.

3.3.3 When All Parameters Are Fuzzy Random Variable

In Case IX, it is already mentioned that all the parameters of the fuzzy stochastic model are FRVs. Thus not only the parameters of all the constraints but also the parameters of the objectives are FRVs. Now, these probabilistic uncertain natures can be removed from the parameters of the objectives through the expectation or variance model. In this chapter the expectation model and variance model procedures are explained briefly. The conversion of fuzzy stochastic model into fuzzy programming model through expectation and variance model are explained in details in Chapter 6.

This above mentioned conversion procedure is now described when all the parameters of the fuzzy probabilistic constraints of the fuzzy stochastic model follow the following continuous probability distribution:

1.   Normal distribution

3.3.3.1 All Parameters of the Constraints Follow Normal Distribution

In this situation it is assumed that all the parameters of the chance constraints follow normally distributed FRVs. Also the parameters of the objectives are considered as FRVs with some known continuous probability distribution as mentioned in Case IX. The mean and variance of the FRVs are taken as FNs either in triangular form or in trapezoidal form.

If $\tilde{c}_{kj}$, $\left(k = 1, 2, ..., K; j = 1, 2, ..., n\right)$ are FRVs following some known probability distribution, then its mean $E\left(\tilde{c}_{kj}\right)$, $\left(k = 1, 2, ..., K; j = 1, 2, ..., n\right)$ is either triangular or trapezoidal FNs.

Thus the objectives with fuzzy uncertain parameters is developed by considering the mean of each FRV as

$$\text{Maximize } E\left(\tilde{Z}_k\right) \cong \sum_{j=1}^{n} E\left(\tilde{c}_{kj}\right) x_j \; ; \; k = 1, 2, ..., K$$

Similarly, objective with fuzzy parameters can also be obtained by taking the variance of each FRV as

$$\text{Minimize } Var\left(\tilde{Z}_k\right) \cong \sum_{j=1}^{n} Var\left(\tilde{c}_{kj}\right) x_j^2 \; ; \; k = 1, 2, ..., K$$

But the difference is that the objective functions become non-linear in nature.

Now the chance constraints following normal distribution are converted into fuzzy constraint using CCP methodology as follows:

$$\text{Let } \tilde{d}_i \cong \sum_{j=1}^{n} \tilde{a}_{ij} x_j - \tilde{b}_i$$

As $\tilde{a}_{ij}, \left(i = 1, 2, ..., m; j = 1, 2, ... n\right)$ and $\tilde{b}_i, \left(i = 1, 2, ..., m\right)$ are FRVs following normal distribution, then by reproductive property, $\tilde{d}_i$ is also an FRV following normal distribution. Now,

$$\Pr\left(\tilde{d}_i \lesssim \tilde{0}\right) \geq 1 - \alpha_i \,;\; i = 1, 2, ..., m$$

i.e., $\Pr\left|\dfrac{\tilde{d}_i - E\left(\tilde{d}_i\right)}{\sqrt{Var\left(\tilde{d}_i\right)}} \lesssim \dfrac{\tilde{0} - E\left(\tilde{d}_i\right)}{\sqrt{Var\left(\tilde{d}_i\right)}}\right| \geq 1 - \alpha_i \,;\; i = 1, 2, ..., m$

i.e., $\dfrac{\tilde{0} - E\left(\tilde{d}_i\right)}{\sqrt{Var\left(\tilde{d}_i\right)}} \geq \Phi^{-1}\left(1 - \alpha_i\right) \,;\; i = 1, 2, ..., m$

i.e., $E\left(\tilde{d}_i\right) \leq \tilde{0} - \Phi^{-1}\left(1 - \alpha_i\right)\sqrt{Var\left(\tilde{d}_i\right)} \,;\; i = 1, 2, ..., m$

i.e., $\quad \displaystyle\sum_{j=1}^{n} E\left(\tilde{a}_{ij}\right) x_j \leq E\left(\tilde{b}_i\right) + \tilde{0} - \Phi^{-1}\left(1 - \alpha_i\right)\sqrt{\displaystyle\sum_{j=1}^{n} Var\left(\tilde{a}_{ij}\right) x_j^2 + Var\left(\tilde{b}_i\right)} \,;$

$i = 1, 2, ..., m$ (23)

Thus the expectation model of the objective is developed as
Find $X\left(x_1, x_2, ...x_n\right)$ so as to

Maximize $E\left(\tilde{Z}_k\right) \cong \displaystyle\sum_{j=1}^{n} E\left(\tilde{c}_{kj}\right) x_j \,;\; k = 1, 2, ..., K$

subject to

$\displaystyle\sum_{j=1}^{n} E\left(\tilde{a}_{ij}\right) x_j \leq E\left(\tilde{b}_i\right) + \tilde{0} - \Phi^{-1}\left(1 - \alpha_i\right)\sqrt{\displaystyle\sum_{j=1}^{n} Var\left(\tilde{a}_{ij}\right) x_j^2 + Var\left(\tilde{b}_i\right)} \qquad ;$

$i = 1, 2, ..., m$

$x_j \geq 0 \,;\; j = 1, 2, ..., n$ (24)

In the same manner, the variance model of the objectives is developed as
Find $X\left(x_1, x_2, \ldots x_n\right)$ so as to

$$\text{Minimize } Var\left(\tilde{Z}_k\right) \cong \sum_{j=1}^{n} Var\left(\tilde{c}_{kj}\right) x_j^2 \, ; \; k = 1, 2, \ldots\ldots, K$$

subject to

$$\sum_{j=1}^{n} E\left(\tilde{a}_{ij}\right) x_j \leq E\left(\tilde{b}_i\right) + \tilde{0} - \Phi^{-1}\left(1 - \alpha_i\right) \sqrt{\sum_{j=1}^{n} Var\left(\tilde{a}_{ij}\right) x_j^2 + Var\left(\tilde{b}_i\right)} \quad ;$$

$$i = 1, 2, \ldots\ldots, m$$

$$x_j \geq 0 \, ; \; j = 1, 2, \ldots\ldots, n \tag{25}$$

where $E\left(\tilde{c}_{kj}\right)$, $E\left(\tilde{a}_{ij}\right)$, $E\left(\tilde{b}_i\right)$, $Var\left(\tilde{a}_{ij}\right)$, $Var\left(\tilde{b}_i\right)$, $Var\left(\tilde{c}_{kj}\right)$ and $\tilde{0}$ are FNs in triangular or trapezoidal form.

Thus, CCP methodology is discussed elaborately through various continuous probability distributions to develop fuzzy programming model.

Now, in general a fuzzy programming model obtained from any fuzzy stochastic model discussed above can be expressed as
Find $X\left(x_1, x_2, \ldots x_n\right)$ so as to

$$\text{Minimize/maximize } \tilde{Z}_k \cong \sum_{j=1}^{n} \tilde{c}_{kj} x_j \text{ or } Z_k = \sum_{j=1}^{n} c_{kj} x_j \, ; \; k = 1, 2, \ldots\ldots, K$$

subject to

$$\sum_{j=1}^{n} \tilde{a}_{ij} x_j \lesssim \tilde{b}_i \, ; \; i = 1, 2, \ldots, t$$

$$\sum_{j=1}^{n} \tilde{a}_{lj} x_j \gtrsim \tilde{b}_l \, ; \; l = t+1, t+2, \ldots, m$$

$$x_j \geq 0 \, ; \; j = 1, 2, \ldots\ldots, n \tag{26}$$

where $\tilde{c}_{kj}$, $\tilde{a}_{ij}$, $\tilde{a}_{lj}$, $\tilde{b}_i$ and $\tilde{b}_l$ are either triangular or trapezoidal FNs and c_{kj} are crisp numbers.

Thus in this manner mathematical models in hybrid uncertain environment with parameters involving fuzzy probabilistic uncertainties following various continuous probability distributions are converted into fuzzy programming model through CCP methodology.

In the next section the fuzzy programming models are now converted into deterministic model using various defuzzification techniques (which are described elaborately in Chapter 2).

3.4 DEVELOPMENT OF DETERMINISTIC MODEL FROM FUZZY PROGRAMMING MODEL

In the previous section it is clearly explained that how a fuzzy programming model is developed from the fuzzy stochastic model through CCP methodology. In this section the fuzzy objectives and/or fuzzy constraints are converted to its equivalent deterministic form using different defuzzification techniques or on the basis of the tolerance of the FNs. It is already stated that defuzzification of FNs is a mapping from the set of FNs to the set of real numbers, i.e. for each FN there exist a real number and based on that real number fuzzy uncertain parameters are replaced by the crisp parameters. Using this concept a deterministic model is developed from a fuzzy programming model capturing various uncertainties that every decision maker face in solving real life decision making problems. Defuzzification of FNs can be done in various ways. Some well-known defuzzification methods of FNs are discussed in the following subsection.

1. Decomposition of FNs on the basis of tolerance ranges.
2. Defuzzification of FNs using probability density function.
3. Defuzzification by using α – cut of an FN.
4. Canonical form of an FN.
5. Centroid of an FN.
6. Nearest symmetric triangular defuzzification.

3.4.1 Decomposition of Fuzzy Numbers on the Basis of Tolerance Ranges

A trapezoidal FN can be represented by a 4-tuple of real numbers as $\tilde{a} = \left(a^1, a^2, a^3, a^4\right)$, the membership function of whose takes the form

$$
\mu_{\tilde{a}}(x) = \begin{cases} \dfrac{x - a^1}{a^2 - a^1} & if \quad a^1 \leq x \leq a^2 \\ 1 & if \quad a^2 \leq x \leq a^3 \\ \dfrac{a^4 - x}{a^4 - a^3} & if \quad a^3 \leq x \leq a^4 \\ 0 & otherwise \end{cases} ,
$$

where a^1 and a^4 denote, respectively, the left and right tolerance values of the FN $\tilde{a}$. If $a^2 = a^3$, then the trapezoidal FN becomes a triangular FN.

Now, in the fuzzy programming model all the parameters are FNs either in trapezoidal or in triangular form. Based on the left and right tolerance of all the FNs, $\tilde{c}_{kj} = \left(c_{kj}^1, c_{kj}^2, c_{kj}^3, c_{kj}^4\right)$, $\tilde{a}_{ij} = \left(a_{ij}^1, a_{ij}^2, a_{ij}^3, a_{ij}^4\right)$, $\tilde{a}_{lj} = \left(a_{lj}^1, a_{lj}^2, a_{lj}^3, a_{lj}^4\right)$, $\tilde{b}_i = \left(b_i^1, b_i^2, b_i^3, b_i^4\right)$ and $\tilde{b}_l = \left(b_l^1, b_l^2, b_l^3, b_l^4\right)$, the membership function of each of them is constructed as

$$
\mu_{\tilde{c}_{kj}}(x) = \begin{cases} \dfrac{x - c_{kj}^1}{c_{kj}^2 - c_{kj}^1} & if \quad c_{kj}^1 \leq x \leq c_{kj}^2 \\ 1 & if \quad c_{kj}^2 \leq x \leq c_{kj}^3 \\ \dfrac{c_{kj}^4 - x}{c_{kj}^4 - c_{kj}^3} & if \quad c_{kj}^3 \leq x \leq c_{kj}^4 \\ 0 & otherwise \end{cases} ,
$$

$$\mu_{\tilde{a}_{ij}}\left(x\right) = \begin{cases} \dfrac{x - a_{ij}^1}{a_{ij}^2 - a_{ij}^1} & if \quad a_{ij}^1 \le x \le a_{ij}^2 \\ 1 & if \quad a_{ij}^2 \le x \le a_{ij}^3 \\ \dfrac{a_{ij}^4 - x}{a_{ij}^4 - a_{ij}^3} & if \quad a_{ij}^3 \le x \le a_{ij}^4 \\ 0 & otherwise \end{cases}$$

$$\mu_{\tilde{a}_{lj}}\left(x\right) = \begin{cases} \dfrac{x - a_{lj}^1}{a_{lj}^2 - a_{lj}^1} & if \quad a_{lj}^1 \le x \le a_{lj}^2 \\ 1 & if \quad a_{lj}^2 \le x \le a_{lj}^3 \\ \dfrac{a_{lj}^4 - x}{a_{lj}^4 - a_{lj}^3} & if \quad a_{lj}^3 \le x \le a_{lj}^4 \\ 0 & otherwise \end{cases} \quad ,$$

$$\mu_{\tilde{b}_{i}}\left(x\right) = \begin{cases} \dfrac{x - b_{i}^1}{b_{i}^2 - b_{i}^1} & if \quad b_{i}^1 \le x \le b_{i}^2 \\ 1 & if \quad b_{i}^2 \le x \le b_{i}^3 \\ \dfrac{b_{i}^4 - x}{b_{i}^4 - b_{i}^3} & if \quad b_{i}^3 \le x \le b_{i}^4 \\ 0 & otherwise \end{cases}$$

$$\mu_{\tilde{b}_{l}}\left(x\right) = \begin{cases} \dfrac{x - b_{l}^1}{b_{l}^2 - b_{l}^1} & if \quad b_{l}^1 \le x \le b_{l}^2 \\ 1 & if \quad b_{l}^2 \le x \le b_{l}^3 \\ \dfrac{b_{l}^4 - x}{b_{l}^4 - b_{l}^3} & if \quad b_{l}^3 \le x \le b_{l}^4 \\ 0 & otherwise \end{cases}$$

Based on these membership functions, the Model can be described as Find $X\left(x_1, x_2, \ldots x_n\right)$ so as to

Minimize/maximize $z_k^1 = \sum_{j=1}^{n} \left(c_{kj}^1 + \left(c_{kj}^2 - c_{kj}^1 \right) \beta \right) x_j$; $k = 1, 2, \ldots\ldots, K$

Minimize/maximize $z_k^2 = \sum_{j=1}^{n} \left(c_{kj}^4 - \left(c_{kj}^4 - c_{kj}^3 \right) \beta \right) x_j$; $k = 1, 2, \ldots\ldots, K$

subject to

$$\sum_{j=1}^{n} \left(a_{ij}^1 + \left(a_{ij}^2 - a_{ij}^1 \right) \beta \right) x_j \leq \left(b_i^1 + \left(b_i^2 - b_i^1 \right) \beta \right); \; i = 1, 2, \ldots, t$$

$$\sum_{j=1}^{n} \left(a_{ij}^4 - \left(a_{ij}^4 - a_{ij}^3 \right) \beta \right) x_j \leq \left(b_i^4 - \left(b_i^4 - b_i^3 \right) \beta \right); \; i = 1, 2, \ldots, t$$

$$\sum_{j=1}^{n} \left(a_{lj}^1 + \left(a_{lj}^2 - a_{lj}^1 \right) \beta \right) x_j \geq \left(b_l^1 + \left(b_l^2 - b_l^1 \right) \beta \right); \; l = t+1, t+2, \ldots, m$$

$$\sum_{j=1}^{n} \left(a_{lj}^4 - \left(a_{lj}^4 - a_{lj}^3 \right) \beta \right) x_j \geq \left(b_l^4 - \left(b_l^4 - b_l^3 \right) \beta \right); \; l = t+1, t+2, \ldots, m$$

$x_j \geq 0$; $j = 1, 2, \ldots\ldots, n$, $0 \leq \beta \leq 1$ \hfill (27)

Here β represents the degree of fuzziness involved with parameters of the system constraints.

In this procedure each objective is decomposed into two objectives. Also each constraint is decomposed into two constraints. Thus a multi-objective mathematical programming model in crisp environment is generated from the fuzzy programming model based on the tolerance of the FNs. Now the deterministic model is solved to find the best and worst value of each objective.

3.4.2 Defuzzification of Fuzzy Numbers Using Proportional Probability Density Function

Let $\tilde{a} = \left(a^1, \ a^2, a^3, a^4\right)$ be any trapezoidal FN. In the previous chapter it is already stated that for each FN there corresponds a probability density function $f_{\tilde{a}}(x)$ and this probability density function is termed as proportional probability density function. The defuzzification of the trapezoidal FN $\tilde{a}$ using proportional probability density function is evaluated as

$$V\left(\tilde{a}\right) = \frac{1}{3}\left(a^4 + a^3 + a^1 + a^2 + \frac{\left(a^1 a^2 - a^3 a^4\right)}{\left(a^4 + a^3 - a^1 - a^2\right)}\right).$$

If the FN is of triangular form, then $a^3 = a^2$. Thus the defuzzified value in this case is given by

$$V\left(\tilde{a}\right) = \frac{1}{3}\left(a^4 + a^2 + a^1\right).$$

Based on these defuzzified value of FNs, a deterministic model is developed as follows:

Find $X\left(x_1, x_2, \ldots x_n\right)$ so as to

Minimize/maximize

$$V\left(\tilde{Z}_k\right) = \sum_{j=1}^{n}\left(\frac{1}{3}\left(c_{kj}^4 + c_{kj}^3 + c_{kj}^2 + c_{kj}^1 + \frac{\left(c_{kj}^1 c_{kj}^2 - c_{kj}^3 c_{kj}^4\right)}{\left(c_{kj}^4 + c_{kj}^3 - c_{kj}^1 - c_{kj}^2\right)}\right)\right)x_j \quad ;$$
$$k = 1, 2, \ldots, K$$

subject to

$$\sum_{j=1}^{n}\left(\frac{1}{3}\left(a_{ij}^4 + a_{ij}^3 + a_{ij}^2 + a_{ij}^1 + \frac{\left(a_{ij}^1 a_{ij}^2 - a_{ij}^3 a_{ij}^4\right)}{\left(a_{ij}^4 + a_{ij}^3 - a_{ij}^1 - a_{ij}^2\right)}\right)\right)x_j$$
$$\leq \left(\frac{1}{3}\left(b_i^4 + b_i^3 + b_i^2 + b_i^1 + \frac{\left(b_i^1 b_i^2 - b_i^3 b_i^4\right)}{\left(b_i^4 + b_i^3 - b_i^1 - b_i^2\right)}\right)\right) \quad ; \ i = 1, 2, \ldots, t$$

$$\sum_{j=1}^{n} \left[\frac{1}{3} \left(a_{lj}^4 + a_{lj}^3 + a_{lj}^2 + a_{lj}^1 + \frac{\left(a_{lj}^1 a_{lj}^2 - a_{lj}^3 a_{lj}^4 \right)}{\left(a_{lj}^4 + a_{lj}^3 - a_{lj}^1 - a_{lj}^2 \right)} \right) \right] x_j$$
$$\geq \left[\frac{1}{3} \left(b_l^4 + b_l^3 + b_l^2 + b_l^1 + \frac{\left(b_l^1 b_l^2 - b_l^3 b_l^4 \right)}{\left(b_l^4 + b_l^3 - b_l^1 - b_l^2 \right)} \right) \right] \quad ; l = t+1, t+2, \dots, m$$

$$x_j \geq 0 \; ; \; j = 1, 2, \dots\dots, n \tag{28}$$

Now the deterministic model is solved to achieve their best and worst values as in the earlier cases.

3.4.3 Defuzzification by Using α-Cut of a Fuzzy Number

Let $\tilde{a} = \left(a^1, a^2, a^3, a^4 \right)$ be a trapezoidal FN. The α – cut of the FN $\tilde{a}$ is given by

$$\tilde{a}[\alpha] = \left[a^1 + \left(a^2 - a^1 \right)\alpha, a^4 - \left(a^4 - a^3 \right)\alpha \right].$$

Then the defuzzified value of the FN $\tilde{a}$ is calculated as

$$V\left(\tilde{a} \right) = c \int_0^1 \left[a^1 + \left(a^2 - a^1 \right)\alpha \right] d\alpha + \left(1 - c \right) \int_0^1 \left[a^4 - \left(a^4 - a^3 \right)\alpha \right] d\alpha$$

$$= c \left[\frac{\left(a^1 + a^2 \right)}{2} \right] + \left(1 - c \right) \left[\frac{\left(a^3 + a^4 \right)}{2} \right], \; \left(0 \leq c \leq 1 \right)$$

Using the above defuzzification method, the fuzzy programming model is converted into deterministic model as

Find $X\left(x_1, x_2, \dots x_n \right)$ so as to

Minimize/maximize $\quad V\left(\tilde{Z}_k\right) = \sum_{j=1}^{n}\left(c\left[\frac{\left(c_{kj}^1 + c_{kj}^2\right)}{2}\right] + \left(1 - c\right)\left[\frac{\left(c_{kj}^3 + c_{kj}^4\right)}{2}\right]\right)x_j \, ;$

$k = 1, 2, \ldots\ldots, K$

subject to

$$\sum_{j=1}^{n}\left(c\left[\frac{\left(a_{ij}^1 + a_{ij}^2\right)}{2}\right] + \left(1 - c\right)\left[\frac{\left(a_{ij}^3 + a_{ij}^4\right)}{2}\right]\right)x_j \leq c\left[\frac{\left(b_i^1 + b_i^2\right)}{2}\right] + \left(1 - c\right)\left[\frac{\left(b_i^3 + b_i^4\right)}{2}\right] \quad ;$$

$i = 1, 2, \ldots, t$

$$\sum_{j=1}^{n}\left(c\left[\frac{\left(a_{lj}^1 + a_{lj}^2\right)}{2}\right] + \left(1 - c\right)\left[\frac{\left(a_{lj}^3 + a_{lj}^4\right)}{2}\right]\right)x_j \quad ; \, l = t+1, t+2, \ldots, m$$

$$\geq c\left[\frac{\left(b_i^1 + b_i^2\right)}{2}\right] + \left(1 - c\right)\left[\frac{\left(b_i^3 + b_i^4\right)}{2}\right]$$

$x_j \geq 0 \, ; \, j = 1, 2, \ldots\ldots, n$ \hfill (29)

3.4.4 Canonical Form of a Fuzzy Number

If $\tilde{a} = \left(a^1, a^2, a^3, a^4\right)$ be a trapezoidal FN, then α – cut of the FN $\tilde{a}$ is given by

$$\tilde{a}\left[\alpha\right] = \left[a^1 + \left(a^2 - a^1\right)\alpha, a^4 - \left(a^4 - a^3\right)\alpha\right].$$

In canonical form of an FN, the defuzzified value of $\tilde{a}$ is formulated as

$$V\left(\tilde{a}\right) = \int_0^1 \left(a^1 + \left(a^2 - a^1\right)\alpha\right)\alpha d\alpha + \int_0^1 \left(a^4 - \left(a^4 - a^3\right)\alpha\right)\alpha d\alpha$$

$$= \frac{\left[a^1 + 2a^2 + 2a^3 + a^4\right]}{6}$$

Based on this defuzzified value, the fuzzy programming model is modified as Find $X\left(x_1, x_2, \ldots . x_n\right)$ so as to

Minimize/maximize $V\left(\tilde{Z}_k\right) = \sum_{j=1}^{n} \frac{\left[c_{kj}^1 + 2c_{kj}^2 + 2c_{kj}^3 + c_{kj}^4\right]}{6} x_j$; $k = 1, 2, \ldots\ldots, K$

subject to

$$\sum_{j=1}^{n} \frac{\left[a_{ij}^1 + 2a_{ij}^2 + 2a_{ij}^3 + a_{ij}^4\right]}{6} x_j \le \frac{\left[b_i^1 + 2b_i^2 + 2b_i^3 + b_i^4\right]}{6} ; \quad i = 1, 2, \ldots, t$$

$$\sum_{j=1}^{n} \frac{\left[a_{lj}^1 + 2a_{lj}^2 + 2a_{lj}^3 + a_{lj}^4\right]}{6} x_j \ge \frac{\left[b_l^1 + 2b_l^2 + 2b_l^3 + b_l^4\right]}{6} ; \quad l = t+1, t+2, \ldots, m$$

$$x_j \ge 0 ; \quad j = 1, 2, \ldots\ldots, n \tag{30}$$

3.4.5 Centroid of a Fuzzy Number

If $\tilde{a} = \left(a^1, a^2, a^3, a^4\right)$ be a trapezoidal FN, then the centroid point $\left(x_0\left(\tilde{a}\right), y_0\left(\tilde{a}\right)\right)$ of the trapezium is

$$x_0\left(\tilde{a}\right) = \frac{1}{3}\left(a^4 + a^3 + a^1 + a^2 + \frac{\left(a^1 a^2 - a^3 a^4\right)}{\left(a^4 + a^3 - a^1 - a^2\right)}\right)$$

and

$$y_0\left(\tilde{a}\right) = \frac{1}{3}\left(1 + \frac{a^3 - a^2}{\left(a^4 + a^3 - a^1 - a^2\right)}\right).$$

Thus the defuzzified value is

$$V\left(\tilde{a}\right) = \frac{1}{3}\sqrt{\left(\left(a^4 + a^3 + a^1 + a^2 + \frac{\left(a^1 a^2 - a^3 a^4\right)}{\left(a^4 + a^3 - a^1 - a^2\right)}\right)\right)^2 + \left(\left(1 + \frac{a^3 - a^2}{\left(a^4 + a^3 - a^1 - a^2\right)}\right)\right)^2}.$$

This defuzzified value of the FN represents the distance of the centroid point from the origin.

Now the fuzzy programming model is converted into deterministic model by replacing the fuzzy parameters by their defuzzified values as follows.

Find $X\left(x_1, x_2, \ldots x_n\right)$ so as to

Minimize/maximize

$$V\left(\tilde{Z}_k\right) = \sum_{j=1}^{n} \frac{1}{3} \sqrt{\left(\left(c_{kj}^4 + c_{kj}^3 + c_{kj}^1 + c_{kj}^2 + \frac{\left(c_{kj}^1 c_{kj}^2 - c_{kj}^3 c_{kj}^4\right)}{\left(c_{kj}^4 + c_{kj}^3 - c_{kj}^1 - c_{kj}^2\right)}\right)\right)^2 + \left(\left(1 + \frac{c_{kj}^3 - c_{kj}^2}{\left(c_{kj}^4 + c_{kj}^3 - c_{kj}^1 - c_{kj}^2\right)}\right)\right)^2} \; x_j \qquad ;$$

$$k = 1, 2, \ldots \ldots, K$$

subject to

$$\sum_{j=1}^{n} \left(\frac{1}{3} \sqrt{\left(a_{ij}^4 + a_{ij}^3 + a_{ij}^1 + a_{ij}^2 + \frac{\left(a_{ij}^1 a_{ij}^2 - a_{ij}^3 a_{ij}^4\right)}{\left(a_{ij}^4 + a_{ij}^3 - a_{ij}^1 - a_{ij}^2\right)}\right)^2 + \left(1 + \frac{a_{ij}^3 - a_{ij}^2}{\left(a_{ij}^4 + a_{ij}^3 - a_{ij}^1 - a_{ij}^2\right)}\right)^2} \; x_j \right)$$

$$\leq \frac{1}{3} \sqrt{\left(b_i^4 + b_i^3 + b_i^1 + b_i^2 + \frac{\left(b_i^1 b_i^2 - b_i^3 b_i^4\right)}{\left(b_i^4 + b_i^3 - b_i^1 - b_i^2\right)}\right)^2 + \left(1 + \frac{b_i^3 - b_i^2}{\left(b_i^4 + b_i^3 - b_i^1 - b_i^2\right)}\right)^2}$$

$; i = 1, 2, \ldots, t$

$$\sum_{j=1}^{n} \left[\frac{1}{3} \sqrt{\left(a_{lj}^4 + a_{lj}^3 + a_{lj}^1 + a_{lj}^2 + \frac{\left(a_{lj}^1 a_{lj}^2 - a_{lj}^3 a_{lj}^4 \right)}{\left(a_{lj}^4 + a_{lj}^3 - a_{lj}^1 - a_{lj}^2 \right)} \right)^2 + \left(1 + \frac{a_{lj}^3 - a_{lj}^2}{\left(a_{lj}^4 + a_{lj}^3 - a_{lj}^1 - a_{lj}^2 \right)} \right)^2} \; x_j \right]$$

$$\geq \frac{1}{3} \sqrt{\left(b_l^4 + b_l^3 + b_l^1 + b_l^2 + \frac{\left(b_l^1 b_l^2 - b_l^3 b_l^4 \right)}{\left(b_l^4 + b_l^3 - b_l^1 - b_l^2 \right)} \right)^2 + \left(1 + \frac{b_l^3 - b_l^2}{\left(b_l^4 + b_l^3 - b_l^1 - b_l^2 \right)} \right)^2}$$

$; l = t+1, t+2, \ldots, m$

$x_j \geq 0$; $j = 1, 2, \ldots\ldots, n$ (31)

3.4.6 Nearest Symmetric Triangular Defuzzification

This defuzzification methodology is already discussed in Chapter 2. In this technique the defuzzified value of a trapezoidal FN $\tilde{a} = \left(a^1, a^2, a^3, a^4 \right)$ is obtained as

$$V\left(\tilde{a} \right) = \frac{\left(a^1 + a^2 + a^3 + a^4 \right)}{4}.$$

Using this defuzzified value of the FN, the fuzzy programming model converted into deterministic model as follows:

Find $X\left(x_1, x_2, \ldots x_n \right)$ so as to

Minimize/maximize $V\left(\tilde{Z}_k \right) = \sum_{j=1}^{n} \frac{\left(c_{kj}^1 + c_{kj}^2 + c_{kj}^3 + c_{kj}^4 \right)}{4} x_j$; $k = 1, 2, \ldots\ldots, K$

subject to

$$\sum_{j=1}^{n} \frac{\left(a_{ij}^1 + a_{ij}^2 + a_{ij}^3 + a_{ij}^4 \right)}{4} x_j \leq \frac{\left(b_i^1 + b_i^2 + b_i^3 + b_i^4 \right)}{4} \; ; \; i = 1, 2, \ldots, t$$

$$\sum_{j=1}^{n} \frac{\left(a_{lj}^1 + a_{lj}^2 + a_{lj}^3 + a_{lj}^4\right)}{4} x_j \geq \frac{\left(b_l^1 + b_l^2 + b_l^3 + b_l^4\right)}{4} ; \ l = t+1, t+2, \ldots, m$$

$$x_j \geq 0 ; \ j = 1, 2, \ldots, n \tag{32}$$

Thus based on various defuzzification methods discussed above, a fuzzy programming model is transformed into deterministic model considering different uncertainties as much as possible.

In the following section, a solution procedure is illustrated in the form of an algorithm to find a most suitable compromise solution acceptable to all the decision makers.

3.5 SOLUTION PROCEDURE

The solution procedure for solving a multi-objective fuzzy stochastic programming problem when the parameters are involved with the forms of FRVs or FNs or crisp numbers is presented below:

1. Obtain a multi-objective fuzzy programming model from multi-objective fuzzy stochastic programming model by applying CCP methodology.
2. Applying different defuzzification techniques the multi-objective fuzzy programming model is converted to an equivalent deterministic model as explained in previous section.
3. Solve each modified objective independently under the modified set of system constraints to find a best and worst solution of each objective. Let Z_k^b and Z_k^w ; $(k = 1, 2, \ldots, K)$ be the best and worst values of the objectives when the parameters of the objectives are crisp numbers. If the coefficients of the objectives are FNs or FRVs, then let $V\left(\tilde{Z}_k\right)^b$ and $V\left(\tilde{Z}_k\right)^w, (k = 1, 2, \ldots, K)$ be the best and worst values of the k-th objective.
4. Express the fuzzy goals of the k-th objective as

$V\left(\tilde{Z}_k\right) \gtrsim V\left(\tilde{Z}_k\right)^b$ or $Z_k \gtrsim Z_k^b; k = 1, 2, \ldots, K$ (for maximization type objectives) or,

$$V\left(\tilde{Z}_k\right) \lesssim V\left(\tilde{Z}_k\right)^b \text{ or } Z_k \lesssim Z_k^{\ b}; k = 1,2,\ldots,K \text{ (for minimizing type objectives)}$$

5. Construct the membership function of the k-th objective as

$$\mu_{Z_k}\left(x\right) = \begin{cases} 0 & \text{if} \quad Z_k \leq Z_k^w \\ \dfrac{Z_k - Z_k^w}{Z_k^b - Z_k^w} & \text{if } Z_k^w \leq Z_k \leq Z_k^b \\ 1 & \text{if} \quad Z_k \geq Z_k^b \end{cases}$$

i.e.,

$$\mu_{V\left(\tilde{Z}_k\right)} = \begin{cases} 0 & \text{if} \quad V\left(\tilde{Z}_k\right) \leq V\left(\tilde{Z}_k\right)^w \\ \dfrac{\left[V\left(\tilde{Z}_k\right) - V\left(\tilde{Z}_k\right)^w\right]}{\left[V\left(\tilde{Z}_k\right)^b - V\left(\tilde{Z}_k\right)^w\right]} & \text{if} \quad V\left(\tilde{Z}_k\right)^w \leq V\left(\tilde{Z}_k\right) \leq V\left(\tilde{Z}_k\right)^b \\ 1 & \text{if} \quad V\left(\tilde{Z}_k\right) \geq V\left(\tilde{Z}_k\right)^b \end{cases}$$

(for maximization type objectives) ;$k = 1,2,\ldots,K$

and

$$\mu_{Z_k}\left(x\right) = \begin{cases} 0 & \text{if} \quad Z_k \geq Z_k^w \\ \dfrac{Z_k^w - Z_k}{Z_k^w - Z_k^b} & \text{if } Z_k^b \leq Z_k \leq Z_k^w \\ 1 & \text{if} \quad Z_k \leq Z_k^b \end{cases}$$

i.e.,

$$
\mu_{DV(\tilde{Z}_k)} = \begin{cases} 0 & if & V\left(\tilde{Z}_k\right) \geq V\left(\tilde{Z}_k\right)^w \\ \dfrac{\left[V\left(\tilde{Z}_k\right)^w - V\left(\tilde{Z}_k\right)\right]}{\left[V\left(\tilde{Z}_k\right)^w - V\left(\tilde{Z}_k\right)^b\right]} & if & V\left(\tilde{Z}_k\right)^b \leq V\left(\tilde{Z}_k\right) \leq V\left(\tilde{Z}_k\right)^w \\ 1 & if & V\left(\tilde{Z}_k\right) \leq V\left(\tilde{Z}_k\right)^b \end{cases}
$$

(for minimization type objectives) $;k = 1,2,...,K$

6. Using the above membership functions the priority based FGP model / weighted FGP model is developed as

Priority Based Fuzzy Goal Programming Model:
Find $X\left(x_1, x_2, ...x_n\right)$ so as to

Min D $= P_1\left(d^-\right), P_2\left(d^-\right),... P_I\left(d^-\right)$

and satisfy

$$
\frac{Z_k - Z_k^w}{Z_k^b - Z_k^w} + d_k^- - d_k^+ = 1 \, \text{for} \ k = 1, 2, ..., K
$$

i.e.,

$$
\frac{\left[V\left(\tilde{Z}_k\right) - V\left(\tilde{Z}_k\right)^w\right]}{\left[V\left(\tilde{Z}_k\right)^b - V\left(\tilde{Z}_k\right)^w\right]} + d_k^- - d_k^+ = 1 \, \text{for} \ k = 1, 2, ..., K \text{ (for maximization type objectives)}
$$

and

$$
\frac{Z_k^w - Z_k}{Z_k^w - Z_k^b} + d_k^- - d_k^+ = 1 \, \text{for} \ k = 1, 2, ..., K
$$

i.e.,

$$\frac{\left[V\left(\tilde{Z}_k\right)^w - V\left(\tilde{Z}_k\right)\right]}{\left[V\left(\tilde{Z}_k\right)^w - V\left(\tilde{Z}_k\right)^b\right]} + d_k^- - d_k^+ = 1 \text{ for } k = 1, 2, \ldots, K \text{ (for minimization type}$$

objectives)

subject to the set of modified constraints given in the above deterministic models

$$d_k^-, d_k^+ \geq 0 \; ; d_k^-.d_k^+ = 0 \; k = 1, 2, \ldots, K \tag{33}$$

where D represents I priority achievement functions consisting of the weighted under deviational variables, d_k^-. The priority factors have the relationship

$$P_1 >>> P_2 >>> \ldots P_i >>> \ldots >>> P_I$$

which implies that the goals at the highest priority level will achieve the goal values to the extent possible before considering the achievement of the goals at the lower priority levels. The priority function $P_i\left(d^-\right)$ has the form:

$$P_i\left(d^-\right) = \sum_{k=1}^{K} w_{ik}^- d_k^-,$$

where $w_{ik}^- \geq 0$ represents the numerical weights of importance of the goals at the i-th priority level P_i, and which are determined as:

$$w_{ik}^- = \frac{1}{\left(Z_k^b - Z_k^w\right)} \text{ i.e., } w_{ik}^- = \frac{1}{\left[V\left(\tilde{Z}_k\right)^b - V\left(\tilde{Z}_k\right)^w\right]} \text{ (for maximizing type}$$

objectives)

and

$$w_{ik}^- = \frac{1}{\left(Z_k^w - Z_k^b\right)} \text{ i.e., } w_{ik}^- = \frac{1}{\left(V\left(\tilde{Z}_k\right)^w - V\left(\tilde{Z}_k\right)^b\right)} \text{ (for minimizing type}$$

objectives).

Weighted Fuzzy Goal Programming Model:
Find $X\left(x_1, x_2, \ldots x_n\right)$ so as to

$$\text{Minimize } D = \sum_{k=1}^{K} w_k d_k^-$$

and satisfy

$$\frac{Z_k - Z_k^w}{Z_k^b - Z_k^w} + d_k^- - d_k^+ = 1 \text{ for } k = 1, 2, \ldots, K$$

or,

$$\frac{\left[V\left(\tilde{Z}_k\right) - V\left(\tilde{Z}_k\right)^w\right]}{\left[V\left(\tilde{Z}_k\right)^b - V\left(\tilde{Z}_k\right)^w\right]} + d_k^- - d_k^+ = 1 \text{ for } k = 1, 2, \ldots, K \text{ (for maximization type}$$

objectives)

and

$$\frac{Z_k^w - Z_k}{Z_k^w - Z_k^b} + d_k^- - d_k^+ = 1 \text{ for } k = 1, 2, \ldots, K$$

i.e.,

$$\frac{\left[V\left(\tilde{Z}_k\right)^w - V\left(\tilde{Z}_k\right)\right]}{\left[V\left(\tilde{Z}_k\right)^w - V\left(\tilde{Z}_k\right)^b\right]} + d_k^- - d_k^+ = 1 \text{ for } k = 1, 2, \ldots, K \text{ (for minimization type}$$

objectives)

subject to the set of modified constraints given in the above deterministic models

$$d_k^-, d_k^+ \geq 0 \; ; d_k^- . d_k^+ = 0 \; k = 1, 2, \ldots, K \tag{34}$$

where $w_k^- \geq 0$ represents the numerical weights of importance of the $k-$th goals, which are determined as:

$$w_k^- = \frac{1}{\left(Z_k^b - Z_k^w\right)} \text{ i.e., } w_k^- = \frac{1}{\left[V\left(\tilde{Z}_k\right)^b - V\left(\tilde{Z}_k\right)^w\right]} \text{ (for maximizing type objectives)}$$

and

$$w_k^- = \frac{1}{\left(Z_k^w - Z_k^b\right)} \text{ i.e., } w_k^- = \frac{1}{\left[V\left(\tilde{Z}_k\right)^w - V\left(\tilde{Z}_k\right)^b\right]} \text{ (for minimizing type}$$

objectives).

All FGP models (priority based and weighted) so obtained is now solved using the *software* LINGO or others to find a compromise solution acceptable to all the decision makers in the decision making context.

3.6 NUMERICAL ILLUSTRATIONS

To demonstrate the feasibility and efficiency of the developed approaches, the following numerical examples with parameters as FNs and FRVs are considered.

3.6.1 Numerical Example 1

In this example a multi-objective fuzzy stochastic programming model, with left sided parameters of the constraints are FNs and right sided parameters of the constraints are Weibull distributed FRVs, are considered and solved using the methodology discussed previously in this chapter.

A fuzzy stochastic mathematical programming problem with two objective functions and two unknowns is presented as

Find $X\left(x_1, x_2\right)$ so as to

Maximize $Z_1 = 3x_1 + 7x_2$

Maximize $Z_2 = 9x_1 + 4x_2$

subject to

$$Pr\left[\tilde{1}x_1 + \tilde{1}x_2 \lesssim \tilde{b}_1\right] \geq 0.85,$$

$$Pr\left[\tilde{3}x_1 + \tilde{2}x_2 \lesssim \tilde{b}_2\right] \geq 0.75,$$

$$Pr\left[\tilde{2}x_1 + \tilde{1}x_2 \lesssim \tilde{b}_3\right] \geq 0.72$$

$$x_1, x_2 \geq 0 \tag{35}$$

Here $\tilde{b}_1, \tilde{b}_2, \tilde{b}_3$ are independent FRVs following Weibull distribution. The parameters of the distribution are taken as triangular FNs with the form

$$\tilde{\lambda}_1 = \widetilde{0.5} = \left(0.4, 0.5, 0.6\right), \tilde{\beta}_1 = \widetilde{186} = \left(184, 186, 188\right),$$

$$\tilde{\lambda}_2 = \widetilde{0.5} = \left(0.4, 0.5, 0.6\right), \tilde{\beta}_2 = \widetilde{118} = \left(115, 118, 121\right),$$

$$\tilde{\lambda}_3 = \widetilde{0.25} = \left(0.20, 0.25, 0.30\right), \tilde{\beta}_3 = \widetilde{589} = \left(585, 589, 593\right).$$

Using CCP methodology, the fuzzy stochastic model is modified into fuzzy programming model as explained in subsection 3.2.1., as

Find $X\left(x_1, x_2\right)$ so as to

Maximize $Z_1 = 3x_1 + 7x_2$

Maximize $Z_2 = 9x_1 + 4x_2$

subject to

$$\tilde{1}x_1 + \tilde{1}x_2 \lesssim \widetilde{186}\left(\ln\left(1.176\right)\right)^{\frac{1}{0.5}}$$

$$\tilde{3}x_1 + \tilde{2}x_2 \lesssim \widetilde{118}\left(\ln\left(1.333\right)\right)^{\frac{1}{0.5}}$$

$$\tilde{2}x_1 + \tilde{1}x_2 \lesssim \widetilde{589}\left(\ln\left(1.389\right)\right)^{\frac{1}{0.25}}$$

$$x_1, x_2 \geq 0 \tag{36}$$

All the left sided parameters of the constraints are taken as trapezoidal FNs of the form

$$\tilde{1} = \left(0.2, 0.8, 1, 1.2\right), \tilde{1} = \left(0.4, 1, 1.6, 2\right), \tilde{3} = \left(1, 2, 3, 4\right),$$
$$\tilde{2} = \left(0.5, 1.5, 2.5, 3\right), \tilde{2} = \left(1, 1.8, 2.2, 3\right), \tilde{1} = \left(0.5, 1, 1.5, 2\right)^{.}$$

Now applying the defuzzification method of FNs, the multi-objective linear programming model is constructed as

Find $X\left(x_1, x_2\right)$ so as to

Maximize $Z_1 = 3x_1 + 7x_2$

Maximize $Z_2 = 9x_1 + 4x_2$

subject to

$$0.78\,x_1 + 1.24x_2 \leq 4.92$$

$$2.67\,x_1 + 1.86x_2 \leq 9.78$$

$$2\,x_1 + 1.25x_2 \leq 6.86$$

$$x_1, x_2 \geq 0 \tag{37}$$

Each objective is now solved independently under the modified set of system constraint to find the best and worst values of each objective.

Thus $Z_1^b = 27.77$, at the solution point $X_1^B = (x_1, x_2) = (0, 3.968)$ and $Z_2^b = 30.87$, at the solution point $X_2^B = (x_1, x_2) = (3.43, 0)$ are found.

So, the pay-off matrix of the objectives is given by

	X_1^B	X_2^B
Z_1	27.77	10.29
Z_2	30.87	15.872

From the pay-off matrix it is clearly seen that the worst value of the objectives are $Z_1^w = 10.29$ and $Z_2^w = 15.872$.

Then the fuzzy goals of the objectives are found as: $Z_1 \gtrsim 27.77$, $Z_2 \gtrsim 15.872$.

Now, the membership function is constructed for each objective based on the fuzzy goals. Finally a FGP model is developed and solved using Software LINGO (ver. 11) to find a most suitable solution acceptable to all the decision makers.

Find X(x_1, x_2)

min= 0.057* d_1^-+ 0.067*d_2^-;

0.172*x_1+0.400*x_2-0.589+ d_1^-- d_1^+=1;

0.600*x_1+0.267*x_2-1.058+ d_2^-- d_2^+=1;

$0.78{*}x_1 + 1.24{*}x_2 <= 4.92;$

$2.67{*}x_1 + 1.86{*}x_2 <= 9.78;$

$2{*}x_1 + 1.25{*}x_2 <= 6.86;$

where

$d_1^-, d_1^+, d_2^-, d_2^+ >= 0$ with $d_1^- {*} d_1^+, d_2^- {*} d_2^+ = 0.$ (38)

Solving the above weighted FGP problem the compromise solution of both the objectives are obtained as

$Z_1 = 25.54$ and $Z_2 = 25.96$ at the solution point $(x_1, x_2) = (1.56, 2.98)$. The membership value of the objectives are found as $\mu_{Z_1} = 0.87$ and $\mu_{Z_2} = 0.70$. From this fact it is clear that the above described methodology yields a compromise solution that is acceptable to all the decision makers and the achieved compromise solution is very close to the optimal solution of all the objectives which are obtained by solving each objective, independently.

This fact can also be clear from the diagrammatic representation in Figure 1.

Figure 1. Comparison of solutions

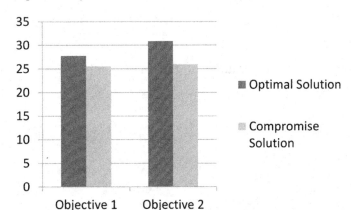

3.6.2 Numerical Example 2

Consider a multi-objective fuzzy stochastic linear programming problem in which all the parameters are FRVs following normal distribution

$$\text{Maximize } \tilde{Z}_k \cong \sum_{j=1}^{3} \tilde{c}_{kj} x_j \text{ ; } k = 1, 2, 3.$$

subject to

$$\Pr\left[\sum_{j=1}^{3} \tilde{a}_{ij} x_j \lesssim \tilde{b}_i\right] \geq 1 - \alpha_i \text{ ; } i = 1, 2.$$

$$x_j \geq 0 \tag{39}$$

Here $\tilde{c}_{kj} \left(k = 1, 2, 3; j = 1, 2, 3\right)$, $\tilde{a}_{ij} \left(i = 1, 2; j = 1, 2, 3\right)$ and $\tilde{b}_i \left(i = 1, 2\right)$ are FRVs following normal distribution and $\alpha_1 = 0.05$ and $\alpha_2 = 0.10$.

The mean of the FRVs $\tilde{c}_{kj} \left(k = 1, 2, 3; j = 1, 2, 3\right)$ are given by

$$E\left(\tilde{c}_{11}\right) = \tilde{5}, E\left(\tilde{c}_{12}\right) = \tilde{6}, E\left(\tilde{c}_{13}\right) = \tilde{3}, E\left(\tilde{c}_{21}\right) = \tilde{7}, E\left(\tilde{c}_{22}\right) = \tilde{2}, E\left(\tilde{c}_{23}\right) = \tilde{4}, E\left(\tilde{c}_{31}\right) = \tilde{2}, E\left(\tilde{c}_{32}\right) = \tilde{3}$$

and $E\left(\tilde{c}_{33}\right) = \tilde{8}$.

Also, the mean and variance of the FRVs $\tilde{a}_{ij} \left(i = 1, 2; j = 1, 2, 3\right)$ and $\tilde{b}_i \left(i = 1, 2\right)$ are

$$E\left(\tilde{a}_{11}\right) = \tilde{1}, E\left(\tilde{a}_{12}\right) = \tilde{3}, E\left(\tilde{a}_{13}\right) = \widetilde{-9}, E\left(\tilde{a}_{21}\right) = \tilde{5}, E\left(\tilde{a}_{22}\right) = \tilde{1}, E\left(\tilde{a}_{23}\right) = \tilde{6}, E\left(\tilde{b}_1\right) = \tilde{8}, E\left(b_2\right) = \tilde{7}$$

and

$$Var\left(\tilde{a}_{11}\right) = \widetilde{25}, Var\left(\tilde{a}_{12}\right) = \widetilde{16}, Var\left(\tilde{a}_{13}\right) = \tilde{4}, Var\left(\tilde{a}_{21}\right) = \widetilde{16},$$
$$Var\left(\tilde{a}_{22}\right) = \widetilde{25}, Var\left(\tilde{a}_{23}\right) = \tilde{7}, Var\left(\tilde{b}_1\right) = \tilde{3}, Var\left(b_2\right) = \tilde{9}.$$

Using CCP methodology, the constraints with FRVs are converted into fuzzy constraints as follows

$$\tilde{1}x_1 + \tilde{3}x_2 + \widetilde{-9}x_3 \lesssim \tilde{8} - 1.645\sqrt{\widetilde{25}x_1^2 + \widetilde{16}x_2^2 + \tilde{4}x_3^2 + \tilde{3}}$$

$$\tilde{5}x_1 + \tilde{1}x_2 + \tilde{6}x_3 \lesssim \tilde{7} - 1.285\sqrt{\widetilde{16}x_1^2 + \widetilde{25}x_2^2 + \tilde{7}x_3^2 + \tilde{9}} \qquad (40)$$

Thus the expectation model of the multi-objective fuzzy stochastic programming model is presented as

Maximize $\tilde{Z}_1 \cong \tilde{5}x_1 + \tilde{6}x_2 + \tilde{3}x_3$

Maximize $\tilde{Z}_2 \cong \tilde{7}x_1 + \tilde{2}x_2 + \tilde{4}x_3$

Maximize $\tilde{Z}_3 \cong \tilde{2}x_1 + \tilde{3}x_2 + \tilde{8}x_3$

subject to

$$\tilde{1}x_1 + \tilde{3}x_2 + \widetilde{-9}x_3 \lesssim \tilde{8} - 1.645\sqrt{\widetilde{25}x_1^2 + \widetilde{16}x_2^2 + \tilde{4}x_3^2 + \tilde{3}}$$

$$\tilde{5}x_1 + \tilde{1}x_2 + \tilde{6}x_3 \lesssim \tilde{7} - 1.285\sqrt{\widetilde{16}x_1^2 + \widetilde{25}x_2^2 + \tilde{7}x_3^2 + \tilde{9}}$$

$$x_1, x_2, x_3 \geq 0 \qquad (41)$$

To reduce the complexity, all the FNs are considered as symmetric triangular FNs of the following form

$$\tilde{2} = (1.95, 2, 2.05), \tilde{3} = (2.5, 3, 3.5), \tilde{4} = (3.8, 4, 4.2), \tilde{5} = (4.95, 5, 5.05), \tilde{6} = (5.9, 6, 6.1),$$

$$\tilde{7} = (6.95, 7, 7.05), \tilde{8} = (7.9, 8, 8.1), \widetilde{-9} = (-9.05, -9, -8.95), \widetilde{25} = (24, 25, 26),$$

$$\widetilde{16} = (14, 16, 18), \tilde{1} = (.95, 1, 1.05), \tilde{9} = (8.5, 9, 9.5).$$

After applying the method of defuzzification to the multi-objective fuzzy programming model, the multi-objective non-linear programming model in crisp environment is formed as

Maximize $Z_1 = 5x_1 + 6x_2 + 3x_3$

Maximize $Z_2 = 7x_1 + 2x_2 + 4x_3$

Maximize $Z_3 = 2x_1 + 3x_2 + 8x_3$

subject to

$$x_1 + 3x_2 - 9x_3 \leq 8 - 1.645\sqrt{25x_1^2 + 16x_2^2 + 4x_3^2 + 3}$$

$$5x_1 + x_2 + 6x_3 \leq 7 - 1.285\sqrt{16x_1^2 + 25x_2^2 + 7x_3^2 + 9}$$

$$x_1, x_2, x_3 \geq 0 \tag{42}$$

As in the previous example, each objective is now solved independently under the modified set of system constraints to find the best and worst value of each objective.

$Z_1^b = 4.579$ at the point $\left(x_1, x_2, x_3\right) = \left(0.01, 0.75, 0\right)$ and $Z_1^w = 0$ at $\left(x_1, x_2, x_3\right) = \left(0, 0, 0\right)$.

$Z_2^b = 3.454$ at the point $\left(x_1, x_2, x_3\right) = \left(0.46, 0.13, 0\right)$ and $Z_2^w = 0$ at $\left(x_1, x_2, x_3\right) = \left(0, 0, 0\right)$.

$Z_3^b = 3.933$ at the point $\left(x_1, x_2, x_3\right) = \left(0, 0.17, 0.43\right)$ and $Z_3^w = 0$ at $\left(x_1, x_2, x_3\right) = \left(0, 0, 0\right)$.

Thus the fuzzy membership goal of each objective is developed as

$Z_1 \gtrsim 4.579$, $Z_2 \gtrsim 3.454$ and $Z_3 \gtrsim 3.933$.

Now the membership goals are converted into membership functions to form the weighted FGP model. The FGP model is then solved using LINGO (ver. 11) software or others to find compromise solution of all the objectives. The FGP model written in LINGO code is presented as

min= 0.218* d_1^-+ 0.290*d_2^- + 0.254*d_3^-;

1.092*x_1+1.310*x_2+0.655*x_3+ d_1^-- d_1^+= 1;

2.027*x_1+0.579*x_2+1.158*x_3+ d_2^-- d_2^+= 1;

0.509*x_1+0.763*x_2+2.034*x_3+ d_3^-- d_3^+= 1;

x_1+3*x_2-9*x_3+1.645*y <= 8;

5*x_1+x_2+6*x_3+1.285*z <= 7;

y^2-25*x_1^2-16*x_2^2-4*x_3^2= 3;

z^2-16*x_1^2-25*x_2^2-7*x_3^2= 9;

where

d_1^-, d_1^+, d_2^-, d_2^+, d_3^-, d_3^+ >= 0 with d_1^- * d_1^+, d_2^- * d_2^+, d_3^- * d_3^+= 0.　　　(43)

Solving the above FGP model using LINGO software the compromise solution of the objectives are obtained as

$Z_1 = 3.644$, $Z_2 = 2.79$, and $Z_3 = 2.8$ at the solution point $(x_1, x_2, x_3) = (0.202, 0.356, 0.166)$. Also, the membership values of the objectives are calculated as $\mu_{Z_1} = 0.8$, $\mu_{Z_2} = 0.81$ and $\mu_{Z_3} = 0.71$. These are summarised in the Table 1.

Table 1. Values of the objectives

Objective	Solution Point	Objective Value	Membership Value
Z_1	$x_1 = 0.202$	3.644	0.8
Z_2	$x_2 = 0.356$ $x_3 = 0.166$	2.79	0.81
Z_3		2.8	0.71

3.7 CONCLUSION

This chapter presents methodologies for solving fuzzy probabilistic multi-objective programming problems involving some well-known continuous FRVs and FNs using FGP technique. This method captures both type of uncertainties like fuzziness and randomness, simultaneously. This model is also flexible enough to introduce the tolerance limits to the fuzzy goals initially to arrive at its satisfactory decisions on the basis of the needs and desires of the DMs. The readers after going through this chapter can realize that

1. Authors in this chapter provided main emphasise on multi-objective linear programming problems under fuzzy stochastic uncertain environment.
2. The parameters of the problems are taken as either crisp numbers or FNs or FRVs with some well-known probability distribution.
3. CCP methodology is applied to form fuzzy programming model from the fuzzy stochastic programming model. Instead of applying CCP methodology, two stage programming technique can also be implemented.
4. The fuzzy parameters of the mathematical programming models are taken as either triangular FNs or trapezoidal FNs, for simplicity. But other forms of FNs such as Gaussian FNs, intuitionistic FNs, type-II FNs, Pythagorean FNs can also be used as FNs.
5. All the FRVs considered in this chapter are taken as continuous FRVs. But discrete FRVs can also be taken in place of continuous FRVs.

REFERECES

Biswal, M. P., Biswal, N. P., & Li, D. (1998). Probabilistic linear programming problems with exponential random variables: A technical note. *European Journal of Operational Research, 111*(3), 589–597. doi:10.1016/S0377-2217(97)90319-2

Biswas, A., & Modak, N. (2011). A fuzzy goal programming method for solving chance constrained programming with fuzzy parameters. *Communications in Computer and Information Science, 140*, 187–196. doi:10.1007/978-3-642-19263-0_23

Biswas, A., & Modak, N. (2012). Using fuzzy goal programming technique to solve multiobjective chance constrained programming problems in a fuzzy environment. *International Journal of Fuzzy System Applications, 2*(1), 71–80. doi:10.4018/ijfsa.2012010105

Charnes, A., & Cooper, W. W. (1959). Chance Constrained Programming. *Management Science, 6*(1), 73–79. doi:10.1287/mnsc.6.1.73

Chen, H. K. (1994). A Note on a Fuzzy Goal Programming Algorithm by Tiwari, Dharmar and Rao. *Fuzzy Sets and Systems, 62*(3), 287–290. doi:10.1016/0165-0114(94)90112-0

De, A. K., Dewan, S., & Biswas, A. (2018). A Unified approach for fuzzy multiobjective Stochastic Programming with Cauchy and extreme value distributed fuzzy random variables. *Intelligent Decision Technologies, 12*(1), 81–91. doi:10.3233/IDT-170312

Dong, F., Liu, Y., Qian, L., Sheng, H., Yang, Y., Guo, H., & Zhao, L. (2014). Interactive decision procedure for watershed nutrient load reduction: An integrated chance constrained programming model with risk–cost tradeoff. *Environmental Modelling & Software, 61*, 166–173. doi:10.1016/j.envsoft.2014.07.014

Fechner, G. T. (1897). *Kollektivmasslehre*. Engelmann.

Galton, F. (1879). The geometric mean in vital and social statistics. *Proceedings of the Royal Society, 29*(196-199), 365–367. doi:10.1098/rspl.1879.0060

Hock, W., & Schittkowski, K. (1981). Test examples for nonlinear programming codes. Lecture Notes in Economics and Mathematical Systems, 187. doi:10.1007/978-3-642-48320-2

Katagiri, H., Kato, K., & Uno, T. (2017). Possibility/Necessity Based Probabilistic Expectation Models for Linear Programming Problems with Discrete Fuzzy Random Variables. *Symmetry*, *9*(11), 1–34. doi:10.3390ym9110254

Kataoka, S. (1963). A stochastic programming model. *Econometrica*, *31*(1/2), 181–196. doi:10.2307/1910956

Kwakernaak, H. (1978). Fuzzy random variable –I. Definitions and theorems. *Information Sciences*, *15*(1), 1–29. doi:10.1016/0020-0255(78)90019-1

Lai, Y. J., & Hwang, C. L. (1994). *Fuzzy Multiple Objective Decision Making: Methods and Applications*. Berlin: Springer Verlag. doi:10.1007/978-3-642-57949-3

Liu, B. (2001). Fuzzy random chance-constrained programming. *IEEE Transactions on Fuzzy Systems*, *9*(5), 713–720. doi:10.1109/91.963757

Luhandjula, M. K. (1996). Fuzziness and randomness in an optimization framework. *Fuzzy Sets and Systems*, *77*(3), 291–297. doi:10.1016/0165-0114(95)00043-7

Luhandjula, M. K., & Roubert, J. W. (2010). On some optimization models in a fuzzy stochastic environment. *European Journal of Operational Research*, *207*(3), 1433–1441. doi:10.1016/j.ejor.2010.07.016

Mohammed, W. (2000). Chance constrained fuzzy goal programming with right-hand side uniform random variable coefficients. *Fuzzy Sets and Systems*, *109*(1), 107–110. doi:10.1016/S0165-0114(98)00151-1

Nematian, J. (2012). A New Method for Multi-Objective Linear Programming Models with Fuzzy Random Variables. *Journal of Uncertain Systems*, *6*(1), 38–50.

Prekopa, A. (1973). Contribution to the theory of stochastic programming. *Mathematical Programming*, *4*(1), 202–221. doi:10.1007/BF01584661

Sahoo, N. P., & Biswal, M. P. (2005). Computation of some stochastic linear programming problems with cauchy and extreme value distributions. *International Journal of Computer Mathematics*, *82*(6), 685–698. doi:10.1080/00207160412331336080

Sakawa, M., Kato, K., & Nishizaki, I. (2003). An interactive fuzzy satisficing method for multiobjective stochastic linear programming problems through an expectation model. *European Journal of Operational Research*, *145*(3), 665–672. doi:10.1016/S0377-2217(02)00150-9

Sinha, S. B., Biswal, M. P., & Hulsurkar, S. (1998). Fuzzy programming approach to multiobjective probabilistic linear programming problems where only bi's are probabilistic. *The Journal of Fuzzy Mathematics*, *6*(1), 63–73.

Weber, H. (1834). *De Pulsa Resorptione Audituet Tactu. In Annotationes Anatomicaeet Physiologicae*. Koehler.

Yano, H., & Sakawa, M. (2012). Interactive multiobjective fuzzy random linear programming through fractile criteria. *Advances in Fuzzy Systems*. doi:10.1155/2012/521080

ZareMehrjerdi, Y. (1986). *A chance constrained goal programming model of stochastic vehicle routine problem* (Unpublished Dissertation). Oklahoma State University.

Zhou, M. (2015). An interval fuzzy chance constrained programming model for sustainable urban land-use planning and land use policy analysis. *Land Use Policy*, *42*, 479–491. doi:10.1016/j.landusepol.2014.09.002

Chapter 4
Development of Fuzzy Multi-Objective Stochastic Fractional Programming Models

ABSTRACT

In this chapter, two methodologies for solving multi-objective linear fractional stochastic programming problems containing fuzzy numbers (FNs) and fuzzy random variables (FRVs) associated with the system constraints are developed. In the model formulation process, the fuzzy probabilistic constraints are converted into equivalent fuzzy constraints by applying chance constrained programming (CCP) technique in a fuzzily defined probabilistic decision-making situation. Then two techniques, α-cut and defuzzification methods, are used to convert the model into the corresponding deterministic model. In the method of using α-cut for FNs, the tolerance level of FNs is considered, and the constraints are reduced to constraints with interval coefficients. Alternatively, in using defuzzification method, FNs are replaced by their defuzzified values. Consequently, the constraints are modified into constraints in deterministic form. In the next step, the constraints with interval coefficients are customized into its equivalent form by using the convex combination of each interval. If the parameters of the objectives are triangular FNs, then on the basis of their tolerance ranges each objective is decomposed into three objectives with crisp coefficients. Then each objective is solved independently to find their best and worst values and those values are used to construct membership function of each objective. Finally, the compromise solution of multi-objective linear fractional CCP problems is obtained by applying any of the approaches: priority-based fuzzy goal programming (FGP) method, Zimmermann's approach, γ-connective process, or minimum bounded sum operator technique. To demonstrate the efficiency of the above-described techniques, two illustrative examples, studied previously, are solved, and the solutions are compared with the existing methodology.

DOI: 10.4018/978-1-5225-8301-1.ch004

4.1 FUZZY STOCHASTIC FRACTIONAL PROGRAMMING MODEL

Mathematical models in which objective functions are appeared as the ratio of two functions are known as fractional programming problem (FPP) (Craven, 1988). Based on the linearity condition of the objectives and constraints, FPPs are classified into two categories; if the objective functions and constraints are linear in form, then that kind of mathematical models are called linear FPPs, otherwise if nonlinearity appears, those are called non-linear FPPs. Considering the ratio form of the objectives, fractional programming has attracted the attention of researchers in the past. There are several applications of fractional programming in solving different real life decision making problems, viz., production planning, financial and corporate planning, health care and hospital planning where several rates need to be optimized, simultaneously. The first monograph in fractional programming was published by Bitran and Novaes (1973) that extensively covers applications, theoretical results and algorithms for single-ratio fractional programs. Fractional programming (Schaible, 1981; Schaible and Ibaraki, 1983; Stancu - Minasian, 1997) deals with the optimization of one or several ratios of functions. These ratios of functions in FPP may be the ratio of purchasing cost and selling cost, ratio of production of two major crops, ratio of death and birth of people of certain region, ratio of full time workers and part time workers, ratio of salary and bonus etc. Hughes (1993) introduced a geometric approach for finding interior efficient solutions in bi-criterion linear FPPs. In some real-life situations, the decision makers may not be able to accurately exert their conclusion due to that (1) they may not possess the precise or sufficient level of knowledge of the problem; (2) they are unable to discriminate explicitly the amount to which one alternative is better than others. i.e., some amounts of uncertainties involve with these problems. Fuzzy programming and stochastic programming are useful techniques to handle these uncertainties.

One well-defined methodology for treating problems with probabilistic constraints is known as CCP. Charnes and Cooper (1962) proposed the E-model (expectation optimization model), the V-model (variance minimization model) and the P-model (probability maximization model) for solving stochastic problems. Thereafter, different methodological aspects of CCP were discussed by Kataoka (1963), Miller and Wagner (1965), Panne and Pop (1963), Prekopa (1973), and other researchers. The basic idea of all stochastic programming models is to convert the probabilistic nature of the problem into an equivalent deterministic model depending on the specified confidence levels and the nature of the distribution followed by the random variables. In recent years, Helmy et al. (2015) proposed multilevel multi-objective FPPs in stochastic environment. Also, Nasseri and Bavandi (2017) suggested an interval parameter CCP approach for FPPs.

If the decision makers do not have any clear knowledge of the problem, then the parameters of the problem may be expressed as FNs rather than crisp numbers. If the problems involve FNs as parameters or fuzzy inequalities or both, then fuzzy programming model is applied to handle these problems. Zimmermann (1976) proposed a decision making model based on fuzzy set theory. Thereafter, a plenty of works have been done (Zadeh, 1965; Dubois and Prade, 1980) from the view point of its potential application in different real life planning problems (Pal and Moitra, 2003). Saad (1995) presented a solution procedure for solving linear fractional programs having fuzzy parameters in the right side of the constraints. Pareto-optimality for multi-objective linear FPPs with fuzzy parameter was discussed by Sakawa and Yano (1992). Chakraborty and Gupta (2002) discussed fuzzy set theoretic approach to multi-objective linear FPP by transformation of variables. Sadjadi et al. (2005) studied fuzzy inventory problem involving multi-objective linear fractional objectives. An FGP approach for solving multi-objective fractional fuzzy goals was presented by Pal et al. (2003). FGP approach to different real life problems is found in the papers presented by Biswas and Pal (2005), and others. Mehrjerdi (2011) Solved FPP through fuzzy goal setting and approximation. Iskander (2004) proposed a fuzzy weighted additive approach for solving stochastic FGP problems. Chan (2005) proposed an FGP approach for solving fractional programming with absolute-value functions. The main difference between FGP and goal programming is that goal programming requires the decision maker to set definite aspiration values for each goal while in the FGP these are specified in an imprecise manner (Sinha, Rao and Mangaraj, 1988). Osman et al. (2017) developed an FGP model for stochastic fuzzy multilevel multi-objective FPP. A redundancy detection algorithm for fuzzy stochastic multi-objective linear FPPs was proposed by Shiraz et al. (2017). It is worthy to mention here that the problem of fractional CCP defined in this chapter is open up new ways in the field of fuzzy stochastic decision making arena.

In this chapter two methodologies are developed to solve a multi-objective fuzzy linear fractional CCP (FCCP) problem consisting of FRVs associated with right side values of the system constraints. Also all the parameters of the system constraints are considered as triangular FNs. The general CCP technique is used to convert the chance constraint into equivalent fuzzy constraints. For the first model α-cut of the FNs associated with the system constraints is used to reduce the problem to a multi-objective FPP with interval coefficients. Then considering the fuzzy aspects of the model, the problem is decomposed on the basis of their tolerance ranges of fuzzy parameters. For the second model each objectives are decomposed into three objectives on the basis of the tolerance ranges of triangular FNs. The individual optimal solution of each objective are found to construct the membership function of them after using the convex combination of the interval in the system constraints the problem. Finally, for the first model a priority based FGP model is used for achieving the highest membership degree of each of the defined fuzzy goals to the extent possible and for the second model three fuzzy approaches is used to find the compromise solution of all the objectives. To illustrate the developed models two examples are solved and solutions are compared with the existing methodology.

4.2. MULTI-OBJECTIVE FUZZY LINEAR STOCHASTIC FRACTIONAL PROGRAMMING MODEL

In this chapter multi-objective fuzzy linear stochastic FPP is expressed in the following two forms. In both the models the fuzzy probabilistic constraints involve FRVs with some known continuous probability distribution. In the first model the parameters of the objectives are considered as crisp numbers where as in the second model the parameters are taken as FNs in triangular form.

4.2.1. Multi-Objective Fuzzy Linear Stochastic Fractional Programming Model With Crisp Objectives

In this subsection a fuzzy stochastic fractional programming model with k number of objectives is presented in the following form

Find $X(x_1, x_2, \ldots, x_n)$ so as to

$$\text{Maximize } Z_k = \frac{\sum_{j=1}^{n} c_{kj} x_j + \gamma_k}{\sum_{j=1}^{n} d_{kj} x_j + \delta_k} \text{ for } k = 1, 2, \ldots, K$$

subject to

$$\Pr(\sum_{j=1}^{n} \tilde{A}_{ij} x_j \le \tilde{b}_i) \ge 1 - \beta_i, \ i = 1, 2, \ldots, m$$

$$\sum_{j=1}^{n} \tilde{A}_{tj} x_j \le \tilde{b}_t, \ t = m + 1, m + 2, \ldots, l$$

$$\sum_{j=1}^{n} \tilde{A}_{sj} x_j \ge \tilde{b}_s, \ s = l + 1, l + 2, \ldots, p$$

$$x_j \ge 0 \,; j = 1, 2, ., ., n \,; c_{kj}, d_{kj}, \gamma_k, \delta_k \in \mathbb{R} \tag{1}$$

where the parameters $\tilde{b}_i, (i = 1, 2, .., m)$ represents FRVs, and the other parameters

$$\tilde{A}_{ij}, \tilde{A}_{tj}, \tilde{A}_{sj}, \tilde{b}_t, \tilde{b}_s \left(i = 1, 2, .., m \,; t = m + 1, m + 2, \ldots, l; s = l + 1, l + 2, \ldots, p \right)$$

are taken as FNs and β_i denotes the probability value i.e., any real number lying in the interval $[0, 1]$.

4.2.2. Fuzzy Programming Model Construction

In this subsection it is assumed that FRV, $\tilde{b}_i, (i = 1, 2, .., m)$ follows exponential distribution. As $\tilde{b}_i$ is an exponentially distributed FRV, the parameter of the distribution must be represented by an FN. The probability density function of exponential distribution is written as

$$f\left(b_i; \tilde{\lambda}_i\right) = \tilde{\lambda}_i exp\left(-\tilde{\lambda}_i b_i\right)$$

where the support of $\tilde{b}_i$ is defined on the set of positive real numbers; $\lambda_i \in \tilde{\lambda}_i[\alpha]$, $\tilde{\lambda}_i[\alpha]$ being the α – cut of the FN, $\tilde{\lambda}_i$, whose support is also the set of positive real numbers. The mean and variance of the FRV, $\tilde{b}_i$, is given by

$$m_{\tilde{b}_i} = E\left(\tilde{b}_i\right) = \frac{1}{\tilde{\lambda}_i} \text{ and } \sigma_{\tilde{b}_i}^2 = Var\left(\tilde{b}_i\right) = \frac{1}{\tilde{\lambda}_i^2} \text{, respectively.}$$

Considering CCP methodology (as described in Chapter 3) in a fuzzy decision making environment by using the concept of α-cut for fuzzy sets, the chance constraints is modified as

$$\Pr\left(\sum_{j=1}^{n}\tilde{A}_{ij}x_j \leq \tilde{b}_i\right) \geq 1 - \beta_i$$

i.e., $\Pr\left(\tilde{A}_i \leq \tilde{b}_i\right) \geq 1 - \beta_i$, where $\tilde{A}_i \cong \sum_{j=1}^{n}\tilde{A}_{ij}x_j$; $i = 1, 2, \ldots, m$

i.e., $\left\{\int_{u_i}^{\infty}\lambda_i exp\left(-\lambda_i b_i\right)db_i : u_i \in \tilde{A}_i[\alpha], \lambda_i \in \tilde{\lambda}_i[\alpha]\right\} \geq 1 - \beta_i$; $i = 1, 2, \ldots, m$

i.e., $u_i \leq -\frac{1}{\lambda_i}\ln\left(1 - \beta_i\right)$; $i = 1, 2, \ldots, m : u_i \in \tilde{A}_i[\alpha], \lambda_i \in \tilde{\lambda}_i[\alpha]$

Since it is true for all elements of the α – cut, the constraint becomes

$$\tilde{A}_i[\alpha] \leq -\frac{1}{\tilde{\lambda}_i[\alpha]}\ln\left(1 - \beta_i\right) ; i = 1, 2, \ldots, m$$

Using first decomposition theorem, the constraint is modified as

$$\sum_{j=1}^{n}\tilde{A}_{ij}x_j \leq -\frac{1}{\tilde{\lambda}_i}\ln\left(1 - \beta_i\right)$$

Hence the problem (1) is converted into the equivalent FP model as

$$\text{Maximize } Z_k = \frac{\sum_{j=1}^{n} c_{kj} x_j + \gamma_k}{\sum_{j=1}^{n} d_{kj} x_j + \delta_k} \; ; \; k = 1, 2, ..., K$$

subject to

$$\sum_{j=1}^{n} \tilde{A}_{ij} x_j \leq -\frac{1}{\lambda_i} \ln\left(1 - \beta_i\right)$$

$$\sum_{j=1}^{n} \tilde{A}_{tj} x_j \leq \tilde{b}_t$$

$$\sum_{j=1}^{n} \tilde{A}_{sj} x_j \geq \tilde{b}_s \; ; i = 1, 2, ..., m; t = m + 1, m + 2, ..., l; s = l + 1, l + 2, ..., p$$

$$x_j \geq 0 \; ; \; j = 1, 2, ..., n \tag{2}$$

The model (2) still involves some amounts of uncertainty, but these uncertainties are not possibilistic type. The above model termed as fuzzy programming model whose parameters are represented by some FNs. On the basis of tolerance ranges of different fuzzy parameters, the model is decomposed by using α-cuts for FNs. In the current decision making context, the coefficients involved with the system constraints of the problem are considered as triangular FNs. Also the mean of the random variable $\tilde{b}_i$ is taken as triangular FN. A triangular FN $\tilde{a}$ can be represented by a triple $\left(a^L, a, a^R\right)$ with membership function of the form

$$
\mu_{\tilde{a}}\left(x\right) = \begin{cases} \dfrac{x - a^{L}}{a - a^{L}} & if \quad a^{L} \leq x \leq a \\[2mm] \dfrac{a^{R} - x}{a^{R} - a} & if \quad a \leq x \leq a^{R} \\[2mm] \quad 0 & otherwise \end{cases}
$$

where a^{L}, a^{R} denote the respective left and right tolerance values of the FN, $\tilde{a}$. From the concept of FNs, it is also clear that any α-cut of an FN always represents a closed interval. Thus α-cut of $\tilde{a}$ is presented as

$$
{}^{\alpha}a = \left[a^{L} + \left(a - a^{L} \right)\alpha \; , a^{R} - \left(a^{R} - a \right)\alpha \right].
$$

The α-cut of different fuzzy parameters $\tilde{A}_{ij}$, $\tilde{A}_{tj}$, $\tilde{A}_{sj}, \tilde{b}_{t}, \tilde{b}_{s}, \dfrac{1}{\tilde{\lambda}_{i}}$ involved with the model are considered as:

$$
{}^{\alpha}A_{ij} = \left[A_{ij}^{L} + \left(A_{ij} - A_{ij}^{L} \right)\alpha, A_{ij}^{R} - \left(A_{ij}^{R} - A_{ij} \right)\alpha \right] = \left[e_{ij}, f_{ij} \right] \text{ for}
$$
$$
i = 1, 2, .., m \;\; ; j = 1, 2, .., n
$$

$$
{}^{\alpha}A_{tj} = \left[A_{tj}^{L} + \left(A_{tj} - A_{tj}^{L} \right)\alpha, A_{tj}^{R} - \left(A_{tj}^{R} - A_{tj} \right)\alpha \right] = \left[g_{tj}, h_{tj} \right] \text{ for}
$$
$$
t = m+1, m+2, .., l \;\; ; j = 1, 2, .., n
$$

$$
{}^{\alpha}A_{sj} = \left[A_{sj}^{L} + \left(A_{sj} - A_{sj}^{L} \right)\alpha, A_{sj}^{R} - \left(A_{sj}^{R} - A_{sj} \right)\alpha \right] = \left[u_{sj}, v_{sj} \right] \text{ for}
$$
$$
s = l+1, l+2, .., p \;\; ; j = 1, 2, .., n
$$

$$
{}^{\alpha}b_{t} = \left[b_{t}^{L} + \left(b_{t} - b_{t}^{L} \right)\alpha, b_{t}^{R} - \left(b_{t}^{R} - b_{t} \right)\alpha \right] = \left[r_{t}, s_{t} \right] \text{ for } t = m+1, m+2, .., l
$$

$$
{}^{\alpha}b_{s} = \left[b_{s}^{L} + \left(b_{s} - b_{s}^{L} \right)\alpha, b_{s}^{R} - \left(b_{s}^{R} - b_{s} \right)\alpha \right] = \left[p_{s}, q_{s} \right] \text{ for } s = l+1, l+2, .., p
$$

$$
{}^{\alpha}\left(\frac{1}{\lambda_{i}} \right) = \left[\frac{1}{\lambda_{i}^{L}} + \left(\frac{1}{\lambda_{i}} - \frac{1}{\lambda_{i}^{L}} \right)\alpha, \frac{1}{\lambda_{i}^{R}} - \left(\frac{1}{\lambda_{i}^{R}} - \frac{1}{\lambda_{i}} \right)\alpha \right] = \left[\gamma_{i}, \delta_{i} \right] \text{ for } i = 1, 2, ..., m
$$

On the basis of the α – cuts of FNs, model (2) is expressed in terms of interval parameters as

$$\text{Maximize } Z_k = \frac{\sum_{j=1}^{n} c_{kj} x_j + \gamma_k}{\sum_{j=1}^{n} d_{kj} x_j + \delta_k}; \ k = 1, 2, ..., K$$

subject to

$$\sum_{j=1}^{n} \left[e_{ij}, f_{ij} \right] x_j + \left[\gamma_i, \delta_i \right] \ln \left(1 - \beta_i \right) \leq 0$$

$$\sum_{j=1}^{n} \left[g_{tj}, h_{tj} \right] x_j - \left[r_t, s_t \right] \leq 0$$

$$\sum_{j=1}^{n} \left[u_{sj}, v_{sj} \right] x_j - \left[p_s, q_s \right] \geq 0 \qquad\qquad ;$$

$$i = 1, 2, ..., m; t = m + 1, m + 2, .., l; s = l + 1, l + 2, .., p$$

$$x_j \geq 0; \ j = 1, 2, ..., n \qquad\qquad (3)$$

Taking convex combination of each interval, model (3) is converted into the following form as

$$\text{Maximize } Z_k = \frac{\sum_{j=1}^{n} c_{kj} x_j + \gamma_k}{\sum_{j=1}^{n} d_{kj} x_j + \delta_k}; \ k = 1, 2, ..., K$$

$$\sum_{j=1}^{n} \left[\lambda_{ij} x_j \left(e_{ij} - f_{ij} \right) + f_{ij} x_j \right] + \left[w_i \left(\gamma_i - \delta_i \right) + \delta_i \right] \ln \left(1 - \beta_i \right) \leq 0$$

$$\sum_{j=1}^{n} \left[\theta_{tj} x_j \left(g_{tj} - h_{tj} \right) + h_{tj} x_j \right] - \left[\mu_t \left(r_t - s_t \right) + s_t \right] \leq 0$$

$$\sum_{j=1}^{n}\left[\varsigma_{sj}x_{j}\left(u_{sj}-v_{sj}\right)+v_{sj}x_{j}\right]-\left[\eta_{s}\left(p_{s}-q_{s}\right)+q_{s}\right]\geq0$$

$$x_{j}\geq0\,;\ j=1,2,\ldots,n\,,0\leq\lambda_{ij}\leq1$$

$$0\leq w_{i}\leq1\,;0\leq\theta_{tj}\leq1\,;\ 0\leq\mu_{t}\leq1;0\leq\varsigma_{sj}\leq1\,;$$

$$0\leq\eta_{s}\leq1\,for\ i=1,2,\ldots,m;t=m+1,m+2,\ldots,l;s=l+1,l+2,\ldots,p \qquad (4)$$

Now since $\left(e_{ij}-f_{ij}\right)\leq0$ and $0\leq\lambda_{ij}\leq1$, it follows that

$$\sum_{j=1}^{n}e_{ij}x_{j}\leq\sum_{j=1}^{n}\left[\lambda_{ij}x_{j}\left(e_{ij}-f_{ij}\right)+f_{ij}x_{j}\right].$$

Similarly, since $\left(\gamma_{i}-\delta_{i}\right)\leq0$, $0\leq w_{i}\leq1$ and $\ln\left(1-\beta_{i}\right)\leq0$, it is observed that

$$\delta_{i}\ln\left(1-\beta_{i}\right)\leq\left[w_{i}\left(\gamma_{i}-\delta_{i}\right)+\delta_{i}\right]\ln\left(1-\beta_{i}\right).$$

Thus

$$\sum_{j=1}^{n}e_{ij}x_{j}+\delta_{i}\ln\left(1-\beta_{i}\right)\leq\sum_{j=1}^{n}\left[\lambda_{ij}x_{j}\left(e_{ij}-f_{ij}\right)+f_{ij}x_{j}\right]+\left[w_{i}\left(\gamma_{i}-\delta_{i}\right)+\delta_{i}\right]\ln\left(1-\beta_{i}\right)\leq0.$$

Applying the same arguments to the remaining constraints the above model takes the following form as

$$\text{Maximize } Z_{k}=\frac{\sum_{j=1}^{n}c_{kj}x_{j}+\gamma_{k}}{\sum_{j=1}^{n}d_{kj}x_{j}+\delta_{k}}\,;\ k=1,2,\ldots,K$$

subject to

$$\sum_{j=1}^{n} e_{ij} x_j + \delta_i ln \left(1 - \beta_i \right) \leq 0$$

$$\sum_{j=1}^{n} g_{tj} x_j - s_t \leq 0$$

$$\sum_{j=1}^{n} v_{sj} x_j - p_s \leq 0 \quad i = 1, 2, ..., m; t = m+1, m+2, .., l; s = l+1, l+2, .., p$$

$$x_j \geq 0; \ j = 1, 2, ..., n \tag{5}$$

Now the model is solved by considering each objective independently under the modified set of system constraints to find the aspiration level of the objectives.

4.2.3. Characterization of Membership Functions

Let

$$\left[x_k^b \ ; Z_k^b \right] = \left[x_{k1}^b, x_{k2}^b, .., x_{kn}^b \ ; Z_k^b \right]$$

and

$$\left[x_k^w ; Z_k^w \right] = \left[x_{k1}^w, x_{k2}^w, .., x_{kn}^w \ ; Z_k^w \right]$$

for $k = 1, 2, .., K$ be the best and worst values of the k-th objective obtained by solving each objective, independently.

Hence the fuzzy objective goal for each of the objectives is expressed as:

$Z_k \gtrsim Z_k^b$ for $k = 1, 2, .., K$.

Considering best and worst values of each objectives the membership functions are constructed as

$$\mu_{Z_k}(x) = \begin{cases} 0 & if \quad Z_k \le Z_k^w \\ \dfrac{Z_k - Z_k^w}{Z_k^b - Z_k^w} & if \ Z_k^w \le Z_k \le Z_k^b \\ 1 & if \quad Z_k \ge Z_k^b \end{cases} \tag{6}$$

Since the membership functions are fractional in form, the Taylor's series linear approximation technique is used to linearize the membership functions in the following subsection.

4.2.4. Linearization of Membership Function Using Taylor Series Approximation

To linearize the membership functions by using Taylor series linear approximation technique, the initial point is considered as the solution point at which the best solution arrived by each of the individual objectives.

Thus applying linearizing technique the defined membership functions are approximated as

$$\mu_{Z_k}(x) \cong \mu_{Z_k(x)}\Big|_{x_k^b} + \left(x_1 - x_{k1}^b\right)\left(\frac{\partial}{\partial x_1}\mu_{Z_k(x)}\right)\Big|_{x_k^b} + \dots + \left(x_n - x_{kn}^b\right)\left(\frac{\partial}{\partial x_n}\mu_{Z_k(x)}\right)\Big|_{x_k^b} = \tau_{Z_k}(x),$$

say, for

$$k = 1, 2, \dots, K \tag{7}$$

An FGP model based on priority structure is formulated in the next subsection to find the best compromise solution of the objectives in the hybrid uncertain decision making context.

4.2.5. Priority Based Fuzzy Goal Programming Model Formulation

In the previous chapter it is already stated that in priority based FGP or weighted FGP, the membership functions are transformed into flexible membership goals by assigning unity as the aspiration level and introducing under- and over- deviational variables to each of them. The under deviational variables are minimized on the basis of priority of importance of the objectives in the decision making environment. The priority based FGP model is stated as

Find $X\left(x_1, x_2, \ldots x_n\right)$ so as to

$$\text{Min } D = P_1\left(d^-\right), P_2\left(d^-\right), \ldots P_I\left(d^-\right)$$

and satisfy

$$\tau_{Z_k(x)} + d_k^- - d_k^+ = 1;$$

$$\sum_{j=1}^{n} e_{ij} x_j + \delta_i \ln\left(1 - \beta_i\right) \le 0$$

$$\sum_{j=1}^{n} g_{tj} x_j - s_t \le 0$$

$$\sum_{j=1}^{n} v_{sj} x_j - p_s \le 0 \ i = 1, 2, \ldots, m; t = m+1, m+2, \ldots, l; s = l+1, l+2, \ldots, p$$

$$x_j \ge 0; \ j = 1, 2, \ldots, n; \tag{8}$$

where D represents I priority achievement function consisting of the weighted under deviational variables, d_k^-. The priority factors have the relationship

$$P_1 >>> P_2 >>> \ldots P_i >>> \ldots >>> P_I$$

which implies that the goals at the highest priority level will achieve the goal values to the extent possible before considering the achievement of the goals at the lower priority levels. The priority function $P_i\left(d^-\right)$ has the form:

$$P_i\left(d^-\right) = \sum_{k=1}^{K} w_{ik}^- d_k^-,$$

where $w_{ik}^- \geq 0$ represents the numerical weights of importance of the goals at the i-th priority level P_i, and which are determined as:

$$w_{ik}^- = \frac{1}{\left(Z_k^b - Z_k^w\right)}.$$

The developed model is now being solved to find the most satisfactory solution in the decision making environment.

4.2.6. Solution Algorithm

The solution algorithm for solving multi-objective fuzzy linear fractional programming model in probabilistic environment with the parameters of the objectives are crisp numbers can be presented as follows:

Step 1: Using CCP technique, the fuzzy probabilistic constraints are converted into fuzzy constraints.

Step 2: The α – cut of each FN is considered to convert the fuzzy constraints into constraints with interval parameters.

Step 3: The convex combination of each interval is taken to find the deterministic form of the constraints.

Step 4: The best and worst value of each objective is then found in isolation under the modified set of system constraints.

Step 5: The membership functions of each objectives are now developed on the basis of their best and worst values.

Step 6: Finally the compromise solution of all the objectives is then found by applying FGP technique.

Step 7: Stop.

4.2.7. Multi-Objective Fuzzy Linear Stochastic Fractional Programming Model With Fuzzy Objectives

The maximization type multiple objective linear probabilistic FPP with parameters as FNs is expressed in the following form

Find $X\left(x_1, x_2, \ldots, x_n\right)$ so as to

$$\text{Max } \tilde{Z}_k \cong \frac{\sum_{j=1}^{n} \tilde{c}_{jk} x_j + \tilde{u}_k}{\sum_{j=1}^{n} \tilde{d}_{jk} x_j + \tilde{v}_k}; k = 1, 2, \ldots, K$$

subject to

$$\Pr\left(\sum_{j=1}^{n} \tilde{a}_{ij} x_j \leq \tilde{b}_i\right) \geq 1 - \gamma_i; i = 1, 2, \ldots, l$$

$$\sum_{j=1}^{n} \tilde{a}_{tj} x_j \geq \tilde{b}_t; t = l+1, l+2, \ldots, m$$

$$x_j \geq 0; j = 1, 2, \ldots, n \tag{9}$$

Here the parameters

$$\tilde{c}_{jk}, \tilde{u}_k, \tilde{d}_{jk}, \tilde{v}_k, \tilde{a}_{ij}, \tilde{a}_{tj}, \tilde{b}_t$$
$$(j = 1, 2, \ldots, n; k = 1, 2, \ldots, K; i = 1, 2, \ldots, l; t = l+1, l+2, \ldots, m)$$

are considered as triangular FNs and the right sided parameters $\tilde{b}_i$ ($i = 1, 2, \ldots, l$) of the probabilistic constraints are FRVs. The mean $E\left(\tilde{b}_i\right)$ of the FRVs $\tilde{b}_i$ ($i = 1, 2, \ldots, l$) are also considered as triangular FNs and $\gamma_i \in [0, 1]$.

In this portion it is assumed that FRVs follow same probability distribution as in the model discussed earlier in this chapter. Applying CCP technique, the probabilistic constraints in (9) are modified (as described in chapter 3) into the following form

$$\sum_{j=1}^{n} \tilde{a}_{ij} x_j \leq -E\left(\tilde{b}_i\right)\ln\left(1 - \gamma_i\right); i = 1, 2, \ldots, l \tag{10}$$

Thus the fuzzy linear stochastic fractional programming model is modified into fuzzy programming model as
Find $X\left(x_1, x_2, \ldots, x_n\right)$ so as to

$$\text{Max } \tilde{Z}_k \cong \frac{\sum_{j=1}^{n} \tilde{c}_{jk} x_j + \tilde{u}_k}{\sum_{j=1}^{n} \tilde{d}_{jk} x_j + \tilde{v}_k}; k = 1, 2, \ldots, K$$

subject to

$$\sum_{j=1}^{n} \tilde{a}_{ij} x_j \leq -E\left(\tilde{b}_i\right) \ln\left(1 - \gamma_i\right); i = 1, 2, \ldots, l$$

$$\sum_{j=1}^{n} \tilde{a}_{tj} x_j \geq \tilde{b}_t; t = l+1, l+2, \ldots, m$$

$$x_j \geq 0; j = 1, 2, \ldots, n \tag{11}$$

Since all the parameters are considered as triangular FNs, these are expressed in the following form as

$$\tilde{c}_{jk} = \left(c_{jk}^L, c_{jk}, c_{jk}^R\right), \tilde{u}_k = \left(u_k^L, u_k, u_k^R\right), \tilde{d}_{jk} = \left(d_{jk}^L, d_{jk}, d_{jk}^R\right), \tilde{v}_k = \left(v_k^L, v_k, v_k^R\right), \tilde{a}_{ij} = \left(a_{ij}^L, a_{ij}, a_{ij}^R\right),$$

$$E\left(\tilde{b}_i\right) = \left(E\left(b_i\right)^L, E\left(b_i\right), E\left(b_i\right)^R\right), \tilde{a}_{tj} = \left(a_{tj}^L, a_{tj}, a_{tj}^R\right), \tilde{b}_t = \left(b_t^L, b_t, b_t^R\right)$$

$$\left(j = 1, 2, \ldots, n; k = 1, 2, \ldots, K; i = 1, 2, \ldots, l; t = l+1, l+2, \ldots, m\right).$$

Considering those FNs, Model (11) becomes
Find $X\left(x_1, x_2, \ldots, x_n\right)$ so as to

$$\text{Max } \tilde{Z}_k \cong \frac{\sum_{j=1}^{n} \left(c_{jk}^L, c_{jk}, c_{jk}^R\right) x_j + \left(u_k^L, u_k, u_k^R\right)}{\sum_{j=1}^{n} \left(d_{jk}^L, d_{jk}, d_{jk}^R\right) x_j + \left(v_k^L, v_k, v_k^R\right)}; k = 1, 2, \ldots, K$$

subject to

$$\sum_{j=1}^{n}\left(a_{ij}^{L},a_{ij},a_{ij}^{R}\right)x_{j} \leq -\left[E\left(b_{i}\right)^{L},E\left(b_{i}\right),E\left(b_{i}\right)^{R}\right]\ln\left(1-\gamma_{i}\right); i=1,2,\ldots,l$$

$$\sum_{j=1}^{n}\left(a_{tj}^{L},a_{tj},a_{tj}^{R}\right)x_{j} \geq \left(b_{t}^{L},b_{t},b_{t}^{R}\right); t=l+1,l+2,\ldots,m$$

$$x_{j} \geq 0; j=1,2,\ldots,n \tag{12}$$

Applying defuzzification of FNs (described in chapter 2) using α – cuts to all the triangular FNs in the constraints, the equivalent deterministic form of the constraints are obtained as

$$\sum_{j=1}^{n}R\left(a_{ij}^{L},a_{ij},a_{ij}^{R}\right)x_{j} \leq -R\left[\left(E\left(b_{i}\right)^{L},E\left(b_{i}\right),E\left(b_{i}\right)^{R}\right)\right]\ln\left(1-\gamma_{i}\right); i=1,2,\ldots,l$$

$$\sum_{j=1}^{n}R\left(a_{tj}^{L},a_{tj},a_{tj}^{R}\right)x_{j} \geq R\left(b_{t}^{L},b_{t},b_{t}^{R}\right); t=l+1,l+2,\ldots,m \tag{13}$$

i.e.,

$$\sum_{j=1}^{n}\left(\frac{a_{ij}^{L}+4a_{ij}+a_{ij}^{R}}{6}\right)x_{j} \leq -\left(\frac{\left(E\left(b_{i}\right)^{L}+4E\left(b_{i}\right)+E\left(b_{i}\right)^{R}\right)}{6}\right)\ln\left(1-\gamma_{i}\right); i=1,2,\ldots,l$$

$$\sum_{j=1}^{n}\left(\frac{a_{tj}^{L}+4a_{tj}+a_{tj}^{R}}{6}\right)x_{j} \geq \left(\frac{b_{t}^{L}+4b_{t}+b_{t}^{R}}{6}\right); t=l+1,l+2,\ldots,m \tag{14}$$

On the basis of the tolerance ranges of triangular FNs each objective is decomposed into three objectives. Similarly, if trapezoidal FNs are considered then each objective are decomposed into four objectives. Similarly for hexagonal, octagonal FNs each objective is decomposed into six and eight objectives, respectively. From this fact it is clear that number of objectives depend on the nature of the FNs. Thus in this case objectives are decomposed as

$$\text{Max } Z_k^L = \frac{\sum_{j=1}^n c_{jk}^L x_j + u_k^L}{\sum_{j=1}^n d_{jk}^R x_j + v_k^R}; k = 1, 2, \ldots, K$$

$$\text{Max } Z_k = \frac{\sum_{j=1}^n c_{jk} x_j + u_k}{\sum_{j=1}^n d_{jk} x_j + v_k}; k = 1, 2, \ldots, K$$

$$\text{Max } Z_k^R = \frac{\sum_{j=1}^n c_{jk}^R x_j + u_k^R}{\sum_{j=1}^n d_{jk}^L x_j + v_k^L}; k = 1, 2, \ldots, K$$

Hence the multi-objective linear FPP in crisp environment is expressed in the following form

Find $X\left(x_1, x_2, \ldots, x_n\right)$ so as to

$$\text{Max } Z_k^L = \frac{\sum_{j=1}^n c_{jk}^L x_j + u_k^L}{\sum_{j=1}^n d_{jk}^R x_j + v_k^R}; k = 1, 2, \ldots, K$$

$$\text{Max } Z_k = \frac{\sum_{j=1}^n c_{jk} x_j + u_k}{\sum_{j=1}^n d_{jk} x_j + v_k}; k = 1, 2, \ldots, K$$

$$\text{Max } Z_k^R = \frac{\sum_{j=1}^n c_{jk}^R x_j + u_k^R}{\sum_{j=1}^n d_{jk}^L x_j + v_k^L}; k = 1, 2, \ldots, K$$

subject to

$$\sum_{j=1}^n \left(\frac{a_{ij}^L + 4a_{ij} + a_{ij}^R}{6}\right) x_j \leq -\left(\frac{\left[\left(E\left(b_i\right)^L + 4E\left(b_i\right) + E\left(b_i\right)^R\right)\right]}{6}\right) \ln\left(1 - \gamma_i\right); i = 1, 2, \ldots, l$$

$$\sum_{j=1}^{n} \left(\frac{a_{tj}^L + 4a_{tj} + a_{tj}^R}{6} \right) x_j \geq \left(\frac{b_t^L + 4b_t + b_t^R}{6} \right); t = l+1, l+2, \dots, m$$

$$x_j \geq 0; j = 1, 2, \dots, n . \tag{15}$$

Now the problem is solved as a single objective linear FPP under the modified system constraints by taking one objective function at a time and ignoring all other objectives. Let $\left(Z_k^L\right)^b, (Z_k^L)^w; \left(Z_k^R\right)^b, (Z_k^R)^w; \left(Z_k\right)^b, \left(Z_k\right)^w$ be the best and worst values of the objectives Z_k^L, Z_k^R and Z_k, respectively.

On the basis of their best and worst values, the membership function is then developed as

$$\mu_{Z_k^L} = \begin{cases} 0 & if \quad Z_k^L \leq (Z_k^L)^w \\ \dfrac{Z_k^L - (Z_k^L)^w}{(Z_k^L)^b - (Z_k^L)^w} & if \quad (Z_k^L)^w \leq Z_k^L \leq (Z_k^L)^b; k = 1, 2, \dots, K \\ 1 & if \quad Z_k^L \geq (Z_k^L)^b \end{cases} \tag{16}$$

$$\mu_{Z_k^R} = \begin{cases} 0 & if \quad Z_k^R \leq (Z_k^R)^w \\ \dfrac{Z_k^R - (Z_k^R)^w}{(Z_k^R)^b - (Z_k^R)^w} & if \quad (Z_k^R)^w \leq Z_k^R \leq (Z_k^R)^b; k = 1, 2, \dots, K \\ 1 & if \quad Z_k^R \geq (Z_k^R)^b \end{cases} \tag{17}$$

$$\mu_{Z_k} = \begin{cases} 0 & if \quad Z_k \leq \left(Z_k\right)^w \\ \dfrac{Z_k - \left(Z_k\right)^w}{\left(Z_k\right)^b - \left(Z_k\right)^w} & if \quad \left(Z_k\right)^w \leq Z_k \leq \left(Z_k\right)^b; k = 1, 2, \dots, K \\ 1 & if \quad Z_k \geq \left(Z_k\right)^b \end{cases} \tag{18}$$

It is already mentioned that the compromise solution of all the objectives are obtained by the three major approaches, viz., goal programming approach, interactive approach and fuzzy approach. The model developed in the earlier section of this chapter is solved by applying FGP approach. Now the fractional programming model developed in this section is now solved by applying fuzzy approach. Again the fuzzy approach in this chapter is described in three different ways.

1. Zimmermann's technique
2. $\gamma-$connective technique
3. Minimum bounded sum operator technique

   In this chapter the compromise solutions are obtained by all the above mentioned techniques.

4.2.7.1. Using Zimmermann's Technique

Let $\lambda = \min\left\{\mu_{Z_k^L}, \mu_{Z_k^R}, \mu_{Z_k}\right\}; k = 1, 2, \dots, K$

Then multi-objective nonlinear programming problem can be described as how to make a reasonable plan so that the decision maker is most satisfied with all objectives. That is, there should be the highest degree of balance among objectives. This can be modeled as follows:

Max λ

such that

$\mu_{Z_k^L} \geq \lambda; k = 1, 2, \dots, K$

$\mu_{Z_k^R} \geq \lambda; k = 1, 2, \dots, K$

$\mu_{Z_k} \geq \lambda; k = 1, 2, \dots, K$

subject to

$$\sum_{j=1}^{n}\left(\frac{a_{ij}^{L}+4a_{ij}+a_{ij}^{R}}{6}\right)x_{j} \leq -\left(\frac{\left(\left(E\left(b_{i}\right)^{L}+4E\left(b_{i}\right)+E\left(b_{i}\right)^{R}\right)\right)}{6}\right)\ln\left(1-\gamma_{i}\right); i = 1, 2, ..., l$$

$$\sum_{j=1}^{n}\left(\frac{a_{tj}^{L}+4a_{tj}+a_{tj}^{R}}{6}\right)x_{j} \geq \left(\frac{b_{t}^{L}+4b_{t}+b_{t}^{R}}{6}\right); t = l+1, l+2, ..., m$$

$$x_{j} \geq 0; j = 1, 2, ..., n .\tag{19}$$

This further reduces to

Max ϕ

such that

$$\frac{Z_{k}^{L}-(Z_{k}^{L})^{w}}{(Z_{k}^{L})^{b}-(Z_{k}^{L})^{w}} \geq \lambda; k = 1, 2, ..., K$$

$$\frac{Z_{k}^{R}-(Z_{k}^{R})^{w}}{(Z_{k}^{R})^{b}-(Z_{k}^{R})^{w}} \geq \lambda; k = 1, 2, ..., K$$

$$\frac{Z_{k}-\left(Z_{k}\right)^{w}}{\left(Z_{k}\right)^{b}-\left(Z_{k}\right)^{w}} \geq \lambda; k = 1, 2, ..., K$$

subject to

$$\sum_{j=1}^{n}\left(\frac{a_{ij}^{L}+4a_{ij}+a_{ij}^{R}}{6}\right)x_{j} \leq -\left(\frac{\left(E\left(b_{i}\right)^{L}+4E\left(b_{i}\right)+E\left(b_{i}\right)^{R}\right)}{6}\right)\ln\left(1-\gamma_{i}\right); i=1,2,...,l$$

$$\sum_{j=1}^{n}\left(\frac{a_{tj}^{L}+4a_{tj}+a_{tj}^{R}}{6}\right)x_{j} \geq \left(\frac{b_{t}^{L}+4b_{t}+b_{t}^{R}}{6}\right); t=l+1, l+2,...,m$$

$$x_{j} \geq 0; j=1,2,...,n \tag{20}$$

This model is now solved using *software* (LINGO. 14) to find the most acceptable compromise solution in the decision making context.

4.2.7.2. Using γ – Connective Technique

In this technique the γ – connective, $\gamma \in [0,1]$ is developed as follows

$$\phi = \left[\prod_{k=1}^{K}\frac{\left(Z_{k}^{L}-(Z_{k}^{L})^{w}\right)}{\left((Z_{k}^{L})^{b}-(Z_{k}^{L})^{w}\right)}\right]^{1-\gamma}\left[\prod_{k=1}^{K}\frac{\left(Z_{k}^{R}-(Z_{k}^{R})^{w}\right)}{\left((Z_{k}^{R})^{b}-(Z_{k}^{R})^{w}\right)}\right]^{1-\gamma}\left[\prod_{k=1}^{K}\frac{\left(Z_{k}-(Z_{k})^{w}\right)}{\left((Z_{k})^{b}-(Z_{k})^{w}\right)}\right]^{1-\gamma}$$

$$\left[1-\left(\prod_{k=1}^{K}\left(1-\frac{\left(Z_{k}^{L}-(Z_{k}^{L})^{w}\right)}{\left((Z_{k}^{L})^{b}-(Z_{k}^{L})^{w}\right)}\right)\right)\right]^{\gamma}\left[1-\left(\prod_{k=1}^{K}\left(1-\frac{\left(Z_{k}^{R}-(Z_{k}^{R})^{w}\right)}{\left((Z_{k}^{R})^{b}-(Z_{k}^{R})^{w}\right)}\right)\right)\right]^{\gamma}\left[1-\left(\prod_{k=1}^{K}\left(1-\frac{\left(Z_{k}-(Z_{k})^{w}\right)}{\left((Z_{k})^{b}-(Z_{k})^{w}\right)}\right)\right)\right]^{\gamma}$$

Then the model is reduced to the following form as

Max φ

subject to

$$\sum_{j=1}^{n} \left(\frac{a_{ij}^{L} + 4a_{ij} + a_{ij}^{R}}{6} \right) x_j \leq - \left(\frac{\left[E\left(b_i\right)^L + 4E\left(b_i\right) + E\left(b_i\right)^R \right]}{6} \right) \ln\left(1 - \gamma_i\right); i = 1, 2, \ldots, l$$

$$\sum_{j=1}^{n} \left(\frac{a_{tj}^{L} + 4a_{tj} + a_{tj}^{R}}{6} \right) x_j \geq \left(\frac{b_t^L + 4b_t + b_t^R}{6} \right); t = l+1, l+2, \ldots, m$$

$$x_j \geq 0; j = 1, 2, \ldots, n \tag{21}$$

This model is also solved by using the *software* (LINGO. 14) to find the best compromise solution to all the objectives.

4.2.7.3. Using Minimum Bounded Sum Operator Technique

In this method the minimum bounded sum operator is constructed as

$$\psi = \left[\gamma \min\left\{ \mu_{Z_k^L}, \mu_{Z_k^R}, \mu_{Z_k} \right\} + \left(1 - \gamma\right) \min\left(1, \sum_{k=1}^{K} \left(\mu_{Z_k^L} + \mu_{Z_k^R} + \mu_{Z_k} \right) \right) \right]$$

Thus the model becomes

$$\text{Max } \psi = \left[\gamma \min\left\{ \mu_{Z_k^L}, \mu_{Z_k^R}, \mu_{Z_k} \right\} + \left(1 - \gamma\right) \min\left(1, \sum_{k=1}^{K} \left(\mu_{Z_k^L} + \mu_{Z_k^R} + \mu_{Z_k} \right) \right) \right]$$

subject to

$$\sum_{j=1}^{n} \left(\frac{a_{ij}^{L} + 4a_{ij} + a_{ij}^{R}}{6} \right) x_{j} \leq - \left(\frac{\left[E\left(b_{i}\right)^{L} + 4E\left(b_{i}\right) + E\left(b_{i}\right)^{R} \right]}{6} \right) \ln\left(1 - \gamma_{i}\right); i = 1, 2, \dots, l$$

$$\sum_{j=1}^{n} \left(\frac{a_{tj}^{L} + 4a_{tj} + a_{tj}^{R}}{6} \right) x_{j} \geq \left(\frac{b_{t}^{L} + 4b_{t} + b_{t}^{R}}{6} \right); t = l+1, l+2, \dots, m$$

$$x_{j} \geq 0; j = 1, 2, \dots, n \tag{22}$$

Using equation (22) the model can also be written as

$$\text{Max } \psi = \left[\gamma\eta + \left(1 - \gamma\right)\nu \right]$$

subject to

$$\sum_{j=1}^{n} \left(\frac{a_{ij}^{L} + 4a_{ij} + a_{ij}^{R}}{6} \right) x_{j} \leq - \left(\frac{\left[E\left(b_{i}\right)^{L} + 4E\left(b_{i}\right) + E\left(b_{i}\right)^{R} \right]}{6} \right) \ln\left(1 - \gamma_{i}\right); i = 1, 2, \dots, l$$

$$\sum_{j=1}^{n} \left(\frac{a_{tj}^{L} + 4a_{tj} + a_{tj}^{R}}{6} \right) x_{j} \geq \left(\frac{b_{t}^{L} + 4b_{t} + b_{t}^{R}}{6} \right); t = l+1, l+2, \dots, m$$

$$\frac{\left(Z_{k}^{L} - (Z_{k}^{L})^{w} \right)}{\left((Z_{k}^{L})^{b} - (Z_{k}^{L})^{w} \right)} \geq \eta$$

$$\frac{\left(Z_{k}^{R} - (Z_{k}^{R})^{w} \right)}{\left((Z_{k}^{R})^{b} - (Z_{k}^{R})^{w} \right)} \geq \eta$$

$$\frac{\left(Z_k - \left(Z_k\right)^w\right)}{\left(\left(Z_k\right)^b - \left(Z_k\right)^w\right)} \geq \eta$$

$$\sum_{k=1}^{K} \left[\frac{\left(Z_k^L - (Z_k^L)^w\right)}{\left((Z_k^L)^b - (Z_k^L)^w\right)} + \frac{\left(Z_k^R - (Z_k^R)^w\right)}{\left((Z_k^R)^b - (Z_k^R)^w\right)} + \frac{\left(Z_k - \left(Z_k\right)^w\right)}{\left(\left(Z_k\right)^b - \left(Z_k\right)^w\right)} \right] \geq \nu$$

$$\nu \leq 1$$

$$x_j \geq 0; j = 1, 2, \ldots, n \qquad\qquad (23)$$

This model is also solved by using the same *software* (LINGO. 14) to find the most satisfactory solution to all the objectives in the fuzzy stochastic uncertain decision making environment.

In the next section the procedure for solving multi-objective fuzzy linear stochastic FPP, developed in this chapter are summarized as an algorithm.

4.2.8. Solution Algorithm

In general the solution algorithm for solving the multi-objective fuzzy linear stochastic fractional programming model with the objective being maximized can be presented as follows:

Step 1: Using CCP technique, the fuzzy probabilistic constraints are converted into constraints involving only fuzzy uncertainty.

Step 2: Defuzzification of FNs using α – cut is applied to all the FNs of the fuzzy constraints to find its equivalent deterministic form.

Step 3: On the basis of tolerance ranges of the triangular FNs of the objectives, each objective is decomposed into three objectives.

Step 4: The individual optimal value of each decomposed objective is then found in isolation under the modified set of system constraints to find their best and worst solutions.

Step 5: The membership functions of each objectives are now developed on the basis of their best and worst values.

Step 6: Finally, the most satisfactory solution of all the objectives is found by using three techniques, *viz.* Zimmermann's technique, γ – connective technique and minimum bounded sum operator technique.

Step 7: Stop.

4.3. NUMERICAL ILLUSTRATION

In this section two numerical examples are presented to explain both the multi-objective fuzzy stochastic fractional programming model. In both the models right side parameters of the fuzzy chance constraints are taken as exponentially distributed FRVs.

4.3.1. Numerical Example 1

To illustrate the proposed approach a modified form of the multi-objective FPP, considered previously by Chakraborty and Gupta (2002), is considered in an imprecisely defined probabilistic decision making arena as

$$\text{Maximize } Z_1 = \frac{-3x_1 + 2x_2}{x_1 + x_2 + 3}$$

$$\text{Maximize } Z_2 = \frac{7x_1 + x_2}{5x_1 + 2x_2 + 1}$$

subject to

$$\tilde{1}x_1 + \widetilde{-1}x_2 \geq \tilde{1}$$

$$\Pr(\tilde{2}x_1 + \tilde{3}x_2 \leq \tilde{b}_1) \geq 0.50$$

$$\tilde{1}x_1 \geq \tilde{3}$$

$$x_1, x_2 \geq 0 \tag{24}$$

Here $\tilde{b}_1$ denotes independent FRV following exponential distribution with mean represented by a triangular FN $m_{\tilde{b}_1} = \widetilde{15} = (14.95, 15, 15.05)$. Also $\widetilde{-1}, \tilde{1}, \tilde{2}, \tilde{3}$ are taken as triangular FNs with the form

$$\widetilde{-1} = (-1.05, -1, -0.95), \tilde{1} = (0.95, 1, 1.05),$$
$$\tilde{2} = (1.5, 2, 2.5), \tilde{3} = (2.5, 3, 3.5), \tilde{1} = (0.5, 1, 1.5).$$

The α-cut of the respective triangular FNs $\widetilde{-1}, \tilde{1}, \tilde{2}, \tilde{3}, \widetilde{15}$ and $\tilde{1}$ are presented as follows:

$$^{\alpha}(-1) = [-1.95 + 0.05\alpha, -0.95 - 0.05\alpha], \ {}^{\alpha}1 = [0.95 + 0.05\alpha, 1.05 - 0.05\alpha],$$

$$^{\alpha}2 = [1.5 + 0.5\alpha, 2.5 - 0.5\alpha],$$

$$^{\alpha}3 = [2.5 + 0.5\alpha, 3.5 - 0.5\alpha],$$

$$^{\alpha}15 = [14.95 + 0.05\alpha, 15.05 - 0.05\alpha],$$

$$^{\alpha}1 = [0.5 + 0.5\alpha, 1.5 - 0.5\alpha]$$

Using CCP technique and α-cut of triangular FNs the problem (24) is reduced to the following form as

$$\text{Maximize } Z_1 = \frac{-3x_1 + 2x_2}{x_1 + x_2 + 3}$$

$$\text{Maximize } Z_2 = \frac{7x_1 + x_2}{5x_1 + 2x_2 + 1}$$

subject to

$$\left[0.95 + 0.05\alpha, 1.05 - 0.05\alpha\right] x_1 + \left[-1.05 + 0.05\alpha, -0.95 - 0.05\alpha\right] x_2$$
$$\geq \left[0.95 + 0.05\alpha, 1.05 - 0.05\alpha\right]$$

$$\left[1.5 + 0.5\alpha, 2.5 - 0.5\alpha\right] x_1 + \left[2.5 + 0.5\alpha, 3.5 - 0.5\alpha\right] x_2$$
$$\leq -\left[14.95 + 0.05\alpha, 15.05 - 0.05\alpha\right] \ln\left(0.50\right)$$

$$\left[0.5 + 0.5\alpha, 1.5 - 0.5\alpha\right] x_1 \geq \left[2.5 + 0.5\alpha, 3.5 - 0.5\alpha\right],$$

$$x_1, \; x_2 \geq 0. \tag{25}$$

On the basis of the proposed methodology *i.e.*, using the concept of $\alpha -$ cut of FNs and taking the convex combination of the intervals, the problem (25) is reduced to

$$\text{Maximize } Z_1 = \frac{-3x_1 + 2x_2}{x_1 + x_2 + 3}$$

$$\text{Maximize } Z_2 = \frac{7x_1 + x_2}{5x_1 + 2x_2 + 1}$$

subject to

$$\left(-0.95 - 0.05\alpha\right) x_2 + \left(1.05 - 0.05\alpha\right) x_1 \geq 0.95 + 0.05\alpha,$$

$$\left(1.5 + 0.5\alpha\right) x_1 + \left(2.5 + 0.5\alpha\right) x_2 - 0.357\left(15.05 - 0.05\alpha\right) \leq 0,$$

$$\left(1.5 - 0.5\alpha\right) x_1 \geq \left(2.5 + 0.5\alpha\right),$$

$$x_1, x_2 \geq 0 \quad ; 0 \leq \alpha \leq 1. \tag{26}$$

Now each objective is now solved individually with respect to the system constraints defined in (26) to find the best and worst values of the objectives.

The achieved best and worst objective values are found as

$Z_1^b = -0.5873$, $Z_1^w = -1.6322$ and $Z_2^b = 1.3260$, $Z_2^w = 1.1346$.

On the basis of the tolerance values of the objectives, the membership functions corresponding to the objectives are constructed as

$$\mu_{Z_1(x)} = \frac{Z_1(x) + 1.6322}{1.0499} \tag{27}$$

$$\mu_{Z_2(x)} = \frac{Z_2(x) - 1.1346}{0.1914} \tag{28}$$

As membership functions are fractional in nature, therefore, the membership functions are then converted into equivalent linear membership functions by linearization technique. In this chapter to linearize the non-linear membership functions, first order Taylor series linear approximation method about the best solution point of the individual objectives is used. The approximated linear objectives are presented as

$$\tau_{Z_1(x)} = 0.99 - 0.38(x_1 - 1.85) + 0.42(x_2 - 1.04)$$

and

$$\tau_{Z_2(x)} = 0.99 + 0.102(x_1 - 3.58) - 0.63(x_2 - 0)$$

The approximated linear membership functions are then converted into fuzzy goals by assigning unity as their desired goal levels. A priority based FGP model under which the most satisfactory solution is achieved is presented as

Find $X(x_1, x_2)$

Min D= $P_1(0.957d_1^-), P_2(5.224d_2^-)$

subject to

$$0.99 - 0.38\left(x_1 - 1.85\right) + 0.42\left(x_2 - 1.04\right) + d_1^- - d_1^+ = 1,$$

$$0.99 + 0.102\left(x_1 - 3.58\right) - 0.63x_2 + d_2^- - d_2^+ = 1,$$

$$\left(-0.95 - 0.05\alpha\right)x_2 + \left(1.05 - 0.05\alpha\right)x_1 \geq \left(0.95 + 0.05\alpha\right),$$

$$\left(1.5 + 0.5\alpha\right)x_1 + \left(2.5 + 0.5\alpha\right)x_2 - 0.357\left(15.05 - 0.05\alpha\right) \leq 0,$$

$$\left(1.5 - 0.5\alpha\right)x_1 \geq \left(2.5 + 0.5\alpha\right),$$

$$x_1, x_2 \geq 0 \quad ; 0 \leq \alpha \leq 1. \tag{29}$$

Now the model (29) is solved to find the satisfactory solution in the decision making context.

The *software* LINGO (Ver. 11.0) is used to solve the problem.

The optimal solution of the problem (29) is obtained as

$$x_1 = 1.733 \,, \; x_2 = 0.916.$$

The achieved objective values of the given problem is found as

$$Z_1 = -0.596 \text{ and } Z_2 = \qquad\qquad\qquad 1.15.$$

with the achieved membership values

$$\mu_{Z_1} = 0.992 \text{ and } \mu_{Z_2} = 0.994.$$

Chakraborty and Gupta (2002) also solved the above FPP without considering the uncertain nature of the parameters associated with the problem. In their example all the parameters are considered as crisp numbers. The multi-objective FPP considered by Chakraborty and Gupta (2002) is as follows:

$$\text{Max } Z_1\left(x\right) = \frac{-3x_1 + 2x_2}{x_1 + x_2 + 3}$$

$$\text{Max } Z_2\left(x\right) = \frac{7x_1 + x_2}{5x_1 + 2x_2 + 1}$$

subject to

$$x_1 - x_2 \geq 1$$

$$2x_1 + 3x_2 \leq 15$$

$$x_1 \geq 3$$

$$x_1, x_2 \geq 0 \tag{30}$$

As the first objective function $Z_1\left(x\right) \leq 0$ for each x within the feasible region and the second objective function $Z_1\left(x\right) \geq 0$ for each x in the feasible region, then using the above fact and using the transformation $y = xt$, $t > 0$, both the objective functions are converted into linear functions without the fractional part. Therefore, the multi-objective FPP converted into a linear programming problem as

$$\text{Max } f_1\left(y,t\right) = y_1 + y_2 + 3t$$

$$\text{Max } f_2\left(y,t\right) = 7y_1 + y_2$$

subject to

$$3y_1 - 2y_2 \leq 1$$

$$5y_1 + 2y_2 + t \leq 1$$

$$y_1 - y_2 - t \geq 0$$

$$2y_1 + 3y_2 - 15t \leq 0$$

$$y_1 - 3t \geq 0$$

$$y_1, y_2, t \geq 0 \tag{31}$$

According to Chakraborty and Gupta (2002) the fuzzy goals of the objectives are

$$f_1(y,t) \gtrsim \frac{1}{2} \text{ and } f_2(y,t) \gtrsim \frac{7}{5}.$$

Therefore, the membership functions are developed as

$$\mu_1 = \begin{cases} 0 & if \quad y_1 + y_2 + 3t \leq 0 \\ 2(y_1 + y_2 + 3t) & if \quad 0 < y_1 + y_2 + 3t \leq \frac{1}{2} \\ 1 & if \quad y_1 + y_2 + 3t > \frac{1}{2} \end{cases}$$

$$\mu_2 = \begin{cases} 0 & if \quad 7y_1 + y_2 \leq 0 \\ \frac{5}{7}(7y_1 + y_2) & if \quad 0 < 7y_1 + y_2 < \frac{7}{5} \\ 1 & if \quad 7y_1 + y_2 \geq \frac{7}{5} \end{cases}$$

Based on the above membership functions, the crisp linear programming model is formed using Zimmermann's min operator as

Max λ

subject to

$$2y_1 + 2y_2 + 6t - \lambda \geq 0$$

$$35y_1 + 5y_2 - 7\lambda \geq 0$$

$$3y_1 - 2y_2 \leq 1$$

$$5y_1 + 2y_2 + t \leq 1$$

$$y_1 - y_2 - t \geq 0$$

$$2y_1 + 3y_2 - 15t \leq 0$$

$$y_1 - 3t \geq 0$$

$$y_1, y_2, t, \lambda \geq 0 \qquad\qquad (32)$$

The solution obtained by using standard *software* package as

$y_1 = 0.15, y_2 = 0.10, t = 0.05$ and $\lambda = 0.8$.

Table 1. Solution comparisons

	Solution Point	**Objective Value**	**Membership Value**
Proposed method	$x_1 = 1.733$ $x_2 = 0.916$	$Z_1 = -0.596$ $Z_2 = 1.15$	$\mu_{Z_1} = 0.992$ $\mu_{Z_2} = 0.994$
Chakraborty and Gupta's method (2002)	$x_1 = 3$ $x_2 = 2$	$Z_1 = -0.625$ $Z_2 = 1.15$	$\mu_{Z_1} = 0.25$ $\mu_{Z_2} = 1$

Thus the solution obtained by using the methodology developed by Chakraborty and Gupta (2002) was found as $x_1 = 3$, $x_2 = 2$ with the corresponding objective values $Z_1 = -0.625$, $Z_2 = 1.15$.

The comparison of the solutions obtained by the proposed methodology and by Chakraborty and Gupta (2002) are summarized in Table 1.

Since the objectives of the problem are of maximization type, the comparison of the solutions reflect that a better decision is obtained by applying the methodology discussed in this chapter in terms of achieving better objective values in the fuzzy chance constrained decision making environment. It is very clear that if the uncertain behaviors of the parameters be included in the problem then the problem becomes much complicated. From the above discussion it is clear that the methodology discussed in this chapter captures not only the uncertainties but also generates better outcomes of the objectives. Further considering the achieved membership values obtained by the objectives it is also establishing the superiority of the proposed approach over others from the view point of achieving better compromise solution in the decision making horizon.

4.3.2. Numerical Example 2

The following multi-objective fuzzy linear stochastic FPP is considered to investigate the potentiality of the proposed approach.

Find $X\left(x_1, x_2\right)$ so as to

$$\text{Max } \tilde{Z}_1 \cong \frac{\tilde{c}_{11}x_1 + \tilde{c}_{21}x_2 + \tilde{u}_1}{\tilde{d}_{11}x_1 + \tilde{d}_{21}x_2 + \tilde{v}_1}$$

$$\text{Max } \tilde{Z}_2 \cong \frac{\tilde{c}_{12}x_1 + \tilde{c}_{22}x_2 + \tilde{u}_2}{\tilde{d}_{12}x_1 + \tilde{d}_{22}x_2 + \tilde{v}_2}$$

subject to

$$\Pr\left(\tilde{a}_{11}x_1 + \tilde{a}_{12}x_2 \lesssim \tilde{b}_1\right) \geq 0.78$$

$$\tilde{a}_{21}x_1 + \tilde{a}_{22}x_2 \gtrsim \tilde{b}_2$$

$$x_1, x_2 \geq 0 \qquad (33)$$

Here

$$\tilde{c}_{11},\ \tilde{c}_{21},\ \tilde{c}_{12},\ \tilde{c}_{22},\ \tilde{d}_{11},\ \tilde{d}_{21},\ \tilde{d}_{12},\ \tilde{d}_{22},\ \tilde{a}_{11},\ \tilde{a}_{21},\ \tilde{a}_{12},\ \tilde{a}_{22},\ \tilde{u}_1,\ \tilde{u}_2,\ \tilde{v}_1,\ \tilde{v}_2,\ \tilde{b}_2$$

are all triangular FNs and $\tilde{b}_1$ is exponentially distributed FRV.

Applying CCP technique to the probabilistic constraint as described in section 4.2.2., the constraint modifies to

$$\tilde{a}_{11}x_1 + \tilde{a}_{12}x_2 \lesssim -E\left(\tilde{b}_1\right)\ln\left(0.78\right)$$

Table 2. Values of objective parameters

Objective	Parameter
1st	$\tilde{c}_{11} = \tilde{4} = \left(3,4,5\right),\ \tilde{c}_{21} = \tilde{6} = \left(5,6,7\right),\ \tilde{d}_{11} = \tilde{2} = \left(1,2,3\right),$ $\tilde{d}_{21} = \tilde{3} = \left(2,3,4\right)$ $\tilde{u}_1 = \tilde{3} = \left(2,3,4\right),\ \tilde{v}_1 = \tilde{4} = \left(3,4,5\right)$
2nd	$\tilde{c}_{12} = \tilde{2} = \left(1,2,3\right),\ \tilde{c}_{22} = \tilde{3} = \left(2,3,4\right),\ \tilde{d}_{12} = \tilde{1} = \left(0.5,1,1.5\right),$ $\tilde{d}_{22} = \tilde{2} = \left(1,2,3\right),$ $\tilde{u}_2 = \tilde{5} = \left(3,5,6\right),\ \tilde{v}_2 = \tilde{6} = \left(5,6,7\right)$

Table 3. Values of parameters of the constraints

Constraint	Parameter
1st	$\tilde{a}_{11} = \tilde{3} = \left(2,3,4\right),\ \tilde{a}_{12} = \tilde{5} = \left(3,5,6\right),$ $E\left(\tilde{b}_1\right) = \widetilde{100} = \left(90,100,110\right)$
2nd	$\tilde{a}_{21} = \tilde{1} = \left(0.5,1,1.5\right),\ \tilde{a}_{22} = \tilde{2} = \left(1,2,3\right),$ $\tilde{b}_2 = \tilde{8} = \left(7,8,9\right)$

Thus the fuzzy programming model is developed as

Find $X\left(x_1, x_2\right)$ so as to

$$\text{Max } \tilde{Z}_1 \cong \frac{\tilde{c}_{11}x_1 + \tilde{c}_{21}x_2 + \tilde{u}_1}{\tilde{d}_{11}x_1 + \tilde{d}_{21}x_2 + \tilde{v}_1}$$

$$\text{Max } \tilde{Z}_2 \cong \frac{\tilde{c}_{12}x_1 + \tilde{c}_{22}x_2 + \tilde{u}_2}{\tilde{d}_{12}x_1 + \tilde{d}_{22}x_2 + \tilde{v}_2}$$

subject to

$$\tilde{a}_{11}x_1 + \tilde{a}_{12}x_2 \lesssim -E\left(\tilde{b}_1\right)\ln\left(0.78\right)$$

$$\tilde{a}_{21}x_1 + \tilde{a}_{22}x_2 \gtrsim \tilde{b}_2$$

$$x_1, x_2 \geq 0 \tag{34}$$

The parameters of the two objectives and the two constraints which are considered here are presented in Tables 2 and 3.

Applying the defuzzification technique of FNs to all the parameters of the constraints, the fuzzy constraints are modified into deterministic constraints. Also as described in the model formulation each objective are decomposed into three objectives on the basis of the tolerance ranges of the triangular FNs. Thus the multi-objective linear fractional programming model is formed as

Find $X\left(x_1, x_2\right)$ so as to

$$\text{Max } Z_1^L = \frac{3x_1 + 5x_2 + 2}{3x_1 + 4x_2 + 5}$$

$$\text{Max } Z_1 = \frac{4x_1 + 6x_2 + 3}{2x_1 + 3x_2 + 4}$$

$$\text{Max } Z_1^R = \frac{5x_1 + 7x_2 + 4}{x_1 + 2x_2 + 3}$$

$$\text{Max } Z_2^L = \frac{x_1 + 2x_2 + 3}{1.5x_1 + 3x_2 + 7}$$

$$\text{Max } Z_2 = \frac{2x_1 + 3x_2 + 5}{x_1 + 2x_2 + 6}$$

$$\text{Max } Z_2^R = \frac{3x_1 + 4x_2 + 6}{0.5x_1 + x_2 + 5}$$

subject to

$$3x_1 + 4.83x_2 \leq 25$$

$$x_1 + 2x_2 \geq 7.83$$

$$x_1, x_2 \geq 0$$

Figure 1. Comparison between best and worst solutions

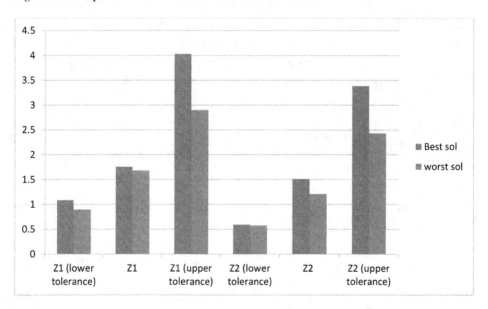

where

$$\tilde{Z}_1 = \left(Z_1^L, Z_1, Z_1^R \right) \text{ and } \tilde{Z}_2 = \left(Z_2^L, Z_2, Z_2^R \right) \tag{35}$$

Each objective is now solved independently under the system constraints to find the best and worst solutions. The solutions are found as

$$(Z_1^L)^b = 1.084 \text{ at } \left(0, 5.18\right) \text{ and } (Z_1^L)^w = 0.895 \text{ at } \left(7.83, 0\right);$$

$$\left(Z_1\right)^b = 1.758 \text{ at } \left(8.33, 0\right) \text{ and } \left(Z_1\right)^w = 1.682 \text{ at } \left(0, 3.92\right);$$

$$(Z_1^R)^b = 4.029 \text{ at } \left(8.33, 0\right) \text{ and } (Z_1^R)^w = 2.900 \text{ at } \left(0, 3.92\right);$$

$$(Z_2^L)^b = 0.593 \text{ at } \left(0, 5.18\right) \text{ and } (Z_2^L)^w = 0.578 \text{ at } \left(5.36, 1.23\right);$$

$$\left(Z_2\right)^b = 1.512 \text{ at } \left(8.33, 0\right) \text{ and } \left(Z_2\right)^w = 1.211 \text{ at } \left(0, 3.92\right); \text{ and}$$

$$(Z_2^R)^b = 3.382 \text{ at } \left(8.33, 0\right) \text{ and } (Z_2^R)^w = 2.430 \text{ at } \left(0, 3.92\right)$$

The comparison between the best and worst solutions of all the objectives are described in the Figure 1.

On the basis of best and worst solutions of all the objectives the membership functions are developed as

$$\mu_{Z_1^L} = 5.291 \left(Z_1^L - 0.895 \right)$$

$$\mu_{Z_1} = 13.158 \left(Z_1 - 1.682 \right)$$

$$\mu_{Z_1^R} = 0.886 \left(Z_1^R - 2.900 \right)$$

$$\mu_{Z_2^L} = 66.667 \left(Z_2^L - 0.578 \right),$$

$$\mu_{Z_2} = 3.322\left(Z_2 - 1.211\right),$$

$$\mu_{Z_2^R} = 1.050\left(Z_2^R - 2.430\right)$$

Also the membership functions can also be written as

$$\mu_{Z_1^L} = 5.291\left(\frac{3x_1 + 5x_2 + 2}{3x_1 + 4x_2 + 5} - 0.895\right)$$

$$\mu_{Z_1} = 13.158\left(\frac{4x_1 + 6x_2 + 3}{2x_1 + 3x_2 + 4} - 1.682\right)$$

$$\mu_{Z_1^R} = 0.886\left(\frac{5x_1 + 7x_2 + 4}{x_1 + 2x_2 + 3} - 2.900\right);$$

$$\mu_{Z_2^L} = 66.667\left(\frac{x_1 + 2x_2 + 3}{1.5x_1 + 3x_2 + 7} - 0.578\right)$$

$$\mu_{Z_2} = 3.322\left(\frac{2x_1 + 3x_2 + 5}{x_1 + 2x_2 + 6} - 1.211\right)$$

$$\mu_{Z_2^R} = 1.050\left(\frac{3x_1 + 4x_2 + 6}{0.5x_1 + x_2 + 5} - 2.430\right) \tag{36}$$

Now the most satisfactory compromise solution of all the objectives is obtained by the three fuzzy approaches, *viz.*, a) Zimmermann's technique, b) γ – connective technique and c) Minimum bounded sum operator technique.

Using Zimmermann's Technique

In this technique, the above model is transformed to the following model using the above defined membership function as

Max λ

so as to

$$\frac{3x_1 + 5x_2 + 2}{3x_1 + 4x_2 + 5} \geq 0.189\lambda + 0.895$$

$$\frac{4x_1 + 6x_2 + 3}{2x_1 + 3x_2 + 4} \geq 0.076\lambda + 1.682$$

$$\frac{5x_1 + 7x_2 + 4}{x_1 + 2x_2 + 3} \geq 1.129\lambda + 2.9$$

$$\frac{x_1 + 2x_2 + 3}{1.5x_1 + 3x_2 + 7} \geq 0.015\lambda + 0.578$$

$$\frac{2x_1 + 3x_2 + 5}{x_1 + 2x_2 + 6} \geq 0.301\lambda + 1.211$$

Figure 2. Comparison between best and compromise solution

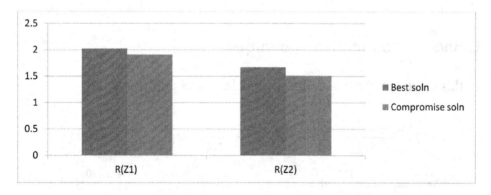

$$\frac{3x_1 + 4x_2 + 6}{0.5x_1 + x_2 + 5} \geq 0.952\lambda + 2.430$$

subject to

$$3x_1 + 4.83x_2 \leq 25$$

$$x_1 + 2x_2 \geq 7.83$$

$$x_1, x_2 \geq 0 \tag{37}$$

Solving this model using *software* package (LINGO. 14), the compromise solution point is obtained as $x_1 = 4.00, x_2 = 2.69$ with satisfactory level $\lambda = 0.50$. At this solution point the objective values are obtained as

$$Z_1^L = 0.99, Z_1 = 1.75, Z_1^R = 3.46, Z_2^L = 0.59, Z_2 = 1.37, Z_2^R = 2.9.$$

Thus $\tilde{Z}_1 = (0.99, 1.75, 3.46)$ and $\tilde{Z}_2 = (0.59, 1.37, 2.97)$.

The defuzzified values of the objectives are $R(\tilde{Z}_1) = 1.91$ and $R(\tilde{Z}_2) = 1.51$.

The comparison between the best solution and compromise solution are shown in Figure 2.

Using γ – Connective Technique

In this technique the γ – connective technique is constructed as

$$\phi = \frac{\left[14343.7 \frac{\left(\frac{3x_1 + 5x_2 + 2}{3x_1 + 4x_2 + 5} - 0.895\right)\left(\frac{4x_1 + 6x_2 + 3}{2x_1 + 3x_2 + 4} - 1.682\right)\left(\frac{5x_1 + 7x_2 + 4}{x_1 + 2x_2 + 3} - 2.9\right)}{\left(\frac{x_1 + 2x_2 + 3}{1.5x_1 + 3x_2 + 7} - 0.578\right)\left(\frac{2x_1 + 3x_2 + 5}{x_1 + 2x_2 + 6} - 1.211\right)\left(\frac{3x_1 + 4x_2 + 6}{0.5x_1 + x_2 + 5} - 2.430\right)}\right]^{1-\gamma}}{\left[1 - 14343.7 \frac{\left(\frac{3.25x_1 + 5.42x_2 + 2.17}{3x_1 + 4x_2 + 5}\right)\left(\frac{7.03x_1 + 10.55x_2 + 5.27}{2x_1 + 3x_2 + 4}\right)\left(\frac{20.14x_1 + 28.2x_2 + 16.12}{x_1 + 2x_2 + 3}\right)}{\left(\frac{0.59x_1 + 1.19x_2 + 1.78}{1.5x_1 + 3x_2 + 7}\right)\left(\frac{3.02x_1 + 4.54x_2 + 7.56}{x_1 + 2x_2 + 6}\right)\left(\frac{10.15x_1 + 13.53x_2 + 20.29}{0.5x_1 + x_2 + 5}\right)}\right]^{\gamma}}$$

Then the model is reduced to

Max

$$
\left[14343.7 \left(\frac{3x_1 + 5x_2 + 2}{3x_1 + 4x_2 + 5} - 0.895 \right) \left(\frac{4x_1 + 6x_2 + 3}{2x_1 + 3x_2 + 4} - 1.682 \right) \left(\frac{5x_1 + 7x_2 + 4}{x_1 + 2x_2 + 3} - 2.9 \right) \right]^{1-\gamma}
$$
$$
\left[\left(\frac{x_1 + 2x_2 + 3}{1.5x_1 + 3x_2 + 7} - 0.578 \right) \left(\frac{2x_1 + 3x_2 + 5}{x_1 + 2x_2 + 6} - 1.211 \right) \left(\frac{3x_1 + 4x_2 + 6}{0.5x_1 + x_2 + 5} - 2.430 \right) \right]
$$
$$
\left[1 - 14343.7 \left(\frac{3.25x_1 + 5.42x_2 + 2.17}{3x_1 + 4x_2 + 5} \right) \left(\frac{7.03x_1 + 10.55x_2 + 5.27}{2x_1 + 3x_2 + 4} \right) \left(\frac{20.14x_1 + 28.2x_2 + 16.12}{x_1 + 2x_2 + 3} \right) \right]^{\gamma}
$$
$$
\left[\left(\frac{0.59x_1 + 1.19x_2 + 1.78}{1.5x_1 + 3x_2 + 7} \right) \left(\frac{3.02x_1 + 4.54x_2 + 7.56}{x_1 + 2x_2 + 6} \right) \left(\frac{10.15x_1 + 13.53x_2 + 20.29}{0.5x_1 + x_2 + 5} \right) \right]
$$

subject to

$$3x_1 + 4.83x_2 \leq 25$$

$$x_1 + 2x_2 \geq 7.83$$

Figure 3. Comparison between solutions

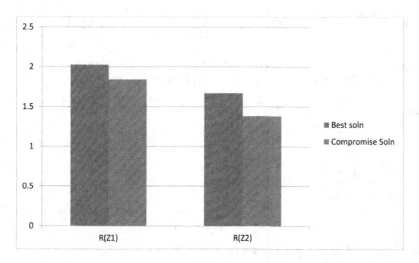

$x_1, x_2 \geq 0$ (38)

If the model is also solved by using software (LINGO. 14) then the compromise solutions are obtained as $x_1 = 0, x_2 = 5.18$. At this solution point the objective values are obtained as

$$Z_1^L = 1.08, Z_1 = 1.74, Z_1^R = 3.01, Z_2^L = 0.59, Z_2 = 1.26, Z_2^R = 2.62.$$

Thus $\tilde{Z}_1 = (1.08, 1.74, 3.01)$ and $\tilde{Z}_2 = (0.59, 1.26, 2.62)$.

The defuzzified values of the objectives are $R(\tilde{Z}_1) = 1.84$ and $R(\tilde{Z}_2) = 1.38$.

The comparison between the best solution and compromise solution are shown in Figure 3.

Using Minimum Bounded Sum Operator Technique

In this technique the model is converted to

$$\text{Max } \left[\gamma \eta + (1 - \gamma) \nu \right]$$

such that

$$5.291 \left(\frac{3x_1 + 5x_2 + 2}{3x_1 + 4x_2 + 5} - 0.895 \right) + 13.158 \left(\frac{4x_1 + 6x_2 + 3}{2x_1 + 3x_2 + 4} - 1.682 \right)$$
$$+ 0.886 \left(\frac{5x_1 + 7x_2 + 4}{x_1 + 2x_2 + 3} - 2.900 \right) + 66.667 \left(\frac{x_1 + 2x_2 + 3}{1.5x_1 + 3x_2 + 7} - 0.578 \right)$$
$$+ 3.322 \left(\frac{2x_1 + 3x_2 + 5}{x_1 + 2x_2 + 6} - 1.211 \right) + 1.050 \left(\frac{3x_1 + 4x_2 + 6}{0.5x_1 + x_2 + 5} - 2.430 \right) \geq \nu$$

$$5.291 \left(\frac{3x_1 + 5x_2 + 2}{3x_1 + 4x_2 + 5} - 0.895 \right) \geq \eta$$

$$0.886 \left(\frac{5x_1 + 7x_2 + 4}{x_1 + 2x_2 + 3} - 2.900 \right) \geq \eta$$

$$66.667 \left(\frac{x_1 + 2x_2 + 3}{1.5x_1 + 3x_2 + 7} - 0.578 \right) \geq \eta$$

$$3.322 \left(\frac{2x_1 + 3x_2 + 5}{x_1 + 2x_2 + 6} - 1.211 \right) \geq \eta$$

$$1.050 \left(\frac{3x_1 + 4x_2 + 6}{0.5x_1 + x_2 + 5} - 2.430 \right) \geq \eta$$

subject to

$$3x_1 + 4.83x_2 \leq 25$$

$$x_1 + 2x_2 \geq 7.83$$

$$x_1, x_2 \geq 0 \tag{39}$$

As like earlier models, if the above model is also solved by using the *Software* (LINGO.14.0), then the compromise solution is obtained as

Table 4. Comparison of solutions

Technique	Solution Point	Objective Value	Ranking Value
Zimmermann's technique	$x_1 = 4.00, x_2 = 2.69$	$\tilde{Z}_1 = (0.99, 1.75, 3.46)$ $\tilde{Z}_2 = (0.59, 1.37, 2.97)$	$R(\tilde{Z}_1) = 1.91$ $R(\tilde{Z}_2) = 1.51$
γ − connective technique	$x_1 = 0, x_2 = 5.18$	$\tilde{Z}_1 = (1.08, 1.74, 3.01)$ $\tilde{Z}_2 = (0.59, 1.26, 2.62)$	$R(\tilde{Z}_1) = 1.84$ $R(\tilde{Z}_2) = 1.38$
Minimum bounded sum operator technique	$x_1 = 4.00, x_2 = 2.69$	$\tilde{Z}_1 = (0.99, 1.75, 3.46)$ $\tilde{Z}_2 = (0.59, 1.37, 2.97)$	$R(\tilde{Z}_1) = 1.91$ $R(\tilde{Z}_2) = 1.51$

Figure 4. Values of objectives

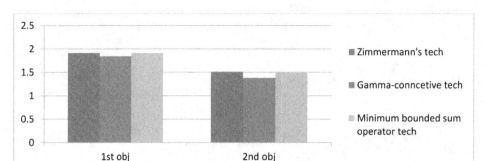

$x_1 = 4.00, x_2 = 2.69$.

At this solution point the objective values are obtained as

$Z_1^L = 0.99, Z_1 = 1.75, Z_1^R = 3.46, Z_2^L = 0.59, Z_2 = 1.37, Z_2^R = 2.97$.

Thus $\tilde{Z}_1 = (0.99, 1.75, 3.46)$ and $\tilde{Z}_2 = (0.59, 1.37, 2.97)$.

The defuzzified values of the objectives are $R(\tilde{Z}_1) = 1.91$ and $R(\tilde{Z}_2) = 1.51$.

This shows that the compromise solution obtained by using Minimum Bounded Sum Operator Technique and by using Zimmermann's technique produced identical solutions.

The comparative study of the obtained compromise solutions by the three different techniques are given in Table 4.

The comparison are also shown in Figure 4.

It is clear from the table and from the diagram that Zimmermann's technique and Minimum bounded sum operator technique provide identical and better compromise solutions of the first and second objectives than the compromise solution obtained by using γ–connective technique. Also, it is to be noted here that other types of conclusion may be made for the other numerical examples. Thus all these fuzzy approaches are equally important for solving multi-objective decision making problems.

4.4 RESULTS AND CONCLUSION

This chapter presents two efficient methodologies for solving multi-objective fuzzy linear FPP in an imprecisely defined probabilistic decision making environment. Both the methodologies capture the probabilistic uncertainty as well as the imprecision involved with the parameters which are frequently occurred in the model formulation process of any decision making problem. Both the developed models can be extended in a stochastic decision making environment in which all the parameters of the models would be represented by FRVs following different probability distributions (continuous or discrete). In this chapter all the fuzzy parameters are considered in triangular form. These methodologies can be extended by considering other form of FNs, viz., hexagonal FNs, octagonal FNs, intuitionistic FNs, type-II FNs, etc. The compromise solution of the first model is obtained by applying FGP technique and the compromise solution of the second model is obtained by the three fuzzy approaches, *viz.*, Zimmermann's technique, γ – connective technique and minimum bounded sum operator technique. It can also be applied in a hierarchical decision making environment for achieving compromise solution in the decision making context. However, it is hoped that the developed methodologies shown in this chapter may widen the scope of solving multi-objective FPPs under the simultaneous occurrence of fuzziness and randomness in some decision making environment.

REFERENCES

Biswas, A., & Pal, B. B. (2005). Application of fuzzy goal programming technique to land use planning in agricultural system. *Omega, 33*(5), 391–398. doi:10.1016/j.omega.2004.07.003

Bitran, G. R., & Noveas, A. G. (1973). Linear programming with a fractional objective function. *Operations Research, 21*(1), 22–29. doi:10.1287/opre.21.1.22

Chakraborty, M., & Gupta, S. (2002). Fuzzy mathematical programming for multiobjective linear fractional programming problem. *Fuzzy Sets and Systems, 125*(3), 335–342. doi:10.1016/S0165-0114(01)00060-4

Chan, C. T. (2005). Fractional programming with absolute-value functions: A fuzzy goal programming approach. *Applied Mathematics and Computation, 167*(1), 508–515. doi:10.1016/j.amc.2004.07.014

Charnes, A., & Cooper, W. W. (1962). Chance constrained programming. *Management Science, 6*(1), 73–79. doi:10.1287/mnsc.6.1.73

Craven, B. D. (1988). *Fractional Programming*. Berlin: Heldermann Verlag.

Dubois, D., & Prade, H. (1980). *Fuzzy Sets and Systems: Theory and Applications*. New York: Academic Press.

Helmy, Y. M., Emam, O. E., & Abdelwahab, A. M. (2015). On Stochastic Multi-Level Multi-Objective Fractional Programming Problems. *Journal of Statistics Applications & Probability, 4*(1), 93–101.

Hughes, J. B. (1993). Interior efficient solutions in bicriterion linear fractional programming—A geometric approach. *Mathematical and Computer Modelling, 17*(6), 23–28. doi:10.1016/0895-7177(93)90192-2

Iskander, M. G. (2004). A fuzzy weighted additive approach for stochastic fuzzy goal programming. *Applied Mathematics and Computation, 154*(2), 543–553. doi:10.1016/S0096-3003(03)00734-3

Kataoka, S. (1963). A stochastic programming model. *Econometrica, 31*(1/2), 181–196. doi:10.2307/1910956

Mehrjerdi, Y. Z. (2011). Solving fractional programming problem through fuzzy goal setting and approximation. *Applied Soft Computing, 11*(2), 1735–1742. doi:10.1016/j.asoc.2010.05.016

Miller, L. B., & Wagner, H. (1965). Chance-Constrained Programming with Joint Constraints. *Operations Research, 13*(6), 930–945. doi:10.1287/opre.13.6.930

Nasseri, S. H., & Bavandi, S. (2017). A suggested approach for stochastic interval-valued linear fractional programming problem. *International Journal of Applied Operational Research, 7*(1), 23–31.

Osman, M. S., Emam, O. E., & El Sayed, M. A. (2017). Stochastic Fuzzy Multi-level Multi-objective Fractional Programming Problem: A FGP Approach. *OPSEARCH, 54*(4), 816–840. doi:10.100712597-017-0307-8

Pal, B. B., & Moitra, B. N. (2003). A Goal Programming Procedure for Solving Problems with Multiple Fuzzy Goals Using Dynamic Programming. *European Journal of Operational Research*, *144*(3), 480–491. doi:10.1016/S0377-2217(01)00384-8

Pal, B. B., Moitra, B. N., & Maulik, U. (2003). A goal programming procedure for fuzzy multiobjective linear fractional programming. *Fuzzy Sets and Systems*, *139*(2), 395–405. doi:10.1016/S0165-0114(02)00374-3

Panne, V. D., & Popp, W. (1963). Minimum Cost Cattle Feed under Probabilistic Protein Constraints. *Management Science*, *9*(3), 405–430. doi:10.1287/mnsc.9.3.405

Prekopa, A. (1973). Contribution to the Theory of Stochastic Programming. *Mathematical Programming*, *4*(1), 202–221. doi:10.1007/BF01584661

Saad, O. M. (1995). On the solution of fuzzy linear fractional programs. *The 30th Annual Conference*, 1–9.

Sadjadi, S. J., Aryanejad, M. B., & Sarfaraz, A. (2005). A fuzzy approach to solve a multi-objective linear fractional inventory model. *Journal of Industrial Engineering International*, *1*(1), 43–47.

Sakawa, M., Yano, H., & Takahashi, J. (1992). Pareto optimality for multiobjective linear fractional programming problems with fuzzy parameters. *Information Sciences*, *63*(1-2), 33–53. doi:10.1016/0020-0255(92)90061-C

Schaible, S. (1981). Fractional Programming: Applications and Algorithms. *European Journal of Operational Research*, *7*(2), 111–120. doi:10.1016/0377-2217(81)90272-1

Schaible, S., & Ibaraki, T. (1983). Fractional Programming, Invited Review. *European Journal of Operational Research*, *12*(4), 325–338. doi:10.1016/0377-2217(83)90153-4

Shiraz, R. K., Charles, V., Tavana, M., & Caprio, D. D. (2017). A redundancy detection algorithm for fuzzy stochastic multi-objective linear fractional programming problems. *Stochastic Analysis and Applications*, *35*(1), 40–62. doi:10.1080/07362994.2016.1248780

Sinha, S. B., Rao, K. A., & Mangaraj, B. K. (1988). *Fuzzy programming in multi-criteria decision systems: a case study in agricultural planning*. Socio-Economic Planning.

Stancu-Minasian, M. (1997). *Fractional Programming*. Dordrecht: Kluwer Academic Publishers. doi:10.1007/978-94-009-0035-6

Zadeh, L. A. (1965). Fuzzy sets. *Information and Control*, *8*(3), 338–353. doi:10.1016/S0019-9958(65)90241-X

Zimmermann, H. J. (1976). Description and optimization of fuzzy systems. *International Journal of General Systems*, *2*(4), 209–215. doi:10.1080/03081077608547470

Chapter 5
Methodology for Solving Multi-Objective Quadratic Programming Problems in a Fuzzy Stochastic Environment

ABSTRACT

This chapter presents two methodologies for solving quadratic programming problems with multiple objectives under fuzzy stochastic environments. The right side parameters of the chance constraints of both the models are chosen as fuzzy random variables (FRVs) following different probability distributions. Like the previous chapters, chance constrained programming (CCP) methodology is employed to the fuzzy chance constraints to develop fuzzy programming model. In the first model, α – cut of fuzzy sets and fuzzy partial order relations are incorporated to the fuzzy programming model to develop an equivalent deterministic model. For the second model, defuzzification method of fuzzy numbers (FNs), which are presented in Chapter 2, are taken into consideration to generate equivalent quadratic programming model in a crisp environment. As the objective functions are quadratic in nature, it is easy to understand that the membership functions obtained through methodological development process are also quadratic in nature. To linearize the quadratic membership functions, linearization techniques are employed in this chapter. Finally, for achieving the maximum degree of each of the membership goals of the objectives, a fuzzy goal programming (FGP) approach is developed for the linearized membership goals and solved by minimizing under-deviational variables and satisfying modified system constraints in fuzzy stochastic decision-making environments. To illustrate the acceptability of the developed methodology presented in this chapter, some numerical examples are included.

DOI: 10.4018/978-1-5225-8301-1.ch005

5.1 QUADRATIC PROGRAMMING MODEL IN FUZZY STOCHASTIC ENVIRONMENT

In single objective mathematical programming model only one objective is considered subject to some set of system constraints. Most of the times this type of mathematical programming models fails to represent practical situations properly as real life decision making problem in various fields of science, engineering and management etc., involve multiple conflicting objectives. Mathematical programming problems with multiple objectives are termed as multi-objective programming. The authors throughout this book discuss different types of multi-objective programming problems. Hwang and Masud (1979) classified the methods for solving multi-objective optimization problems into three categories, viz., priori methods, interactive methods and posteriori methods. In the literature, a variety of algorithms (Chen and Chou, 1996; Gass and Roy, 2003; Ida, 2005; Li et al., 2006) for finding efficient solutions to multi-objective optimization problems were proposed. Also, in multi-objective environments some additional preference information is needed from the decision makers (DMs) for getting better solution from a set of efficient solutions. Again, it is found that the objectives of various practical decision making problems may not be represented by linear functions, these objectives includes some non-linear natures, especially, quadratic natures. To handle such mathematical programming problems the authors present some methodology to solve quadratic programming problems. Multi-objective quadratic programming is considered as a special case of non-linear programming in which either the objectives or constraints or both are quadratic in nature. Korhonen and Yu (1997) discussed a reference direction approach to solve multi-objective quadratic programming problems. Ammar and Khalifa (2003) studied quadratic programming to solve portfolio optimization problems. In 2014, Brito et al. (2014) proposed a new approach for multi-objective quadratic optimization. In recent years, Fliege and Vaz (2016) and Ansary and Panda (2018) developed a methodology for solving multi-objective quadratic programming problems based on sequential quadratic programming technique. Syaripuddin et al. (2017) extended Wolfe's method for solving quadratic programming problems by taking model parameters as interval coefficients.

In the preceding chapters the authors already mentioned that in conventional linear programming model it is necessary that the parameters are known precisely. But real world context, however, the parameters are seldom known exactly and, hence, have to be estimated. Therefore, some kind of uncertainty may involve with these problems. These uncertain parameters may be possibilistic or probabilistic in nature. Also some situation arises when these uncertain parameters are represented as a combination of both possibilistic and probabilistic uncertainties. The context that arises due to the simultaneous presence of randomness and fuzziness is known as hybrid fuzzy environment.

The possibilistic uncertainty involved inherently with the DMs' ambiguous understanding of the nature of parameters associated with the problem. As stated earlier, fuzzy set theory, introduced by Zadeh (1965), are used to represent possibilistic uncertainties. Zimmermann (1978) showed that the solutions obtained by fuzzy linear programming are always efficient. Abo-Sinha (2001) discussed multi-objective optimization for solving non-linear multi-objective bi-level programming problems in fuzzy environment. Aggarwal and Sharma (2013) proposed a procedure for solving non-convex multi-objective quadratic programming under fuzzy environment. Gabr (2015) analyzed quadratic and non-linear programming models in fully fuzzy environment. Recently, Khalifa (2017) studied a multi- objective quadratic programming problem with possibilistic variables coefficients matrix in the objective functions.

To resolve the randomness or probabilistic uncertainties, Dantzig (1955) introduced stochastic programming using the concept of probability theory. It is already cited that although CCP and two- stage programming are the two main approaches of stochastic programming, throughout the book the authors emphasize on CCP methodology. Charnes and Cooper (1959) first introduced the CCP models. Various characteristics of CCP technique were further investigated by Kataoka (1963), Geoffrion (1967), Prekopa (1973), and other researchers in the past. Emam et al. (2015) proposed an algorithm to solve bi-level multi-objective large scale quadratic programming problem with stochastic parameter in the objective functions.

With these developments in computational resources and scientific computing techniques many complicated optimization models representing several real life problems are solved efficiently. In the process of deriving models of CCP it is also important to consider that the possible values of the random parameters under the occurrence of events are uncertain and these uncertain hyper parameters are represented as FNs. Realizing the above fact, the concept of fuzzy CCP was introduced. Fuzzy CCP problem is a CCP problem in the presence of ambiguous information. Many researchers like Liu and Iwamura (1998), Luhandjula (1983, 2003) and others derived different methods to solve CCP problems. Most of the parameters of this type of problems involve fuzziness and randomness concurrently. It is easy for the readers to understand that through FRVs the joint occurrence of fuzziness and randomness can be represented efficiently. The concept of FRVs was first introduced by Zadeh (1968) and further developed by Kwakernaak (1978), Kratschmer (2001) according to different requirements of measurability. Buckley (2003, 2004) defined fuzzy probability using FNs as parameters in probability density function and probability mass function. These FNs are obtained from the set of confidence intervals. The approach of fuzzy probability theory developed by Buckley is different from his predecessors and also comfortable for computational point of view.

Again, the authors in this book already stated that there are several methods used, in general, to solve multi-objective decision making problems with hybrid uncertainty, viz., fuzzy linear programming (Zimmermann, 1991; Liang, 2006), compromise programming (Zeleny, 1982; Romero, 1990), interactive approaches (Zeleny, 1982; Liang, 2008), FGP (Narasimhan, 1980; Tabucanon, 1988; Giannikos, 1998), etc. However, the most efficient solution technique to solve these types of problems is FGP method and for finding a compromise solution FGP methodology is adopted in this book. FGP makes easiness by allowing vague aspirations of the DMs. Modak and Biswas (2011, 2012) developed FGP approach for solving multi-objective stochastic models.

In this chapter methodologies for solving fuzzy stochastic multi-objective quadratic programming problems are aimed to be developed with parameters of the chance constraints representing FRVs following different continuous probability distributions. In the first model the fuzzy stochastic programming problem is first converted into fuzzy programming model through CCP methodology. After that, deterministic model is developed based on $\alpha - $ cut of FNs and fuzzy partial order relation. The piecewise linear approximation method is used to solve fuzzy multi-objective quadratic programming problems. In the second model the left side parameters of the constraints as well as the parameter of the objectives are taken as FNs. The CCP technique is employed to the chance constraints to convert the problem into a multi-objective quadratic programming involving only fuzzy uncertainty. Then defuzzification of FNs which are described in Chapter 2 of the book are used to develop multi-objective quadratic programming models in crisp environment. Finally, for both the models FGP approach is used for getting compromise solutions.

This FGP approach helps the DMs to achieve maximum degree of each of the membership goals of the objectives by minimizing under-deviational variables in the fuzzy stochastic decision making environment.

5.2 FUZZY MULTI-OBJECTIVE QUADRATIC CHANCE CONSTRAINED PROGRAMMING MODEL FORMULATION

In this chapter two multi-objective quadratic programming models are presented in fuzzy stochastic environment. In Chapter 3, authors presented mathematical models in which objective functions are assumed as linear functions. Chapter 4 discussed a mathematical model in which objective functions are fractional in nature. Now, in this chapter it is assumed that the objective functions are quadratic in nature. In previous chapters the authors already illustrated that the objectives can be either in deterministic form or due to lack of knowledge about the parameters the DMs either expressed objectives in fuzzy form or in fuzzy probabilistic form. In the first model it is assumed that the parameters of the quadratic objective are taken as crisp numbers. The left side parameters of the constraints are FNs and the right side parameters of the constraints are continuous FRVs with fuzzy probability. In the second model the parameters of the quadratic objectives are considered as FNs. The left side parameters of the constraints are FNs and the right side parameters are taken as FRVs following known probability distribution.

Thus the generic forms of fuzzy multi-objective CCP models with quadratic objectives are presented as follows:

5.2.1 Model I

Find $X\left(x_1, x_2, \cdots\cdots, x_n\right)$ so as to

Maximize $Z_k = \sum_{j=1}^{n} c_j^{(k)} x_j + \frac{1}{2}\sum_{j=1}^{n}\sum_{l=1}^{n} d_{jl}^{(k)} x_j x_l$; $k = 1, 2, \cdots\cdots, K$

subject to

$$\widetilde{Pr}\left(\sum_{j=1}^{n}\tilde{a}_{ij}x_j \lesssim \tilde{b}_i\right) \gtrsim \tilde{p}_i \, ; \, i = 1, 2, \cdots\cdots, m$$

$$x_j \geq 0; \; j = 1, 2, \cdots\cdots, n : \; 0 \leq p_i \leq 1 \; ; \; p_i \in \tilde{p}_i[\alpha] \tag{1}$$

Here the parameters $c_j^{(k)}$, $d_{jl}^{(k)}$ of the objectives are crisp numbers and also the left sided parameters $\tilde{a}_{ij}$ of the constraints are FNs. Also the parameter $\tilde{b}_i$ is FRV with density function $f\left(b_i; \tilde{\theta}_i\right)$, $\tilde{\theta}_i$ is a fuzzy parameter and $\tilde{p}_i$ are FNs, $\gtrsim$ and $\lesssim$ represent greater than or equal, and less than or equal, respectively, in fuzzy sense. It is obvious to prove that these fuzzy relations are fuzzy partial order relations.

5.2.2 Model II

Find $X\left(x_1, x_2, \ldots, x_n\right)$ so as to

$$\text{Max } \tilde{Z}_k \cong \sum_{j=1}^{n} \tilde{c}_{kj} x_j + \frac{1}{2} \sum_{j=1}^{n} \sum_{l=1}^{n} \tilde{d}_{kjl} x_j x_l; \; k = 1, 2, \ldots, K$$

subject to

$$\Pr\left(\sum_{j=1}^{n} \tilde{a}_{ij} x_j \lesssim \tilde{b}_i\right) \geq 1 - p_i; \; i = 1, 2, \ldots, m$$

$$x_j, \; x_l \geq 0; \; j = 1, 2, \ldots, n \; ; l = 1, 2, \ldots, n \tag{2}$$

Here $\tilde{b}_i \left(i = 1, 2, \ldots, m\right)$ also represents FRVs following some continuous probability distributions. The coefficients of the objectives $\tilde{c}_{kj}$ and $\tilde{d}_{kjl}$

$$\left(j = 1, 2, \ldots, n \; ; l = 1, 2, \ldots, n \; ; k = 1, 2, \ldots, K\right)$$

are taken as FNs. The left side parameters of the constraints

$$\tilde{a}_{ij}\left(i = 1, 2, \ldots, m; j = 1, 2, \ldots, n\right)$$

are also considered as FNs and $p_i \in [0, 1]$.

In the following part of the chapter both the multi-objective quadratic programming models in fuzzy stochastic environment are converted into their equivalent deterministic form.

5.3 MULTI-OBJECTIVE QUADRATIC PROGRAMMING MODEL FORMULATION

In this section the fuzzy stochastic quadratic programming model presented in (1) are modified to form its equivalent deterministic model.

To convert the model presented in (1) to its equivalent deterministic form, the following methodology is adopted.

Let $\sum_{j=1}^{n} \tilde{a}_{ij} x_j = \tilde{u}_i$. As $\tilde{a}_{ij}$'s are FNs, then $\tilde{u}_i$ is also a FN of the same form.

Then the probabilistic constraints are reduced to the following form

$$\widetilde{Pr}\left(\sum_{j=1}^{n} \tilde{a}_{ij} x_j \lesssim \tilde{b}_i\right) = \widetilde{Pr}\left(\tilde{u}_i \lesssim \tilde{b}_i\right)$$

which is also an FN.

The authors already stated in Chapter 2 that $\alpha - \text{cut}$ of an FN is a closed interval. So it's $\alpha - \text{cut}$ is given by

$$\widetilde{Pr}\left(\tilde{u}_i \lesssim \tilde{b}_i\right)[\alpha] = \left\{\int_{u_i}^{\infty} f\left(b_i;\theta_i\right) db_i : \theta_i \in \tilde{\theta}_i[\alpha], u_i \in \tilde{u}_i[\alpha]\right\},$$

where $\tilde{\theta}_i$ is the fuzzy parameter of the FRV, $\tilde{b}_i$.

In this model it is assumed that the FRV $\tilde{b}_i$ follows Weibull distribution. Then its probability density function is written as

$$f\left(b_i\;;\tilde{\beta}_i\;,\tilde{\lambda}_i\right) = \left(\frac{v_i}{s_i}\right)\left(\frac{b_i}{s_i}\right)^{v_i-1} e^{-\left(\frac{b_i}{s_i}\right)^{v_i}} \;, \; v_i \in \tilde{\lambda}_i[\alpha], s_i \in \tilde{\beta}_i[\alpha]$$

where the support of $\tilde{b}_i$ is the set of non-negative real numbers. Here $\tilde{\lambda}_i[\alpha], \tilde{\beta}_i[\alpha]$ are the α–cut of FNs $\tilde{\lambda}_i, \tilde{\beta}_i$ whose support are the set of positive real numbers. Therefore,

$$\widetilde{Pr}\left(\tilde{u}_i \lesssim \tilde{b}_i\right)[\alpha] = \left\{ \int\limits_{u_i}^{\infty} \left(\frac{v_i}{s_i}\right)\left(\frac{b_i}{s_i}\right)^{v_i-1} e^{-\left(\frac{b_i}{s_i}\right)^{v_i}} db_i : v_i \in \tilde{\lambda}_i[\alpha], s_i \in \tilde{\beta}_i[\alpha], u_i \in \tilde{u}_i[\alpha] \right\}$$

$$= \left\{ e^{-\left(\frac{u_i}{s_i}\right)^{v_i}} : v_i \in \tilde{\lambda}_i[\alpha], s_i \in \tilde{\beta}_i[\alpha], u_i \in \tilde{u}_i[\alpha] \right\}. \tag{3}$$

Here the fuzzy parameters $\tilde{u}_i$ together with the parameters $\tilde{\lambda}_i, \tilde{\beta}_i$ of the FRV $\tilde{b}_i$ and $\tilde{p}_i$ are all taken as triangular FNs. Other type of FNs can also be taken in this methodology. Thus these fuzzy parameters $\tilde{u}_i, \tilde{\lambda}_i, \tilde{\beta}_i, \tilde{p}_i$ are expressed as follows:

$$\tilde{u}_i = \left(u_i^L, u_i, u_i^R\right), \quad \tilde{\beta}_i = \left(\beta_i^L, \beta_i, \beta_i^R\right), \quad \tilde{\lambda}_i = \left(\lambda_i^L, \lambda_i, \lambda_i^R\right), \quad \tilde{p}_i = \left(p_i^L, p_i, p_i^R\right);$$
$$\left(i = 1, 2, \cdots\cdots, m\right)$$

Since the α – cut of FNs is a closed interval, then the α – cut of these FNs are expressed as follows:

$$\tilde{\beta}_i[\alpha] = \left[\beta_i^L + \left(\beta_i - \beta_i^L\right)\alpha, \beta_i^R - \left(\beta_i^R - \beta_i\right)\alpha\right]$$

$$\tilde{\lambda}_i[\alpha] = \left[\lambda_i^L + \left(\lambda_i - \lambda_i^L\right)\alpha, \lambda_i^R - \left(\lambda_i^R - \lambda_i\right)\alpha\right]$$

$$\tilde{u}_i[\alpha] = \left[u_i^L + \left(u_i - u_i^L\right)\alpha, u_i^R - \left(u_i^R - u_i\right)\alpha\right]$$

$$\tilde{p}_i[\alpha] = \left[p_i^L + \left(p_i - p_i^L\right)\alpha, p_i^R - \left(p_i^R - p_i\right)\alpha\right]; \left(i = 1, 2, \cdots\cdots, m\right)$$

Thus using the above α – cuts, (3) can be written in the following form as

$$\widetilde{Pr}\left(\tilde{u}_i \lesssim \tilde{b}_i\right)[\alpha] = \left\{ e^{-\left(\frac{\tilde{u}_i[\alpha]}{\tilde{\beta}_i[\alpha]}\right)^{\tilde{\lambda}_i[\alpha]}} \quad ; 0 \le \alpha \le 1 \right\}$$

As the support of the FNs $\tilde{\lambda}_i, \tilde{\beta}_i$ are positive real numbers, the above $\alpha-$ cuts can be written in the following form

$$\widetilde{Pr}\left(\tilde{u}_i \lesssim \tilde{b}_i\right)[\alpha] = \left[e^{-\left(\frac{u_i^R - \left(u_i^R - u_i\right)\alpha}{\beta_i^L + \left(\beta_i - \beta_i^L\right)\alpha}\right)^{\lambda_i^R - \left(\lambda_i^R - \lambda_i\right)\alpha}} \quad , e^{-\left(\frac{u_i^L + \left(u_i - u_i^L\right)\alpha}{\beta_i^R - \left(\beta_i^R - \beta_i\right)\alpha}\right)^{\lambda_i^L + \left(\lambda_i - \lambda_i^L\right)\alpha}} \right].$$

Hence the probabilistic constraints $\widetilde{Pr}\left(\sum_{j=1}^{n}\tilde{a}_{ij}x_j \lesssim \tilde{b}_i\right) \gtrsim \tilde{p}_i$, in terms of $\alpha-$ cut are expressed as follows:

$$\left[e^{-\left(\frac{u_i^R - \left(u_i^R - u_i\right)\alpha}{\beta_i^L + \left(\beta_i - \beta_i^L\right)\alpha}\right)^{\lambda_i^R - \left(\lambda_i^R - \lambda_i\right)\alpha}} \quad , e^{-\left(\frac{u_i^L + \left(u_i - u_i^L\right)\alpha}{\beta_i^R - \left(\beta_i^R - \beta_i\right)\alpha}\right)^{\lambda_i^L + \left(\lambda_i - \lambda_i^L\right)\alpha}} \right] \ge \left[p_i^L + \left(p_i - p_i^L\right)\alpha, p_i^R - \left(p_i^R - p_i\right)\alpha\right]$$

$$(4)$$

i.e., $\quad e^{-\left(\frac{u_i^R - \left(u_i^R - u_i\right)\alpha}{\beta_i^L + \left(\beta_i - \beta_i^L\right)\alpha}\right)^{\lambda_i^R - \left(\lambda_i^R - \lambda_i\right)\alpha}} \ge \left(p_i^L + \left(p_i - p_i^L\right)\alpha\right)$

and

$$e^{-\left(\frac{u_i^L + \left(u_i - u_i^L\right)\alpha}{\beta_i^R - \left(\beta_i^R - \beta_i\right)\alpha}\right)^{\lambda_i^L + \left(\lambda_i - \lambda_i^L\right)\alpha}} \ge \left(p_i^R - \left(p_i^R - p_i\right)\alpha\right)$$

i.e.,

$$\left(\frac{u_i^R - \left(u_i^R - u_i\right)\alpha}{\beta_i^L + \left(\beta_i - \beta_i^L\right)\alpha}\right)^{\lambda_i^R - \left(\lambda_i^R - \lambda_i\right)\alpha} \leq -\ln\left(p_i^L + \left(p_i - p_i^L\right)\alpha\right)$$

and

$$\left(\frac{u_i^L + \left(u_i - u_i^L\right)\alpha}{\beta_i^R - \left(\beta_i^R - \beta_i\right)\alpha}\right)^{\lambda_i^L + \left(\lambda_i - \lambda_i^L\right)\alpha} \leq -\ln\left(p_i^R - \left(p_i^R - p_i\right)\alpha\right); \left(i = 1, 2, \cdots\cdots, m\right)$$

$$\left(\frac{u_i^R - \left(u_i^R - u_i\right)\alpha}{\beta_i^L + \left(\beta_i - \beta_i^L\right)\alpha}\right) \leq \ln\left(\frac{1}{p_i^L + \left(p_i - p_i^L\right)\alpha}\right)^{\frac{1}{\left(\lambda_i^R - \left(\lambda_i^R - \lambda_i\right)\alpha\right)}}$$

and

$$\left(\frac{u_i^L + \left(u_i - u_i^L\right)\alpha}{\beta_i^R - \left(\beta_i^R - \beta_i\right)\alpha}\right) \leq \ln\left(\frac{1}{p_i^R - \left(p_i^R - p_i\right)\alpha}\right)^{\frac{1}{\lambda_i^L + \left(\lambda_i - \lambda_i^L\right)\alpha}}$$

i.e.,

$$\sum_{j=1}^{n}\left[a_{ij}^R - \left(a_{ij}^R - a_{ij}\right)\alpha\right]x_j \leq \left(\beta_i^L + \left(\beta_i - \beta_i^L\right)\alpha\right)\ln\left(\frac{1}{p_i^L + \left(p_i - p_i^L\right)\alpha}\right)^{\frac{1}{\left(\lambda_i^R - \left(\lambda_i^R - \lambda_i\right)\alpha\right)}}$$

and

$$\sum_{j=1}^{n}\left[a_{ij}^L + \left(a_{ij} - a_{ij}^L\right)\alpha\right]x_j \leq \left(\beta_i^R - \left(\beta_i^R - \beta_i\right)\alpha\right)\ln\left(\frac{1}{p_i^R - \left(p_i^R - p_i\right)\alpha}\right)^{\frac{1}{\lambda_i^L + \left(\lambda_i - \lambda_i^L\right)\alpha}}$$

(5)

Hence the deterministic model of the corresponding fuzzy multi-objective CCP model with quadratic objectives is derived as follows:

Find $X\left(x_1, x_2, \cdots\cdots, x_n\right)$ so as to

$$\text{Maximize } Z_k = \sum_{j=1}^{n} c_j^{(k)} x_j + \frac{1}{2} \sum_{j=1}^{n} \sum_{l=1}^{n} d_{jl}^{(k)} x_j x_l \, ; \ k = 1, 2, \cdots\cdots, K$$

subject to

$$\sum_{j=1}^{n} \left[a_{ij}^{R} - \left(a_{ij}^{R} - a_{ij} \right) \alpha \right] x_j \leq \left(\beta_i^{L} + \left(\beta_i - \beta_i^{L} \right) \alpha \right) \ln \left(\frac{1}{p_i^{L} + \left(p_i - p_i^{L} \right) \alpha} \right)^{\frac{1}{\left(\lambda_i^{R} - \left(\lambda_i^{R} - \lambda_i \right) \alpha \right)}}$$

$$\sum_{j=1}^{n} \left[a_{ij}^{L} + \left(a_{ij} - a_{ij}^{L} \right) \alpha \right] x_j \leq \left(\beta_i^{R} - \left(\beta_i^{R} - \beta_i \right) \alpha \right) \ln \left(\frac{1}{p_i^{R} - \left(p_i^{R} - p_i \right) \alpha} \right)^{\frac{1}{\lambda_i^{L} + \left(\lambda_i - \lambda_i^{L} \right) \alpha}}$$

$$x_j \geq 0 \, ; \ \left(j = 1, 2, \cdots\cdots, n \right) \left(i = 1, 2, \cdots\cdots, m \right) 0 \leq \alpha \leq 1 . \tag{6}$$

Now the above model is solved using FGP technique in the next section.

5.4 METHODOLOGY FOR FINDING COMPROMISE SOLUTION

In this section the membership goals are constructed to find the most commensurable solution in a conflicting and multi-objective decision making context. To find the membership goal of the objectives, the model is solved by considering each objective independently under the modified set of system constraints; and the aspiration level of each objective is calculated in isolation.

Let $x_k^{B} = \left(x_{k1}^{B}, x_{k2}^{B}, \cdots\cdots, x_{kn}^{B} \right)$ be the point at which the $k - th$ objective $Z_k \, ; \left(k = 1, 2, \cdots\cdots, K \right)$ attains its best value subject to the set of modified system constraints.

Using the best solutions

$$x_k^{B} = \left(x_{k1}^{B}, x_{k2}^{B}, \cdots\cdots, x_{kn}^{B} \right) ; \left(k = 1, 2, \cdots\cdots, K \right)$$

the value of all the objectives Z_k ; $\left(k = 1, 2, \cdots\cdots, K\right)$ is calculated as $Z_k^B = Z_k\left(x_k^B\right)$. Hence a payoff matrix is constructed as follows:

$$
\begin{array}{c}
\begin{array}{cccc}
Z_1(x) & Z_2(x) & \cdots & Z_K(x)
\end{array} \\
\begin{array}{c}
x_1^B \\
x_2^B \\
\vdots \\
\vdots \\
x_K^B
\end{array}
\begin{bmatrix}
Z_1^B & Z_2\left(x_1^B\right) & \cdots & Z_K\left(x_1^B\right) \\
Z_1\left(x_2^B\right) & Z_2^B & \cdots & Z_k\left(x_2^B\right) \\
\vdots & \vdots & \vdots & \vdots \\
\vdots & \vdots & \vdots & \vdots \\
Z_1\left(x_K^B\right) & Z_2\left(x_K^B\right) & \cdots & Z_k^B
\end{bmatrix}
\end{array}
\tag{7}
$$

Then the fuzzy goal of the $k - th$ objective is expressed as

$$
\sum_{j=1}^{n} c_j^{(k)} x_j + \frac{1}{2} \sum_{j=1}^{n}\sum_{l=1}^{n} d_{jl}^{(k)} x_j x_l \gtrsim Z_k^B \, ; \text{ for } k = 1, 2, \cdots\cdots, K \, .
$$

In the previous chapters the worst value of each objective is obtained by solving the objective under modified system constraints. But in this chapter the worst value of each objective is calculated by considering the best solution point of other objectives, i.e., the worst value of the first objective $Z_1(x)$ is the least entry of the first column of the above pay-off matrix and similarly for others.

Thus Z_k^W is calculated as

$$
Z_k^W = \min\left\{ Z_k\left(x_1^B\right), Z_k\left(x_2^B\right), \cdots\cdots, Z_k\left(x_K^B\right)\right\}
$$

for $k = 1, 2, \cdots\cdots, K$.

Therefore, the membership function for each of the objectives is written as

$$\mu_{Z_k}(x) = \begin{cases} 0 & \text{if} \quad Z_k \leq Z_k^W \\[2mm] \dfrac{\sum_{j=1}^{n} c_j^{(k)} x_j + \dfrac{1}{2}\sum_{j=1}^{n}\sum_{l=1}^{n} d_{jl}^{(k)} x_j x_l - Z_k^W}{Z_k^B - Z_k^W} & \text{if} \quad Z_k^W \leq Z_k \leq Z_k^B \\[2mm] 1 & \text{if} \quad Z_k \geq Z_k^B \end{cases}$$

(8)

In FGP model formulation process of the problem, the quadratic membership functions defined above are considered as flexible quadratic membership goals by introducing under- and over- deviational variables to each of them and thereby assigning the highest membership value (unity) as the aspiration level to each of them. Also, it is evident that full achievement of all the membership goals is not possible in a multi-objective decision making context. So the under-deviational variables are minimized to achieve the goal values of objectives in the decision making environment.

Thus an FGP model is formulated as

Find $X(x_1, x_2, \ldots x_n)$ so as to

$$\text{Min } D = \sum_{k=1}^{K} w_k d_k^{-}$$

and satisfy

$$\frac{Z_k - Z_k^w}{Z_k^b - Z_k^w} + d_k^{-} - d_k^{+} = 1 \text{ for } k = 1, 2, \ldots, K$$

$$\sum_{j=1}^{n} \left[a_{ij}^R - \left(a_{ij}^R - a_{ij} \right)\alpha \right] x_j \leq \left(\beta_i^L + \left(\beta_i - \beta_i^L \right)\alpha \right) \ln \left(\frac{1}{p_i^L + \left(p_i - p_i^L \right)\alpha} \right)^{\frac{1}{\left(\lambda_i^R - \left(\lambda_i^R - \lambda_i \right)\alpha \right)}}$$

$$\sum_{j=1}^{n} \left[a_{ij}^L + \left(a_{ij} - a_{ij}^L \right)\alpha \right] x_j \leq \left(\beta_i^R - \left(\beta_i^R - \beta_i \right)\alpha \right) \ln \left(\frac{1}{p_i^R - \left(p_i^R - p_i \right)\alpha} \right)^{\frac{1}{\left(\lambda_i^L + \left(\lambda_i - \lambda_i^L \right)\alpha \right)}}$$

$$x_j \geq 0; \left(j = 1, 2, \cdots\cdots, n\right)\left(i = 1, 2, \cdots\cdots, m\right) 0 \leq \alpha \leq 1. \tag{9}$$

where $w_k^- \geq 0$ represents the numerical weights of the goals which are determined as:

$$w_k^- = \frac{1}{\left(Z_k^b - Z_k^w\right)}.$$

The developed model (9) is solved to find the most satisfactory solution in the hybrid uncertain decision making environment.

5.5 LINEARIZATION OF THE QUADRATIC MEMBERSHIP GOALS

Since the membership goals are quadratic in nature, so a linearization technique is necessary to linearize the membership goals. In this chapter two linearization techniques are adopted, viz., piecewise approximation technique and Taylor series approximation technique. For the first model i.e., in this section quadratic membership goals are linearized through piecewise approximation technique. Then the developed model is solved to achieve the most suitable solution in the decision making arena. In piecewise approximation methodology the quadratic membership goals are expressed with the form as follows:

$$\frac{\sum_{j=1}^{n} f_{kj}\left(x_j\right) - Z_k^W}{Z_k^B - Z_k^W} + d_k^- - d_k^+ = 1; \left(k = 1, 2, \cdots\cdots, K\right) \tag{10}$$

Now the quadratic functions $f_{kj}\left(x_j\right)$ are linearized by taking the grid points $a_{jp}\left(p = 0, 1, \cdots\cdots, p_j\right)$ for the variable $x_j\left(j = 1, 2, \cdots\cdots, n\right)$. The variable x_j are expressed by introducing a new variable, $y_{jp}; \left(p = 1, 2, \cdots\cdots, p_j\right)$ as $x_j = \sum_{p=0}^{p_j} a_{jp} y_{jp}$, where $\sum_{p=0}^{p_j} y_{jp} = 1$ with a_{j0} as a lower bound of the variable x_j which is obtained by solving each objective, independently, and a_{jp} as an upper bound of the variable x_j which is obtained by solving each objective, independently. Then piecewise approximated linear form of the quadratic function $f_{kj}\left(x_j\right)$ is expressed as follows:

$$F_{kj} = \sum_{p=0}^{p_j} y_{jp} f_{kj}\left(a_{jp}\right)$$
(11)

Using the above relation (11) the linear FGP model is presented as follows:

Minimize $D = \sum_{k=1}^{K} w_k d_k^-$

so as to satisfy

$$\frac{\sum_{j=1}^{n} F_{kj}\left(x_j\right) - Z_k^W}{Z_k^B - Z_k^W} + d_k^- - d_k^+ = 1 \, ; \, \left(k = 1, 2, \cdots\cdots, K\right)$$

subject to

$$\sum_{j=1}^{n}\left[\left(a_{ij}^R - \left(a_{ij}^R - a_{ij}\right)\alpha\right)\left(\sum_{p=0}^{p_j} a_{jp} y_{jp}\right)\right] \le \left(\beta_i^L + \left(\beta_i - \beta_i^L\right)\alpha\right)\ln\left(\frac{1}{p_i^L + \left(p_i - p_i^L\right)\alpha}\right)^{\frac{1}{\left(\lambda_i^R - \left(\lambda_i^R - \lambda_i\right)\alpha\right)}}$$

$$\sum_{j=1}^{n}\left[\left(a_{ij}^L + \left(a_{ij} - a_{ij}^L\right)\alpha\right)\left(\sum_{p=0}^{p_j} a_{jp} y_{jp}\right)\right] \le \left(\beta_i^R - \left(\beta_i^R - \beta_i\right)\alpha\right)\ln\left(\frac{1}{p_i^R - \left(p_i^R - p_i\right)\alpha}\right)^{\frac{1}{\lambda_i^L + \left(\lambda_i - \lambda_i^L\right)\alpha}}$$

$$y_{jp} \ge 0 \, ; j = 1, 2, \cdots\cdots, n; i = 1, 2, \cdots\cdots, m; p = 1, 2, \cdots\cdots, p_j \, ; 0 \le \alpha \le 1.$$

where

$$F_{kj}\left(x_j\right) = \sum_{p=0}^{p_j} y_{jp} f_{kj}\left(a_{jp}\right)$$
(12)

At most two y_{jp} may be positive and if two are positive, they must be consecutive.

To ensure the above conditions binary variable $Z_{jp}\left(j = 1, 2, .., n \; ; p = 0, 1, .., p_j - 1\right)$ are to be introduced. The required restriction are then appeared as

$$y_{j0} \leq Z_{j0} \; ; y_{jp} \leq Z_{jp-1} + Z_{jp} \, , \left(p = 0, 1, .., p_j - 1\right);$$

$$y_{jp_j} \leq Z_{jp_j-1} \; ; \sum_{j=0}^{p_j-1} Z_{jp} = 1 \,. \tag{13}$$

Finally, the developed linear model (13) obtained by piecewise linearization methodology is solved to find the most satisfactory solution in the decision making environment.

5.5.1 Solution Algorithm of Model I

The methodology for solving FMOCCP model of the form 5.1, is summarized by the following algorithm.

Step 1: Using α – cut of FNs, each fuzzy probabilistic constraint with fuzzy probability is converted into two constraints in crisp environment.

Step 2: The individual optimal value of each objective is found in isolation under modified set of system constraints.

Step 3: The worst value of each objective is evaluated at the best solution point of the other objectives.

Step 4: The quadratic fuzzy membership function of each of each the objectives are developed based on the best and worst values.

Step 5: The non-linear membership functions are linearize using linearization technique.

Step 6: The linear membership goals are developed from linear membership goals.

Step 7: FGP approach is deployed to achieve maximum degree of the membership goals of each of the objectives.

Step 8: Solutions obtained by solving non-linear membership goals and by using piecewise linear approximation method is compared using distance function.

Step 9: Stop.

5.6 FORMULATION OF QUADRATIC PROGRAMMING MODEL WITH SEVERAL OBJECTIVES

In this section deterministic model is developed for the multi-objective quadratic programming model presented in (2). In the previous model the readers already seen that the chance constraints involve fuzzy probability and α – cut of FNs is used to form quadratic programming model with interval parameters. After that the deterministic model is constructed by comparing the interval parameters of the model. At first CCP methodology is applied to convert the fuzzy probabilistic constraints into fuzzy constraints according to the nature of the probability distribution. In this model it is assumed that the FRV $\tilde{b}_i$ involved with chance constraints follows Frechet distribution.

Using CCP, probabilistic constraints involving Frechet distributed FRVs are modified as follows

$$\Pr\left(\sum_{j=1}^{n}\tilde{a}_{ij}x_j \lesssim \tilde{b}_i\right) \geq 1 - p_i \,;\; \left(i = 1, 2, .., m\right)$$

i.e., $\Pr\left(\tilde{A}_i \lesssim \tilde{b}_i\right) \geq 1 - p_i$, where $\tilde{A}_i \cong \sum_{j=1}^{n}\tilde{a}_{ij}x_j$

Since $\tilde{b}_i$ is Frechet distributed FRVs with fuzzy shape parameters $\tilde{\delta}_i$, $\tilde{\eta}_i$ and $\tilde{\mu}_i$, then its probability density function involving fuzzy parameters is written as

$$f\left(b_i \,;\tilde{\mu}_i \,, \tilde{\delta}_i, \tilde{\eta}_i\right) = \frac{r_i}{q_i}\left(\frac{b_i - d_i}{q_i}\right)^{-1-r_i} e^{-\left(\frac{b_i - d_i}{q_i}\right)^{-r_i}} ,\; r_i \in \tilde{\mu}_i\left[\alpha\right], q_i \in \tilde{\delta}_i\left[\alpha\right], d_i \in \tilde{\eta}_i\left[\alpha\right]$$

Figure 1. Density graph of Frechet distribution

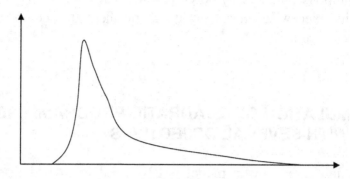

where $b_i \geq d_i$. Here $\tilde{\mu}_i[\alpha], \tilde{\delta}_i[\alpha]$ and $\tilde{\eta}_i[\alpha]$ are the α–cut of FNs $\tilde{\mu}_i, \tilde{\delta}_i$ and $\tilde{\eta}_i$, respectively. The support of $\tilde{\mu}_i, \tilde{\delta}_i$ are the set of positive real numbers and the support of $\tilde{\eta}_i$ is the set of real numbers.

The probability density curve of the Frechet distribution is given by Figure 1. Now,

$$\int_{h_i}^{\infty} \frac{r_i}{q_i} \left(\frac{b_i - d_i}{q_i} \right)^{-1-r_i} e^{-\left(\frac{b_i - d_i}{q_i} \right)^{-r_i}} db_i \geq 1 - p_i \,;\; r_i \in \tilde{\mu}_i[\alpha], q_i \in \tilde{\delta}_i[\alpha], d_i \in \tilde{\eta}_i[\alpha]$$

and $h_i \in \tilde{A}_i[\alpha]$ and $h_i \geq d_i$

i.e., $h_i \leq d_i + q_i \dfrac{1}{\ln\left(\dfrac{1}{p_i}\right)^{\frac{1}{r_i}}} \,;\; r_i \in \tilde{\mu}_i[\alpha], q_i \in \tilde{\delta}_i[\alpha], d_i \in \tilde{\eta}_i[\alpha]$ and $h_i \in \tilde{A}_i[\alpha]$ and

$h_i \geq d_i$

Since, this inequality is true for all $\alpha \in (0,1]$ i.e, as the inequality is valid for every elements of the $\alpha -$ cut, the expression can be written in terms of $\alpha -$ cut as

$$\tilde{A}_i[\alpha] \leq \tilde{\eta}_i[\alpha] + \tilde{\delta}_i[\alpha] \frac{1}{\ln\left(\dfrac{1}{p_i}\right)^{\frac{1}{\tilde{\mu}_i[\alpha]}}} \text{ and } \tilde{A}_i[\alpha] \geq \tilde{\eta}_i[\alpha]\,;\; (i = 1, 2, .., m) \tag{14}$$

Now using first decomposition theorem, the above equation is reduced to the following form as

$$\tilde{A}_i \le \tilde{\eta}_i + \tilde{\delta}_i \frac{1}{\ln\left(\dfrac{1}{p_i}\right)^{\frac{1}{\bar{\mu}_i}}} \text{ and } \tilde{A}_i \ge \tilde{\eta}_i \,;\; \left(i = 1, 2, .., m\right) \tag{15}$$

i.e., $\displaystyle\sum_{j=1}^{n} \tilde{a}_{ij} x_j \lesssim \tilde{\eta}_i + \tilde{\delta}_i \frac{1}{\ln\left(\dfrac{1}{p_i}\right)^{\frac{1}{\bar{\mu}_i}}} \text{ and } \displaystyle\sum_{j=1}^{n} \tilde{a}_{ij} x_j \gtrsim \tilde{\eta}_i \,;\; \left(i = 1, 2, .., m\right)$ (16)

Hence the fuzzy multi-objective CCP model (2) with quadratic objective functions, is converted into the equivalent fuzzy multi-objective problem by using the derived methodology as

Find $X\left(x_1, x_2, \ldots, x_n\right)$ so as to

$$\text{Max } \tilde{Z}_k \cong \sum_{j=1}^{n} \tilde{c}_{kj} x_j + \frac{1}{2} \sum_{j=1}^{n} \sum_{l=1}^{n} \tilde{d}_{kjl} x_j x_l \,;\; k = 1, 2, \ldots, K$$

subject to

$$\sum_{j=1}^{n} \tilde{a}_{ij} x_j \lesssim \tilde{\eta}_i + \tilde{\delta}_i \frac{1}{\ln\left(\dfrac{1}{p_i}\right)^{\frac{1}{\bar{\mu}_i}}}$$

and

$$\sum_{j=1}^{n} \tilde{a}_{ij} x_j \gtrsim \tilde{\eta}_i \,;\; \left(i = 1, 2, .., m\right)$$

$$x_j \ge 0 \,;\; j = 1, 2, \ldots, n \tag{17}$$

Here the parameters of the quadratic objective functions $\tilde{c}_{kj}$, $\tilde{d}_{kjl}$, $\tilde{a}_{ij}$ (

$$j = 1, 2, \ldots, n \;\; ; l = 1, 2, \ldots, n \;\; ; k = 1, 2, \ldots, K \; ; i = 1, 2, \ldots, m \,)$$

are taken as triangular FNs. Also it is supposed that the parameters $\tilde{\mu}_i$, $\tilde{\delta}_i$ and $\tilde{\eta}_i$ of the Frechet distributed FRVs are considered as triangular FNs. Since the reciprocal of an FN is again an FN of the same type, then $\dfrac{1}{\tilde{\mu}_i}$ is also triangular FNs and these triangular FNs can be expressed as

$$\tilde{c}_{kj} = \left(c_{kj}^L, c_{kj}, c_{kj}^R \right) ; \tilde{d}_{kjl} = \left(d_{kjl}^L, d_{kjl}, d_{kjl}^R \right) ; \tilde{a}_{ij} = \left(a_{ij}^L, a_{ij}, a_{ij}^R \right) \;\;;$$

$$\tilde{\eta}_i = \left(\eta_i^{\,L}, \eta_i, \eta_i^{\,R} \right) \;\; ; \; \frac{1}{\tilde{\mu}_i} = \left(\left(\frac{1}{\mu_i} \right)^L, \frac{1}{\mu_i}, \left(\frac{1}{\mu_i} \right)^R \right) ; \tilde{\delta}_i = \left(\delta_i^{\,L}, \delta_i, \delta_i^{\,R} \right) \tag{18}$$

After the nature of the fuzzy parameters in fuzzy programming model is specified, the fuzzy parameters are now defuzzified according to some defuzzified methodology described in Chapter 2 to find an equivalent crisp value of each FNs. Thus the equivalent crisp values of the FNs of model (17) are obtained by the method of defuzzification (*viz.*, canonical form of an FN) of the triangular FN using $\alpha -$ cuts are given as

$$V\left(\tilde{c}_{kj} \right) = \frac{c_{kj}^L + 4c_{kj} + c_{kj}^R}{6} \;\; ; V\left(\tilde{d}_{kjl} \right) = \frac{d_{kjl}^L + 4d_{kjl} + d_{kjl}^R}{6} \;\;;$$

$$V\left(\tilde{a}_{ij} \right) = \frac{a_{ij}^L + 4a_{ij} + a_{ij}^R}{6} \;\; ; \;\; V\left(\tilde{\eta}_i \right) = \frac{\eta_i^{\,L} + 4\eta_i + \eta_i^{\,R}}{6} \;;$$

$$V\left(\frac{1}{\tilde{\mu}_i} \right) = \frac{(\frac{1}{\mu_i})^L + 4\frac{1}{\mu_i} + \left(\frac{1}{\mu_i} \right)^R}{6} \;\; ; V\left(\tilde{\delta}_i \right) = \frac{\delta_i^{\,L} + 4\delta_i + \delta_i^{\,R}}{6}$$

$$j = 1, 2, \ldots, n \;\; ; i = 1, 2, \ldots, m \;\; ; l = 1, 2, \ldots, n \; ; k = 1, 2, \ldots, K \tag{19}$$

Thus the equivalent deterministic model of the fuzzy multi-objective CCP as described in model (17) is stated as

Find $X\left(x_1, x_2, \ldots, x_n\right)$ so as to

$$\text{Max } V\left(\tilde{Z}_k\right) = \sum_{j=1}^{n} V\left(\tilde{c}_{kj}\right) x_j + \frac{1}{2} \sum_{j=1}^{n} \sum_{l=1}^{n} V\left(\tilde{d}_{kjl}\right) x_j x_l \; ; \; k = 1, 2, \ldots, K$$

subject to

$$\sum_{j=1}^{n} V\left(\tilde{a}_{ij}\right) x_j \leq V\left(\tilde{\eta}_i\right) + V\left(\tilde{\delta}_i\right) \frac{1}{\ln\left(\dfrac{1}{p_i}\right)^{V\left(\frac{1}{\tilde{\mu}_i}\right)}}$$

and

$$\sum_{j=1}^{n} V\left(\tilde{a}_{ij}\right) x_j \geq V\left(\tilde{\eta}_i\right); \; \left(i = 1, 2, \ldots, m\right)$$

$$x_j \geq 0; \; j = 1, 2, \ldots, n \tag{20}$$

or,

Find $X\left(x_1, x_2, \ldots, x_n\right)$ so as to

$$\text{Max } V\left(\tilde{Z}_k\right) = \sum_{j=1}^{n} \left[\frac{c_{kj}^L + 4c_{kj} + c_{kj}^R}{6}\right] x_j + \frac{1}{2} \sum_{j=1}^{n} \sum_{l=1}^{n} \left[\frac{d_{kjl}^L + 4d_{kjl} + d_{kjl}^R}{6}\right] x_j x_l \; ;$$

$$k = 1, 2, \ldots, K$$

subject to

$$\sum_{j=1}^{n} \left[\frac{a_{ij}^L + 4a_{ij} + a_{ij}^R}{6}\right] x_j \leq \left[\frac{\eta_i^L + 4\eta_i + \eta_i^R}{6}\right] + \left[\frac{\delta_i^L + 4\delta_i + \delta_i^R}{6}\right] \frac{1}{\ln\left(\dfrac{1}{p_i}\right)^{\frac{(\frac{1}{\mu_i})^L + 4\frac{1}{\mu_i} + \left(\frac{1}{\mu_i}\right)^R}{6}}}$$

and

$$\sum_{j=1}^{n} \left(\frac{a_{ij}^{L} + 4a_{ij} + a_{ij}^{R}}{6} \right) x_j \geq \left(\frac{\eta_i^{L} + 4\eta_i + \eta_i^{R}}{6} \right); \ (i = 1, 2, .., m)$$

$$x_j \geq 0; \ j = 1, 2, ..., n \tag{21}$$

In multi-objective programming it can reasonably be assumed that the DMs try to optimize each of their objectives under modified set of system constraints in multi-objective environment. To know the independent optimal value of the objectives, like the previous chapters each objective of the model (21) is now solved independently under the same set of system constraints as defined in (21).

Let

$$\left[x^{kb} \ ; V \left(Z_k \right)^b \right] = \left[x_1^{kb}, x_2^{kb}, ..., x_n^{kb} \ ; V \left(Z_k \right)^b \right]$$

be the best independent solutions of the k – th objective. The readers already seen that in the previous model the worst values of the objectives are calculated from the pay-off matrix. But in this model the worst value of each objective is obtained by calculating the minimum value of each objective under modified set of system constraints.

Thus the worst value of the k – th objective is evaluated as

$$\left[x^{kw} \ ; V \left(Z_k \right)^w \right] = \left[x_1^{kw}, x_2^{kw}, ..., x_n^{kw} \ ; V \left(Z_k \right)^w \right] (k = 1, 2, ..., K)$$

Hence, the fuzzy goal for each of the k – th objective is expressed as:

$$\sum_{j=1}^{n} \left(\frac{c_{kj}^{L} + 4c_{kj} + c_{kj}^{R}}{6} \right) x_j + \frac{1}{2} \sum_{j=1}^{n} \sum_{l=1}^{n} \left(\frac{d_{kjl}^{L} + 4d_{kjl} + d_{kjl}^{R}}{6} \right) x_j x_l \gtrsim V \left(Z_k \right)^b \text{ for }$$

$$k = 1, 2, ... K \tag{22}$$

Thus the membership function for each of the objectives is formulated as

$$\mu_{V(z_k(x))} = \begin{cases} 0 & if & V\left(Z_k\right) \le V\left(Z_k\right)^w \\[2em] \dfrac{\displaystyle\sum_{j=1}^{n}\left(\dfrac{c_{kj}^L + 4c_{kj} + c_{kj}^R}{6}\right)x_j + \dfrac{1}{2}\displaystyle\sum_{j=1}^{n}\sum_{l=1}^{n}\left(\dfrac{d_{kjl}^L + 4d_{kjl} + d_{kjl}^R}{6}\right)x_j x_l - V\left(Z_k\right)^w}{V\left(Z_k\right)^b - V\left(Z_k\right)^w} & if & V\left(Z_k\right)^w \le V(Z_k) \le V\left(Z_k\right)^b \\[2em] 1 & if & V\left(Z_k\right) \ge V\left(Z_k\right)^b \end{cases}$$

$$\left(k = 1, 2, \ldots, K\right) \tag{23}$$

From the above expression it is clear that membership function of the objective is quadratic in nature and it is easy to understand that instead of using quadratic functions it is easy to handle linear functions.

So, in the next subsection the quadratic membership functions defined above are to be linearized using Taylor series linear approximation technique as presented in the previous model.

5.6.1 Linearization by Taylor Series Approximation

In this chapter piecewise linear approximation technique, described earlier, is applied to linearize quadratic membership functions. In this subsection Taylor's series linear approximation technique (Bazarra et al., 1993) is applied to convert the defined non-linear membership functions to linear forms and thereby obtaining most suitable solution in the decision making arena.

For expanding the Taylor series a point is needed about which the Taylor series is expressed. In this model the best solution point of each objective is taken as the initial point of the Taylor's series approximation. Thus applying linearizing technique the defined membership functions are approximated as

$$\mu_{V(Z_k(x))} \cong \mu_{V(Z_k(\,x))}\Big|_{x^{kb}} + \left(x_1 - x_1^{kb}\right)\left(\frac{\partial}{\partial x_1}\mu_{V(Z_k(x))}\right)\Big|_{x^{kb}} + \ldots + \left(x_n - x_n^{kb}\right)\left(\frac{\partial}{\partial x_n}\mu_{V(Z_k(x))}\right)\Big|_{x^{kb}}$$

$$= \tau_{V(Z_k(x))}, \text{ say, for } k = 1, 2, \dots, K. \tag{24}$$

Now for the compromise solution it is necessary to develop a model based on the linearized membership functions and the modified form of system constraints.

For developing such model the linear membership function defined above are now converted into the membership goals by introducing under- and over- deviational variables and assigning the highest membership value (unity) as the aspiration level to each of them. Thus the linearize FGP model of the corresponding multi-objective quadratic programming model (21) is presented as:

Find $X\left(x_1, x_2, \dots x_n\right)$ so as to

$$\text{Min } D = \sum_{k=1}^{n} w_k d_k^-$$

and satisfy

$$\tau_{V(Z_k(x))} + d_k^- - d_k^+ = 1; \; k = 1, 2, \dots, K$$

subject to

$$\sum_{j=1}^{n} \left(\frac{a_{ij}^L + 4a_{ij} + a_{ij}^R}{6}\right) x_j \le \left(\frac{\eta_i^L + 4\eta_i + \eta_i^R}{6}\right) + \left(\frac{\delta_i^L + 4\delta_i + \delta_i^R}{6}\right)\left(\frac{1}{\ln\left(\frac{1}{p_i}\right)^{\frac{\left(\frac{1}{\mu_i}\right)^L + 4\frac{1}{\mu_i} + \left(\frac{1}{\mu_i}\right)^R}{6}}}\right)$$

and

$$\sum_{j=1}^{n} \left(\frac{a_{ij}^L + 4a_{ij} + a_{ij}^R}{6}\right) x_j \ge \left(\frac{\eta_i^L + 4\eta_i + \eta_i^R}{6}\right); \; \left(i = 1, 2, \dots, m\right)$$

$$x_j \geq 0; \ j = 1, 2, \ldots, n \tag{25}$$

$$d_k^-, d_k^+ \geq 0 \text{ with } d_k^- . d_k^+ = 0$$

where

$$w_k = \frac{1}{V\left(Z_k\right)^b - V\left(Z_k\right)^w} \left(k = 1, 2, \ldots, K\right)$$

represents fuzzy weight corresponding to the membership goals of the DMs.

The derived model (25) is then solved using min-sum goal programming to achieve most compromise solution in a decision making context.

5.6.2 Solution Algorithm for Model II

The methodology for solving fuzzy multi-objective CCP model with quadratic objectives of the form (2), is summarized by the following algorithm.

Step 1: Applying CCP technique the constraints involving fuzzy stochastic uncertainty are converted into constraints involving only fuzzy uncertainty.
Step 2: Defuzzification of FNs using $\alpha - $ cut is applied to find the crisp value of the FNs.
Step 3: The individual optimal value of each of the objective is found in isolation.
Step 4: The quadratic fuzzy membership function of each of each the objectives are formed.
Step 5: Using Taylor series approximation technique the non-linear membership functions are linearized.
Step 6: The linear membership functions are converted into linear membership goals.
Step 7: FGP approach is deployed to achieve maximum degree of the membership goals of each of the objectives.
Step 8: Stop.

To illustrate the described approaches two numerical examples are provided and solved in the next section.

5.7 NUMERICAL EXAMPLES

In this section two numerical examples are discussed to exhibit the acceptability of both the methodologies.

5.7.1 Numerical Example 1

To demonstrate the efficiency of the methodology (1), the following numerical example is considered. In this example objectives are quadratic functions with crisp parameters and the fuzzy chance constraints involve fuzzy probability. Thus the example can be expressed in the following form

Maximize $Z_1 = 7x_1 + 3x_2 - 2x_1^2 - 2x_2^2$

Maximize $Z_2 = 8x_1 + 9x_2 - 3x_1^2 - 2x_2^2$

Maximize $Z_3 = 5x_1 + x_2 - x_1^2 - x_2^2$

Subject to

$$\widetilde{Pr}\left(\tilde{1}x_1 + \tilde{4}x_2 \lesssim \tilde{b}_1\right) \gtrsim \widetilde{0.90}$$

$$\widetilde{Pr}\left(\tilde{1}x_1 + \tilde{1}x_2 \lesssim \tilde{b}_2\right) \gtrsim \widetilde{0.91}$$

$$x_1, x_2 \geq 0 \tag{26}$$

Here $\tilde{b}_1, \tilde{b}_2$ are Weibull distributed FRVs and the parameters of the chance constraints $\tilde{1}, \tilde{4}, \tilde{1}, \tilde{1}, \widetilde{0.90}, \widetilde{0.91}$ are all considered as triangular FNs. The parameters

$$\tilde{\ae}_1 = \tilde{5}, \quad \tilde{\ae}_1^2 = \widetilde{586}, \quad \tilde{\ae}_2 = \widetilde{3.5}, \quad \tilde{\ae}_2^2 = \widetilde{1089}$$

of the fuzzy Weibull distribution are also taken as triangular FNs.

The above triangular fuzzy parameters are expressed in the following respective form:

$$\tilde{1} = (0.90, 1, 1.05), \tilde{4} = (3.25, 4, 4.15), \tilde{1} = (0.85, 1, 1.1), \tilde{1} = (0.95, 1, 1.05),$$

$$\widetilde{0.90} = (0.80, 0.90, 1), \widetilde{0.91} = (0.75, 0.91, 1.1), \tilde{5} = (4, 5, 6),$$

$$\widetilde{586} = (584, 586, 588), \widetilde{3.5} = (3, 3.5, 4), \widetilde{1089} = (1085, 1089, 1093).$$

The α – cut of the above triangular FNs are given by

$$\tilde{1}[\alpha] = [0.90 + 0.1\alpha, 1.05 - 0.05\alpha], \tilde{4}[\alpha] = [3.25 + 0.75\alpha, 4.15 - 0.15\alpha],$$

$$\tilde{1}[\alpha] = [0.85 + 0.15\alpha, 1.1 - 0.1\alpha], \tilde{1}[\alpha] = [0.95 + 0.05\alpha, 1.05 - 0.05\alpha],$$

$$\widetilde{0.90}[\alpha] = [0.80 + 0.1\alpha, 1 - 0.1\alpha], \widetilde{0.91}[\alpha] = [0.75 + 0.16\alpha, 1.1 - 0.19\alpha],$$

$$\tilde{5}[\alpha] = [4 + \alpha, 6 - \alpha], \widetilde{586}[\alpha] = [584 + 2\alpha, 588 - 2\alpha],$$

$$\widetilde{3.5}[\alpha] = [3 + 0.5\alpha, 4 - 0.5\alpha], \widetilde{1089}[\alpha] = [1085 + 4\alpha, 1093 - 4\alpha].$$

Using the above α – cuts and applying CCP methodology the above model is reduced to the following form as follows:

Maximize $Z_1 = 7x_1 + 3x_2 - 2x_1^2 - 2x_2^2$

Maximize $Z_2 = 8x_1 + 9x_2 - 3x_1^2 - 2x_2^2$

Maximize $Z_3 = 5x_1 + x_2 - x_1^2 - x_2^2$

subject to

$$\left(\left(0.90 + 0.1\alpha\right)x_1 + \left(3.25 + 0.75\alpha\right)x_2\right) \leq \left(588 - 2\alpha\right)\left[\ln\left(\frac{1}{1 - 0.1\alpha}\right)\right]^{\frac{1}{(4+\alpha)}}$$

$$\left(\left(1.05 - 0.05\alpha\right)x_1 + \left(4.15 - 0.15\alpha\right)x_2\right) \leq \left(584 + 2\alpha\right)\left[\ln\left(\frac{1}{0.80 + 0.1\alpha}\right)\right]^{\frac{1}{(6-\alpha)}}$$

$$\left(\left(0.85 + 0.15\alpha\right)x_1 + \left(0.95 + 0.05\alpha\right)x_2\right) \leq \left(1093 - 4\alpha\right)\left[\ln\left(\frac{1}{1.1 - 0.19\alpha}\right)\right]^{\frac{1}{(3+0.5\alpha)}}$$

$$\left(\left(1.1 - 0.1\alpha\right)x_1 + \left(1.05 - 0.05\alpha\right)x_2\right) \leq \left(1085 + 4\alpha\right)\left[\ln\left(\frac{1}{0.75 + 0.16\alpha}\right)\right]^{\frac{1}{(4-0.5\alpha)}}$$

$$x_1, x_2 \geq 0 ; \ 0 \leq \alpha \leq 1. \tag{27}$$

Now, each nonlinear objective is considered independently and is solved with respect to the system constraints defined in (27) to find individual optimal values of the objectives. The results are obtained as

$$Z_1^b = 7.25 \text{ at } \left(x_1, x_2\right) = (1.75, 0.75\,);$$

$$Z_2^b = 15.458 \text{ at } \left(x_1, x_2\right) = (1.333, 2.25\,)$$

and

$$Z_3^b = 6.5 \text{, at } \left(x_1, x_2\right) = \left(2.5, 0.5\right).$$

The pay-off matrix is thus be constructed as follows:

$$
\begin{array}{c}
\quad\quad\quad Z_1 \quad\quad Z_2 \quad\quad Z_3 \\
\begin{array}{l}
(1.75, 0.75) \\
(1.333, 2.25) \\
(2.5, 0.5)
\end{array}
\begin{bmatrix}
7.25 & 10.437 & 5.876 \\
2.402 & 15.458 & 2.076 \\
6 & 5.25 & 6.5
\end{bmatrix} .
\end{array}
$$

Then the fuzzy goals of the objectives are found as follows:

$Z_1 \gtrsim 7.25,\ Z_2 \gtrsim 15.458,\ Z_3 \gtrsim 6.5.$

So constructing the quadratic membership goals of the respective objectives, the FGP model is constructed as

Minimize $D = 0.206 d_1^- + 0.098 d_2^- + 0.226 d_3^-$

so as to satisfy

$$
\mu_{Z_1}\left(x\right) = 1.442 x_1 + 0.618 x_2 - 0.412 x_1^2 - 0.412 x_2^2 - 0.495 + d_1^- - d_1^+ = 1
$$

$$
\mu_{Z_2}\left(x\right) = 0.784 x_1 + 0.882 x_2 - 0.294 x_1^2 - 0.196 x_2^2 - 0.515 + d_2^- - d_2^+ = 1
$$

$$
\mu_{Z_3}\left(x\right) = 1.13 x_1 + 0.226 x_2 - 0.226 x_1^2 - 0.226 x_2^2 - 0.469 + d_3^- - d_3^+ = 1
$$

subject to the system constraints defined in (27) (28)

Now the above FGP model at first is solved directly without linearization using *software* LINGO (Ver. 13) to find the compromise solution in the hybrid uncertain decision making context. The solutions are achieved as $x_1 = 1.91, x_2 = 0.85$ with the achieved objective values $Z_1 = 7.108, Z_2 = 12.541$ and $Z_3 = 5.7$. The achieved membership values corresponding to the fuzzy goals are obtained as $\mu_1 = 0.97$, $\mu_2 = 0.71$ and $\mu_3 = 0.82$.

Again, the model is solved using piecewise linear approximation technique to the nonlinear membership goals as described below.

In piecewise linear approximation technique, at first, each of the objectives are expressed as the sum of separable functions which are shown in the Table 1,

The membership goals can now be written as follows:

Table 1. Separable functions associated with the objectives

$f_{11}\left(x_1\right)$	$7x_1 - 2x_1^2$
$f_{12}\left(x_2\right)$	$3x_2 - 2x_2^2$
$f_{21}\left(x_1\right)$	$8x_1 - 3x_1^2$
$f_{22}\left(x_2\right)$	$9x_2 - 2x_2^2$
$f_{31}\left(x_1\right)$	$5x_1 - x_1^2$
$f_{32}\left(x_2\right)$	$x_2 - x_2^2$

$$0.206\left(f_{11}\left(x_1\right) + f_{12}\left(x_2\right) - 2.402\right) + d_1^- - d_1^+ = 1$$

$$0.098\left(f_{21}\left(x_1\right) + f_{22}\left(x_2\right) - 5.25\right) + d_2^- - d_2^+ = 1$$

$$0.226\left(f_{31}\left(x_1\right) + f_{32}\left(x_2\right) - 2.076\right) + d_3^- - d_3^+ = 1$$

To linearize the functions using piecewise linear approximation technique, the set of grid points for the variables x_1 and x_2 are needed. In this example the range of x_1 is divided into two equal subintervals and the range of x_2 is divided into four equal subintervals.

Thus the grid points are found as $\{1.333, 1.916, 2.5\}$ and $\{0.5, 0.938, 1.376, 1.814, 2.25\}$.

Using the grid points on the above mentioned membership goals, the FGP model (28) is rewritten in the following form as

Minimize $D = 0.206d_1^- + 0.098d_2^- + 0.226d_3^-$

so as to satisfy

$$0.206\left(F_{11}\left(x_{1}\right)+F_{12}\left(x_{2}\right)-2.402\right)+d_{1}^{-}-d_{1}^{+}=1$$

$$0.098\left(F_{21}\left(x_{1}\right)+F_{22}\left(x_{2}\right)-5.25\right)+d_{2}^{-}-d_{2}^{+}=1$$

$$0.226\left(F_{31}\left(x_{1}\right)+F_{32}\left(x_{2}\right)-2.076\right)+d_{3}^{-}-d_{3}^{+}=1$$

subject to

$$\frac{\left(\begin{array}{l}\left(0.90+0.1\alpha\right)\left(1.333y_{10}+1.916y_{11}+2.5y_{13}\right)+\left(3.25+0.75\alpha\right)\\\left(0.5y_{20}+0.938y_{21}+1.376y_{22}+1.814y_{23}+2.25y_{24}\right)\end{array}\right)}{\left(588-2\alpha\right)\left[\ln\left(\dfrac{1}{1-0.1\alpha}\right)\right]^{\frac{1}{(4+\alpha)}}} \leq$$

$$\frac{\left(\begin{array}{l}\left(1.05-0.05\alpha\right)\left(1.333y_{10}+1.916y_{11}+2.5y_{13}\right)+\left(4.15-0.15\alpha\right)\\\left(0.5y_{20}+0.938y_{21}+1.376y_{22}+1.814y_{23}+2.25y_{24}\right)\end{array}\right)}{\left(584+2\alpha\right)\left[\ln\left(\dfrac{1}{0.80+0.1\alpha}\right)\right]^{\frac{1}{(6-\alpha)}}} \leq$$

$$\frac{\left(\left(0.85+0.15\alpha\right)\left(1.333y_{10}+1.916y_{11}+2.5y_{13}\right)+\left(0.95+0.05\alpha\right)\left(\begin{array}{l}0.5y_{20}+0.938y_{21}+1.376y_{22}+\\1.814y_{23}+2.25y_{24}\end{array}\right)\right)}{}$$
$$\leq\left(1093-4\alpha\right)\left[\ln\left(\dfrac{1}{1.1-0.19\alpha}\right)\right]^{\frac{1}{(3+0.5\alpha)}}$$

$$\left(\left(1.1-0.1\alpha\right)\left(1.333y_{10}+1.916y_{11}+2.5y_{13}\right)+\left(1.05-0.05\alpha\right)\left(\begin{array}{l}0.5y_{20}+0.938y_{21}+1.376y_{22}+\\1.814y_{23}+2.25y_{24}\end{array}\right)\right)$$
$$\leq\left(1085+4\alpha\right)\left[\ln\left(\dfrac{1}{0.75+0.16\alpha}\right)\right]^{\frac{1}{(4-0.5\alpha)}}$$

where

$$F_{11}=5.777\mathrm{y}_{10}+6.07\mathrm{y}_{11}+5\mathrm{y}_{12}$$

$$F_{12} = y_{20} + 1.054y_{21} + 0.341y_{22} - 1.139y_{23} - 3.375y_{24}$$

$$F_{21} = 5.333y_{10} + 4.315y_{11} + 1.25y_{12}$$

$$F_{22} = 4y_{20} + 6.682y_{21} + 8.597y_{22} + 9.745y_{23} + 10.125y_{24}$$

$$F_{31} = 4.888y_{10} + 5.9095y_{11} + 6.25y_{12}$$

$$F_{32} = 0.25y_{20} + 0.058y_{21} - 0.517y_{22} - 1.476y_{23} - 2.812y_{24}$$

with

$$y_{10} + y_{11} + y_{12} = 1$$

$$y_{20} + y_{21} + y_{22} + y_{23} + y_{24} = 1$$

$$y_{10} \leq Z_{10}; \ y_{11} \leq Z_{10} + Z_{11}; \ y_{12} \leq Z_{11}$$

$$y_{20} \leq Z_{20}; \ y_{21} \leq Z_{20} + Z_{21}; \ y_{22} \leq Z_{21} + Z_{22}; \ y_{23} \leq Z_{22} + Z_{23}; \ y_{24} \leq Z_{23}$$

$$y_{1p} \geq 0 \big(p = 0, 1, 2 \big) \text{ and } y_{2p} \geq 0 \big(p = 0, 1, 2, 3, 4 \big).$$

Table 2. Comparison of results

	Solution Points	Objective Values	Membership Values	Euclidean Distance
without linearization	$x_1 = 1.91$ $x_2 = 0.85$	$Z_1 = 7.108$ $Z_2 = 12.541$ $Z_3 = 5.7$	$\mu_1 = 0.97$ $\mu_2 = 0.71$ $\mu_3 = 0.82$	$d = 0.34$
using Piecewise linear approximation method	$x_1 = 1.92$ $x_2 = 0.938$	$Z_1 = 7.124$ $Z_2 = 12.997$ $Z_3 = 5.967$	$\mu_1 = 0.97$ $\mu_2 = 0.76$ $\mu_3 = 0.88$	$d = 0.27$

Also the variables $Z_{1p}\left(p = 0, 1\right)$, $Z_{2p}\left(p = 0, 1, 2, 3\right)$ are binary variables and satisfy the following conditions

$$Z_{10} + Z_{11} = 1$$

$$Z_{20} + Z_{21} + Z_{22} + Z_{23} = 1. \tag{29}$$

Now solving the above model using *software* LINGO (Ver. 13) the solutions are found as $x_1 = 1.916$, $x_2 = 0.938$ with objective values $Z_1 = 7.124$, $Z_2 = 12.997$ and $Z_3 = 5.967$.

The solutions achieved through piecewise linearization method and without using any linearization technique are summarized in the following Table 2. The superior solution is measured using Euclidean distance function (Yu, 1973) for group decision making which is given by $d = \left\{\sum_{k=1}^{3}\left(1 - \mu_k\right)^2\right\}^{\frac{1}{2}}$, i.e.,

for both the solutions the value d is calculated and the methodology that gives minimum value of d gives the better solution than the other methodology.

The comparison reflects that better solution is obtained in the process of piecewise linear approximation method than without using linearization technique. This indicated that for nonlinear programming problems use of linearization process is necessary for achieving more acceptable solutions.

5.7.2 Numerical Example 2

This numerical example is considered to explain the methodological development of the model (2). This example involves two fuzzy chance constraints involving Frechet distribution. Thus the quadratic programming problem is expressed as

Find $X\left(x_1, x_2\right)$ so as to

$$\text{Max } \tilde{Z}_k \cong \sum_{j=1}^{2}\tilde{c}_{kj}x_j + \frac{1}{2}\sum_{j=1}^{2}\sum_{l=1}^{2}\tilde{d}_{kjl}x_j x_l ; \quad k = 1, 2$$

subject to

Table 3. Value of parameters of the Frechet distribution

Shape Parameter	Specific Probability Level
$\tilde{\delta}_1 = \tilde{6} = \left(5.8, 6, 6.2\right)$ $\dfrac{1}{\tilde{\mu}_1} = \widetilde{2.8} = \left(2.75, 2.8, 2.85\right)$ $\tilde{\eta}_1 = \widetilde{29} = \left(28, 29, 30\right)$	$p_1 = 0.22$
$\tilde{\delta}_2 = \tilde{5} = \left(4, 5, 6\right)$ $\dfrac{1}{\tilde{\mu}_2} = \widetilde{2.7} = \left(2.6, 2.7, 2.8\right)$ $\tilde{\eta}_2 = \widetilde{15} = \left(14, 15, 16\right)$	$p_2 = 0.24$

Table 4. Values of the coefficients of the objectives and constraints

First Objective	Second Objective	First Constraints	Second Constraints
$\tilde{c}_{12} = \tilde{5} = \left(4, 5, 6\right),$ $\tilde{d}_{111} = \widetilde{25} = \left(23, 25, 27\right),$ $\tilde{d}_{122} = \widetilde{10} = \left(9, 10, 11\right)$ and other coefficients are considered as zero	$\tilde{c}_{21} = \widetilde{24} = \left(23, 24, 25\right),$ $\tilde{c}_{22} = \tilde{3} = \left(2.95, 3, 3.05\right),$ $\tilde{d}_{222} = \widetilde{22} = \left(21, 22, 23\right)$ and other coefficients are considered as zero	$\tilde{a}_{11} = \tilde{4} = \left(2, 4, 6\right)$ $\tilde{a}_{12} = \tilde{8} = \left(7.5, 8, 8.5\right)$	$\tilde{a}_{21} = \tilde{6} = \left(5.95, 6, 6.05\right),$ $\tilde{a}_{22} = \tilde{2} = \left(1.5, 2, 2.5\right)$

$$\mathrm{Pr}\left(\sum_{j=1}^{2} \tilde{a}_{ij} x_j \lesssim \tilde{b}_i\right) \geq 1 - p_i; \; i = 1, 2$$

$$x_1, \; x_2 \geq 0. \tag{30}$$

Here $\tilde{b}_1$ and $\tilde{b}_2$ represents Frechet distributed FRVs. The parameters of Frechet distribution are given in Table 3.

In this example it is assumed that the coefficients of the objectives and the left side coefficients of the constraints are triangular FNs. Thus the different fuzzy parameters which are associated with the objectives and system constraints are represented in Table 4.

Applying CCP technique to the fuzzy probabilistic constraints and then using defuzzification method of FNs to the fuzzy parameters of the objectives and modified fuzzy constraints of the model (30) as described in this paper, the model reduces to the following form as

$$\text{Max } V(\tilde{Z}_1) = 25x_1^2 + 5x_2 + 10x_2^2$$

$$\text{Max } V(\tilde{Z}_2) = 24x_1 + 22x_2^2 + 3x_2$$

Subject to

$$4x_1 + 8x_2 \leq 34.17$$

$$6x_1 + 2x_2 \leq 19.38$$

$$x_1, x_2 \geq 0. \tag{31}$$

Like the previous model each objective is now solved independently with respect to the modified set of system constraints presented in (31) to find the best value of the objectives. Unlike the previous model the worst values of this model is also obtained by finding the minimum value of the objectives. The results are obtained as

$$x_1 = 3.23, x_2 = 0 \text{ with } V\left(\tilde{Z}_1\right)^b = 260.82;$$

$$\text{and } x_1 = 0, x_2 = 4.27 \text{ with } V\left(\tilde{Z}_2\right)^b = 414.17;$$

The worst values of the objective of the respective DMs are calculated as

$$V\left(\tilde{Z}_1\right)^w = 0 \text{ and } V\left(\tilde{Z}_2\right)^w = 0$$

Then the fuzzy goals of the objectives are found as:

$$V\left(\tilde{Z}_1\right)^b \gtrsim 260.82 \tag{32}$$

$$V\left(\tilde{Z}_2\right)^b \gtrsim 414.17 . \tag{33}$$

Therefore, the membership functions of the leader and follower are appeared as

$$\mu_{V\left(Z_1(x)\right)} = 0.096x_1^2 + 0.019x_2 + 0.038x_2^2 \tag{34}$$

$$\mu_{V\left(Z_2(x)\right)} = 0.058x_1 + 0.053x_2^2 + 0.007x_2 \tag{35}$$

The non-linear membership functions are first linearized by Taylor series approximation technique and the linearized forms are appeared as

$$\tau_{V\left(Z_1(x)\right)} = 1 + 0.62\left(x_1 - 3.23\right) + 0.02x_2 \tag{36}$$

$$\tau_{V\left(Z_2(x)\right)} = 1 + 0.06x_1 + 0.46\left(x_2 - 4.27\right) \tag{37}$$

Now the FGP model is constructed, after converting the linear membership function into linear membership goals.

The above FGP model is solved using *software* LINGO (*Ver. 13*) to find the best compromise solution in the decision making context.

The achieved solutions are presented in Table 5.

Table 5. Compromise solutions of the objectives

Objective	Solution Point	Expected Value of Objective	Membership Value
$\tilde{Z}_1$	$x_1 = 2.17$ $x_2 = 3.19$	$V\left(\tilde{Z}_1\right) = 235.43$	$\mu_{V\left(Z_1(x)\right)} = 0.90$
$\tilde{Z}_2$		$V\left(\tilde{Z}_2\right) = 285.52$	$\mu_{V\left(Z_2(x)\right)} = 0.70$

From this table it is clear that the compromise solution of the objectives obtained by the methodology discussed in the second part of the chapter is highly acceptable to the DMs in terms of the high membership value (close to 1) in hybrid uncertain decision making environment.

5.8 CONCLUSION

In this chapter, two fuzzy multi-objective quadratic CCP models are presented and solved in a hierarchical decision making environment for finding most satisfactory solution to all the objectives for overall benefit of the organization. The method described can able to solve fuzzy multi-objective quadratic programming problems with other types of continuous and discrete probability distributions. The developed model can be extended to solve hierarchical decision making problems with bilevel, multilevel and fractional programming problems. Also this developed technique can be used to solve non-linear decision making problems in a fully fuzzified domain. The developed technique can also be used to solve the fuzzy stochastic multi-objective quadratic programming model with parameters taken as FNs other than triangular FNs, viz., trapezoidal FNs, Gaussian FNs, hexagonal FNs, octagonal FNs, intuitionistic FNs, type-II FNs, interval valued FNs, interval type-II FNs, Pythagorean FNs, etc., which are discussed in the introduction section of this book. The methodology explained in this chapter can be applied to different real life problems for obtaining most satisfactory solution in mult-objective decision making environment.

REFERENCES

Abo-Sinha, M. A. (2001). A bi-level non-linear multi-objective decision making under fuzziness. *Operation Research Society of India*, *38*(5), 484–495.

Aggarwal, S., & Sharma, U. (2013). A Computational Procedure For Solving A Non-Convex Multi-Objective Quadratic Programming Under Fuzzy Environment. *International Journal of Pure and Applied Mathematics*, *89*(4), 511–529. doi:10.12732/ijpam.v89i4.6

Ammar, E. E., & Khalifa, H. A. (2003). Fuzzy portfolio optimization a quadratic programming approach. *Chaos, Solitons, and Fractals*, *18*(5), 1045–1054. doi:10.1016/S0960-0779(03)00071-7

Ansary, A. T., & Panda, G. (2018). A sequential quadratically constrained quadratic programming technique for a multi-objective optimization problem. *Engineering Optimization*. doi:10.1080/0305215X.2018.1437154

Bazaraa, M. M., Sherali, H. D., & Shetty, C. M. (1993). *Nonlinear Programming Theory and Algorithms*. New York: John Wiley & Sons.

Biswas, A., & Modak, N. (2011). A fuzzy goal programming method for solving chance constrained programming with fuzzy parameters. *Communications in Computer and Information Science*, *140*, 187–196. doi:10.1007/978-3-642-19263-0_23

Biswas, A., & Modak, N. (2012). Using fuzzy goal programming technique to solve multiobjective chance constrained programming problems in a fuzzy environment. *International Journal of Fuzzy System Applications*, *2*(1), 71–80. doi:10.4018/ijfsa.2012010105

Brito, O., Bennis, F., & Caro, S. (2014). Multiobjective optimization involving quadratic functions. *SIAM Journal on Optimization*, *2014*, 1–11. doi:10.1155/2014/406092

Buckley, J. J. (2003). *New Approach and Applications*. Fuzzy Probabilities. Physica Verlag Heidelberg.

Buckley, J. J., & Eslami, E. (2004a). Uncertain Probabilities – II. *Soft Computing*, *8*(3), 193–199. doi:10.100700500-003-0263-5

Buckley, J. J., & Eslami, E. (2004b). Uncertain Probabilities – III. *Soft Computing*, *8*(3), 200–206. doi:10.100700500-003-0263-5

Charnes, A., & Cooper, W. W. (1959). Chance-constrained programming. *Management Science*, *6*(1), 73–79. doi:10.1287/mnsc.6.1.73

Chen, H. K., & Chou, H. W. (1996). Solving multiobjective linear programming problem, A generic approach. *Fuzzy Sets and Systems*, *82*(1), 35–38. doi:10.1016/0165-0114(95)00277-4

Dantzig, G. B. (1955). Linear programming under uncertainty. *Management Science*, *1*(3-4), 197–206. doi:10.1287/mnsc.1.3-4.197

Emam, O. E., Salama, S. E., & Youssef, A. M. (2015). An Algorithm For Solving Stochastic bi-Level Multi-Objective Large Scale Quadratic Programming Problem. *International Journal of Mathematical Archive*, *6*(1), 144–152.

Fliege, J., & Vaz, A. I. F. (2016). A Method for Constrained Multiobjective Optimization Based on SQP Techniques. *SIAM Journal on Optimization, 26*(4), 2091–2119. doi:10.1137/15M1016424

Gabr, W. I. (2015). Quadratic and nonlinear programming problems solving and analysis in fully fuzzy environment. *Alexandria Engineering Journal, 54*(3), 457–472. doi:10.1016/j.aej.2015.03.020

Gass, S. I., & Roy, P. G. (2003). The compromise hyper sphere for multiobjective linear programming. *European Journal of Operational Research, 144*(3), 459–479. doi:10.1016/S0377-2217(01)00388-5

Geoffrion, A. M. (1967). Stochastic programming with aspiration or fractile criterion. *Management Science, 13*(9), 672–679. doi:10.1287/mnsc.13.9.672

Giannikos, I. (1998). A multiobjective programming model for locating treatment sites and routing hazardous wastes. *European Journal of Operational Research, 104*(2), 333–342. doi:10.1016/S0377-2217(97)00188-4

Hwang, C. L., & Masud, A. S. M. (1979). Multiple objective decision making: Methods and Applications: A state of the art survey. Lecture Notes in Economics and Mathematical Systems, 164. doi:10.1007/978-3-642-45511-7

Ida, M. (2005). Efficient solution generation for multiple objective linear programming based on extreme ray generation method. *European Journal of Operational Research, 160*(1), 242–251. doi:10.1016/j.ejor.2003.08.039

Kataoka, S. (1963). A stochastic programming model. *Econometrica, 31*(1/2), 181–196. doi:10.2307/1910956

Khalifa, H. (2017). On Solutions of Possibilistic Multi- objective Quadratic Programming Problems. *International Journal of Supply and Operations Management, 4*(2), 150–157.

Korhonen, P., & Yu, G. Y. (1997). A reference direction approach to multiple objective quadratic – linear programming. *European Journal of Operational Research, 102*(3), 601–610. doi:10.1016/S0377-2217(96)00245-7

Kratschmer, V. (2001). A Unified Approach to Fuzzy Random Variables. *Fuzzy Sets and Systems, 123*(1), 1–9. doi:10.1016/S0165-0114(00)00038-5

Kwakernaak, H. (1978). Fuzzy Random Variable – I. Definitions and theorems. *Information Sciences, 15*(1), 1–29. doi:10.1016/0020-0255(78)90019-1

Li, X.-Q., Zhang, B., & Li, H. (2006). Computing efficient solutions to fuzzy multiple objective linear programming problems. *Fuzzy Sets and Systems*, *157*(10), 1328–1332. doi:10.1016/j.fss.2005.12.003

Liang, T. F. (2006). Distribution planning decisions using interactive fuzzy multi-objective linear programming. *Fuzzy Sets and Systems*, *157*(10), 1303–1316. doi:10.1016/j.fss.2006.01.014

Liang, T. F. (2008). Interactive multi-objective transportation planning decisions using fuzzy linear programming. *Asia-Pacific Journal of Operational Research*, *25*(01), 11–31. doi:10.1142/S0217595908001602

Liu, B., & Iwamura, I. (1998). Chance Constrained Programming with Fuzzy Parameters. *Fuzzy Sets and Systems*, *94*(2), 227–237. doi:10.1016/S0165-0114(96)00236-9

Luhandjula, M. K. (1983). Linear Programming under randomness and Fuzziness. *Fuzzy Sets and Systems*, *10*(1-3), 45–55. doi:10.1016/S0165-0114(83)80103-1

Luhandjula, M. K. (2003). Mathematical Programming in the Presence of Fuzz Quantities and Random Variables. *Journal of Fuzzy Mathematics*, *11*(1), 27–40.

Narasimhan, R. (1980). On fuzzy goal programming – Some comments. *Decision Sciences*, *11*, 532–538. doi:10.1111/j.1540-5915.1980.tb01142.x

Prekopa, A. (1973). Contribution to the Theory of Stochastic Programming. *Mathematical Programming*, *4*(1), 202–221. doi:10.1007/BF01584661

Romero, C. (1990). *Handbook of Critical Issues in Goal Programming*. Pergamum Press.

Syaripuddin, S., & Fatmawati, H. (2017). Extension of Wolfe Method for Solving Quadratic Programming with Interval Coefficients. *Journal of Applied Mathematics*. . doi:10.1155/2017/9037857

Tabucanon, M. T. (1988). *Multiple criteria decision making in industry*. Elsevier Science Publishing Company, Inc.

Yu, P. L. (1973). A class of solutions for group decision problems. *Management Science*, *19*(8), 936–946. doi:10.1287/mnsc.19.8.936

Zadeh, L. (1968). Probability Measures of Fuzzy Events. *Journal of Mathematical Analysis and Applications*, *23*(2), 421–427. doi:10.1016/0022-247X(68)90078-4

Zadeh, L. A. (1965). Fuzzy sets. *Information and Control*, *8*(3), 338–353. doi:10.1016/S0019-9958(65)90241-X

Zeleny, M. (1982). *Multiple criteria decision making*. McGraw-Hill Book Company.

Zimmermann, H. J. (1978). Fuzzy programming and linear programming with several objective functions. *Fuzzy Sets and Systems*, *1*(1), 45–55. doi:10.1016/0165-0114(78)90031-3

Zimmermann, H. J. (1991). *Fuzzy Set Theory and Its Applications* (2nd ed.). Kluwer Academic Publishers. doi:10.1007/978-94-015-7949-0

Chapter 6
Fully Fuzzified Multi–Objective Stochastic Programming

ABSTRACT

This chapter develops a methodology for solving fully fuzzified multi-objective chance constrained programming (CCP) problems with fuzzy random variables (FRVs) as parameters. In the preceding chapters, it is assumed that the parameters of the multi-objective programming models are uncertain, and these uncertain parameters are expressed through fuzzy numbers (FNs) and FRVs. However, in practical situations, it is also observed that not only the parameters but also the variables of the multi-objective programming problems are uncertain. From that view point, the methodology for solving fully fuzzified multi-objective stochastic programming problems are presented in this chapter. At first the fuzzy probabilistic constraints are modified into fuzzy constraints. Using the defuzzification method of FNs, the different fuzzy parameters and fuzzy variables in the constraints are converted into crisp equivalent parameters and crisp variables. In this chapter, the parameters of the objectives are considered as either symmetric trapezoidal FNs or FRVs whose mean and variances are taken as symmetric trapezoidal FNs. If the parameters of the objectives are FRVs, then expectation model and variance model of the objective is used to find an equivalent form of the objectives whose parameters are only FNs. The ranking function of FNs is then applied to the objectives to convert them into crisp objectives. Then each objective is solved independently under the modified system constraints to construct the membership goals of each objective. Finally, weighted fuzzy goal programming (FGP) model is applied to achieve the most satisfactory solution for the overall benefit of the organization. Two illustrative numerical examples are given to demonstrate the efficiency of the proposed methodology and to compare the solution obtained by the developed methodology with the pre-defined techniques.

DOI: 10.4018/978-1-5225-8301-1.ch006

6.1 MULTI-OBJECTIVE FULLY FUZZIFIED STOCHASTIC PROGRAMMING

The classical multi-objective programming is used to find an optimal solution in many real life decision making problems, especially, in engineering and management. However, in a real world environment the value of many parameters are not precisely known. Usually the values of these parameters are estimated by experts and it cannot be assumed that the knowledge of experts is precise enough. Bellman and Zadeh (1970) proposed the concept of decision making in fuzzy environments. Tanaka et al. (1973) adopted these concepts to solve mathematical programming problems. Zimmermann (1978) first proposed the formulation of fuzzy linear programming problem (FLPP). Delgado et al. (1989) proposed a general model for the FLPPs in which constraints are fuzzy inequality and the parameters of the constraints are FNs but the parameters of the objective functions are crisp. Afterwards, a plenty number of researchers exhibited their interests to solve the FLPPs (Hop, 1991; Liu, 2001; Chiang, 2001). The FLPP can also be solved by multi-objective optimization method (Zhang et al., 2003), penalty method (Jamison and Lodwick, 2001), semi-infinite programming method (Leon and Vercher, 2004). Ganesan and veeramani (2006) proposed a method for solving FLPPs without converting them to crisp linear programming problems (LPP). In recent years, several kinds of fully fuzzified LPPs (FFLPPs) are appeared in the literature. The FLPP in which all the parameters as well as variables are FNs is known as FFLPP. Buckley and Feuring (2000) introduced a method to find the solution for FFLPP by changing the objective function into the multi-objective FLPPs (MOFLPPs). Dehghan et al. (2006) used a computational method to find the exact solution of an FFLPP. Allahviranloo et al. (2008) proposed a method for solving FFLPP by using a kind of defuzzification method. Kaur and Kumar (2011) proposed a new method for solving FFLPP in which some or all the parameters are represented by unrestricted L-R FNs. Hosseinzadeh and Edalatpanah (2016) proposed a methodology for solving FFLPP by using the lexicography method. Das et al. (2017) developed a mathematical model for solving FFLPP with trapezoidal FNs. Recently, Sharma and Agarwal (2018) developed methodology for solving MOFLPP using nearest interval approximation of FNs and interval programming.

Also, as described in preceding chapters, the decision makers (DMs) often face another type of uncertainty known as probabilistic uncertainty.

CCP methodology is one the most useful techniques for dealing with such type of probabilistic uncertainties. The CCP model was first proposed by Charnes and Cooper (1962, 1963). Further the concept of CCP technique was extended by several researchers (Kataoka, 1963; Geoffrion, 1967) for solving different type of problems. With this improvement in computational resources and scientific computing techniques many complex optimization models can now be solved proficiently.

In fuzzy CCP (FCCP), probabilistic and fuzzy aspects are combined together to derive an efficient model to describe real-life planning problems where uncertainty and imprecision of information co-occur. From the view point of different real life applications associated with fuzzy chance constrained optimization problems, development of different innovative techniques has attracted more attention to the researcher (Iskander, 2006; Liu, 2001). In the recent years Biswas and De (2015) developed a method for solving fully fuzzified CCP problems (FFCCPP) with exponentially distributed FRVs. In that paper the fuzzy parameters are converted into crisp nature by the defuzzification techniques or ranking techniques. Generally, ranking functions are used in the context of finding expected value of an FN. Thus selection of ranking functions for finding the expected value of FNs is an important issue in the decision making process under fuzzy environment. The ranking of FNs was first proposed by Jain (1976). Later on Yager (1981) proposed four indices which may be employed for the purpose of ordering fuzzy quantities in $[0,1]$. In 1998 Cheng (1998) developed a method for ranking FNs using distance method. For ranking generalized trapezoidal FNs Chen and Chen (2007) proposed a method in the context of fuzzy risk analysis. Kumar et al. (2011) proposed a technique for ranking L-R type FNs.

Goal programming (GP) was originally introduced by Charnes and Cooper (1977) for solving multi-objective linear programming models. This approach allows the simultaneous solution of a system of complex objectives. The solution of the problem requires the establishment among these multiple objectives. The principal concept for linear GP is to assign specific numeric goal for each objective. The objective function is then formulated and a solution is sought which minimizes the weighted sum of deviations from their respective goal. GP problems can be categorized according to the importance of each objective. In non-preemptive GP all the goals are of equal importance. Preemptive GP has a hierarchy of priority levels for the goals, in which goal of greater importance receive greater attention in general GP models consist of three components: an objective function, a set of goal constraints, and non-negativity requirements. However, the target value associated with each goal could be fuzzy in many real-world applications. Under this context FGP technique (Hannan, 1980; Narasimhan, 1980) is used as a competent tool for making decision in an imprecisely defined probabilistic multi-objective decision making arena. FGP technique for solving CCP problems involving FRVs have been presented by Biswas and Modak (2011, 2012). To the best of authors' knowledge an efficient solution technique for solving multi-objective fully fuzzified CCP (MOFFCCP) following normal distribution from the view point of its potential use in different planning problems involving fuzzy parameters is yet to appear in the literature.

In this chapter an MOFFCCPP with FRVs as parameters are developed. In the model formulation process the coefficients of the objectives are considered as either symmetric trapezoidal FNs or FRVs. The left side parameters of the system constraints are taken as symmetric trapezoidal FNs. The variables are also considered as fuzzy variables. The expectation model and variance model is applied to the objectives to convert the fuzzy stochastic objectives into fuzzy objectives. Using the concept of ranking function of FNs, the problem is transferred into an equivalent deterministic model. The individual optimal value of each objective is found in isolation to find their best and worst solutions. On the basis of the best and worst solutions the membership functions of the objectives are constructed. Finally, FGP approach is used for achieving the best compromise solution to the extent possible in the decision making context.

6.1.1. Fully Fuzzified Chance Constrained Programming Model

In this chapter fully fuzzified stochastic programming models are expressed in two forms. In the first model multiple objectives are considered as linear functions in which the parameters and variables are considered as symmetric trapezoidal FNs and trapezoidal fuzzy variables, respectively. Also the parameters of the chance constraints are FRVs following some continuous probability distribution. In the second model the coefficients of the objectives are treated as FRVs whose mean and variances are symmetric trapezoidal FNs. Thus a MOFFCCPP with normally distributed FRVs is presented in the following two forms as

6.1.1.1 Form (I)

Find $\tilde{X}\left(\tilde{x}_1,\ \tilde{x}_2,\ ...,\ \tilde{x}_n\right)$ so as to

Maximize $\tilde{Z}_k \cong \sum\limits_{j=1}^{n} \tilde{c}_{kj}\tilde{x}_j ; k = 1, 2, ..., K$

subject to

$$Pr\left(\sum_{j=1}^{n}\tilde{a}_{ij}\tilde{x}_j \lesssim \tilde{b}_i\right) \geq 1 - \gamma_i ; i = 1, 2, ..., m$$

$$\tilde{x}_j \gtrsim \tilde{0}; j = 1, 2, ..., n \tag{1}$$

where $\tilde{b}_i, \left(i = 1, 2, ..., m\right)$ represents FRV following some probability distributions,

$$\tilde{c}_{kj} = \left(c_{kj}^1, c_{kj}^2, \beta_{kj}, \beta_{kj}\right), \tilde{a}_{ij} = \left(a_{ij}^1, a_{ij}^2, d_{ij}, d_{ij}\right), \tilde{x}_j$$
$$= \left(x_j^1, x_j^2, \delta_j, \delta_j\right)\left(k = 1, 2, ..., K \ ; j = 1, 2, ..., n \ ; i = 1, 2, ..., m\right)$$

are symmetric trapezoidal FNs and trapezoidal fuzzy variables, respectively, and γ_i denotes any real number lies in $\left[0,1\right]$. Here $\cong, \gtrsim, \lesssim$ denotes equality, greater than or equal and less than or equal in fuzzy sense.

6.1.1.2 Form (II)

Find $\tilde{X}\left(\tilde{x}_1,\ \tilde{x}_2,\ ...,\ \tilde{x}_n\right)$ so as to

Maximize $\tilde{Z}_k \cong \sum\limits_{j=1}^{n} \tilde{c}_{kj}\tilde{x}_j ; k = 1, 2, ..., K$

subject to

$$Pr\left(\sum_{j=1}^{n}\tilde{a}_{ij}\tilde{x}_{j}\lesssim\tilde{b}_{i}\right)\geq 1-\gamma_{i}; i=1,2,\ldots,m$$

$$\tilde{x}_{j}\gtrsim\tilde{0}; j=1,2,\ldots,n \tag{2}$$

where

$$\tilde{c}_{kj},\left(k=1,2,\ldots,K; j=1,2,\ldots,n\right),\tilde{b}_{i},\left(i=1,2,\ldots,m\right)$$

represents FRV,

$$\tilde{a}_{ij}=\left(a_{ij}^{1},a_{ij}^{2},d_{ij},d_{ij}\right),\ \tilde{x}_{j}=\left(x_{j}^{1},x_{j}^{2},\delta_{j},\delta_{j}\right)\left(j=1,2,\ldots,n\ ;i=1,2,\ldots,m\right)$$

are symmetric trapezoidal FNs and trapezoidal fuzzy variables, respectively, and γ_{i} denotes any real number lies in $\left[0,1\right]$. The mean and variance of the FRV $\tilde{c}_{kj}$ is

$$E\left(\tilde{c}_{kj}\right)=\tilde{m}_{\tilde{c}_{kj}}=\left(m_{c_{kj}^{1}},m_{c_{kj}^{2}},\ \alpha_{kj},\alpha_{kj}\right)$$

and

$$Var\left(\tilde{c}_{kj}\right)=\tilde{\sigma}_{\tilde{c}_{kj}}^{2}=\left(\sigma_{c_{kj}^{1}}^{2},\sigma_{c_{kj}^{2}}^{2},\ \theta_{kj},\theta_{kj}\right).\left(k=1,2,\ldots,K; j=1,2,\ldots,n\right)$$

The solution methodology for the model (1) and model (2) are described successively in the next section.

6.2 CONSTRUCTION OF FUZZY PROGRAMMING MODEL HAVING FUZZY PARAMETERS

The conversion of MOFFCCPP into a multi-objective FFLP model is presented in this section. It is already mentioned that CCP is a technique used to remove the probabilistic nature from the constraints. In this section it is assumed that

FRVs follow normal distribution. As $\tilde{b}_i$ is normally distributed FRV, its probability density function is expressed as

$$f\left(b_i \; ; \tilde{m}_i, \tilde{\sigma}_i\right) = \frac{1}{\sqrt{2\pi t}} e^{-\frac{(b_i - s)^2}{2t^2}},$$

where the support of $\tilde{b}_i$ is defined on the set of real numbers, $s \in \tilde{m}_i [\alpha]$ and $t \in \tilde{\sigma}_i [\alpha]$; $\tilde{m}_i [\alpha]$ and $\tilde{\sigma}_i [\alpha]$ are the α-cut of the FN $\tilde{m}_i$ and $\tilde{\sigma}_i$, respectively. The mean and variance of the FRV $\tilde{b}_i$ are given by $E\left(\tilde{b}_i\right) = \tilde{m}_{\tilde{b}_i}$ and $Var\left(\tilde{b}_i\right) = \tilde{\sigma}_{\tilde{b}_i}^2$. The mean $E\left(\tilde{b}_i\right)$ and variance $Var\left(\tilde{b}_i\right)$ are also considered as symmetric trapezoidal FNs which are expressed as

$$E\left(\tilde{b}_i\right) = \left(m_i^1, m_i^2, \mu_i, \mu_i\right)$$

and

$$Var\left(\tilde{b}_i\right) = \left(v_i^1, v_i^2, \tau_i, \tau_i\right)\left(i = 1, 2, \ldots, m\right).$$

Then the standard deviation of $\tilde{b}_i$ is given by

$$\sigma_{\tilde{b}_i} = \left(\sqrt{v_i^1 - \tau_i}, \sqrt{v_i^1}, \sqrt{v_i^2}, \sqrt{v_i^2 + \tau_i}\right).$$

Applying CCP technique, the constraints in the multi-objective FFLP problem (1) is transformed into the following form as

$$Pr\left(\sum_{j=1}^{n} \tilde{a}_{ij} \tilde{x}_j \lesssim \tilde{b}_i\right) \geq 1 - \gamma_i \text{ or, } Pr\left(\tilde{A}_i \lesssim \tilde{b}_i\right) \geq 1 - \gamma_i$$

(where $\tilde{A}_i = \sum_{j=1}^{n} \tilde{a}_{ij} \tilde{x}_j ; i = 1, 2, \ldots, m$)

i.e. $Pr\left(\tilde{b}_i \lesssim \tilde{A}_i\right) \leq \gamma_i$

i.e. $\Pr\left(\dfrac{\tilde{b}_i - E\left(\tilde{b}_i\right)}{\sqrt{Var\left(\tilde{b}_i\right)}} \lesssim \dfrac{\tilde{A}_i - E\left(\tilde{b}_i\right)}{\sqrt{Var\left(\tilde{b}_i\right)}}\right) \leq \gamma_i$

i.e. $\Phi\left(\dfrac{\tilde{A}_i - E\left(\tilde{b}_i\right)}{\sqrt{Var\left(\tilde{b}_i\right)}}\right) \leq \gamma_i$

i.e. $\tilde{A}_i \leq E\left(\tilde{b}_i\right) + \sqrt{Var\left(\tilde{b}_i\right)}\Phi^{-1}\left(\gamma_i\right)$

i.e. $\displaystyle\sum_{j=1}^{n} \tilde{a}_{ij}\tilde{x}_j \leq E\left(\tilde{b}_i\right) + \sqrt{Var\left(\tilde{b}_i\right)}\Phi^{-1}\left(\gamma_i\right)$ (3)

Hence the multi-objective FFLP model (1) in fuzzy environment is written as

Maximize $\tilde{Z}_k \cong \displaystyle\sum_{j=1}^{n} \tilde{c}_{kj}\tilde{x}_j ; k = 1, 2, \ldots, K$

subject to

$\displaystyle\sum_{j=1}^{n} \tilde{a}_{ij}\tilde{x}_j \leq E\left(\tilde{b}_i\right) + \sqrt{Var\left(\tilde{b}_i\right)}\Phi^{-1}\left(\gamma_i\right) ; i = 1, 2, \ldots, m$

$\tilde{x}_j \gtrsim \tilde{0} ; j = 1, 2, \ldots, n$ (4)

Here the function $\Phi(\cdot)$ represents the cumulative distribution function of the standard normal fuzzy random variate.

6.2.1. Use of Ranking Function to Develop Deterministic Model

In this subsection the ranking function is used to convert the FP model into a deterministic form. Different defuzzification techniques of FNs were exists in the literature which helps to find the crisp value of FNs. Using the linearity property of ranking function, the above model (4) is written as

$$\text{Maximize } R(\tilde{Z}_k) = \sum_{j=1}^{n} R\left(\tilde{c}_{kj}\right) R\left(\tilde{x}_j\right); k = 1, 2, \ldots, K$$

subject to

$$\sum_{j=1}^{n} R\left(\tilde{a}_{ij}\right) R\left(\tilde{x}_j\right) \leq R\left(E\left(\tilde{b}_i\right)\right) + R\left(\sqrt{Var\left(\tilde{b}_i\right)}\right) \Phi^{-1}\left(\gamma_i\right); i = 1, 2, \ldots, m$$

$$R\left(\tilde{x}_j\right) \geq 0; j = 1, 2, \ldots, n.$$

Considering the FNs and fuzzy variables as trapezoidal type, the problem is expressed as

$$\text{Maximize } R(\tilde{Z}_k) = \sum_{j=1}^{n} R\left(\left(c_{kj}^1, c_{kj}^2, \beta_{kj}, \beta_{kj}\right)\right) R\left(\left(x_j^1, x_j^2, \delta_j, \delta_j\right)\right); k = 1, 2, \ldots, K$$

subject to

$$\sum_{j=1}^{n} R\left(\left(a_{ij}^1, a_{ij}^2, d_{ij}, d_{ij}\right)\right) R\left(\left(x_j^1, x_j^2, \delta_j, \delta_j\right)\right) \leq R\left(\left(m_i^1, m_i^2, \mu_i, \mu_i\right)\right) + R\left(\sqrt{\left(v_i^1, v_i^2, \tau_i, \tau_i\right)}\right) \Phi^{-1}\left(\gamma_i\right)$$
$$; i = 1, 2, \ldots, m$$

$$R\left(\left(x_j^1, x_j^2, \delta_j, \delta_j\right)\right) \geq 0; j = 1, 2, \ldots, n \tag{5}$$

Alternatively, the model can be written as

Maximize

$$R(\tilde{Z}_k) = \sum_{j=1}^{n} R\left(\left(c_{kj}^1 - \beta_{kj}, c_{kj}^1, c_{kj}^2, c_{kj}^2 + \beta_{kj}\right)\right) R\left(\left(x_j^1 - \delta_j, x_j^1, x_j^2, x_j^2 + \delta_j\right)\right); k = 1, 2, \ldots, K$$

subject to

$$\sum_{j=1}^{n} R\left(\left(a_{ij}^1 - d_{ij}, a_{ij}^1, a_{ij}^2, a_{ij}^2 + d_{ij}\right)\right) R\left(\left(x_j^1 - \delta_j, x_j^1, x_j^2, x_j^2 + \delta_j\right)\right) \leq$$

$$R\left(\left(m_i^1 - \mu_i, m_i^1, m_i^2, m_i^2 + \mu_i\right)\right) + R\left(\sqrt{v_i^1 - \tau_i}, v_i^1, v_i^2, v_i^2 + \tau_i\right) \Phi^{-1}\left(\gamma_i\right)$$

$$; i = 1, 2, \ldots, m$$

$$R\left(\left(x_j^1 - \delta_j, x_j^1, x_j^2, x_j^2 + \delta_j\right)\right) \geq 0; j = 1, 2, \ldots, n. \tag{6}$$

Applying the square root of symmetric trapezoidal FNs, the model (6) is modified to

Maximize

$$R(\tilde{Z}_k) = \sum_{j=1}^{n} R\left(\left(c_{kj}^1 - \beta_{kj}, c_{kj}^1, c_{kj}^2, c_{kj}^2 + \beta_{kj}\right)\right) R\left(\left(x_j^1 - \delta_j, x_j^1, x_j^2, x_j^2 + \delta_j\right)\right); k = 1, 2, \ldots, K$$

subject to

$$\sum_{j=1}^{n} R\left(\left(a_{ij}^1 - d_{ij}, a_{ij}^1, a_{ij}^2, a_{ij}^2 + d_{ij}\right)\right) R\left(\left(x_j^1 - \delta_j, x_j^1, x_j^2, x_j^2 + \delta_j\right)\right) \leq$$

$$R\left(\left(m_i^1 - \mu_i, m_i^1, m_i^2, m_i^2 + \mu_i\right)\right) + R\left(\sqrt{v_i^1 - \tau_i}, \sqrt{v_i^1}, \sqrt{v_i^2}, \sqrt{v_i^2 + \tau_i}\right) \Phi^{-1}\left(\gamma_i\right)$$

$$; i = 1, 2, \ldots, m$$

$$R\left(\left(x_j^1 - \delta_j, x_j^1, x_j^2, x_j^2 + \delta_j\right)\right) \geq 0; j = 1, 2, \ldots, n \tag{7}$$

Using the definition of ranking function of trapezoidal FNs, the above model (7) is rewritten as

Maximize

$$R\left(\tilde{Z}_k\right) = \sum_{j=1}^{n}\left\{(a\,/\,2)\left(2c_{kj}^1 - \beta_{kj}\right) + \left((1-a)\,/\,2\right)\left(2c_{kj}^2 + \beta_{kj}\right)\right\}\begin{bmatrix}(a\,/\,2)\left(2x_j^1 - \delta_j\right) \\ +\left((1-a)\,/\,2\right)\left(2x_j^2 + \delta_j\right)\end{bmatrix}$$

$$k = 1, 2, ..., K$$

subject to

$$\sum_{j=1}^{n}\left\{(a\,/\,2)\left(2a_{ij}^1 - d_{ij}\right) + \left((1-a)\,/\,2\right)\left(2a_{ij}^2 + d_{ij}\right)\right\}$$

$$\left\{(a\,/\,2)\left(2x_j^1 - \delta_j\right) + \left((1-a)\,/\,2\right)\left(2x_j^2 + \delta_j\right)\right\} \le \left\{(a\,/\,2)\left(2m_i^1 - \mu_i\right) + \left((1-a)\,/\,2\right)\left(2m_i^2 + \mu_i\right)\right\} +$$

$$\left\{(a\,/\,2)\left(\sqrt{v_i^1 - \tau_i} + \sqrt{v_i^1}\right) + \left((1-a)\,/\,2\right)\left(\sqrt{v_i^2} + \sqrt{v_i^2 + \tau_i}\right)\right\}\Phi^{-1}\left(\gamma_i\right)$$

$$; i = 1, 2, ..., m$$

$$\left\{(a\,/\,2)\left(2x_j^1 - \delta_j\right) + \left((1-a)\,/\,2\right)\left(2x_j^2 + \delta_j\right)\right\} \ge 0\, j = 1, 2, ..., n$$

$$x_j^1 \le x_j^2$$

$$0 \le a \le 1 \qquad\qquad\qquad\qquad\qquad\qquad\qquad\qquad (8)$$

where $R(\tilde{Z}_k)$ denotes the defuzzified value of the k − th objective $\tilde{Z}_k$.

6.2.2. Weighted Fuzzy Goal Programming Model

Let

$$\left[\tilde{x}_k^b; R\left(\tilde{Z}_k\right)^b\right] = \left[\left(\tilde{x}_{k1}^b, \tilde{x}_{k2}^b, ..., \tilde{x}_{kn}^b\right); R\left(\tilde{Z}_k\right)^b\right] (k = 1, 2, ..., K)$$

be the best values of the k − th objective obtained by solving each objective independently under the derived set of system constraints. The worst values, $R\left(\tilde{Z}_k\right)^w$ ($k = 1, 2, ..., K$), of the k − th objective is calculated as

$$R\left(\tilde{Z}_k\right)^w = \min\left\{R\left(\tilde{Z}_k\right)\Big|_{\left(\tilde{x}_{l1}^b, \tilde{x}_{l2}^b, \ldots, \tilde{x}_{ln}^b\right)}; l = 1, 2, \ldots, k : l \neq k\right\}$$

Hence the fuzzy goal for each objective is expressed as

$$R\left(\tilde{Z}_k\right) \gtrsim R\left(\tilde{Z}_k\right)^b; k = 1, 2, \ldots, K \tag{9}$$

Thus the membership function for each of the objectives can be written as

$$\mu_{R\left(\tilde{Z}_k\right)} = \begin{cases} 0 & \text{if} & R\left(\tilde{Z}_k\right) \leq R\left(\tilde{Z}_k\right)^w \\ \dfrac{\left[R\left(\tilde{Z}_k\right) - R\left(\tilde{Z}_k\right)^w\right]}{\left[R\left(\tilde{Z}_k\right)^b - R\left(\tilde{Z}_k\right)^w\right]} & \text{if} & R\left(\tilde{Z}_k\right)^w \leq R\left(\tilde{Z}_k\right) \leq R\left(\tilde{Z}_k\right)^b \\ 1 & \text{if} & R\left(\tilde{Z}_k\right) \geq R\left(\tilde{Z}_k\right)^b \end{cases} \tag{10}$$

In weighted FGP model formulation process, the membership functions are first converted into flexible membership goals by introducing under- and over- deviational variables to each of them and thereby assigning the highest membership value (unity) as the aspiration level to each of them. Also it is evident that full achievement of all the membership goals is not possible in a multi-objective decision making context. So the under-deviational variables are minimized to achieve the goal values of objectives in the decision making environment.

Thus a weighted FGP model is formulated as

Find $\tilde{X}\left(\tilde{x}_1, \tilde{x}_2, \ldots, \tilde{x}_n\right)$ so as to

Minimize $D = \sum_{k=1}^{K} w_k d_k^-$

subject to

$$\mu_{R\left(\tilde{Z}_k\right)} + d_k^- - d_k^+ = 1; k = 1, 2, \ldots, K$$

$$\sum_{j=1}^{n}\left\{(a/2)\left(2a_{ij}^{1}-d_{ij}\right)+\left((1-a)/2\right)\left(2a_{ij}^{2}+d_{ij}\right)\right\}$$

$$\left\{(a/2)\left(2x_{j}^{1}-\delta_{j}\right)+\left((1-a)/2\right)\left(2x_{j}^{2}+\delta_{j}\right)\right\}\leq\left\{(a/2)\left(2m_{i}^{1}-\mu_{i}\right)+\left((1-a)/2\right)\left(2m_{i}^{2}+\mu_{i}\right)\right\}+$$

$$\left\{(a/2)\left(\sqrt{v_{i}^{1}-\tau_{i}}+\sqrt{v_{i}^{1}}\right)+\left((1-a)/2\right)\left(\sqrt{v_{i}^{2}}+\sqrt{v_{i}^{2}+\tau_{i}}\right)\right\}\Phi^{-1}\left(\gamma_{i}\right)$$

$$;i=1,2,...,m$$

$$\left\{(a/2)\left(2x_{j}^{1}-\delta_{j}\right)+\left((1-a)/2\right)\left(2x_{j}^{2}+\delta_{j}\right)\right\}\geq 0; j=1,2,...,n$$

$$x_{j}^{1}\leq x_{j}^{2}$$

$$0\leq a\leq 1,\tag{11}$$

where $w_{k}\geq 0$ represents the numerical weights of the goals which are determined as:

$$w_{k}=\frac{p}{\left[R\left(\tilde{Z}_{k}\right)^{b}-R\left(\tilde{Z}_{k}\right)^{w}\right]}.\ k=1,2,...,K; p>0\tag{12}$$

The developed model (11) is solved to find the most satisfactory solution in the decision making context.

6.2.3. Solution Algorithm

In general the solution algorithm of the MOFFCCPP from the view point of maximizing the objective is presented as follows:

Step 1: Using CCP technique, the probabilistic constraints are converted into constraints involving fuzzy values.
Step 2: Ranking technique of symmetrical trapezoidal FNs using $\alpha-$ cut is then employed to both the objectives and constraints to find the multi-objective linear programming model in deterministic form.
Step 3: The individual optimal value of each objective is found in isolation to find their best and worst solutions.
Step 4: Construct the fuzzy membership goals corresponding to each objectives.

Step 5: The membership functions are developed on the basis of their best and worst values.

Step 6: Finally, FGP approach is applied to achieve maximum degree of each of the membership goals.

Step 7: Stop.

6.3. FORMULATION OF FUZZY PROGRAMMING MODEL HAVING PARAMETER AS FRVS

In this case the parameters of the objectives are treated as FRVs following normal distribution. Thus in this situation the model takes the form

Find $\tilde{X}\left(\tilde{x}_1, \tilde{x}_2, \ldots, \tilde{x}_n\right)$ so as to

Maximize $\tilde{Z}_k \cong \sum_{j=1}^{n} \tilde{c}_{kj} \tilde{x}_j; k = 1, 2, \ldots, K$

subject to

$$Pr\left(\sum_{j=1}^{n} \tilde{a}_{ij} \tilde{x}_j \lesssim \tilde{b}_i\right) \geq 1 - \gamma_i; i = 1, 2, \ldots, m$$

$$\tilde{x}_j \gtrsim \tilde{0}; j = 1, 2, \ldots, n \tag{13}$$

where

$$\tilde{c}_{kj}\left(k = 1, 2, \ldots, K; j = 1, 2, \ldots, n\right), \tilde{b}_i\left(i = 1, 2, \ldots, m\right)$$

represent normally distributed FRVs.

The expectation model and the variance model of the objectives are used to convert the objectives into fuzzy objectives.

6.3.1. Conversion of Fuzzy Stochastic Objectives into Fuzzy Objectives Through Expectation Model

Taking the expectation value of all the FRVs associated with the objectives, the model (13) is modified as

$$\text{Maximize } E(\tilde{Z}_k) \cong \sum_{j=1}^{n} E\left(\tilde{c}_{kj}\right) \tilde{x}_j; k = 1, 2, \ldots, K$$

i.e., Maximize $E(\tilde{Z}_k) \cong \sum_{j=1}^{n} \tilde{m}_{\tilde{c}_{kj}} \tilde{x}_j; k = 1, 2, \ldots, K$

$$\text{i.e., Maximize } E(\tilde{Z}_k) \cong \sum_{j=1}^{n} \left(m_{c_{kj}^1}, m_{c_{kj}^2}, \alpha_{kj}, \alpha_{kj} \right) \tilde{x}_j; k = 1, 2, \ldots, K \tag{14}$$

Here $E(\tilde{Z}_k)$ denotes the expectation of the $k-$th objective $\tilde{Z}_k$.

6.3.2. Chance Constrained Programming Model

By applying the CCP technique to the fuzzy probabilistic constraints, the fuzzy probabilistic constraints are transformed into fuzzy constraints as described in section 6.2 as

$$\sum_{j=1}^{n} \tilde{a}_{ij} \tilde{x}_j \lesssim E\left(\tilde{b}_i\right) + \sqrt{Var\left(\tilde{b}_i\right)} \Phi^{-1}\left(\gamma_i\right)$$

Thus the expectation model of the model (13) is developed as
Find $\tilde{X}\left(\tilde{x}_1, \tilde{x}_2, \ldots, \tilde{x}_n\right)$ so as to

$$\text{Maximize } E(\tilde{Z}_k) \cong \sum_{j=1}^{n} \left(m_{c_{kj}^1}, m_{c_{kj}^2}, \alpha_{kj}, \alpha_{kj} \right) \tilde{x}_j; k = 1, 2, \ldots, K$$

subject to

$$\sum_{j=1}^{n} \tilde{a}_{ij} \tilde{x}_{j} \lesssim E\left(\tilde{b}_{i}\right) + \sqrt{Var\left(\tilde{b}_{i}\right)} \Phi^{-1}\left(\gamma_{i}\right)$$

$$\tilde{x}_{j} \gtrsim \tilde{0}; j = 1, 2, ..., n \,. \tag{15}$$

6.3.3. Conversion to Deterministic Model

As described in subsection 6.2.1, ranking function of FNs is applied to all the FNs in both the objectives and constraints to find the equivalent deterministic model of the fuzzy stochastic problem. Thus the model becomes

Find $\tilde{X}\left(\tilde{x}_{1},\ \tilde{x}_{2},\ ...,\ \tilde{x}_{n}\right)$ so as to

$$\text{Maximize}\ R(E(\tilde{Z}_{k})) = \sum_{j=1}^{n} R\left(m_{c_{kj}^{1}}, m_{c_{kj}^{2}},\ \alpha_{kj}, \alpha_{kj}\right) R(\tilde{x}_{j})\ ; k = 1, 2, ..., K$$

subject to

$$\sum_{j=1}^{n} R\left(\tilde{a}_{ij}\right) R\left(\tilde{x}_{j}\right) \leq R\left(E\left(\tilde{b}_{i}\right)\right) + R\left(\sqrt{Var\left(\tilde{b}_{i}\right)}\right) \Phi^{-1}\left(\gamma_{i}\right); i = 1, 2, ..., m$$

$$R\left(\tilde{x}_{j}\right) \geq 0; j = 1, 2, ..., n \tag{16}$$

Or,

Find $\tilde{X}\left(\tilde{x}_{1}, \tilde{x}_{2}, ..., \tilde{x}_{n}\right)$ so as to

Maximize

$$R\left(E(\tilde{Z}_{k})\right) = \sum_{j=1}^{n} \left[\begin{matrix} \left(a\ /\ 2\right)\left(2m_{c_{kj}^{1}} - \alpha_{kj}\right) \\ +\left(\left(1-a\right)\ /\ 2\right)\left(2m_{c_{kj}^{2}} + \alpha_{kj}\right) \end{matrix} \right] \left[\begin{matrix} \left(a\ /\ 2\right)\left(2x_{j}^{1} - \delta_{j}\right) \\ +\left(\left(1-a\right)\ /\ 2\right)\left(2x_{j}^{2} + \delta_{j}\right) \end{matrix} \right]$$

$; k = 1, 2, ..., K$

subject to

$$\sum_{j=1}^{n}\left\{ \left(a\,/\,2 \right)\left(2a_{ij}^{1} - d_{ij} \right) + \left(\left(1 - a \right)/\,2 \right)\left(2a_{ij}^{2} + d_{ij} \right) \right\}$$

$$\left\{ \left(a\,/\,2 \right)\left(2x_{j}^{1} - \delta_{j} \right) + \left(\left(1 - a \right)/\,2 \right)\left(2x_{j}^{2} + \delta_{j} \right) \right\} \le \left\{ \left(a\,/\,2 \right)\left(2m_{i}^{1} - \mu_{i} \right) + \left(\left(1 - a \right)/\,2 \right)\left(2m_{i}^{2} + \mu_{i} \right) \right\} +$$

$$\left\{ \left(a\,/\,2 \right)\left(\sqrt{v_{i}^{1}} - \tau_{i} + \sqrt{v_{i}^{1}} \right) + \left(\left(1 - a \right)/\,2 \right)\left(\sqrt{v_{i}^{2}} + \sqrt{v_{i}^{2} + \tau_{i}} \right) \right\} \Phi^{-1}\left(\gamma_{i} \right)$$

$$;i = 1, 2, \ldots, m$$

$$\left\{ \left(a\,/\,2 \right)\left(2x_{j}^{1} - \delta_{j} \right) + \left(\left(1 - a \right)/\,2 \right)\left(2x_{j}^{2} + \delta_{j} \right) \right\} \ge 0 \, j = 1, 2, \ldots, n$$

$$x_{j}^{1} \le x_{j}^{2}$$

$$0 \le a \le 1. \tag{17}$$

Now each modified objective is solved under the set of modified system constraints (as described in the section 6.2.2.) to find their best and worst solutions. The membership functions on the basis of their best and worst solutions are formed as developed in the subsection 6.2.2. as

$$\mu_{R\left(E\left(\tilde{Z}_{k} \right) \right)} = \begin{cases} 0 & \text{if} & R\left(E\left(\tilde{Z}_{k} \right) \right) \le R\left(E\left(\tilde{Z}_{k} \right) \right)^{w} \\ \dfrac{\left[R\left(E\left(\tilde{Z}_{k} \right) \right) - R\left(E\left(\tilde{Z}_{k} \right) \right)^{w} \right]}{\left[R\left(E\left(\tilde{Z}_{k} \right) \right)^{b} - R\left(E\left(\tilde{Z}_{k} \right) \right)^{w} \right]} & \text{if} & R\left(E\left(\tilde{Z}_{k} \right) \right)^{w} \le R\left(E\left(\tilde{Z}_{k} \right) \right) \le R\left(E\left(\tilde{Z}_{k} \right) \right)^{b} \\ 1 & \text{if} & R\left(E\left(\tilde{Z}_{k} \right) \right) \ge R\left(E\left(\tilde{Z}_{k} \right) \right)^{b} \end{cases} \tag{18}$$

Now on the basis of these membership functions the FGP model is formed to find the most compromise solutions of all the objectives as seen in subsection 6.2.2.

Find $\tilde{X}\left(\tilde{x}_{1}, \tilde{x}_{2}, \ldots, \tilde{x}_{n} \right)$ so as to

Minimize $D = \sum_{k=1}^{K} w_{k} d_{k}^{-}$

subject to

$$\frac{\left[R\left(E\left(\tilde{Z}_k\right)\right) - R\left(E\left(\tilde{Z}_k\right)\right)^w\right]}{\left[R\left(E\left(\tilde{Z}_k\right)\right)^b - R\left(E\left(\tilde{Z}_k\right)\right)^w\right]} + d_k^- - d_k^+ = 1 \; ; \; k = 1, 2, \ldots, K$$

$$\sum_{j=1}^{n} \left\{ (a/2)\left(2a_{ij}^1 - d_{ij}\right) + \left((1-a)/2\right)\left(2a_{ij}^2 + d_{ij}\right) \right\}$$

$$\left\{ (a/2)\left(2x_j^1 - \delta_j\right) + \left((1-a)/2\right)\left(2x_j^2 + \delta_j\right) \right\} \le \left\{ (a/2)\left(2m_i^1 - \mu_i\right) + \left((1-a)/2\right)\left(2m_i^2 + \mu_i\right) \right\} +$$

$$\left\{ (a/2)\left(\sqrt{v_i^1 - \tau_i} + \sqrt{v_i^1}\right) + \left((1-a)/2\right)\left(\sqrt{v_i^2} + \sqrt{v_i^2 + \tau_i}\right) \right\} \Phi^{-1}\left(\gamma_i\right)$$

$$; i = 1, 2, \ldots, m$$

$$\left\{ (a/2)\left(2x_j^1 - \delta_j\right) + \left((1-a)/2\right)\left(2x_j^2 + \delta_j\right) \right\} \ge 0 \; ; \; j = 1, 2, \ldots, n$$

$$x_j^1 \le x_j^2$$

$$0 \le a \le 1, \tag{19}$$

where $w_k \ge 0$ represents the numerical weights of the goals which are determined as:

$$w_k = \frac{p}{\left[R\left(E\left(\tilde{Z}_k\right)\right)^b - R\left(E\left(\tilde{Z}_k\right)\right)^w\right]} \cdot k = 1, 2, \ldots, K \; ; p > 0 \tag{20}$$

6.3.4. Variance Model for Constructing Fuzzy Objectives

Taking the variance of all the FRVs present in the objectives, the objective function is modified as

$$\text{Minimize } Var(\tilde{Z}_k) \cong \sum_{j=1}^{n} Var\left(\tilde{c}_{kj}\right)\tilde{x}_j^2; k = 1, 2, \ldots, K$$

i.e., Minimize $Var(\tilde{Z}_k) \cong \sum_{j=1}^{n} \tilde{\sigma}_{\tilde{c}_{kj}}^2 \tilde{x}_j^2; k = 1, 2, ..., K$

i.e., Minimize $Var(\tilde{Z}_k) \cong \sum_{j=1}^{n} \left(\sigma_{c_{kj}^1}^2, \sigma_{c_{kj}^2}^2, \theta_{kj}, \theta_{kj} \right) \tilde{x}_j^2; k = 1, 2, ..., K$

As discussed in the section 6.2, by introducing the condition of chance constrained the constraints can be interpreted as

$$\sum_{j=1}^{n} \tilde{a}_{ij} \tilde{x}_j \lesssim E\left(\tilde{b}_i\right) + \sqrt{Var\left(\tilde{b}_i\right)} \Phi^{-1}\left(\gamma_i\right)$$

By introducing new constraints the variance model is expressed in the form

Minimize $Var(\tilde{Z}_k) \cong \sum_{j=1}^{n} \left(\sigma_{c_{kj}^1}^2, \sigma_{c_{kj}^2}^2, \theta_{kj}, \theta_{kj} \right) \tilde{x}_j^2; k = 1, 2, ..., K$

subject to

$$\sum_{j=1}^{n} \tilde{a}_{ij} \tilde{x}_j \lesssim E\left(\tilde{b}_i\right) + \sqrt{Var\left(\tilde{b}_i\right)} \Phi^{-1}\left(\gamma_i\right)$$

$E(\tilde{Z}_k) \gtrsim \rho_k; k = 1, 2, ..., K$

$\tilde{x}_j \gtrsim \tilde{0}; j = 1, 2, ..., n,$ \hfill (21)

where ρ_k is the expectation level which is acceptable to the DMs and $Var(\tilde{Z}_k)$ denotes the variance of $\tilde{Z}_k$. The constraints $E(\tilde{Z}_k) \gtrsim \rho_k; k = 1, 2, ..., K$ indicate that variance model depend on the expectation model and the expectation level ρ_k is achieved from the expectation model.

6.3.5. Determination of Crisp Model

As expressed in the subsection 6.2.1, the ranking function is applied to all the FNs of the fuzzy programming model to form its equivalent deterministic form.

Minimize

$$R(Var(\tilde{Z}_k)) = \sum_{j=1}^{n} R\left(\sigma^2_{c^1_{kj}}, \sigma^2_{c^2_{kj}}, \theta_{kj}, \theta_{kj}\right) R\left(\left(x^1_j - \delta_j\right)^2, \left(x^1_j\right)^2, \left(x^2_j\right)^2, \left(x^2_j + \delta_j\right)^2\right)$$

$$k = 1, 2, \ldots, K$$

subject to

$$\sum_{j=1}^{n} R\left(\tilde{a}_{ij}\right) R\left(\tilde{x}_j\right) \leq R\left(E\left(\tilde{b}_i\right)\right) + \sqrt{R\left(Var\left(\tilde{b}_i\right)\right)} \Phi^{-1}\left(\gamma_i\right)$$

$$R(E(\tilde{Z}_k)) \geq \rho_k \; ; k = 1, 2, \ldots, K$$

$$R(\tilde{x}_j) \geq 0; j = 1, 2, \ldots, n \qquad\qquad (22)$$

i.e.,

Minimize

$$R(Var(\tilde{Z}_k)) = \sum_{j=1}^{n} R\left(\sigma^2_{c^1_{kj}}, \sigma^2_{c^2_{kj}}, \theta_{kj}, \theta_{kj}\right) R\left(\left(x^1_j - \delta_j\right)^2, \left(x^1_j\right)^2, \left(x^2_j\right)^2, \left(x^2_j + \delta_j\right)^2\right); k = 1, 2, \ldots, K$$

subject to

$$\sum_{j=1}^{n} R\left(\left(a^1_{ij} - d_{ij}, a^1_{ij}, a^2_{ij}, a^2_{ij} + d_{ij}\right)\right) R\left(\left(x^1_j - \delta_j, x^1_j, x^2_j, x^2_j + \delta_j\right)\right) \leq$$
$$R\left(m^1_i - \mu_i, m^1_i, m^2_i, m^2_i + \mu_i\right) + R\left(\sqrt{v^1_i - \tau_i}, \sqrt{v^1_i}, \sqrt{v^2_i}, \sqrt{v^2_i + \tau_i}\right) \Phi^{-1}\left(\gamma_i\right)$$
$$; i = 1, 2, \ldots, m$$

$$\sum_{j=1}^{n} R\left(m_{c^1_{kj}}, m_{c^2_{kj}}, \alpha_{kj}, \alpha_{kj}\right) R\left(\left(x^1_j - \delta_j, x^1_j, x^2_j, x^2_j + \delta_j\right)\right) \geq \rho_k \; ; k = 1, 2, \ldots, K$$

$$R\left(\left(x_j^1 - \delta_j, x_j^1, \ x_j^2, \ x_j^2 + \delta_j\right)\right) \geq 0; j = 1, 2, \ldots, n \tag{23}$$

i.e.,

Minimize

$$R(Var(\tilde{Z}_k)) = \sum_{j=1}^{n} \left\{ \left(\frac{a}{2}\right)\left(2\sigma_{c_{kj}^1}^2 - \theta_{kj}\right) + \left(\frac{1-a}{2}\right)\left(2\sigma_{c_{kj}^2}^2 + \theta_{kj}\right) \right\} \left[\begin{array}{l} \left(\dfrac{a}{2}\right)\left[\left(x_j^1 - \delta_j\right)^2 + \left(x_j^1\right)^2\right] + \\ \left(\dfrac{1-a}{2}\right)\left[\left(x_j^2\right)^2 + \left(x_j^2 + \delta_j\right)^2\right] \end{array} \right]$$

$;k = 1, 2, \ldots, K$

subject to

$$\sum_{j=1}^{n} \left\{(a/2)\left(2a_{ij}^1 - d_{ij}\right) + \left((1-a)/2\right)\left(2a_{ij}^2 + d_{ij}\right)\right\} \left\{(a/2)\left(2x_j^1 - \delta_j\right) + \left((1-a)/2\right)\left(2x_j^2 + \delta_j\right)\right\}$$

$$\leq \left\{(a/2)\left(2m_i^1 - \mu_i\right) + \left((1-a)/2\right)\left(2m_i^2 + \mu_i\right)\right\} +$$

$$\left\{(a/2)\left(\sqrt{v_i^1 - \tau_i} + \sqrt{v_i^1}\right) + \left((1-a)/2\right)\left(\sqrt{v_i^2} + \sqrt{v_i^2 + \tau_i}\right)\right\} \Phi^{-1}\left(\gamma_i\right)$$

$;i = 1, 2, \ldots, m$

$$\sum_{j=1}^{n} \left\{(a/2)\left(2m_{c_{kj}^1} - \alpha_{kj}\right) + \left((1-a)/2\right)\left(2m_{c_{kj}^2} + \alpha_{kj}\right)\right\} \left[\begin{array}{l} (a/2)\left(2x_j^1 - \delta_j\right) \\ + \left((1-a)/2\right)\left(2x_j^2 + \delta_j\right) \end{array} \right] \geq \rho_k$$

$;k = 1, 2, \ldots, K$

$$\left\{(a/2)\left(2x_j^1 - \delta_j\right) + \left((1-a)/2\right)\left(2x_j^2 + \delta_j\right)\right\} \geq 0 \, j = 1, 2, \ldots, n$$

$$x_j^1 \leq x_j^2$$

$$0 \leq a \leq 1 \tag{24}$$

The above expressed variance model is solved independently to find its best and worst values. As in the variance model all objectives are minimized, therefore, the best value of each objective indicate the minimum value of the objectives and the worst value specify the maximum value of the objectives. As described in the previous sections the membership function of each objective is developed depending on their best and worst values.

Thus the membership function of the $k-$th objective $R(Var(\tilde{Z}_k))$ is appeared as

$$\mu_{R(Var(\tilde{Z}_k))} = \begin{cases} 0 & if & R(Var(\tilde{Z}_k)) \geq R(Var(\tilde{Z}_k))^w \\ \dfrac{R(Var(\tilde{Z}_k))^w - R(Var(\tilde{Z}_k))}{R(Var(\tilde{Z}_k))^w - R(Var(\tilde{Z}_k))^b} & if & R(Var(\tilde{Z}_k))^b \leq R(Var(\tilde{Z}_k)) \leq R(Var(\tilde{Z}_k))^w \\ 1 & if & R(Var(\tilde{Z}_k)) \leq R(Var(\tilde{Z}_k))^b \end{cases}$$

$; k = 1, 2, \ldots, K$

As explained in the subsection 6.2.2, the compromise solution is obtained by applying FGP technique. The FGP model for the above defined variance model is developed as

Find $\tilde{X}\left(\tilde{x}_1, \tilde{x}_2, \ldots, \tilde{x}_n\right)$ so as to

Minimize $D = \displaystyle\sum_{k=1}^{K} w_k d_k^-$

subject to

$$\frac{R(Var(\tilde{Z}_k))^w - R(Var(\tilde{Z}_k))}{R(Var(\tilde{Z}_k))^w - R(Var(\tilde{Z}_k))^b} + d_k^- - d_k^+ = 1 \; ; \; k = 1, 2, \ldots, K$$

$$\sum_{j=1}^{n} \left\{ (a/2)\left(2a_{ij}^1 - d_{ij}\right) + \left((1-a)/2\right)\left(2a_{ij}^2 + d_{ij}\right) \right\} \left\{ (a/2)\left(2x_j^1 - \delta_j\right) + \left((1-a)/2\right)\left(2x_j^2 + \delta_j\right) \right\} \leq$$
$$\left\{ (a/2)\left(2m_i^1 - \mu_i\right) + \left((1-a)/2\right)\left(2m_i^2 + \mu_i\right) \right\} +$$
$$\left\{ (a/2)\left(\sqrt{v_i^1 - \tau_i} + \sqrt{v_i^1}\right) + \left((1-a)/2\right)\left(\sqrt{v_i^2} + \sqrt{v_i^2 + \tau_i}\right) \right\} \Phi^{-1}\left(\gamma_i\right)$$
$; i = 1, 2, \ldots, m$

$$\sum_{j=1}^{n} \left\{ \begin{bmatrix} (a/2)\left(2m_{c_{kj}^1} - \alpha_{kj}\right) \\ +((1-a)/2)\left(2m_{c_{kj}^2} + \alpha_{kj}\right) \end{bmatrix} \begin{bmatrix} (a/2)\left(2x_j^1 - \delta_j\right) \\ +((1-a)/2)\left(2x_j^2 + \delta_j\right) \end{bmatrix} \right\} \geq \rho_k \; ; k = 1, 2, \ldots, K$$

$$\left\{ (a/2)\left(2x_j^1 - \delta_j\right) + ((1-a)/2)\left(2x_j^2 + \delta_j\right) \right\} \geq 0; j = 1, 2, \ldots, n$$

$$x_j^1 \leq x_j^2$$

$$0 \leq a \leq 1, \tag{25}$$

where $w_k \geq 0$ represents the numerical weights of the goals which are determined as:

$$w_k = \frac{\mathrm{p}}{\left(R(Var(\tilde{Z}_k))^w - R(Var(\tilde{Z}_k))^b\right)} \cdot k = 1, 2, \ldots, K; p > 0 \tag{26}$$

6.3.6. Solution Algorithm

The solution algorithm of the MOFFCCPP in which the parameters of the objectives are FRVs following normal distribution is summarized as follows

Step 1: Using CCP technique the probabilistic constraints are converted into constraints involving only fuzzy parameters.

Step 2:

    a. For the expectation model, the expectation of the FRVs involved with the objectives is considered.

    b. For the variance model, both expectation and variance of the FRVs present in the objectives are taken.

Step 3: Defuzzification of symmetrical trapezoidal FNs is applied to all types of objectives as well as constraints to find an equivalent deterministic model of the MOFFCCPP.

Step 4: Individual optimal value of each objective is found in isolation to find their best and worst solutions.

Step 5: Construct the fuzzy membership goals corresponding to each objectives.

Step 6: The membership functions are developed on the basis of their best and worst values.

Step 7: Finally, FGP approach is applied to achieve the most acceptable compromise solution to all the objectives.

Step 8: Stop.

Before illustrating the developed methodologies through numerical examples, the expectation and variance model of the multi-objective fuzzy stochastic programming problems developed by Sakawa et al. (2011) are discussed briefly in the following section.

6.4 MULTI-OBJECTIVE FUZZY STOCHASTIC MODEL

Consider a fuzzy stochastic programming problem with K number of objectives as follows

Minimize $z_1(\boldsymbol{x}) = \overline{c}_1 \boldsymbol{x}$

$$\dotfill$$

Minimize $z_k(\boldsymbol{x}) = \overline{c}_k \boldsymbol{x}$

Subject to

$$P\left(a_1 \boldsymbol{x} \leq \overline{b}_1\right) \geq \beta_1$$

$$P\left(a_m \boldsymbol{x} \leq \overline{b}_m\right) \geq \beta_m$$

$$\boldsymbol{x} \geq 0 \tag{27}$$

where $\boldsymbol{x}$ is an $n-$ dimensional decision variable column vector, $\overline{c}_l \; ; l = 1, 2, \ldots k$ are $n-$ dimensional random variable row vectors with finite mean $E\left(\overline{c}_l\right)$

and $n \times n$ positive definite variance covariance matrices $V_l \ \left(l = 1, 2, \ldots k\right)$ and $\overline{b}_l \left(l = 1, 2, \ldots, k\right)$ is an n – dimensional random variable column vector whose elements are mutually independent.

6.4.1 Expectation Model

Using CCP methodology, the expectation model of the above model is developed as

Minimize $z_1^E \left(\boldsymbol{x}\right) = E\left(z_1\left(\boldsymbol{x}\right)\right) = E\left(\overline{c}_1\right)\boldsymbol{x}$

....

Minimize $z_k^E \left(\boldsymbol{x}\right) = E\left(z_k\left(\boldsymbol{x}\right)\right) = E\left(\overline{c}_k\right)\boldsymbol{x}$

subject to

$$\sum_{j=1}^{n} a_{ij}x_j \leq m_{\overline{b}_i} + \sigma_{\overline{b}_i}\Phi^{-1}\left(1 - \beta_i\right); \ i = 1, 2, \ldots, m$$

$\boldsymbol{x} \geq 0$ \hfill (28)

Here Φ^{-1} is the inverse function of the distribution function of the standard normal distribution $N\left(0, 1\right)$.

The methodology developed by Sakawa et al. (2011) for solving the above model is explained in the form of an algorithm.

6.4.2 Solution Algorithm

The procedure of interactive fuzzy satisficing method for the expectation model is as follows:

Step 1: Ask the DM to specify the satisficing probability levels β_i, $i = 1, 2, \ldots, m$
Step 2: Calculate the individual minima and maxima of $\left(\overline{c}_l\right)\boldsymbol{x}$, $l = 1, 2, \ldots, k$
   by solving the LPPs

Step 3: Ask the DM to specify the membership functions μ_l $l = 1, 2, ..., k$ for the expectations of the objective functions by using the individual minima and maxima obtained in step 2 as a reference.

Step 4: Set the initial reference membership levels at 1s, i.e., $\hat{\mu}_l = 1$, $l = 1, 2, ..., k$ which can be viewed as the ideal values.

Step 5: For the current reference membership levels $\hat{\mu}_l$, solve the following minimax problem.

Minimize ν

subject to

$$\hat{\mu}_1 - \mu_1\left(z_1^E\left(\boldsymbol{x}\right)\right) \leq \nu$$

$$\cdots\cdots\cdots\cdots\cdots\cdots\cdots\cdots\cdots\cdots\cdots$$

$$\hat{\mu}_k - \mu_k\left(z_k^E\left(\boldsymbol{x}\right)\right) \leq \nu$$

$$\sum_{j=1}^{n} a_{ij} x_j \leq m_{\overline{b}_i} + \sigma_{\overline{b}_i}\Phi^{-1}\left(1 - \beta_i\right); \quad i = 1, 2, ..., m$$

$$\boldsymbol{x} \geq 0 \tag{29}$$

For the achieved optimal solution $\boldsymbol{x}^*$, if there are inactive constraints in the first $\left(k - 1\right)$ constraints of above model, replace $\hat{\mu}_l$ for the inactive constraints with $\mu_l\left(z_l^E\left(\boldsymbol{x}^*\right)\right) + \nu^*$ and resolve the revised problem. Furthermore, if the solution $\boldsymbol{x}^*$ is not unique, perform the M-Pareto optimality test.

Step 6: The DM is supplied with the corresponding M-Pareto optimal solution and the trade-off rates between the membership functions. If the DM is satisfied with the current membership function values $\mu_l\left(z_l^E\left(\boldsymbol{x}^*\right)\right)$

$(l = 1, 2, ..., k)$, then stop. Otherwise, ask the DM to update the reference membership levels $\hat{\mu}_l$, $l = 1, 2, ..., k$ by taking into account the current membership function values $\mu_l\left(z_l^E\left(x^*\right)\right)$ together with the trade-off rates $-\dfrac{\partial \mu_1}{\partial \mu_l}, (l = 1, 2, ..., k)$ and return to Step 5.

6.4.3 Variance Model

Considering CCP methodology and the expectation model, the variance model can be developed as

$$\text{Minimize } z_1^V\left(x\right) = Var\left(z_1\left(x\right)\right)$$

$$\cdots\cdots\cdots\cdots\cdots\cdots\cdots\cdots$$

$$\text{Minimize } z_k^V\left(x\right) = Var\left(z_k\left(x\right)\right)$$

subject to

$$\sum_{j=1}^{n} a_{ij} x_j \leq m_{\overline{b}_i} + \sigma_{\overline{b}_i} \Phi^{-1}\left(1 - \beta_i\right); \ i = 1, 2, ..., m$$

$$E\left(\overline{c}_l\right) x \leq \gamma_l, \ l = 1, 2, ..., k$$

$$x \geq 0 \tag{30}$$

Now, methodology proposed by Sakawa et al. (2011) for solving the above variance model of the multi-objective fuzzy stochastic model is presented as an algorithm.

6.4.4 Solution Algorithm

The procedure of interactive fuzzy satisficing method for the variance model is

Step 1: Ask the DM to specify the satisficing probability levels β_i, $i = 1, 2, ..., m$

Step 2: Calculate the individual minima and maxima of $\left(\overline{c}_l\right)x$, $l = 1, 2, ..., k$ by solving the LPPs

Step 3: Ask the DM to specify the expectation levels γ_l $\left(l = 1, 2, ..., k\right)$.

Step 4: Calculate the individual minima of $z_l^V\left(x\right)\left(l = 1, 2, ..., k\right)$ by solving the quadratic programming problems, i.e. solving the variance model.

Step 5: Ask the DM to specify the membership functions μ_l $l = 1, 2, ..., k$ with the individual minima $z_{l,min}^V$ obtained in Step 4 in mind.

Step 6: Set the initial reference membership levels at 1s, i.e., $\hat{\mu}_l = 1$, $l = 1, 2, ..., k$ which can be viewed as the ideal values.

Step 7: For the current reference membership levels $\hat{\mu}_l$ $l = 1, 2, ..., k$, solve the following augmented minimax problem.

Minimize ν

subject to

$$\hat{\mu}_1 - \mu_1\left(z_1^V\left(x\right)\right) + \rho\sum_{i=1}^{k}\left\{\hat{\mu}_i - \mu_i\left(z_i^V\left(x\right)\right)\right\} \leq \nu$$

....

$$\hat{\mu}_k - \mu_k\left(z_k^V\left(x\right)\right) + \rho\sum_{i=1}^{k}\left\{\hat{\mu}_i - \mu_i\left(z_i^V\left(x\right)\right)\right\} \leq \nu$$

$$\sum_{j=1}^{n}a_{ij}x_j \leq m_{\overline{b}_i} + \sigma_{\overline{b}_i}\Phi^{-1}\left(1 - \beta_i\right); \ i = 1, 2, ..., m$$

$$E\left(\overline{c}_l\right)x \leq \gamma_l \ l = 1, 2, ..., k$$

$$x \geq 0 \tag{31}$$

where ρ is a sufficiently small positive number.

Step 8: The DM is supplied with the corresponding M-Pareto optimal solution. If the DM is satisfied with the current membership function values $\mu_l\left(z_l^V\left(\boldsymbol{x}\right)\right)$ $\left(l = 1, 2, ..., k\right)$, then stop. Otherwise, ask the DM to update the reference membership levels $\hat{\mu}_l$, $l = 1, 2, ..., k$ by taking into account the current membership function values $\mu_l\left(z_l^V\left(\boldsymbol{x}\right)\right)$ and return to Step 5.

6.5. NUMERICAL EXAMPLES

To illustrate the efficiency of the proposed approach, the following two numerical examples are considered in this section. In the first numerical example the parameters of the objectives are taken as symmetric trapezoidal FNs and in the second numerical illustration the coefficients of the objectives are considered as normally distributed FRVs. In both examples the right side parameters of the constraints are taken as FRVs.

6.5.1. Numerical Example 1

Find $X\left(\tilde{x}_1, \tilde{x}_2\right)$ so as to

Maximize $\tilde{Z}_1 \cong \tilde{7}\tilde{x}_1 + \widetilde{17}\tilde{x}_2$

Maximize $\tilde{Z}_2 \cong \tilde{5}\tilde{x}_1 + \tilde{6}\tilde{x}_2$

subject to

$\text{Pr}\left(\tilde{3}\tilde{x}_1 + \tilde{7}\tilde{x}_2 \lesssim \tilde{b}_1\right) \geq 0.15$

$\text{Pr}\left(\tilde{7}\tilde{x}_1 + \tilde{2}\tilde{x}_2 \lesssim \tilde{b}_2\right) \geq 0.10$

$\tilde{x}_1, \ \tilde{x}_2 \gtrsim \tilde{0} \tag{32}$

Here the coefficients of the objectives as well as system constraints are considered as symmetric trapezoidal FNs with the following form as

$$\tilde{7} = \left(3,5,8,10\right); \widetilde{17} = \left(12,15,18,21\right); \tilde{5} = \left(2,4,6,8\right);$$

$$\tilde{6} = \left(4,6,8,10\right); \tilde{3} = \left(2,3,4,5\right); \tilde{2} = \left(1,2,3,4\right)$$

The mean and variance of normally distributed FRVs are taken as

$$E\left(\tilde{b}_1\right) = \tilde{m}_1 = \tilde{7} = \left(3,5,8,10\right); E\left(\tilde{b}_2\right) = \tilde{m}_2 = \tilde{8} = \left(4,7,9,12\right)$$

$$var\left(\tilde{b}_1\right) = \tilde{\sigma}_1^2 = \tilde{9} = \left(5,8,10,13\right); var\left(\tilde{b}_2\right) = \tilde{\sigma}_2^2 = \widetilde{12} = \left(7,10,12,15\right)$$

Also the variables are expressed as

$$\tilde{x}_1 = \left(x_1^1 - \delta_1, x_1^1, x_1^2, x_1^2 + \delta_1\right); \tilde{x}_2 = \left(x_2^1 - \delta_2, x_2^1, x_2^2, x_2^2 + \delta_2\right)$$

Using the CCP technique and ranking function as described in chapter 2 the above model (32) takes the following form

Maximize
$$R\left(\tilde{Z}_1\right) = \left(4.5 - 2.5a\right)\left(a\left(2x_1^1 - \delta_1\right) + \left(1 - a\right)\left(2x_1^2 + \delta_1\right)\right)$$
$$+ \left(19.5 - 6a\right)\left(a\left(2x_2^1 - \delta_2\right) + \left(1 - a\right)\left(2x_2^2 + \delta_2\right)\right)$$

Maximize
$$R\left(\tilde{Z}_2\right) = \left(3.5 - 2a\right)\left(a\left(2x_1^1 - \delta_1\right) + \left(1 - a\right)\left(2x_1^2 + \delta_1\right)\right)$$
$$+ \left(4.5 - 2a\right)\left(a\left(2x_2^1 - \delta_2\right) + \left(1 - a\right)\left(2x_2^2 + \delta_2\right)\right)$$

subject to

$$\left(2.25 - a\right)\left(a\left(2x_1^1 - \delta_1\right) + \left(1 - a\right)\left(2x_1^2 + \delta_1\right)\right) + \left(4.5 - 2.5a\right)\left(a\left(2x_2^1 - \delta_2\right) + \left(1 - a\right)\left(2x_2^2 + \delta_2\right)\right) \le \left(14.31 - 5.77a\right)$$

$$\left(4.5 - 2.5a\right)\left(a\left(2x_1^1 - \delta_1\right) + \left(1-a\right)\left(2x_1^2 + \delta_1\right)\right) + \left(3.5 - 2a\right)\left(a\left(2x_2^1 - \delta_2\right) + \left(1-a\right)\left(2x_2^2 + \delta_2\right)\right) \le$$
$$\left(13.325 - 6.08a\right)$$

$$\left(a\left(2x_1^1 - \delta_1\right) + \left(1-a\right)\left(2x_1^2 + \delta_1\right)\right) \ge 0$$

$$\left(a\left(2x_2^1 - \delta_2\right) + \left(1-a\right)\left(2x_2^2 + \delta_2\right)\right) \ge 0$$

$$x_1^1 \le x_1^2$$

$$x_2^1 \le x_2^2$$

$$0 \le a \le 1 \tag{33}$$

Now each objective is solved independently with respect to the system constraints as described in subsection 6.2.2 to find the best values of each objective. The solutions are obtained as

$$\left[\tilde{x}_{11}^b, \tilde{x}_{12}^b; R\left(\tilde{Z}_1\right)^b\right] = \left[\tilde{0}, \widetilde{1.06}; 31\right] \text{ and } \left[\tilde{x}_{21}^b, \tilde{x}_{22}^b; R\left(\tilde{Z}_2\right)^b\right] = \left[\widetilde{0.714}, \widetilde{0.703}; 16.98\right].$$

The worst values of the objective are found as $R\left(\tilde{Z}_1\right)^w = 0$ and $R\left(\tilde{Z}_2\right)^w = 0$.

From the achieved optimal solutions of the individual objectives the membership goals are found as

$$R\left(\tilde{Z}_1\right) \gtrsim 31 \text{ and } R\left(\tilde{Z}_2\right) \gtrsim 16.98 .$$

On the basis of the derived aspiration levels of the fuzzy goals, the following membership functions of each of the objectives are derived as

$$\mu_{R\left(\tilde{Z}_1\right)} = 0.032 R\left(\tilde{Z}_1\right) \text{ and } \mu_{R\left(\tilde{Z}_2\right)} = 0.059 R\left(\tilde{Z}_2\right).$$

Hence the FGP model is presented by converting the elicited membership functions into membership goals as

Find $\tilde{X}\left(\tilde{x}_1, \tilde{x}_2\right)$ so as to

Minimize $D = 0.032 d_1^- + 0.059 d_2^-$

so as to

$$0.032 R\left(\tilde{Z}_1\right) + d_1^- - d_1^+ = 1$$

$$0.059 R\left(\tilde{Z}_2\right) + d_2^- - d_2^+ = 1$$

subject to

$$\left(2.25 - a\right)\left(a\left(2x_1^1 - \delta_1\right) + \left(1 - a\right)\left(2x_1^2 + \delta_1\right)\right) + \left(4.5 - 2.5a\right)\left(a\left(2x_2^1 - \delta_2\right) + \left(1 - a\right)\left(2x_2^2 + \delta_2\right)\right) \leq \left(14.31 - 5.77a\right)$$

$$\left(4.5 - 2.5a\right)\left(a\left(2x_1^1 - \delta_1\right) + \left(1 - a\right)\left(2x_1^2 + \delta_1\right)\right) + \left(3.5 - 2a\right)\left(a\left(2x_2^1 - \delta_2\right) + \left(1 - a\right)\left(2x_2^2 + \delta_2\right)\right) \leq \left(13.325 - 6.08a\right)$$

$$\left(a\left(2x_1^1 - \delta_1\right) + \left(1 - a\right)\left(2x_1^2 + \delta_1\right)\right) \geq 0$$

$$\left(a\left(2x_2^1 - \delta_2\right) + \left(1 - a\right)\left(2x_2^2 + \delta_2\right)\right) \geq 0$$

Table 1. Compromise solution of the objectives

	Solution Point	Objective Value	Ranking Value	Membership Value
Solution obtained in the proposed technique	$\tilde{x}_1 =$ $\left(0, 0.712, 0.712, 1.424\right)$ $\tilde{x}_2 =$ $\left(1.009, 1.040, 1.040, 1.071\right)$	$\tilde{Z}_1 = \left(8.36, 19.16, 24.42, 35.22\right)$ $\tilde{Z}_2 = \left(1.06, 9.09, 12.59, 20.62\right)$	$R\left(\tilde{Z}_1\right) = 29.82$ $R\left(\tilde{Z}_2\right) = 16.60$	$\mu_{R\left(\tilde{Z}_1\right)} = 0.96$ $\mu_{R\left(\tilde{Z}_2\right)} = 0.97$

Figure 1. Comparison of solutions

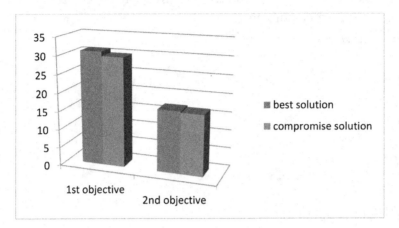

$$x_1^1 \le x_1^2$$

$$x_2^1 \le x_2^2$$

$$0 \le a \le 1 \tag{34}$$

The *software* LINGO (Ver.11.0) is used to solve the problem.

The optimal solution of the problem is found in Table 1.

The comparison between best and compromise solutions are shown Figure 1.

This comparison shows that the compromise solution obtained by proposed methodology is almost identical to the best solution which is obtained when the objectives are solved independently under the modified set of system constraints. Thus the optimization technique described in this chapter is very much acceptable to the DMs as it produces a compromise solution which is very close to the individual optimal solution.

6.5.2. Numerical Example 2

This numerical example is a modified version of the multi-objective fuzzy stochastic problem studied previously by Sakawa et al., (2011), in an imprecisely defined fully fuzzified probabilistic decision making arena.

Find $X\left(\tilde{x}_1, \tilde{x}_2\right)$ so as to

Min $\tilde{Z}_1 \cong \tilde{c}_{11}\tilde{x}_1 + \tilde{c}_{12}\tilde{x}_2$

Min $\tilde{Z}_2 \cong \tilde{c}_{21}\tilde{x}_1 + \tilde{c}_{22}\tilde{x}_2$

subject to

$\Pr\left(\tilde{a}_{11}\tilde{x}_1 + \tilde{a}_{12}\tilde{x}_2 \lesssim \tilde{b}_1\right) \geq 0.80$

$\Pr\left(\tilde{a}_{21}\tilde{x}_1 + \tilde{a}_{22}\tilde{x}_2 \lesssim \tilde{b}_2\right) \geq 0.80$

$\Pr\left(\tilde{a}_{31}\tilde{x}_1 + \tilde{a}_{32}\tilde{x}_2 \lesssim \tilde{b}_3\right) \geq 0.80$

$\tilde{x}_1, \tilde{x}_2 \gtrsim \tilde{0}$ \hfill (35)

Here $\tilde{c}_{11}$, $\tilde{c}_{12}$, $\tilde{c}_{21}$, $\tilde{c}_{22}$, $\tilde{b}_1$, $\tilde{b}_2$, $\tilde{b}_3$ are normally distributed FRVs. The left side parameters $\tilde{a}_{11}$, $\tilde{a}_{12}$, $\tilde{a}_{21}$, $\tilde{a}_{22}$, $\tilde{a}_{31}$, $\tilde{a}_{32}$ of the chance constraints are

Table 2. Values of the fuzzy parameters

FRV	Mean	Variance
$\tilde{c}_{11}$	$E\left(\tilde{c}_{11}\right) = \widetilde{-3} = \left(-5,-3,-2,0\right)$	$Var\left(\tilde{c}_{11}\right) = \tilde{2} = \left(1,2,3,4\right)$
$\tilde{c}_{12}$	$E\left(\tilde{c}_{12}\right) = \widetilde{-8} = \left(-10,-8,-7,-5\right)$	$Var\left(\tilde{c}_{12}\right) = \tilde{3} = \left(2,3,4,5\right)$
$\tilde{c}_{21}$	$E\left(\tilde{c}_{21}\right) = \tilde{5} = \left(4,5,6,7\right)$	$Var\left(\tilde{c}_{21}\right) = \tilde{3} = \left(2,3,4,5\right)$
$\tilde{c}_{22}$	$E\left(\tilde{c}_{22}\right) = \tilde{4} = \left(1,3,4,6\right)$	$Var\left(\tilde{c}_{22}\right) = \tilde{2} = \left(1,2,3,4\right)$
$\tilde{b}_1$	$E\left(\tilde{b}_1\right) = \widetilde{27} = \left(25,27,28,30\right)$	$Var\left(\tilde{b}_1\right) = \tilde{3} = \left(2,3,4,5\right)$
$\tilde{b}_2$	$E\left(\tilde{b}_2\right) = \widetilde{16} = \left(14,16,17,19\right)$	$Var\left(\tilde{b}_2\right) = \tilde{2} = \left(1,2,3,4\right)$
$\tilde{b}_3$	$E\left(\tilde{b}_3\right) = \widetilde{18} = \left(16,18,19,21\right)$	$Var\left(\tilde{b}_3\right) = \tilde{2} = \left(1,2,3,4\right)$

Table 3. Values of left sided parameters

Parameter	Values of the Parameter
$\tilde{a}_{11}$	$\tilde{2} = \left(1, 2, 3, 4\right)$
$\tilde{a}_{12}$	$\tilde{6} = \left(5, 6, 7, 8\right)$
$\tilde{a}_{21}$	$\tilde{3} = \left(2, 3, 4, 5\right)$
$\tilde{a}_{22}$	$\tilde{2} = \left(1, 2, 3, 4\right)$
$\tilde{a}_{31}$	$\tilde{4} = \left(3, 4, 5, 6\right)$
$\tilde{a}_{32}$	$\tilde{1} = \left(0, 1, 2, 3\right)$

symmetric trapezoidal FNs. The variables $\tilde{x}_1$, $\tilde{x}_2$ are also considered as symmetric trapezoidal FNs of the form

$$\tilde{x}_1 = \left(x_1^1 - \delta_1, x_1^1, x_1^2, x_1^2 + \delta_1\right), \quad \tilde{x}_2 = \left(x_2^1 - \delta_2, x_2^1, x_2^2, x_2^2 + \delta_1\right).$$

The mean and variances of all the normally distributed FRVs are also considered as symmetric trapezoidal FNs.

Values of the mean and variance of the FRVs are shown in Table 2.

The values of the left hand side parameters of the chance constraints are presented in Table 3.

Using CCP technique and the ranking of FNs as described in this chapter, the fuzzy probabilistic constraints are modified into fuzzy constraints as

$$\left(1.75 - a\right)\left(a\left(2x_1^1 - \delta_1\right) + \left(1 - a\right)\left(2x_1^2 + \delta_1\right)\right) + \left(3.75 - a\right)\left(a\left(2x_2^1 - \delta_2\right) + \left(1 - a\right)\left(2x_2^2 + \delta_2\right)\right) \leq \left(25.22 - 1.32a\right)$$

$$\left(2.25 - a\right)\left(a\left(2x_1^1 - \delta_1\right) + \left(1 - a\right)\left(2x_1^2 + \delta_1\right)\right) + \left(1.75 - a\right)\left(a\left(2x_2^1 - \delta_2\right) + \left(1 - a\right)\left(2x_2^2 + \delta_2\right)\right) \leq \left(15.06 - 1.32a\right)$$

$$\left(2.75-a\right)\left(a\left(2x_1^1-\delta_1\right)+\left(1-a\right)\left(2x_1^2+\delta_1\right)\right)+\left(1.25-a\right)\left(a\left(2x_2^1-\delta_2\right)+\left(1-a\right)\left(2x_2^2+\delta_2\right)\right)\leq$$
$$\left(17.06-1.32a\right)$$

Applying the ranking function of FNs on the objectives after considering the expectation of all FRVs, the expectation model of the objectives are expressed as

Find $X\left(\tilde{x}_1,\tilde{x}_2\right)$ so as to

Min $\begin{aligned}R\left(E\left(\tilde{Z}_1\right)\right)&=\left(-0.5-1.05a\right)\left(a\left(2x_1^1-\delta_1\right)+\left(1-a\right)\left(2x_1^2+\delta_1\right)\right)\\&+\left(-3-1.5a\right)\left(a\left(2x_2^1-\delta_2\right)+\left(1-a\right)\left(2x_2^2+\delta_2\right)\right)\end{aligned}$

Min $\begin{aligned}R\left(E\left(\tilde{Z}_2\right)\right)&=\left(3.25-a\right)\left(a\left(2x_1^1-\delta_1\right)+\left(1-a\right)\left(2x_1^2+\delta_1\right)\right)\\&+\left(2.5-1.5a\right)\left(a\left(2x_2^1-\delta_2\right)+\left(1-a\right)\left(2x_2^2+\delta_2\right)\right)\end{aligned}$

subject to

$$\left(1.75-a\right)\left(a\left(2x_1^1-\delta_1\right)+\left(1-a\right)\left(2x_1^2+\delta_1\right)\right)+\left(3.75-a\right)\left(a\left(2x_2^1-\delta_2\right)+\left(1-a\right)\left(2x_2^2+\delta_2\right)\right)\leq$$
$$\left(25.22-1.32a\right)$$

$$\left(2.25-a\right)\left(a\left(2x_1^1-\delta_1\right)+\left(1-a\right)\left(2x_1^2+\delta_1\right)\right)+\left(1.75-a\right)\left(a\left(2x_2^1-\delta_2\right)+\left(1-a\right)\left(2x_2^2+\delta_2\right)\right)\leq$$
$$\left(15.06-1.32a\right)$$

$$\left(2.75-a\right)\left(a\left(2x_1^1-\delta_1\right)+\left(1-a\right)\left(2x_1^2+\delta_1\right)\right)+\left(1.25-a\right)\left(a\left(2x_2^1-\delta_2\right)+\left(1-a\right)\left(2x_2^2+\delta_2\right)\right)\leq$$
$$\left(17.06-1.32a\right)$$

$$\left(a\left(2x_1^1-\delta_1\right)+\left(1-a\right)\left(2x_1^2+\delta_1\right)\right)\geq0$$

$$\left(a\left(2x_2^1-\delta_2\right)+\left(1-a\right)\left(2x_2^2+\delta_2\right)\right)\geq0$$

$$x_1^1<x_1^2$$

$$x_2^1 < x_2^2$$

$$0 \le a \le 1 \tag{36}$$

Each objective is now solved under the modified system constraints as described in the subsection 6.3.3 to find the minimum and maximum value of the objectives.

The best value (minimum value) of the objectives is

$$R\left(E\left(\tilde{Z}_1\right)\right)^b = -41.34$$

at

$$\tilde{x}_1 = \widetilde{3.72} = \left(3.18, 3.72, 3.72, 4.26\right)$$

and

$$\tilde{x}_2 = \widetilde{4.03} = \left(2.78, 4.03, 4.03, 5.28\right)$$

and

$$R\left(E\left(\tilde{Z}_2\right)\right)^b = 0$$

at

$$\tilde{x}_1 = \widetilde{0.74} = \left(-0.74, 0.74, 0.74, 2.22\right) \text{ and } \tilde{x}_2 = \widetilde{0.74} = \left(-0.74, 0.74, 0.74, 2.22\right).$$

The worst values of the objectives $R\left(E\left(\tilde{Z}_1\right)\right)$ and $R\left(E\left(\tilde{Z}_2\right)\right)$ are obtained as the solution point

$$\left(\tilde{x}_1, \tilde{x}_2\right) = \left(\widetilde{0.74}, \widetilde{0.74}\right) \text{ and } \left(\tilde{x}_1, \tilde{x}_2\right) = \left(\widetilde{3.72}, \widetilde{4.03}\right),$$

respectively. Thus the worst values of the objective are

$$R\left(E\left(\tilde{Z}_{1}\right)\right)^{w} = 0 \text{ and } R\left(E\left(\tilde{Z}_{2}\right)\right)^{w} = 22.32.$$

Therefore, the fuzzy goals of the objectives are $R\left(E\left(\tilde{Z}_{1}\right)\right) \lesssim -41.34$ and $R\left(E\left(\tilde{Z}_{2}\right)\right) \lesssim 0$.

To find the compromise solution, the FGP model of the above expectation model is constructed as shown in subsection 6.3.4. Thus the FGP model is written as

Find $\tilde{X}\left(\tilde{x}_{1}, \tilde{x}_{2}\right)$ so as to

Minimize $D = 0.024 d_{1}^{-} + 0.045 d_{2}^{-}$

so as to

$$-0.024 R\left(E\left(\tilde{Z}_{1}\right)\right) + d_{1}^{-} - d_{1}^{+} = 1$$

$$-0.045 R\left(E\left(\tilde{Z}_{2}\right)\right) + d_{2}^{-} - d_{2}^{+} = 0$$

subject to

$$\left(1.75 - a\right)\left(a\left(2x_{1}^{1} - \delta_{1}\right) + \left(1 - a\right)\left(2x_{1}^{2} + \delta_{1}\right)\right) + \left(3.75 - a\right)\left(a\left(2x_{2}^{1} - \delta_{2}\right) + \left(1 - a\right)\left(2x_{2}^{2} + \delta_{2}\right)\right) \leq$$
$$\left(25.22 - 1.32a\right)$$

$$\left(2.25 - a\right)\left(a\left(2x_{1}^{1} - \delta_{1}\right) + \left(1 - a\right)\left(2x_{1}^{2} + \delta_{1}\right)\right) + \left(1.75 - a\right)\left(a\left(2x_{2}^{1} - \delta_{2}\right) + \left(1 - a\right)\left(2x_{2}^{2} + \delta_{2}\right)\right) \leq$$
$$\left(15.06 - 1.32a\right)$$

$$\left(2.75 - a\right)\left(a\left(2x_{1}^{1} - \delta_{1}\right) + \left(1 - a\right)\left(2x_{1}^{2} + \delta_{1}\right)\right) + \left(1.25 - a\right)\left(a\left(2x_{2}^{1} - \delta_{2}\right) + \left(1 - a\right)\left(2x_{2}^{2} + \delta_{2}\right)\right) \leq$$
$$\left(17.06 - 1.32a\right)$$

$$\left(a\left(2x_{1}^{1} - \delta_{1}\right) + \left(1 - a\right)\left(2x_{1}^{2} + \delta_{1}\right)\right) \geq 0$$

$$\left(a\left(2x_{2}^{1} - \delta_{2}\right) + \left(1 - a\right)\left(2x_{2}^{2} + \delta_{2}\right)\right) \geq 0$$

$$x_1^1 < x_1^2$$

$$x_2^1 < x_2^2$$

$$0 \le a \le 1,\ d_1^-, d_2^- \ge 0 \text{ and } d_1^- . d_2^- = 0 \tag{37}$$

The *software* LINGO (Ver.13.0) is used to solve the problem.

- **Model Class:** NLP
- **Total Variables:** 11
- **Nonlinear Variables:** 7
- **Integer Variables:** 0
- **Total Constraints:** 12
- **Nonlinear Constraints:** 7
- **Total Non-Zeros:** 55
- **Nonlinear Non-Zeros:** 43

Variables and values:

d_1^- : 0.5396510E-01
d_2^- : 0.3892906
X_1^1 : 0.7119132
δ_1 : 1.423826
X_1^2 : 0.7119132
X_2^1 : 4.403211
δ_2 : 0.1155139

Table 4. Compromise solution of the objectives

	Solution Point	Objective Value	Ranking Value	Membership Value
Solution obtained in the proposed technique	$\tilde{x}_1 =$ $\left(-0.708, 0.712, 0.712, 2.132 \right)$ $\tilde{x}_2 =$ $\left(4.287, 4.403, 4.848, 4.519 \right)$	$\tilde{Z}_1 =$ $\left(-40.06, -38.06, -32.11, -30.11 \right)$ $\tilde{Z}_2 =$ $\left(7.36, 10, 12.17, 14.81 \right)$	$R\left(E\left(\tilde{Z}_1 \right) \right) = -39.11$ $R\left(E\left(\tilde{Z}_2 \right) \right) = 8.69$	$\mu_{R\left(E\left(\tilde{Z}_1 \right) \right)} = 0.95$ $\mu_{R\left(E\left(\tilde{Z}_2 \right) \right)} = 0.62$

X_{2}^{2} : 4.847547

d_{1}^{+} : 0.000000

d_{2}^{+} : 0.000000

a: 1.000000

The optimal solution of the problem is found in Table 4.

If the expectation model be solved by the methodology developed by Sakawa et al. (2011), the achieved objective values are found as $E\left(z_{1}\left(x\right)\right) = -33.51$ and $E\left(z_{2}\left(x\right)\right) = 25.99$. This comparison shows that the methodology presented in this chapter generates better solution than the methodology developed by Sakawa et al. (2011).

In the same manner the variance model of the fully fuzzified stochastic programming can be generated. As in the model formulation described in the previous subsection, the individual optimal value of the objectives is calculated by solving each objective independently under the modified set of system constraints. Then based on the fuzzy membership goals the FGP model is developed as

Find $\tilde{X}\left(\tilde{x}_{1}, \tilde{x}_{2}\right)$ so as to

Minimize $D = 0.03 d_{1}^{-} + 0.033 d_{2}^{-}$

so as to

$$-0.03 R\left(Var\left(\tilde{Z}_{1}\right)\right) + d_{1}^{-} - d_{1}^{+} = 0$$

$$-0.033 R\left(Var\left(\tilde{Z}_{2}\right)\right) + d_{2}^{-} - d_{2}^{+} = 0$$

subject to

$$\left(1.75 - a\right)\left(a\left(2x_{1}^{1} - \delta_{1}\right) + \left(1 - a\right)\left(2x_{1}^{2} + \delta_{1}\right)\right) + \left(3.75 - a\right)\left(a\left(2x_{2}^{1} - \delta_{2}\right) + \left(1 - a\right)\left(2x_{2}^{2} + \delta_{2}\right)\right) \leq \left(25.22 - 1.32a\right)$$

$$\left(2.25 - a\right)\left(a\left(2x_{1}^{1} - \delta_{1}\right) + \left(1 - a\right)\left(2x_{1}^{2} + \delta_{1}\right)\right) + \left(1.75 - a\right)\left(a\left(2x_{2}^{1} - \delta_{2}\right) + \left(1 - a\right)\left(2x_{2}^{2} + \delta_{2}\right)\right) \leq \left(15.06 - 1.32a\right)$$

$$\left(2.75 - a\right)\left(a\left(2x_1^1 - \delta_1\right) + \left(1 - a\right)\left(2x_1^2 + \delta_1\right)\right) + \left(1.25 - a\right)\left(a\left(2x_2^1 - \delta_2\right) + \left(1 - a\right)\left(2x_2^2 + \delta_2\right)\right) \leq$$
$$\left(17.06 - 1.32a\right)$$

$$\left(a\left(2x_1^1 - \delta_1\right) + \left(1 - a\right)\left(2x_1^2 + \delta_1\right)\right) \geq 0$$

$$\left(a\left(2x_2^1 - \delta_2\right) + \left(1 - a\right)\left(2x_2^2 + \delta_2\right)\right) \geq 0$$

$$\left(-0.5 - 1.05a\right)\left(a\left(2x_1^1 - \delta_1\right) + \left(1 - a\right)\left(2x_1^2 + \delta_1\right)\right) + \left(-3 - 1.5a\right)\left(a\left(2x_2^1 - \delta_2\right) + \left(1 - a\right)\left(2x_2^2 + \delta_2\right)\right) \geq$$
$$-41.34$$

$$\left(3.25 - a\right)\left(a\left(2x_1^1 - \delta_1\right) + \left(1 - a\right)\left(2x_1^2 + \delta_1\right)\right) + \left(2.5 - 1.5a\right)\left(a\left(2x_2^1 - \delta_2\right) + \left(1 - a\right)\left(2x_2^2 + \delta_2\right)\right) \geq 0$$

$$x_1^1 < x_1^2$$

$$x_2^1 < x_2^2$$

$$0 \leq a \leq 1, \; d_1^-, d_2^- \geq 0 \text{ and } d_1^-.d_2^- = 0 \tag{38}$$

Solving the above FGP model using the *software* LINGO (Ver.11.0), the compromise solution is achieved as

$$R\left(E\left(\tilde{Z}_1\right)\right) = -8.3, \; R\left(E\left(\tilde{Z}_2\right)\right) = 3.65$$

at the solution point

$$\tilde{x}_1 = \left(-0.22, 1.09, 1.09, 2.4\right) \; \tilde{x}_2 = \left(0.13, 1.32, 1.32, 2.51\right).$$

From this solution it is seen that slightly better value of the second objective is achieved using variance model compared to expectation model. Although expectation model generates much better value of the first objective than the variance model. This indicates that both methodologies are applicable to multi-objective fuzzy stochastic programming problem satisfying all the depending constraints of the problem.

6.6 RESULTS AND DISCUSSION

This chapter introduces new methodologies for solving FFMOCCP involving normally distributed FRVs. As in the preceding chapters, both types of uncertainties like fuzziness and randomness are included in this methodology, simultaneously. The decision variables associated with the problems are also considered as symmetric trapezoidal fuzzy variables. Both expectation and variance model are developed in this chapter and expresses how variance model depends on the expectation model. Based on FGP a compromise decision of the multi-objective problem is achieved. The proposed procedure can be extended to solve quadratic fuzzy multi-objective programming problem, bilevel programming problem, and fractional programming problems. The proposed methodology can be applied to different real life problems for obtaining most satisfactory solution in a hierarchical decision making environment. However it is hoped that the developed methodology may open up new direction into the way of making decision in a fully fuzzified probabilistic decision making arena.

REFERENCES

Allahviranloo, T., Lotfi, F. H., Kiasary, M. K., Kiani, N. A., & Alizadeh, L. (2008). Solving fully fuzzy linear programming problem by the ranking function. *Applied Mathematical Sciences*, 2(1), 19–32.

Bellman, R. E., & Zadeh, L. A. (1970). Decision making in a fuzzy environment. *Management Science*, 17(4), 141–164. doi:10.1287/mnsc.17.4.B141

Biswas, A., & De, A K. (2015). An efficient technique for solving fully fuzzified multiobjective stochastic programming problems. *Advances in Intelligent Systems and Computing*, 339, 497-509. doi.org/10.1007/978-81-322-2250-7_49

Biswas, A., & Modak, N. (2011). A fuzzy goal programming method for solving chance constrained programming with fuzzy parameters. *Communications in Computer and Information Science*, 140, 187–196. doi:10.1007/978-3-642-19263-0_23

Biswas, A., & Modak, N. (2012). Using fuzzy goal programming technique to solve multiobjective chance constrained programming problems in a fuzzy environment. *International Journal of Fuzzy System Applications*, 2(1), 71–80. doi:10.4018/ijfsa.2012010105

Buckley, J., & Feuring, T. (2000). Evolutionary algorithm solution to fuzzy problems: Fuzzy linear programming. *Fuzzy Sets and Systems*, 109(1), 35–53. doi:10.1016/S0165-0114(98)00022-0

Charnes, A., & Cooper, W. W. (1962). Chance-constrained programming. *Management Science*, 6(1), 73–79. doi:10.1287/mnsc.6.1.73

Charnes, A., & Cooper, W. W. (1963). Deterministic equivalents for optimizing and satisfying under chance constraints. *Operations Research*, 11(1), 18–39. doi:10.1287/opre.11.1.18

Charnes, A., & Cooper, W. W. (1977). Goal programming and multiple objective optimizations. *Euro. J. Opl. Res*, 1(1), 39–54. doi:10.1016/S0377-2217(77)81007-2

Chen, S. J., & Chen, S. M. (2007). Fuzzy risk analysis based on the ranking of generalized trapezoidal fuzzy numbers. *Applied Intelligence*, 26(1), 1–11. doi:10.100710489-006-0003-5

Cheng, C. H. (1998). A new approach for ranking fuzzy numbers by distance method. *Fuzzy Sets and Systems*, 95(3), 307–317. doi:10.1016/S0165-0114(96)00272-2

Chiang, J. (2001). Fuzzy linear programming based on statistical confidence interval and interval-valued fuzzy set. *European Journal of Operational Research*, 129(1), 65–86. doi:10.1016/S0377-2217(99)00404-X

Das, S. K., Mandal, T., & Edalatpanah, S. A. (2017). A mathematical model for solving fully fuzzy linear programming problem with trapezoidal fuzzy numbers. *Applied Intelligence*, 46(3), 509–519. doi:10.100710489-016-0779-x

Dehghan, M., Hashemi, B., & Ghatee, M. (2006). Computational methods for solving fully fuzzy linear systems. *Applied Mathematics and Computation*, 179(1), 328–343. doi:10.1016/j.amc.2005.11.124

Delgado, M., Verdegay, J. L., & Vila, M. A. (1989). A general model for fuzzy linear programming. *Fuzzy Sets and Systems*, 29(1), 21–29. doi:10.1016/0165-0114(89)90133-4

Ganesan, K., & Veeramani, P. (2006). Fuzzy linear programs with trapezoidal fuzzy numbers. *Annals of Operations Research, 143*(1), 305–315. doi:10.100710479-006-7390-1

Geoffrion, A. M. (1967). Stochastic programming with aspiration or fractilecriteria. *Management Science, 13*(9), 672–679. doi:10.1287/mnsc.13.9.672

Hannan, E. L. (1980). Linear programming with multiple fuzzy goals. *Fuzzy Sets and Systems, 6*(3), 235–248. doi:10.1016/0165-0114(81)90002-6

Hosseinzadeh, A., & Edalatpanah, S. A. (2016). A New Approach for Solving Fully Fuzzy Linear Programming by Using the Lexicography Method. *Advances in Fuzzy Systems*, 1-6. doi.org/10.1155/2016/1538496

Iskander, M. G. (2006). Exponential membership function in stochastic fuzzy goal programming. *Applied Mathematics and Computation, 173*(2), 782–791. doi:10.1016/j.amc.2005.04.014

Jain, R. (1976). Decision-making in the presence of fuzzy variables. *IEEE Transactions on Systems, Man, and Cybernetics, 6*(10), 698–703.

Jamison, K. D., & Lodwick, W. A. (2001). Fuzzy linear programming using a penalty method. *Fuzzy Sets and Systems, 119*(1), 97–110. doi:10.1016/S0165-0114(99)00082-2

Kataoka, S. (1963). A stochastic programming model. *Econometrica, 31*(1/2), 181–196. doi:10.2307/1910956

Kumar, A., Kaur, J., & Singh, P. (2011). A new method for solving fully fuzzy linear programming problems. *Applied Mathematical Modelling, 35*(2), 817–823. doi:10.1016/j.apm.2010.07.037

Kumar, A., Singh, P., Kaur, P., & Kaur, A. (2011). A new approach for ranking of *L-R* type generalized fuzzy numbers. *Expert Systems with Applications, 38*(9), 10906–10910. doi:10.1016/j.eswa.2011.02.131

Leon, T., & Vercher, E. (2004). Solving a class of fuzzy linear programs by using semi-infinite programming techniques. *Fuzzy Sets and Systems, 146*(2), 235–252. doi:10.1016/j.fss.2003.09.010

Liu, B. (2001). Fuzzy random chance-constrained programming. *IEEE Transactions on Fuzzy Systems, 9*(5), 713–720. doi:10.1109/91.963757

Liu, X. (2001). Measuring the satisfaction of constraints in fuzzy linear programming. *Fuzzy Sets and Systems*, *122*(2), 263–275. doi:10.1016/S0165-0114(00)00114-7

Narasimhan, R. (1980). On fuzzy goal programming–Some comments. *Decision Sciences*, *11*, 532–538. doi:10.1111/j.1540-5915.1980.tb01142.x

Sakawa, M., Nishizaki, I., & Katagiri, H. (2011). *Fuzzy Stochastic Multiobjective Programming*. Springer. doi:10.1007/978-1-4419-8402-9

Sharma, U., & Aggarwal, S. (2018). Solving fully fuzzy multi-objective linear programming problem using nearest interval approximation of fuzzy number and interval programming. *International Journal of Fuzzy Systems*, *20*(2), 488–499. doi:10.100740815-017-0336-8

Tanaka, H., Okuda, T., & Asai, K. (1973). On fuzzy mathematical programming. *Journal of Cybernetics and Systems*, *3*(4), 37–46. doi:10.1080/01969727308545912

Van Hop, N. (2007). Hop van N. Solving fuzzy (stochastic) linear programming problems using superiority and inferiority measures. *Information Sciences*, *177*(9), 1977–1991. doi:10.1016/j.ins.2006.12.001

Yager, R. R. (1981). A procedure for ordering fuzzy subsets of the unit interval. *Information Sciences*, *24*(2), 143–161. doi:10.1016/0020-0255(81)90017-7

Zhang, G., Wu, Y. H., Remias, M., & Lu, J. (2003). Formulation of fuzzy linear programming problems as four-objective constrained optimization problems. *Applied Mathematics and Computation*, *139*(2-3), 383–399. doi:10.1016/S0096-3003(02)00202-3

Zimmerman, H. J. (1978). Fuzzy programming and linear programming with several objective functions. *Fuzzy Sets and Systems*, *1*(1), 45–55. doi:10.1016/0165-0114(78)90031-3

Chapter 7
Fuzzy Multi–Objective Programming With Joint Probability Distribution

ABSTRACT

In this chapter, a fuzzy goal programming (FGP) model is employed for solving multi-objective linear programming (MOLP) problem under fuzzy stochastic uncertain environment in which the probabilistic constraints involves fuzzy random variables (FRVs) following joint probability distribution. In the preceding chapters, the authors explain about linear, fractional, quadratic programming models with multiple conflicting objectives under fuzzy stochastic environment. But the chance constraints in these chapters are considered independently. However, in practical situations, the decision makers (DMs) face various uncertainties where the chance constraints occur jointly. By considering the above fact, the authors presented a solution methodology for fuzzy stochastic MOLP (FSMOLP) with joint probabilistic constraint following some continuous probability distributions. Like the other chapters, chance constrained programming (CCP) methodology is adopted for handling probabilistic constraints. But the difference is that in the earlier chapters chance constraints are considered independently, whereas in this chapter all the chance constraints are taken jointly. Then the transformed problem involving possibilistic uncertainty is converted into a comparable deterministic problem by using the method of defuzzification of the fuzzy numbers (FNs). Objectives are now solved independently under the set of modified system constraints to obtain the best solution of each objective. Then the membership function for each objective is constructed, and finally, a fuzzy goal programming (FGP) model is developed for the achievement of the highest membership goals to the extent possible by minimizing group regrets in the decision-making context.

DOI: 10.4018/978-1-5225-8301-1.ch007

7.1 FUZZY STOCHASTIC PROGRAMMING FOLLOWING JOINT PROBABILITY DISTRIBUTION

Authors in the preceding chapters already clarified the fact that due to the coexistence of imprecision and uncertainty, the DMs have to deal with real life decision-making problems within hybrid uncertain environments. It is necessary to combine both probability theory and possibility theory for a hybrid uncertain decision making problems. Through FRV probabilistic and possibilistic uncertainty can be described simultaneously. FRV is a mapping from a probability space to a collection of fuzzy variables, hence acts as an appropriate and effective tool to deal with hybrid uncertainty in an optimization framework. The concept of FRV was first introduced by Zadeh (1968) using probability measure. After Zadeh, the thought of FRV was advanced by Kwakernaak (1978, 1979) which was further developed by Puri and Ralescu (1986), Liu and Iwamura (1998), Liu and Liu (2003), Buckley and Eslami (2004, 2004[a]) as per the different necessities of measurability.

Fuzzy CCP (FCCP) methodology is applied to those CCP problems in which at least one parameter of the constraints or the objective function has FRVs. CCP with both fuzziness and randomness was examined by Gharraph and Mohammed (1994), Liu and Iwamura (1998) and Mohammed (2000) and others. An interval-parameter dynamic CCP approach for capacity planning under uncertainty was developed by Dai et al. (2012). The researchers employ the FCCP technique to change over hybrid decision making problem into a fuzzy programming problem. As traditional linear programming, Zimmermann (1978) first introduced fuzzy linear programming (FLP). In that approach, LP problems are considered with a fuzzy goal and fuzzy constraints. Zimmermann (1983) proposed an approach for determining suitable values for the aspiration level and admissible violation of the fuzzy goal, rather than leaving this decision to DMs. After the pioneering work on FLP by Zimmermann (1983), several kinds of FLP problems appeared in the literature and different methods have been introduced to take care of such problems. A few of the methods depend on the idea of the penalty method (Jamison and Lodwick, 2001), the satisfaction degree of the constraints (Liu, 2001), the statistical confidence interval (Chiang, 2001), and optimization method with multiple objectives (Zhang et al, 2003). Other kinds of methods are semi-infinite programming method (Leon and Vercher, 2004), the superiority and inferiority of FNs (Hop, 2007), and the degrees of feasibility (Jimenez et al, 2007). Since then FLP has developed in various ways with numerous fruitful applications.

Among the others, the approach of Verdegay (1982) and Chanas (1983) which proposed a parametric programming method for solving FLP is one of the most often used technique. Several researchers (Delgado et al., 1989; Lai and Hwang, 1992; Lai and Hwang, 1992[a]) studied FLP problem with fuzzy goals, fuzzy constraints and fuzzy parameters in a concise manner. FLP with fuzzy variables and the application of ranking functions in FLP were discussed in the literature (Campus and Verdegay, 1989; Cadenas and Verdegay, 2000; Maleki, 2003) by several researchers in the past.

In the preceding chapters CCP methodology is employed to the chance constraints independently. If individual chance constraints are considered, each line of the constraints can be transformed individually. In this situation each chance constraint satisfied different probability level. There is no interaction with the other constraints and accordingly, individual chance constraints are easy to solve in compared to joint probabilistic constraints as they only guarantee that each line satisfies the constraint to a certain confidence level. With joint constraints the set of constraints as a whole is reformulated as one constraint. Joint chance constraint ensures that the constraint as a whole is satisfied to a certain confidence level. However, it is incredibly difficult to solve, even numerically. In 2000, Sinha et al. (2000) proposed a fuzzy programming approach for solving multi-objective probabilistic linear programming problems when the coefficients follow joint normal distribution. After that, Sahoo and Biswal (2005) developed stochastic linear programming problems with Cauchy and extreme value distributions. Ackooij et al., (2011) demonstrated a methodology that deals with joint probabilistic constraints with Gaussian coefficient matrix. Reich (2013) studied a class of mixed-integer programs for solving linear programs with joint probabilistic constraints from random right-hand side vectors with finite distributions. Liu et al. (2016) proposed a methodology that discussed geometric programs with joint probabilistic constraints. Multi-objective stochastic programming problems with joint probabilistic constraints were applied to air quality management (Lv et al., 2011) and to power management (Arnold et al., 2013) in the past. Zhang et al., (2017) proposed an interval multistage joint probabilistic CCP model for crop area planning problem. In recent years Liu et al., (2019) proposed a distributionally robust model with joint chance constraints for optimizing the location, number of ambulances and demand assignment in an EMS system by minimizing the expected total cost.

In this chapter FGP model is adopted for solving fuzzy stochastic multi-objective linear programming problem (FSMOLPP) in which the probabilistic constraints involves FRVs following joint Cauchy and extreme value distribution. In the model formulation process the FSMOLPP is converted into an FP problem with the help of CCP methodology. Then the problem is converted into a comparable deterministic problem by using the method of defuzzification methods of the FNs. After that each objective is solved independently under the set of modified system constraints to obtain the best solution of each objective. Then the membership function for each objective is formed and finally a weighted FGP model is developed for the highest degree achievement of each of the defined membership goals to the extent possible by minimizing group regrets in the decision making context.

7.2 DEVELOPMENT OF FUZZY MULTI-OBJECTIVE PROGRAMMING MODEL WITH JOINT PROBABILISTIC CONSTRAINT

In this section FSMOLPP with joint probabilistic constraint is expressed in the following two forms. In the first model the parameters of multiple objectives are considered as FNs and the chance constraints, involved with FRVs as right sided parameters, following joint probability distribution. In the second model the parameters of the objectives and the right side parameters of the constraints involved with FRVs following joint probability distribution. Other parameters of the model are considered as FNs. Also in the first model constraints are taken as " $\lesssim$ " type and the constraints in second model are selected as " $\gtrsim$ " type to discuss all possible situations. Thus the general form of two FSMOLPPs are expressed as

$$\text{Max } \tilde{Z}_k \cong \sum_{j=1}^{n} \tilde{c}_{kj} x_j \, ; \; k = 1, 2, \dots, K$$

subject to

$$\Pr\left(\sum_{j=1}^{n}\tilde{a}_{1j}x_{j} \lesssim \tilde{b}_{1}, \sum_{j=1}^{n}\tilde{a}_{2j}x_{j} \lesssim \tilde{b}_{2}, \ldots, \sum_{j=1}^{n}\tilde{a}_{mj}x_{j} \lesssim \tilde{b}_{m}\right) \geq 1-\gamma$$

$$x_{j} \geq 0 \; ; \; j=1,2,\ldots,n \tag{1}$$

where

$$\tilde{c}_{kj}, \; \tilde{a}_{ij}\left(k=1,2,\ldots,K; i=1,2,\ldots,m; j=1,2,\ldots,n\right)$$

are FNs and $\tilde{b}_{i}\left(i=1,2,\ldots,m\right)$ are independent FRVs. The parameters of the probabilistic constraints in (1) is a joint probabilistic constraint with a specified probability level $\gamma \in \mathbb{R}$ with $0 \leq \gamma \leq 1$.

$$\text{Max / Min } \tilde{Z}_{k} \cong \sum_{j=1}^{n}\tilde{c}_{kj}x_{j} \; ; \; k=1,2,\ldots,K$$

subject to

$$\Pr\left(\sum_{j=1}^{n}\tilde{a}_{1j}x_{j} \gtrsim \tilde{b}_{1}, \sum_{j=1}^{n}\tilde{a}_{2j}x_{j} \gtrsim \tilde{b}_{2}, \ldots, \sum_{j=1}^{n}\tilde{a}_{mj}x_{j} \gtrsim \tilde{b}_{m}\right) \geq 1-\gamma$$

$$x_{j} \geq 0 \; j=1,2,\ldots,n \tag{2}$$

where

$$\tilde{a}_{ij}\left(i=1,2,\ldots,m; j=1,2,\ldots,n\right)$$

are FNs,

$$\tilde{c}_{kj}\left(k=1,2,\ldots,K; j=1,2,\ldots,n\right)$$

are FRVs and $\tilde{b}_i (i = 1, 2, ..., m)$ are independent FRVs. The probabilistic constraints in (2) is a joint probabilistic constraint with a specified probability level $\gamma \in \mathbb{R}$ with $0 \leq \gamma \leq 1$.

From the chance constraints given in (1) and (2) it is clear to the readers that if individual chance constraints are considered then each of them satisfy different probability level. As in this chapter joint probabilistic constraints are considered, therefore, all the constraints as a whole satisfies a specified probability level.

7.3 DEVELOPMENT OF FUZZY PROGRAMMING MODEL

It is already clear to the reader that the solution of fuzzy stochastic mathematical programming model without transforming into its equivalent deterministic form is a tedious and complicated job. To free from the probabilistic uncertainty generally two well-known methods viz., two stage programming and CCP technique are mainly used. Although in this book authors highlighted CCP methodology and in every chapter CCP methodology is implemented instead of two stage programming technique.

In this section the fuzzy programming model is developed from both the FSMOLP model through CCP methodology from joint probabilistic constraint.

Now the joint probability constraint in (1) is expressed as

$$\Pr\left(\sum_{j=1}^{n}\tilde{a}_{1j}x_j \lesssim \tilde{b}_1, \sum_{j=1}^{n}\tilde{a}_{2j}x_j \lesssim \tilde{b}_2, ..., \sum_{j=1}^{n}\tilde{a}_{mj}x_j \lesssim \tilde{b}_m\right) \geq 1 - \gamma$$

As, the FRVs $\tilde{b}_i, (i = 1, 2, ..., m)$ are mutually independent FRVs, therefore, the constraint can be transformed as

$$\prod_{i=1}^{m}\Pr\left(\tilde{A}_i \lesssim \tilde{b}_i\right) \geq \left(1 - \gamma\right)$$

where

$$\tilde{A}_i \cong \sum_{j=1}^{n}\tilde{a}_{ij}x_j. \tag{3}$$

In the first model it is assumed that all the FRVs in joint probabilistic constraint follows extreme value distribution.

As $\tilde{b}_i$ is extreme value distributed FRV, its probability density function is written as

$$f\left(b_i \ ; \tilde{\beta}_i \ , \tilde{\lambda}_i\right) = \frac{1}{t} e^{-\frac{(b_i - s)}{t}} e^{-e^{-\frac{(b_i - s)}{t}}},$$

where the support of $\tilde{b}_i$ is defined on the set of real numbers; $t \in \tilde{\beta}_i[\alpha], s \in \tilde{\lambda}_i[\alpha]$; $\tilde{\beta}_i[\alpha], \tilde{\lambda}_i[\alpha]$ are the α –cut of the FNs $\tilde{\beta}_i$, $\tilde{\lambda}_i$. The fuzzy parameter $\tilde{\lambda}_i$ is the median of the random variable $\tilde{b}_i$ and $\tilde{\beta}_i$ is the scale parameters of the random variable $\tilde{b}_i$.

Using the probability density function of the extreme value distributed FRV's, the equation (3) are modified to

$$\prod_{i=1}^{m} \left(\int_{u_i}^{\infty} \frac{1}{t} e^{-\frac{(b_i - s)}{t}} e^{-e^{-\frac{(b_i - s)}{t}}} db_i \right) \geq \left(1 - \gamma\right) \text{ where } u_i \in \tilde{A}_i[\alpha], t \in \tilde{\beta}_i[\alpha], s \in \tilde{\lambda}_i[\alpha].$$

$$\prod_{i=1}^{m} \left(1 - e^{-e^{-\frac{(u_i - s)}{t}}} \right) \geq \left(1 - \gamma\right) \text{ where } u_i \in \tilde{A}_i[\alpha], t \in \tilde{\beta}_i[\alpha], s \in \tilde{\lambda}_i[\alpha].$$

Since this inequality is true for all $\alpha \in (0, 1]$, the expression can be written in terms of α-cut as

$$\prod_{i=1}^{m} \left(1 - e^{-e^{-\frac{(\tilde{A}_i[\alpha] - \tilde{\lambda}_i[\alpha])}{\tilde{\beta}_i[\alpha]}}} \right) \geq \left(1 - \gamma\right)$$

Now using first decomposition theorem, the above equation is reduced to the following form as

$$i.e. \ \prod_{i=1}^{m} \left(1 - e^{-e^{-\frac{\left(\sum_{j=1}^{n} \tilde{a}_{ij} x_j - \tilde{\lambda}_i\right)}{\tilde{\beta}_i}}} \right) \geq \left(1 - \gamma\right)$$

269

Hence the FMOCCP model (1), is converted into the equivalent FP problem by using the derived methodology as

$$\text{Max } \tilde{Z}_k \cong \sum_{j=1}^{n} \tilde{c}_{kj} x_j \, ; \; k = 1, 2, \ldots, K$$

subject to

$$\prod_{i=1}^{m} \left(1 - e^{-e^{-\frac{\left[\sum_{j=1}^{n} \tilde{a}_{ij} x_j - \tilde{\lambda}_i \right]}{\tilde{\beta}_i}}} \right) \geq \left(1 - \gamma \right)$$

$$x_j \geq 0 \, ; \; j = 1, 2, \ldots, n \, . \tag{4}$$

In the second model it is considered that the parameters

$$\tilde{c}_{kj} \left(k = 1, 2, \ldots, K \, ; j = 1, 2, \ldots, n \right)$$

of all the objectives are considered as normally distributed FRVs. Let the mean

$$E \left(\tilde{c}_{kj} \right) = m_{\tilde{c}_{kj}} \left(k = 1, 2, \ldots, K \, ; j = 1, 2, \ldots, n \right)$$

associated with FRV

$$\tilde{c}_{kj} \left(k = 1, 2, \ldots, K \, ; j = 1, 2, \ldots, n \right)$$

be considered as FNs. Then the fuzzy E - model of the objectives of the model (2) can be presented as

$$\text{Max / Min } E(\tilde{Z}_k) \cong \sum_{j=1}^{n} E \left(\tilde{c}_{kj} \right) x_j \, ; \; k = 1, 2, \ldots, K \tag{5}$$

From equation (5) it is clear that objective functions are now involved with only possibilistic uncertainties.

Also In the model (2) the right side parameters of the constraints are taken as Cauchy distributed FRVs.

The Cauchy density function $f\left(x;\tilde{\beta},\tilde{\lambda}\right)$ for fuzzily described random variable $\tilde{X}$ with fuzzy parameters $\tilde{\beta}$ and $\tilde{\lambda}$ is expressed as

$$f\left(x;\tilde{\beta},\tilde{\lambda}\right) = \frac{t}{\pi\left[t^2 + \left(x - s\right)^2\right]}, \tag{6}$$

where the support of $\tilde{X}$ is defined on the set of real numbers; $t \in \tilde{\beta}\left[\alpha\right], s \in \tilde{\lambda}\left[\alpha\right]$; $\tilde{\beta}\left[\alpha\right], \tilde{\lambda}\left[\alpha\right]$ being the α –cut of the FNs $\tilde{\beta}, \tilde{\lambda}$, respectively.

Now the joint probability constraints in (2) is expressed as

$$\Pr\left(\sum_{j=1}^{n}\tilde{a}_{1j}x_j \gtrsim \tilde{b}_1, \sum_{j=1}^{n}\tilde{a}_{2j}x_j \gtrsim \tilde{b}_2, ..., \sum_{j=1}^{n}\tilde{a}_{mj}x_j \gtrsim \tilde{b}_m\right) \geq 1 - \gamma$$

As all $\tilde{b}_i$ are independent FRVs, therefore the joint constraint becomes a chance constraint in product form. Therefore, it can be written as

$$\text{i.e.} \prod_{i=1}^{m}\Pr\left(\sum_{j=1}^{n}\tilde{a}_{ij}x_j \gtrsim \tilde{b}_i\right) \geq 1 - \gamma$$

$$\text{i.e.} \prod_{i=1}^{m}\Pr\left(\tilde{A}_i \gtrsim \tilde{b}_i\right) \geq 1 - \gamma, \text{ where } \tilde{A}_i = \sum_{j=1}^{n}\tilde{a}_{ij}x_j$$

$$\text{i.e.} \prod_{i=1}^{m}\left\{\frac{1}{\pi}\int_{-\infty}^{u_i}\frac{t}{t^2 + \left(b_i - s\right)^2}\, db_i : t \in \tilde{\beta}_i\left[\alpha\right], s \in \tilde{\lambda}_i\left[\alpha\right], u_i \in \tilde{A}_i\left[\alpha\right]\right\} \geq 1 - \gamma$$

$$\text{i.e.} \prod_{i=1}^{m}\left(\tan^{-1}\frac{\left(u_i - s\right)}{t} + \frac{\pi}{2}\right) \geq \pi^m\left(1 - \gamma\right) \tag{7}$$

As described in the section 7.3, the expression (7) can be written in terms of $\alpha - \text{cut}$ as

$$\prod_{i=1}^{m} \left(\tan^{-1} \frac{\left(\tilde{A}_i[\alpha] - \tilde{\lambda}_i[\alpha] \right)}{\tilde{\beta}_i[\alpha]} + \frac{\pi}{2} \right) \geq \pi^m \left(1 - \gamma \right) \tag{8}$$

Again applying first decomposition theorem, the above expression reduced to the following form as

$$\text{i.e.} \prod_{i=1}^{m} \left(\tan^{-1} \frac{\left(\sum_{j=1}^{n} \tilde{a}_{ij} x_j - \tilde{\lambda}_i \right)}{\tilde{\beta}_i} + \frac{\pi}{2} \right) \geq \pi^m \left(1 - \gamma \right) \tag{9}$$

Hence the FSMOLP model (2), is converted into its equivalent FP model by using the derived methodology as

$$\text{Max / Min } E(\tilde{Z}_k) \cong \sum_{j=1}^{n} E\left(\tilde{c}_{kj} \right) x_j \,; \quad k = 1, 2, ..., K$$

subject to

$$\prod_{i=1}^{m} \left(\tan^{-1} \frac{\left(\sum_{j=1}^{n} \tilde{a}_{ij} x_j - \tilde{\lambda}_i \right)}{\tilde{\beta}_i} + \frac{\pi}{2} \right) \geq \pi^m \left(1 - \gamma \right)$$

$$x_j \geq 0 \,; \quad j = 1, 2, ..., n \,. \tag{10}$$

where

$$E\left(\tilde{c}_{kj} \right), \, \tilde{a}_{ij}, \tilde{\lambda}_i, \tilde{\beta}_i \, (k = 1, 2, ..., K; i = 1, 2, ..., m; j = 1, 2, ..., n)$$

are all FNs.

From equation (10) it is clear that FP model is developed from FSMOLP model in which the constraints are in multiplicative form. Thus the constraints are non-linear in nature. Therefore, in joint probabilistic constraint non-linear programming model is formed from linear programming through CCP methodology.

7.4 DETERMINISTIC MODEL CONSTRUCTION

In this section deterministic model is constructed from FP model through defuzzification methods described in Chapter 2. In this chapter two defuzzification methods are considered, *viz.*, canonical form of an FN and centroid of an FN. In the first model all fuzzy parameters are defuzzified using canonical form of an FN.

In this model it is assumed that all the fuzzy parameters

$$\tilde{c}_{kj}, \ \tilde{a}_{ij}, \tilde{\lambda}_i, \tilde{\beta}_i \ (k = 1,2,\ldots,K; i = 1,2,\ldots,m; j = 1,2,\ldots,n)$$

are triangular FNs. Then it can be expressed in the following form

$$\tilde{c}_{kj} = \left(c_{kj}^L, c_{kj}, c_{kj}^R \right), \ \tilde{a}_{ij} = \left(a_{ij}^L, a_{ij}, a_{ij}^R \right),$$

$$\tilde{\lambda}_i = \left(\lambda_i^L, \lambda_i, \lambda_i^R \right), \ \tilde{\beta}_i = \left(\beta_i^L, \beta_i, \beta_i^R \right).$$

where the superscript " R " denotes the right tolerance and the superscript " L " denotes the left tolerance of the triangular FNs.

The defuzzified values $V\left(\tilde{c}_{kj}\right), V\left(\tilde{a}_{ij}\right), V(\tilde{\lambda}_i), V(\tilde{\beta}_i)$ of these FNs are obtained as using canonical form of FN as

$$V\left(\tilde{c}_{kj}\right) = \frac{c_{kj}^L + 4c_{kj} + c_{kj}^R}{6},$$

$$V\left(\tilde{a}_{ij}\right) = \frac{a_{ij}^L + 4a_{ij} +, a_{ij}^R}{6},$$

$$V(\tilde{\lambda}_i) = \frac{\lambda_i^L + 4\lambda_i + \lambda_i^R}{6},$$

$$V(\tilde{\beta}_i) = \frac{\beta_i^L + 4\beta_i + \beta_i^R}{6}.$$

Thus the equivalent deterministic model of the fuzzy programming model (10) is stated as

$$\text{Max } V\left(\tilde{Z}_k\right) = \sum_{j=1}^{n} V\left(\tilde{c}_{kj}\right) x_j; \ k = 1, 2, \ldots, K$$

subject to

$$\prod_{i=1}^{m} \left(1 - e^{-e^{-\frac{\left[\sum_{j=1}^{n} V\left(\tilde{a}_{ij}\right) x_j - V(\tilde{\lambda}_i)\right]}{V(\tilde{\beta}_i)}}} \right) \geq \left(1 - \gamma\right)$$

$$x_j \geq 0; \ j = 1, 2, \ldots, n. \tag{11}$$

i.e., $\text{Max } V\left(\tilde{Z}_k\right) = \sum_{j=1}^{n} \frac{c_{kj}^L + 4c_{kj} + c_{kj}^R}{6} x_j; \ k = 1, 2, \ldots, K$

subject to

$$\prod_{i=1}^{m} \left(1 - e^{-e^{-\frac{\left[\sum_{j=1}^{n} \left(\frac{a_{ij}^L + 4a_{ij} + a_{ij}^R}{6} x_j\right) - \left(\frac{\lambda_i^L + 4\lambda_i + \lambda_i^R}{6}\right)\right]}{\left(\frac{\beta_i^L + 4\beta_i + \beta_i^R}{6}\right)}}} \right) \geq \left(1 - \gamma\right)$$

$$x_j \geq 0; \ j = 1, 2, \ldots, n. \tag{12}$$

In the second model all fuzzy parameters are defuzzified based on centroid method of FNs. All fuzzy parameters in this model are assumed to be triangular FNs.

Therefore,

$$E\left(\tilde{c}_{kj}\right),\ \tilde{a}_{ij}, \tilde{\lambda}_i, \tilde{\beta}_i\ (k=1,2,...,K; i=1,2,...,m; j=1,2,...,n)$$

are all triangular FNs with the following form

$$E\left(\tilde{c}_{kj}\right) = \left(E\left(c_{kj}^L\right), E\left(c_{kj}\right), E\left(c_{kj}^R\right)\right),\ \tilde{a}_{ij} = \left(a_{ij}^L, a_{ij}, a_{ij}^R\right),\ \tilde{\lambda}_i = \left(\lambda_i^L, \lambda_i, \lambda_i^R\right),$$
$$\tilde{\beta}_i = \left(\beta_i^L, \beta_i, \beta_i^R\right).$$

The crisp values of these FNs are obtained (Wang et al. (2006)) as

$$V\left(E\left(\tilde{c}_{kj}\right)\right) = \frac{1}{3}\sqrt{\left(E\left(c_{kj}^L\right) + E\left(c_{kj}\right) + E\left(c_{kj}^R\right)\right)^2 + 1}\ ;\ k = 1,2,...,K; j = 1,2,...,n$$

$$V\left(\tilde{a}_{ij}\right) = \frac{1}{3}\sqrt{\left(a_{ij}^L + a_{ij} + a_{ij}^R\right)^2 + 1}\ ;\ i = 1,2,...,m; j = 1,2,...,n$$

$$V\left(\tilde{\lambda}_i\right) = \frac{1}{3}\sqrt{\left(\lambda_i^L + \lambda_i + \lambda_i^R\right)^2 + 1}\ ;\ i = 1,2,...,m$$

$$V\left(\tilde{\beta}_i\right) = \frac{1}{3}\sqrt{\left(\beta_i^L + \beta_i + \beta_i^R\right)^2 + 1}\ ;\ i = 1,2,...,m$$

Thus the equivalent deterministic model of the fuzzy programming problem (12) can be stated as

$$\text{Max / Min } V\left(E(\tilde{Z}_k)\right) = \sum_{j=1}^{n} V\left(E\left(\tilde{c}_{kj}\right)\right) x_j\ ;\ k = 1,2,...,K$$

subject to

$$\prod_{i=1}^{m} \left(\tan^{-1} \frac{\left[\sum_{j=1}^{n} V\left(\tilde{a}_{ij}\right) x_j - V\left(\tilde{\lambda}_i\right) \right]}{V\left(\tilde{\beta}_i\right)} + \frac{\pi}{2} \right) \geq \pi^m \left(1 - \gamma\right)$$

$$x_j \geq 0 \quad j = 1, 2, \ldots, n.$$ (13)

i.e.,

$$\text{Max / Min } V\left(E(\tilde{Z}_k)\right) = \sum_{j=1}^{n} \frac{1}{3} \sqrt{\left(E\left(c_{kj}^L\right) + E\left(c_{kj}\right) + E\left(c_{kj}^R\right) \right)^2 + 1} \, x_j ;$$

$$k = 1, 2, \ldots, K$$

subject to

$$\prod_{i=1}^{m} \left(\frac{\pi}{2} + \tan^{-1} \frac{\left(\sum_{j=1}^{n} \left[\frac{1}{3} \sqrt{\left(a_{ij}^L + a_{ij} + a_{ij}^R \right)^2 + 1} \right] x_j - \left[\frac{1}{3} \sqrt{\left(\lambda_i^L + \lambda_i + \lambda_i^R \right)^2 + 1} \right] \right)}{\frac{1}{3} \sqrt{\left(\beta_i^L + \beta_i + \beta_i^R \right)^2 + 1}} \right) \geq \pi^m \left(1 - \gamma\right)$$

$$x_j \geq 0 \quad j = 1, 2, \ldots, n.$$ (14)

In an optimization problem, the DMs specify the fuzzy goals of each objective on the basis of their aspiration level which are obtained when each objective is solved individually under the system constraints defined in model (14). Let $V\left(\tilde{Z}_k\right)^b$ and $V\left(\tilde{Z}_k\right)^w$; $k = 1, 2, \ldots, K$ be the best and worst values obtained by solving each objective of the first model independently. Hence the fuzzy objective goal for each of the objectives of the first model is expressed as:

$$V\left(\tilde{Z}_k\right) \gtrsim V\left(\tilde{Z}_k\right)^b \text{ for } k = 1, 2, \ldots, K$$ (15)

Such fuzzy goals are now quantified by producing the corresponding membership functions on the basis of the achieved objective values. Thus the membership function for each of the objectives can be written as:

$$\mu_{V(\tilde{Z}_k)}(x) = \begin{cases} 0 & V(\tilde{Z}_k) \leq V(\tilde{Z}_k)^w \\ \dfrac{V(\tilde{Z}_k) - V(\tilde{Z}_k)^w}{V(\tilde{Z}_k)^b - V(\tilde{Z}_k)^w} & V(\tilde{Z}_k)^w \leq V(\tilde{Z}_k) \leq V(\tilde{Z}_k)^b \; ; \; k = 1,2,..,K \\ 1 & V(\tilde{Z}_k) \geq V(\tilde{Z}_k)^b \end{cases}$$

$$(16)$$

In a similar manner, multiple objectives of the second model are now solved to achieve the aspiration level of each objective. The aspiration or target level of the objectives are depends on the maximization or minimization types of objectives.

In the second model both type of objectives i.e., maximization type and minimization type are considered. Therefore, it is necessary to define fuzzy goals for both types of objectives.

- **Fuzzy Goals for Maximization Type of Objectives:** In a maximization type problem, the DMs specify the fuzzy goals in such a manner that the value of objectives should be substantially greater than or equal to some assigned value. To obtain the aspiration level to the fuzzy goals, each objective is solved independently under the modified set of system constraints. Let $V\left(E(\tilde{Z}_k)\right)^b$ (maximum) and $V\left(E(\tilde{Z}_k)\right)^w$ (minimum); $k = 1,2,...,K$ be the best and worst values obtained by solving each objective, independently. Hence the fuzzy objective goal for each of the objectives is expressed as:

$$V\left(E(\tilde{Z}_k)\right) \gtrsim V\left(E(\tilde{Z}_k)\right)^b \text{ (maximum) for } k = 1,2,...,K \qquad (17)$$

- **Fuzzy Goals for Minimization Type of Objectives:** In the case of minimization type problem, the DMs specify the fuzzy goals such that the value of the objectives should be substantially less than or equal to some assigned value. Each objective is now solved separately under the customized set of system constraints to achieve the desired target level to the fuzzy goals. Let $V\left(E(\tilde{Z}_k)\right)^b$ (minimum) and $V\left(E(\tilde{Z}_k)\right)^w$ (maximum); $k = 1, 2, ..., K$ be the best and worst values of the $k-$th objective obtained as described above. Hence the fuzzy objective goal for each of the objectives is expressed as:

$$V\left(E(\tilde{Z}_k)\right) \lesssim V\left(E(\tilde{Z}_k)\right)^b \text{ (minimum) for } k = 1, 2, ..., K \tag{18}$$

7.4.1 Construction of Membership Functions

The above defined fuzzy goals can be quantified by eliciting the corresponding membership functions of each objective on the basis of its best and worst values obtained by solving each objective independently under the modified set of system constraints. Thus the membership function for each of the objectives can be written as:

$$\mu_{V\left(E(\tilde{Z}_k)\right)}\left(x\right) = \begin{cases} 0 & if & V\left(E(\tilde{Z}_k)\right) \leq V\left(E(\tilde{Z}_k)\right)^w \\ \dfrac{V\left(E(\tilde{Z}_k)\right) - V\left(E(\tilde{Z}_k)\right)^w}{V\left(E(\tilde{Z}_k)\right)^b - V\left(E(\tilde{Z}_k)\right)^w} & if & V\left(E(\tilde{Z}_k)\right)^w \leq V\left(E(\tilde{Z}_k)\right) \leq V\left(E(\tilde{Z}_k)\right)^b \\ 1 & if & V\left(E(\tilde{Z}_k)\right) \geq V\left(E(\tilde{Z}_k)\right)^b \end{cases}$$

; $k = 1, 2, ..., K$ (for maximizing objectives) $\tag{19}$

or

$$\mu_{V\left(E(\tilde{Z}_k)\right)}\left(x\right) = \begin{cases} 0 & if & V\left(E(\tilde{Z}_k)\right) \geq V\left(E(\tilde{Z}_k)\right)^w \\ \dfrac{V\left(E(\tilde{Z}_k)\right)^w - V\left(E(\tilde{Z}_k)\right)}{V\left(E(\tilde{Z}_k)\right)^w - V\left(E(\tilde{Z}_k)\right)^b} & if & V\left(E(\tilde{Z}_k)\right)^b \leq V\left(E(\tilde{Z}_k)\right) \leq V\left(E(\tilde{Z}_k)\right)^w \\ 1 & if & V\left(E(\tilde{Z}_k)\right) \leq V\left(E(\tilde{Z}_k)\right)^b \end{cases}$$

; $k = 1, 2, .., K$ (for minimizing objectives) $\tag{20}$

Considering the above membership functions, the FGP model is derived in the following subsection.

7.5 FUZZY GOAL PROGRAMMING MODEL FORMULATION

In this section FGP model is formulated for both the models by considering the above membership functions for each objectives goals. This is done by introducing under- and over- deviational variables and assigning the highest membership value (unity) as the aspiration level to each of them.

In the following, FGP model for both the multi-objective non-linear programming problem is now developed. At first the FGP model for the first deterministic model can be formulated as

$$\text{Min D} = \sum_{k=1}^{K} w_k d_k^-$$

subject to

$$\frac{V\left(\tilde{Z}_k\right) - V\left(\tilde{Z}_k\right)^w}{V\left(\tilde{Z}_k\right)^b - V\left(\tilde{Z}_k\right)^w} + d_k^- - d_k^+ = 1; \; \left(k = 1, 2, ..., K\right)$$

$$\prod_{i=1}^{m} \left(1 - e^{-e^{\frac{\left[\sum_{j=1}^{n} V\left(\hat{a}_{ij}\right)x_j - V\left(\hat{\lambda}_i\right)\right]}{V\left(\hat{\beta}_i\right)}}} \right) \geq \left(1 - \gamma\right)$$

$$x_j \geq 0; \; j = 1, 2, ..., n. \tag{21}$$

where $d_k^-, d_k^+ \geq 0$ and $d_k^- \cdot d_k^+ = 0$ and w_k, $\left(k = 1, 2, ...K\right)$ are the fuzzy weights representing the relative importance of achieving the aspired levels of the goals in the decision making context with the values

$$w_k = \frac{1}{V\left(\tilde{Z}_k\right)^b - V\left(\tilde{Z}_k\right)^w}; \; k = 1, 2, ...K \tag{22}$$

The developed model is solved to find the most satisfactory solution in the fuzzy stochastic decision making environment.

Similarly, the FGP model for the second deterministic model is constructed as

$$\text{Min D} = \sum_{k=1}^{K} w_k d_k^-$$

subject to

$$\mu_{V(E(\tilde{z}_k))} + d_k^- - d_k^+ = 1; \ \left(k = 1, 2, ..., K \right)$$

$$\prod_{i=1}^{m} \left| \tan^{-1} \frac{\left[\sum_{j=1}^{n} V\left(\tilde{a}_{ij}\right) x_j - V\left(\tilde{\lambda}_i\right) \right]}{V\left(\tilde{\beta}_i\right)} + \frac{\pi}{2} \right| \geq \pi^m \left(1 - \gamma \right)$$

$$x_j \geq 0; \ j = 1, 2, ..., n. \tag{23}$$

where $d_k^-, d_k^+ \geq 0$ and $d_k^- \cdot d_k^+ = 0$ and $w_k, \left(k = 1, 2, ...K \right)$ are the fuzzy weights representing the relative importance of achieving the aspired levels of the goals in the decision making context with the values

$$w_k = \frac{1}{V\left(E(\tilde{Z}_k)\right)^b - V\left(E(\tilde{Z}_k)\right)^w} \ ; \ \text{(for maximizing objectives) or}$$

$$w_k = \frac{1}{V\left(E(\tilde{Z}_k)\right)^w - V\left(E(\tilde{Z}_k)\right)^b} \ ; \ \text{(for minimizing objectives) } k = 1, 2, ...K \tag{24}$$

The developed model (21) is solved to find the most satisfactory solution in a fuzzy stochastic decision making environment.

7.6 SOLUTION ALGORITHM

The methodology for describing the fuzzy multi-objective probabilistic programming model with joint probabilistic constraint is summarized in the form of an algorithm as follows:

Step 1: Considering the expectation of all the parameters of the objectives following normal distribution the E-model of the objectives is generated. *(for second model)*

Step 2: The CCP technique is applied to convert the joint probabilistic constraints into constraints involving only fuzzy parameters. *(for both models)*

Step 3: On the basis of nature of the FNs, the multi-objective fuzzy programming model are translated into MOLP model. *(for both models)*

Step 4: The individual best and worst values of each of the objectives is found in isolation under the modified set of system constraints. *(for both models)*

Step 5: The fuzzy membership goals of each of the objectives are constructed on the basis of the aspiration level. *(for both models)*

Step 6: The membership function for each type of objectives are developed depending on their best and worst values. *(for both models)*

Step 7: FGP approach is used to achieve maximum degree of each of the membership goals. *(for both models)*

Step 8: Stop.

7.7 NUMERICAL EXAMPLES

In this section two illustrative examples are provided to demonstrate the FSMOLP models with joint probabilistic constraint described in this chapter. In the first illustration, the FRVs follow extreme value distribution and in the second illustration, the FRVs are Cauchy distributed. Also, the parameters of the objectives of the second example are considered as normally distributed FRVs.

7.7.1 Numerical Example 1

In this example it is assumed that objective parameters and left side parameters of the chance constraints are triangular FNs. The right side parameters of the joint probabilistic constraints follows extreme value distributed FRVs. Thus the problem can be considered as

Find $X\left(x_1, x_2\right)$ so as to

$$\text{Max } \tilde{Z}_1 \cong \tilde{8}x_1 + \tilde{5}x_2$$

$$\text{Max } \tilde{Z}_2 \cong \tilde{2}x_1 + \widetilde{10}x_2$$

subject to

$$\Pr\left(\tilde{5}x_1 + \tilde{2}x_2 \lesssim \tilde{b}_1, \tilde{1}x_1 + \tilde{2}x_2 \lesssim \tilde{b}_2\right) \geq 0.90$$

$$x_1, x_2 \geq 0 \tag{25}$$

Here $\tilde{b}_1$, $\tilde{b}_2$ are independent extreme value distributed FRVs. It is also assumed that the i-th FRV has two known fuzzy parameters $\tilde{\lambda}_i$, $\tilde{\beta}_i$ ($i = 1, 2$). For this problem it is assume that $\tilde{\lambda}_1 = \tilde{6}, \tilde{\beta}_1 = \widetilde{0.5}$ and $\tilde{\lambda}_2 = \tilde{4}, \tilde{\beta}_2 = \widetilde{0.3}$.

All the FNs are taken as symmetric triangular FNs with the following forms

$$\tilde{2} = \left(1.5, 2, 2.5\right), \widetilde{10} = \left(9.95, 10, 10.05\right), \tilde{8} = \left(7, 8, 9\right), \quad \tilde{5} = \left(4.95, 5, 5.05\right)$$

$$\tilde{2} = \left(1.95, 2, 2.05\right), \tilde{1} = \left(0.75, 1, 1.25\right), \tilde{2} = \left(1, 2, 3\right)$$

$$\tilde{6} = \left(5.5, 6, 6.5\right), \widetilde{0.5} = \left(0.4, 0.5, 0.6\right), \tilde{4} = \left(3.9, 4, 4.1\right), \widetilde{0.3} = \left(0.1, 0.3, 0.5\right).$$

Using the proposed methodology the model (6.23) can be written as

$$\text{Max } \tilde{Z}_1 \cong \tilde{8}x_1 + \tilde{5}x_2$$

$$\text{Max } \tilde{Z}_2 \cong \tilde{2}x_1 + \widetilde{10}x_2$$

subject to

$$\left(1 - e^{-e^{-\frac{(\tilde{5}x_1 + \tilde{2}x_2 - \tilde{6})}{0.5}}}\right)\left(1 - e^{-e^{-\frac{\tilde{1}x_1 + \tilde{2}x_2 - \tilde{4}}{0.3}}}\right) \geq 0.90$$

$$x_1, x_2 \geq 0 \tag{26}$$

On the basis of a defuzzification method the above model (26) is expressed as

$$\text{Max } V(\tilde{Z}_1) = 8x_1 + 5x_2$$

$$\text{Max } V(\tilde{Z}_2) = 2x_1 + 10x_2$$

subject to

$$\left(1 - e^{-e^{-\frac{(5x_1 + 2x_2 - 6)}{0.5}}}\right)\left(1 - e^{-e^{-\frac{x_1 + 2x_2 - 4}{0.3}}}\right) \geq 0.90$$

$$x_1, x_2 \geq 0 \tag{27}$$

Now each objective is considered independently and is solved with respect to the system of constraints in (27) to find the best and worst values of the objectives.

The results are obtained as

$$V(\tilde{Z}_1)^b = 11.662 \;, V(\tilde{Z}_1)^w = 0 \;, V(\tilde{Z}_2)^b = 18.479 \;, V(\tilde{Z}_2)^w = 0.$$

Then the fuzzy goals of the objectives are found as

$$V(\tilde{Z}_1) \gtrsim 11.662 \;, V(\tilde{Z}_2) \gtrsim 18.479 \,.$$

Hence the FGP model is presented by elicited the membership goals as

Find $X\left(x_1, x_2\right)$ so as to

Min D $= 0.086d_1^- + 0.054d_2^-$

subject to

$0.688x_1 + 0.43x_2 + d_1^- - d_1^+ = 1$

$0.108x_1 + 0.54x_2 + d_2^- - d_2^+ = 1$

$$\left(1 - e^{-e^{-\frac{(5x_1 + 2x_2 - 6)}{0.5}}}\right)\left(1 - e^{-e^{-\frac{(x_1 + 2x_2 - 4)}{0.3}}}\right) \geq 0.90$$

$x_1, x_2 \geq 0$ \hfill (28)

where $d_1^-, d_1^+, d_2^-, d_2^+ \geq 0$ with $d_1^- . d_1^+,\ d_2^- . d_2^+ = 0$

Finally, the model (28) is solved to find the most satisfactory solution in the decision making context. The *software* LINGO (ver 11) is used to solve the problem.

The optimal solution of the problem (28) is obtained as $x_1 = 0.416, x_2 = 1.647$. The achieved objective values of the given problem is found as

$V(\tilde{Z}_1) = 11.563, V(\tilde{Z}_2) = 17.302$.

The compromise solution obtained by the above methodology is shown in Table 1.

Table 1. Compromise solution of the objectives

Objective Function	Solution Point	Compromise Solution of the Objective	Membership Value
$\tilde{Z}_1$	$x_1 = 0.416$ $x_2 = 1.647$	$V\left(\tilde{Z}_1\right) = 11.563$	$\mu_{V(\tilde{z}_1)} = 0.98$
$\tilde{Z}_2$		$V\left(\tilde{Z}_2\right) = 17.302$	$\mu_{V(\tilde{z}_2)} = 0.94$

From Table 1 it is clear that the compromise solutions of both the objectives are very close to the optimal solution of the objectives. This indicates the acceptability of the methodology presented in this chapter.

7.7.2 Numerical Example 2

To demonstrate the efficiency and acceptability of the model (2), the following problem of a hypothetical chocolate manufacturing company is considered and solved in this subsection.

A hypothetical chocolate manufacturing company produces two types of chocolates: C1 and C2, say. Both the chocolates require milk and choco as the main ingredients. The requirements of milk and choco to produce each chocolate are not exact. Some amounts of fuzziness involved with this requirement. To manufacture each unit of C1 and C2 daily, following quantities are required.

- Each unit of the chocolate 'C1' daily requires around 1 unit of milk and around 3 units of choco.
- Each unit of the chocolate 'C2' daily requires around 3 units of milk and around 2 units of choco.

Due to uncertainty in daily supply of milk and choco, the variables representing daily supply of milk and choco are considered as FRVs $\tilde{b}_1$ and $\tilde{b}_2$ following joint Cauchy distribution with known fuzzy parameters $\tilde{\lambda}_1 = \widetilde{65}$, $\tilde{\beta}_1 = \tilde{3}$ and $\tilde{\lambda}_2 = \widetilde{78}$, $\tilde{\beta}_2 = \tilde{4}$ for FRVs $\tilde{b}_1$ and $\tilde{b}_2$, respectively.

From the past experience, the managers of the company supposed that the profit for selling chocolates C1 and C2 are uncertain. It depends on the fluctuating price of different ingredients. Again, the time for producing chocolates is not certain. It depends on the number of labours and different machineries of the factory. So the parameters representing profit and time for manufacturing chocolates are considered as normally distributed FRVs with known mean and variances.

Further depending on the previous statistical data, the managing director of the company ensures that around 5 units of the chocolate C1 and around 3 units of chocolate C2 are needed daily. Considering all these assumptions the company wants to

1. maximize the total profit.

2. minimize the total production time.

The following terms are used to convert the production planning problem into the proposed FMOLSP model.

- **Index Set:** $i =$ types of Chocolates Ci; $i = 1, 2$
- **Objectives:** Two main goals of this company is to minimize total production time and to maximize total profit which are presented below
  - $\tilde{Z}_1 =$ total production time
  - $\tilde{Z}_2 =$ total profit
- **Decision Variable:** $x_i =$ amount of $i-$th chocolates to be produced by the chocolate manufacturing companies; $(i = 1, 2)$
- **FRVs:** As the production time of each chocolate depends on the number of labours and different machineries, therefore, the production time of the chocolates are not exact. Again the profit from the chocolates depends on the demands of the products on the markets and the selling price of other manufacturers. Also it depends on the wages of the labours and the price of the ingredients. Thus the parameters representing the price of the chocolates and time for manufacturing chocolates are considered as normally distributed FRVs. Finally, as the daily supply of milk and choco are not exact. It depends on the production of milk and choco by the milk and choco producing farm. So these are considered as Cauchy distributed FRVs.
  - $\widetilde{PC}_i =$ profit for selling of the $i-$th chocolate produced by the chocolate manufacturing company which also follows normal distribution; $(i = 1, 2)$
  - $\widetilde{TMC}_i =$ time required for manufacturing $i-$th chocolate produced by the companies which is normally distributed; $(i = 1, 2)$
  - $\widetilde{SM} =$ daily supply of milk which is Cauchy distributed;
  - $\widetilde{SC} =$ daily supply of choco which also follows Cauchy distribution;
- **Fuzzy Parameters:** The amounts of milks and choco required in producing chocolates are uncertain due to imprecise measurements. These parameters are considered as fuzzy. It may be fluctuating i.e. some amounts of vagueness may exist in the quantities of the ingredients. Therefore, some kinds of possibilistic uncertainty may occur. Thus for

more acceptability in real life the parameters representing the amounts of ingredients in chocolates are considered as FNs.

- $\widetilde{AM}_i$ = amount of milk in the $i-$. th chocolate; $(i=1,2)$
- $\widetilde{AC}_i$ = amount of choco in the $i-$th chocolate; $(i=1,2)$.

Thus the FMOLSP model for the chocolate manufacturing industry is formulated as follows

$$\text{Min } \tilde{Z}_1 \cong \sum_{i=1}^{2}\widetilde{TMH}_i x_i$$

$$\text{Max } \tilde{Z}_2 \cong \sum_{i=1}^{2}\widetilde{PC}_i x_i$$

subject to

$$\Pr\left(\sum_{i=1}^{3}\widetilde{AM}_i x_i \leq \widetilde{SM} , \sum_{i=1}^{3}\widetilde{AC}_i x_i \leq \widetilde{SC}\right) \geq 1-\gamma$$

$$x_i \geq 0 \; ; \; i=1,2 \tag{29}$$

Here $\widetilde{PC}_i, \widetilde{TMH}_i (i=1,2)$ are normally distributed FRVs, $\widetilde{SM}, \widetilde{SC}$ are Cauchy distributed FRVs, and $\widetilde{AM}_i$, $\widetilde{AC}_i (i=1,2)$ are triangular FNs.

Taking the expectation of all the parameters of the objectives and applying the CCP technique, the FP model is evaluated as

$$\text{Min } E\left(\tilde{Z}_1\right) \cong \sum_{i=1}^{2}E\left(\widetilde{TMH}_i\right)x_i$$

$$\text{Max } E\left(\tilde{Z}_2\right) \cong \sum_{i=1}^{2}E\left(\widetilde{PC}_i\right)x_i$$

subject to

$$\left(\frac{\pi}{2} - \tan^{-1}\frac{\left(\sum_{i=1}^{3}\widetilde{AM}_{i}x_{i} - \tilde{\lambda}_{1}\right)}{\tilde{\beta}_{1}}\right)\left(\frac{\pi}{2} - \tan^{-1}\frac{\left(\sum_{i=1}^{3}\widetilde{AC}_{i}x_{i} - \tilde{\lambda}_{2}\right)}{\tilde{\beta}_{2}}\right) \geq \pi^{2}\left(1 - \gamma\right)$$

$$x_{i} \geq 0 \; ; \; i = 1,2 \tag{30}$$

The expectation $E\left(\widetilde{PC}_{i}\right)$, $E\left(\widetilde{TMH}_{i}\right)$ of the normally distributed FRVs $\widetilde{PC}_{i}, \widetilde{TMH}_{i}\left(i = 1,2\right)$, the parameters $\tilde{\lambda}_{1}$,$\tilde{\beta}_{1}$ of the Cauchy distributed FRV $\widetilde{SM}$ and the parameters $\tilde{\lambda}_{2}$,$\tilde{\beta}_{2}$ of the Cauchy distributed FRV $\widetilde{SC}$ are taken as triangular FNs.

The values of the parameters are given in Tables 2-4.

Applying the defuzzification technique (Wang et al., 2006) of FNs the deterministic equivalent of FP model (28) is formed. As described in the solution algorithm the objectives of the deterministic model are solved under the system constraints to find the best and worst values of the objectives.

Table 2. Values of the expectation of normally distributed FRVs

$E\left(\widetilde{PC}_{i}\right)$	$E\left(\widetilde{TMH}_{i}\right)$
$E\left(\widetilde{PC}_{1}\right) = \widetilde{19} = \left(18,19,20\right)$	$E\left(\widetilde{TMH}_{1}\right) = \tilde{2} = \left(1.95,2,2.05\right)$
$E\left(\widetilde{PC}_{2}\right) = \widetilde{12} = \left(11,12,13\right)$	$E\left(\widetilde{TMH}_{2}\right) = \tilde{7} = \left(6.55,7,7.45\right)$

Table 3. Values of median and scale parameters of cauchy distributed FRVs

Random Variable	Scale Parameter $\tilde{\beta}_{i}$	Median $\tilde{\lambda}_{i}$
$\widetilde{SM}$	$\tilde{\beta}_{1} = \tilde{3} = \left(2.95,3,3.05\right)$	$\tilde{\lambda}_{1} = \widetilde{65} = \left(64,65,66\right)$
$\widetilde{SC}$	$\tilde{\beta}_{2} = \tilde{4} = \left(3.9,4,4.1\right)$	$\tilde{\lambda}_{2} = \widetilde{78} = \left(76,78,80\right)$

Table 4. Values of the parameters of the constraints

Constraints	Amounts of Milk and Choco in Chocolates
1st constraint	*Amounts of milk* $\widetilde{AM_1} = \tilde{1} = \left(0.95, 1, 1.05\right),$ $\widetilde{AM_2} = \tilde{3} = \left(2.95, 3, 3.05\right)$
2nd constraint	*Amounts of choco* $\widetilde{AC_1} = \tilde{3} = \left(2.5, 3, 3.5\right),$ $\widetilde{AC_2} = \tilde{2} = \left(1.95, 2, 2.05\right)$

The best and worst values of the objectives are shown in Table 5.

Finally, FGP technique is used to find the most compromise and acceptable solution of all the objectives. The compromise solution obtained by applying the proposed methodology are shown in Table 6.

The Comparison between the compromise solution and best solution are shown in Figure 1.

From this diagram it is very much clear that the compromise solution of all the objectives is very close to their best solution values. Thus solution

Table 5. Best and worst solution of the objectives

Objectives	Best Solution	Worst Solution
$\tilde{Z}_1$ (total production time)	$V\left(E(\tilde{Z}_1)\right)^b = 31$	$V\left(E(\tilde{Z}_1)\right)^w = 115$
$\tilde{Z}_2$ (total profit)	$V\left(E(\tilde{Z}_2)\right)^b = 383$	$V\left(E(\tilde{Z}_2)\right)^w = 131$

Table 6. Compromise solution of the objectives

Objectives	Solution Point	Compromise Solution	Membership Value
total production time	$x_1 = 18$ $x_2 = 3$	$V\left(E(\tilde{Z}_1)\right) = 57$	$\mu_{DV\left(E(\tilde{Z}_1)\right)} = 0.71$
total profit		$V\left(E(\tilde{Z}_2)\right) = 378$	$\mu_{DV\left(E(\tilde{Z}_2)\right)} = 0.98$

Figure 1a. Comparison between the solutions: total production time

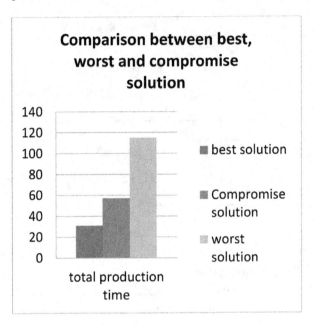

Figure 1b. Comparison between the solutions: profit

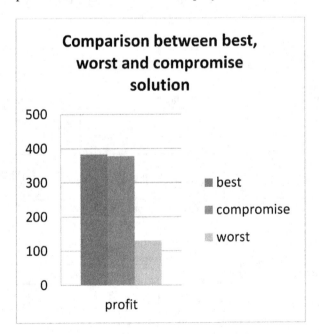

obtained by applying the methodology presented in this chapter is acceptable to the organizations. From the membership value of the objectives it is seen that out of the two objectives, the solutions shows more priorities on the profit than the production time, which is more realistic compare to practical situations. Because every manufacturing industry wants more profit in this competitive market situation. This result indicates that the organization will make a good amount of profit in a very competitive market situation which is one of the most important goals of organization.

7.8 CONCLUSION

This chapter presents methodology for solving FSMOLP problem involving Cauchy distributed and extreme value distributed FRVs following joint probability distribution using FGP technique. Both types of uncertainties like fuzziness and randomness are considered in this chapter simultaneously. The above defined models can be applied to any real life decision making situation in which there is some probabilistic fuzzy parameters follows cauchy and extreme value distribution. Also it is possible to consider other types of FRVs such as logarithmic, binomial, exponential, normal distribution instead of Cauchy and extreme value distribution. Further the proposed methodology can be used to solve fractional programming problem, bilevel or multilevel optimization problems in a fuzzy stochastic decision making arena.

REFERENCES

Arnold, T., Henrion, R., Moller, A., & Vigerske, S. (2014). A mixed-integer stochastic nonlinear optimization problem with joint probabilistic constraints. *Pacific Journal of Optimization, 10*, 5–20.

Buckley, J. J., & Eslami, E. (2004a). Uncertain probabilities-II. *Soft Computing, 8*(3), 193–199. doi:10.100700500-003-0263-5

Buckley, J. J., & Eslami, E. (2004b). Uncertain probabilities-III. *Soft Computing, 8*(3), 200–206. doi:10.100700500-003-0263-5

Cadenas, J. M., & Verdegay, J. L. (2000). Using ranking functions in multi-objective fuzzy linear programming. *Fuzzy Sets and Systems, 111*(1), 47–53. doi:10.1016/S0165-0114(98)00451-5

Campus, L., & Verdegay, J. L. (1989). Linear programming problem and ranking of fuzzy numbers. *Fuzzy Sets and Systems*, *32*(1), 1–11. doi:10.1016/0165-0114(89)90084-5

Chanas, S. (1983). The use of parametric programming in fuzzy linear programming. *Fuzzy Sets and Systems*, *11*(1-3), 243–251. doi:10.1016/S0165-0114(83)80083-9

Chiang, J. (2001). Fuzzy linear programming based on statistical confidence interval and interval-valued fuzzy set. *European Journal of Operational Research*, *129*(1), 65–86. doi:10.1016/S0377-2217(99)00404-X

Dai, C., Li, Y. P., & Huang, G. H. (2012). An interval-parameter chance-constrained dynamic programming approach for capacity planning under uncertainty. *Resources, Conservation and Recycling*, *62*, 37–50. doi:10.1016/j.resconrec.2012.02.010

Delgado, M., Verdegay, J. L., & Vila, M. A. (1989). A general model for fuzzy linear programming. *Fuzzy Sets and Systems*, *29*(1), 21–29. doi:10.1016/0165-0114(89)90133-4

Gharraph, M. K., & Mohammed, W. (1994). Chance constrained linear programming when the coefficients are uniform random variables. *The Egyptian Computer Journal ISSR*, *22*(1), 1–16.

Hop, N. V. (2007). Solving fuzzy (stochastic) linear programming problems using superiority and inferiority measures. *Information Sciences*, *177*(9), 1977–1991. doi:10.1016/j.ins.2006.12.001

Jamison, K. D., & Lodwick, W. A. (2001). Fuzzy linear programming using a penalty method. *Fuzzy Sets and Systems*, *119*(1), 97–110. doi:10.1016/S0165-0114(99)00082-2

Jimenez, M., Arenas, M., Bilbao, A., & Rodrıguez, M. V. (2007). Linear programming with fuzzy parameters: An interactive method resolution. *European Journal of Operational Research*, *177*(3), 1599–1609. doi:10.1016/j.ejor.2005.10.002

Kwakernaak, H. (1978). Fuzzy Random variable-I. Definitions and theorems. *Information Sciences*, *15*(1), 1–29. doi:10.1016/0020-0255(78)90019-1

Kwakernaak, H. (1979). Fuzzy Random variable-II. Algorithms and examples for the discrete case. *Information Sciences, 17*(3), 253–278. doi:10.1016/0020-0255(79)90020-3

Lai, Y. J., & Hwang, C. L. (1992). *Fuzzy mathematical programming methods and applications*. Berlin: Springer-Verlag. doi:10.1007/978-3-642-48753-8

Lai, Y. J., & Hwang, C. L. (1992). Interactive fuzzy linear programming. *Fuzzy Sets and Systems, 45*(2), 169–183. doi:10.1016/0165-0114(92)90116-L

Leon, T., & Vercher, E. (2004). Solving a class of fuzzy linear programs by using semi-infinite programming techniques. *Fuzzy Sets and Systems, 146*(2), 235–252. doi:10.1016/j.fss.2003.09.010

Liu, B., & Iwamura, K. (1998). Chance constrained programming with fuzzy parameters. *Fuzzy Sets and Systems, 94*(2), 227–237. doi:10.1016/S0165-0114(96)00236-9

Liu, J., Lisser, A., & Chen, Z. (2016). Stochastic geometric optimization with joint probabilistic constraints. *Operations Research Letters, 44*(5), 687–691. doi:10.1016/j.orl.2016.08.002

Liu, K., Li, Q., & Zhang, Z. H. (2019). Distributionally robust optimization of an emergency medical service station location and sizing problem with joint chance constraints. *Transportation Research Part B: Methodological, 119*, 79–101. doi:10.1016/j.trb.2018.11.012

Liu, X. (2001). Measuring the satisfaction of constraints in fuzzy linear programming. *Fuzzy Sets and Systems, 122*(2), 263–275. doi:10.1016/S0165-0114(00)00114-7

Liu, Y. K., & Liu, B. (2003). Fuzzy random variables. A scalar expected value operator. *Fuzzy Optimization and Decision Making, 2*(2), 143–160. doi:10.1023/A:1023447217758

Lv, Y., Huang, G. H., Li, Y. P., Yang, Z. F., & Sun, W. (2011). A two-stage inexact joint-probabilistic programming method for air quality management under uncertainty. *Journal of Environmental Management, 92*(3), 813–826. doi:10.1016/j.jenvman.2010.10.027 PMID:21067860

Maleki, H. R. (2003). Ranking functions and their applications to fuzzy linear programming. *Far East Journal of Mathematical Sciences, 4*(3), 283–301.

Mohammed, W. (2000). Chance constrained fuzzy goal programming with right-hand side uniform random variable coefficients. *Fuzzy Sets and Systems, 109*(1), 107–110. doi:10.1016/S0165-0114(98)00151-1

Puri, M. L., & Ralescu, D. A. (1986). Fuzzy random variables. *Journal of Mathematical Analysis and Applications, 114*(2), 409–422. doi:10.1016/0022-247X(86)90093-4

Reich, D. (2013). A linear programming approach for linear programs with probabilistic constraints. *European Journal of Operational Research, 230*(3), 487–494. doi:10.1016/j.ejor.2013.04.049

Sahoo, N. P., & Biswal, M. P. (2005). Computation of some stochastic linear programming problems with Cauchy and extreme value distributions. *International Journal of Computer Mathematics, 82*(6), 685–698. doi:10.1080/00207160412331336080

Sinha, S. B., Hulsurkar, S., & Biswal, M. P. (2000). Fuzzy programming approach to multiobjective probabilistic linear programming problems when the coefficients follow joint normal distribution. *Fuzzy Sets and Systems, 109*(1), 91–96. doi:10.1016/S0165-0114(98)00070-0

van Ackooij, W., Henrion, R., Möller, A., & Zorgati, R. (2011). On joint probabilistic constraints with Gaussian coefficient matrix. *Operations Research Letters, 39*(2), 99–102. doi:10.1016/j.orl.2011.01.005

Verdegay, J. L. (1982). Fuzzy mathematical programming. In M. M. Gupta & E. Sanchez (Eds.), *Fuzzy Information and Decision Processes* (pp. 231–236). Amsterdam: North-Holland.

Wang, Y. M., Yang, J. B., Xu, D. L., & Chin, K. S. (2006). On the centroids of fuzzy numbers. *Fuzzy Sets and Systems, 157*(7), 919–926. doi:10.1016/j.fss.2005.11.006

Zadeh, L. A. (1968). Probability measures of fuzzy events. *Journal of Mathematical Analysis and Applications, 23*(2), 421–427. doi:10.1016/0022-247X(68)90078-4

Zhang, C., Li, M., & Guo, P. (2017). An interval multistage joint probabilistic chance-constrained programming model with left-hand-side randomness for crop area planning under uncertainty. *Journal of Cleaner Production, 167*, 1276–1289. doi:10.1016/j.jclepro.2017.05.191

Zhang, G., Wu, Y. H., Remias, M., & Lu, J. (2003). Formulation of fuzzy linear programming problems as four objective constrained optimization problems. *Applied Mathematics and Computation, 139*(2-3), 383–399. doi:10.1016/S0096-3003(02)00202-3

Zimmermann, H. J. (1978). Fuzzy programming and linear programming with several objective functions. *Fuzzy Sets and Systems, 1*(1), 45–55. doi:10.1016/0165-0114(78)90031-3

Zimmermann, H. J. (1983). Fuzzy Mathematical Programming. *Computers & Operations Research, 10*(4), 291–298. doi:10.1016/0305-0548(83)90004-7

Section 2
Applications

Chapter 8
Fuzzy Multi–Objective Stochastic Models for Municipal Solid Waste Management

ABSTRACT

With rising urbanization and change in lifestyle and food habits of human beings, the amount of municipal solid wastes (MSWs) are now being increasing day by day, and the composition of wastes are now also being changed. Therefore, it is now becoming essential to develop a consistent mathematical model for managing those wastes in a systematic manner. In this context, fuzzy chance constrained programming (FCCP) model becomes useful to handle wastes efficiently through the process of selecting sorting stations, treatment facilities, etc. through an efficient way so that the net system cost of sorting and transporting the wastes would be minimized, and the revenue generated from different sorting stations and different treatment facilities would be to maximized. From that view point, in this chapter, a fuzzy chance constrained programming (CCP) model is developed for MSW management. Most of the parameters involved with this model are imprecisely defined and probabilistically uncertain. So, the parameters of the objectives are considered as FNs, and the right side parameters of the probabilistic constraints involve normally distributed fuzzy random variables (FRVs). To resolve the cases arising due to the multiple occurrences of fuzzy goals, a fuzzy goal programming (FGP) has been adopted. To expound the potential use of the approach, a modified version of a case example, studied previously, is considered and solved. The achieved model solution is discussed elaborately to illustrate the proposed methodology for MSW management.

DOI: 10.4018/978-1-5225-8301-1.ch008

8.1 FORMULATION OF SOLID WASTE MANAGEMENT SYSTEM

Ever since the ancient times, human and animals are using the resources of the earth to support life and disposing the wastes that are discarded as useless or unwanted. In those days, the disposal of wastes did not pose significant problems as the population size was small and a vast expanse of land was available for the assimilation of such wastes.

However, in recent years due to accelerated urbanization and growing population, waste management has become challenging to urban communities (Cheng et al., 2009). Also environmental protection has challenged many regional planners and decision makers. Such challenges are complicated by the rapid socio-economic development associated with increasing contaminant emissions and decreasing resources availabilities (Maqsood and Huang, 2003). As the capacity of the landfill areas gradually decreases, there is arising an increasing demand of other waste treatment facilities such as incinerator, composting facility and recycling facility. Thus those facilities are becoming an integrated part of waste management systems (Tang et al., 2008; Guo et al., 2008; Guo et al., 2009). Also, balancing the conflicts among various system components and considering limitations of the constraints of resources, it is necessary to develop acceptable planning techniques to effectively allocate the available resources (Maqsood et al., 2004). In 2015, Soltani et al. developed a review article in multi-criteria decision-making in the context of MSW management. Mir et al. (2016) developed an optimized MSW management model based on multi criteria decision analysis. Tozlu et al. (2016) proposed a technology to convert waste into energy for MSW management in Gaziantep.

In the context of modelling MSW management problems, probabilistic or possibilistic uncertainties are frequently involved with the amount of disposal of wastes and the costs related to collections, transportations, treatment of wastes, etc. Moreover, these uncertainties may further affect not only interactions among these complex, dynamic and uncertain parameters, but also their associations with economic penalties if the promised targets are violated (Howe et al., 2003). Consequently, various methods have been developed to deal with such uncertainties for planning MSW management systems. Most of them can be dealt with fuzzy, stochastic and interval mathematical programming approaches (Kirca and Erkip, 1988; Zhu and Revelle, 1993; Leimbach, 1996; Chang and Wang, 1994).

Charnes and Cooper (1962, 1963) first introduced the concept of CCP for dealing with probabilistic uncertainties. A bibliographical study has been presented by Infanger (1993) on stochastic programming. Several researchers (Kataoka, 1963; Geoffrion, 1967) further extended the concept of CCP technique for solving different real life problems. With this advancement in computational resources and scientific computing techniques, many complicated optimization models can now be solved efficiently. Guo *et al.*(2008) presented an interval stochastic quadratic programming approach to MSW management.

Another type of uncertainty that the researchers often face is fuzzy (Bellman and Zadeh, 1970) or possibilistic uncertainty. It is worthy to mention here that the possibilistic uncertainties arise if the parameters of the model are not properly defined. Bellman and Zadeh (1970) first introduced the concept of decision making in fuzzy environment. Tanaka *et al.* (1973) extended this concept for solving mathematical programming problems. Afterwards, Delgado *et al.* (1989) presented a general model for solving fuzzy linear programming (FLP) problems in which constraints are involved with fuzzy inequality and the parameters of the constraints are FNs. In order to solve those types of FLP problems, different approaches are presented by several researchers.

In recent years the decision makers feel the presence of probabilistic and possibilistic uncertainty simultaneously. In fuzzy CCP, probabilistic and fuzzy aspects are combined together to derive an efficient model to describe real-life planning problems where uncertainty and imprecision of information co-occur. However, this kind of combination creates a great challenge for the researcher (Iskander, 2006; Liu, 2001) to find an efficient solution method for solving decision making models involving both fuzzy and stochastic terms.

For dealing with the models consisting of an imprecisely defined multiple numbers of objectives, fuzzy goal programming (FGP) technique (Hannan, 1980; Narasimhan, 1980) is appeared as an efficient tool for making proper decisions. FGP technique for solving CCP problems involving FRVs have been recently studied by Biswas and Modak (2011, 2012).

Li *et al.* (2008) developed an inexact stochastic quadratic programming method for MSW management in which the uncertainties relating to operational and transportation costs are expressed in terms of probability distributions and discrete intervals. Afterwards, Guo and Huang (2011) proposed an inexact fuzzy-stochastic quadratic programming approach for waste management under multiple uncertainties. However, the Interval parameter quadratic programming encountered difficulties when the model's right-hand-side coefficients in the constraints are highly uncertain. Wang et al. (2018) presented an interval-valued fuzzy multi-criteria decision making technique for the evaluation of waste-to-energy, MSW treatment, and best available technology in the recent past. Muneeb et al. (2018) described a decentralized bi-level decision planning model for MSW recycling and management with cost reliability under uncertain environment. A fuzzy multi-objective optimization case study based on an anaerobic co-digestion process of food waste leachate and piggery wastewater has recently been presented by Choi et al. (2018).

8.1.1. Major Components in Solid Waste Management System

There are four major components which are frequently involved in an MSW management system. These are sources of waste generation or dumping stations, sorting stations, waste treatment and disposal facilities. Generally, MSW consists of household waste, construction and demolition debris, sanitation residue, and waste from streets. The garbage is generated mainly from residential and commercial complexes. In addition to the above wastes, another type of waste called domestic hazardous waste may also be generated at the household level. These include used aerosol cans, batteries, households, kitchen and drain cleaning agents, car batteries and car care products, cosmetic items, chemical-based insecticides/pesticides, light bulbs, tube-lights and compact fluorescent lamps (CFLs), paint, oil, lubricant and their empty containers, etc. In this system at first MSWs are flows from different dumping stations to different sorting stations. In sorting stations, wastes are separated into two main categories, wet or biodegradable wastes and dry or non-biodegradable wastes. The biodegradable wastes include kitchen waste including food waste of all kinds, cooked and uncooked, including eggshells and bones, flower and fruit waste including juice peels and house-plant waste, garden sweeping or yard waste consisting of green/dry leaves, sanitary wastes, green waste from vegetable & fruit vendors/shops and waste from food & tea stalls/shops etc., whereas, non-biodegradable wastes includes paper and plastic, cardboard and cartons, containers of all kinds excluding those containing hazardous material, packaging of all kinds, glass of all kinds, metals of all kinds, rags, rubber, house sweeping, ashes, foils, wrappings, pouches, sachets and tetra packs (rinsed), discarded electronic items from offices, colonies viz. cassettes, computer diskettes, printer cartridges and electronic parts and discarded clothing, furniture and equipment. Then these wastes are transported from different sorting stations to some specified treatment facilities within multiple periods. Some portions of the total sorted wastes are transferred directly from sorting facility to the waste disposal facility, *viz.*, landfill. The Remaining portions are shifted to the waste treatment facilities, *viz.*, incinerator, composting and recycling. Also, residues generated at the treatment facilities are transferred to the disposal facility. Now, different treatment facilities i.e. landfilling, incinerator facility, composting facility and recycling facility are discussed briefly.

8.1.1.1 Landfilling

A landfill is an engineered pit, in which layers of solid waste are filled, compacted and covered for final disposal. It is lined at the bottom to prevent groundwater pollution. Engineered landfills consist of a lined bottom; a leachate collection and treatment system; groundwater monitoring; gas extraction (the gas is flared or used for energy production) and a cap system. The capacity is planned and the site is chosen based on an environmental risk assessment study. There are also landfills specially designed to encourage anaerobic biodegradation of the organic fraction of the waste for biogas production by monitoring the oxygen conditions and moisture content. Landfills need expert design as well as skilled operators and a proper management to guarantee their functionality.

Figure 1. Images of landfilling

Advantages and Disadvantages of Landfilling

Advantages:

1. Effective disposal method if managed well.
2. Sanitary disposal method if managed effectively.
3. Energy production and fast degradation if designed as a bioreactor landfill.

Disadvantages:

1. Fills up quickly if waste is not reduced and reusable waste is not collected separately and recycled.
2. A reasonably large area is required.
3. Risk of groundwater contamination if not sealed correctly or the liner system is damaged.
4. High costs for high-tech landfills.
5. If not managed well, there is a risk of the landfill degenerating into an open dump.
6. Once the landfill site is shut down monitoring must continue for the following 50 to 100 years

8.1.1.2 Incineration Facility

Incineration is the process of control and complete combustion for burning solid wastes. It is the treatment of waste material by combustion of organic substances present in the waste materials. It converts the waste material into heat, flue gas and ash which are released into the atmosphere without any further treatment for usage.

In incineration plant the recyclable material is segregated and the rest of the material is burnt. There are three main types of combustion technologies used in incineration plant. They are

1. **Rotary Kiln:** A rotary kiln are mainly used for combusting industrial and hazardous wastes, but is also used in some MSW incinerators. The principle design consists of two thermal treatment chambers. A slightly inclined primary chamber where waste is fed in, rotated and thermally decomposed by the heat radiation. The secondary or the re-combustion

Figure 2. Incineration process

chamber positioned at the rear of the kiln where the decomposition air and the rest waste is completely burnt with the supply of secondary air.

2. **Moving Grate:** A moving grate is a typical combustion design of a MSW incinerator. Waste is dropped by a crane on to the descending grate, which moves into the combustion chamber and eventually moves down to drop the burnt residuals into an ash pit at the other end of the grate.

3. **Fluidized Bed:** Fluidized bed combustion has recently increased in application in MSW incinerators, although it is still mainly used for the combustion of hazardous waste. There are different types of fluidized bed combustors such as, bubbling, rotating and circulating fluidized bed.

Advantages and Disadvantages of Incineration Process

Advantages:

1. Waste volumes are reduced by an estimated 80-95%.
2. The need for land and landfill place is greatly reduced.

Disadvantages:

1. An incineration plant involves heavy investment and high operating cost.
2. It requires skilled staff to run and maintain the incineration process.

8.1.1.3 Composting Facility

Composting is a biological degradation process during which conversion of organic matter of the solid wastes into simpler units of carbon and nitrogen takes place. The decomposition of organic materials is carried out primarily by bacteria, yeasts and fungi. Other microorganisms such as ants, nematodes and oligochaete worms are also involved in the process of degradation. In general, the rate of organic matter degradation depends mostly on degrading microbes and their activities. Microorganims through different kinds of substrate specific hydrolytic enzymes promote the degradation of organic matter followed by the solubilisation of these degraded materials into simple water-soluble compounds.

Although composting is a biological process, it is controlled by many physico-chemical parameters. Some of the most influential parameters on composting are temperature, pH, aeration, moisture, size, nature and volume of substrate etc.

Advantages and Disadvantages of Composting Process

Advantages:

1. Compost has an abundance of nutrients and is suitable for a wide variety of end uses, such as landscaping, topsoil blending, and growth media.
2. Compost has less nitrogen than bio-solids from other stabilization processes, due to the loss of ammonia during composting.

Figure 3. Composting process

3. Compost increases the water content and retention of sandy soils.
4. Compost increases aeration and water infiltration of clay soils.

Disadvantages:

1. Windrow and aerated static pile composting require relatively large areas, and odor control is a common problem.
2. Ambient temperatures and weather conditions influence windrow and aerated static pile composting.

8.1.1.4 Recycling Facility

Recycling process of MSW includes collection, sorting and processing of materials obtained from the solid wastes and the transformation or remanufacture of those materials for reuse as new products and/or other productive resources. Recycling effort can be implemented in the residential, commercial and industrial solid wastes.

MSW is comprised of a number of solid waste streams. The two principal solid waste streams that compose MSW are:

Figure 4. Recycling of wastes

1.   **Residential Solid Waste:** Residential solid wastes mean solid wastes that are generated from single-family residences, and multi-family residences. Recyclables prevalent in the residential waste stream include paper, plastics, metals, food scraps, yard trimmings, textiles and personal electronics.

2.   **Commercial Solid Waste:** Solid waste generated from businesses, offices, stores, markets, institutions, government, and other commercial establishments are all included in Commercial solid wastes. Recyclables common in the commercial waste stream include paper, plastic, metals, food, yard trimmings, lumber, textiles, and electronic devices.

Again, different types of costs, *viz.*, transportation costs of the transferring process of the wastes and residues, operational costs related to the treatment and sorting of the wastes are frequently involved with this process. Some revenues are also generated from the sorting stations and from the treatment facilities.

Thus the total process is summarized in Fig. 5.

The problem under consideration is to determine the appropriate distribution of waste flow among these components so as to minimize the net system costs consisting of transportation and operational costs and to maximize the revenue in the planned period.

Figure 5. Components and key factors in the MSW management system

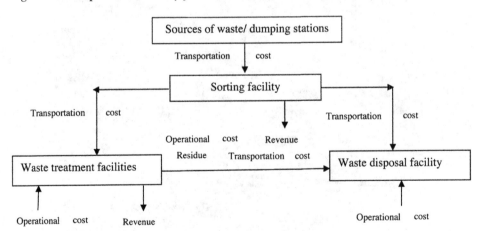

8.1.2. Mathematical Model for Solid Waste Management

The model is formulated with the assumption that solid wastes are transferred from L number of dumping stations to n number of sorting stations and then to m number of treatment and disposal facilities within K periods. The following terms are used to formulate the proposed model.

Index Sets

The following indices are used to frame the model

$l =$ Dumping station; $l = 1, 2, ..., L$;
$i =$ Treatment and disposal facilities; $i = 1, 2, ..., m$; in this case, $i = 1$ for the landfill and $i = 2, 3, ..., m$ for other waste treatment facilities such as recycling, incinerating and composting facilities;
$j =$ Sorting station; $j = 1, 2, ..., n$;
$k =$ Planning period; $k = 1, 2, ..., K$;

Objectives

The two objectives of this study are to minimize the system costs and to maximize the revenues which are presented below.

$\tilde{Z}_1 =$ Net operating cost + Transportation cost;
$\tilde{Z}_2 =$ Net revenue;

Decision Variable

$x_{ijk} =$ Amount of waste from sorting station j to facility i during period k;
$y_{ljk} =$ Amount of waste from dumping station l to sorting station j during period k;

Crisp Parameters

$L_k =$ Length of the planning period k;
$RF_i =$ Residue flow rate from the treatment facility $i (\neq 1)$ to the landfill (% of incoming mass to treatment facilities);

β_{jk} = Probability of waste generation rate $\left(\tilde{W}_{jk}\right)$ in sorting station j during period k;

γ = Probability of landfill capacity;

Fuzzy Parameters

Since the transportation cost of wastes and residues, operation cost of the facility and sorting, revenue from the treatment facility and sorting stations and capacity of the treatment facility are not fixed, it varies time to time, so some kind of possibilistic uncertainty occurs. Also the diversion rate of waste flow may vary due to the nature of the wastes. Thus for more acceptability in real life these parameters are considered as FNs.

$\widetilde{TCW}_{ljk}$ = Transportation cost of waste from dumping station l to sorting station j during period k;

$\widetilde{OS}_{jk}$ = Operational cost of sorting station j during period k;

$\widetilde{RS}_{jk}$ = Revenue from the sorting station j during period k;

$\widetilde{WTC}_{ijk}$ = Waste transportation cost from sorting station j to facility i during period k;

$\widetilde{RTC}_{ik}$ = Residue transportation cost from facility $i(\neq 1)$ to landfill during period k;

$\widetilde{OC}_{ik}$ = Operational cost of facility i during period k;

$\widetilde{RE}_{ik}$ = Revenue from the treatment facility $i(\neq 1)$ during period k;

$\widetilde{TC}_{i}$ = Capacity of waste treatment facility $i(\neq 1)$;

$\widetilde{WD}_{ik}$ = Diversion rate of waste flow to waste treatment facilities in period k;

FRV

The waste generation rate is uncertain in an MSW system. Also, landfill capacity may vary as the model is developed for the long time prospective. So these quantities are considered as FRVs.

$\tilde{W}_{jk}$ = Waste generation rate in sorting station j during period k which is normally distributed;

$\widetilde{LC}$ = Landfill capacity which follows normal distribution;

Thus in an MSW system, considering transportation cost, operation cost, generated revenue are expressible using FNs; and waste generation amounts, landfill capacity are expressible using FRVs, an FMOCCP model is formulated as

Minimize

$$\tilde{Z}_1 \cong \sum_{i=1}^{m}\sum_{j=1}^{n}\sum_{k=1}^{K} L_k \left(\widetilde{WTC}_{ijk} + \widetilde{OC}_{ik} \right) x_{ijk} + \sum_{i=2}^{m}\sum_{j=1}^{n}\sum_{k=1}^{K} L_k \left(\widetilde{RTC}_{ik} + \widetilde{OC}_{1k} \right) RF_i x_{ijk}$$

$$+ \sum_{l=1}^{L}\sum_{j=1}^{n}\sum_{k=1}^{K} L_k \left(\widetilde{TCW}_{ljk} + \widetilde{OS}_{jk} \right) y_{ljk}$$

Maximize $\tilde{Z}_2 \cong \sum_{i=2}^{m}\sum_{j=1}^{n}\sum_{k=1}^{K} L_k \widetilde{RE}_{ik} x_{ijk} + \sum_{l=1}^{L}\sum_{j=1}^{n}\sum_{k=1}^{K} L_k \widetilde{RS}_{jk} y_{ljk}$

subject to

$$\Pr \left(\sum_{j=1}^{n}\sum_{k=1}^{K} L_k \left(x_{1jk} + \sum_{i=2}^{m} RF_i x_{ijk} \right) \lesssim \widetilde{LC} \right) \gtrsim 1 - \gamma \text{ (Landfill capacity constraint)}$$

$$\sum_{j=1}^{n} x_{2jk} \lesssim \widetilde{TC}_2; \forall k \text{ (Incinerator capacity constraints)}$$

$$\sum_{j=1}^{n} x_{3jk} \lesssim \widetilde{TC}_3; \forall k \text{ (Composting facility capacity constraints)}$$

$$\sum_{j=1}^{n} x_{4jk} \lesssim \widetilde{TC}_4; \forall k \text{ (Material recycling facility capacity constraints)}$$

$$\Pr \left(\sum_{i=1}^{m} x_{ijk} \gtrsim \tilde{W}_{jk} \right) \gtrsim \beta_{jk}; \forall j, k \text{ (Waste disposal demand constraints)}$$

$\Pr\left(x_{ijk} \gtrsim \widetilde{WD}_{ik}\tilde{W}_{jk}\right) \gtrsim 1 - \beta_{jk}; \forall j, k, i = 2, 3, ..., m$ (Waste diversion rate constraints)

$$\sum_{l=1}^{L} y_{ljk} \geq \sum_{i=1}^{m} x_{ijk}; \forall j, k$$

$x_{ijk} \geq 0; \forall i, j, k$ (Non-negativity constraints)

$y_{ljk} \geq 0; \forall l, j, k$ (Non-negativity constraints)   (1)

In this model

$$\widetilde{LC}, \tilde{W}_{jk}\left(j = 1, 2, ..., n; k = 1, 2, ..., K\right)$$

are considered as FRVs. The mean $E\left(\widetilde{LC}\right)$ and variance $V\left(\widetilde{LC}\right)$ of the FRV $\widetilde{LC}$ are considered as FNs. Similarly, the mean $E\left(\tilde{W}_{jk}\right)$ and the variance V $\left(\tilde{W}_{jk}\right)$ of the FRV $\tilde{W}_{jk}$ are also taken as FNs.

Again, the possibilistic uncertainties (i) waste transportation cost, (ii) residue transportation cost, (iii) operational cost, (iv) capacity of the treatment facilities and (v) revenue from the sorting and treatment facilities are taken as FNs.

From the above discussion, the readers can understand that the mathematical model of SWM can be expressed as multi-objective linear programming model in hybrid uncertain environment. Different form of multi-objective linear programming model under fuzzy stochastic uncertain environment and their solution methodologies are already elaborately in Chapter 3. Therefore the above mathematical model for SWM can be equivalent to any one of the multi-objective linear programming model discussed in chapter 3 or a combination of some multi-objective linear programming models.

In the following section, a fuzzy programming model of the fuzzy stochastic mathematical programming model of SWM is developed through Chance constrained programming methodology discussed in chapter 3.

8.2 METHODOLOGY FOR SOLVING SOLID WASTE MANAGEMENT MODEL

In this chapter, a weighted FGP model is developed to minimize the net system costs and maximize the revenue generated from different sorting stations and treatment facilities. The right side parameters of the probabilistic constraints are taken as normally distributed FRVs and the coefficients of the objectives and the right side parameter of some other constraints are considered as FNs. In the solution process the probabilistic constraints are converted to fuzzy constraints applying CCP technique in fuzzy environment. Then by considering fuzzy nature of parameters involved with the model, the problem is decomposed on the basis of tolerance values of the parameters. Afterwards each objective is solved independently under the modified system constraints to construct the membership goals of each objective. Finally weighted FGP model is used to achieve the most satisfactory decision in the decision making arena. Then the developed methodology is applied in the context of solid waste management for validating the model.

8.2.1 Development of Solid Waste Management Model

The fuzzy stochastic multi-objective linear programming model representation the mathematical form of SWM in hybrid uncertain decision making context is already presented as

Minimize

$$\tilde{Z}_1 \cong \sum_{i=1}^{m}\sum_{j=1}^{n}\sum_{k=1}^{K}L_k\left(\widetilde{WTC}_{ijk} + \widetilde{OC}_{ik}\right)x_{ijk} + \sum_{i=2}^{m}\sum_{j=1}^{n}\sum_{k=1}^{K}L_k\left(\widetilde{RTC}_{ik} + \widetilde{OC}_{1k}\right)RF_ix_{ijk}$$

$$+\sum_{l=1}^{L}\sum_{j=1}^{n}\sum_{k=1}^{K}L_k\left(\widetilde{TCW}_{ljk} + \widetilde{OS}_{jk}\right)y_{ljk}$$

Maximize $\tilde{Z}_2 \cong \sum_{i=2}^{m}\sum_{j=1}^{n}\sum_{k=1}^{K}L_k\widetilde{RE}_{ik}x_{ijk} + \sum_{l=1}^{L}\sum_{j=1}^{n}\sum_{k=1}^{K}L_k\widetilde{RS}_{jk}y_{ljk}$

subject to

311

$$\Pr\left(\sum_{j=1}^{n}\sum_{k=1}^{K}L_k\left(x_{1jk}+\sum_{i=2}^{m}RF_ix_{ijk}\right)\lesssim \widetilde{LC}\right)\gtrsim 1-\gamma$$

$$\sum_{j=1}^{n}x_{2jk}\lesssim \widetilde{TC}_2;\forall k$$

$$\sum_{j=1}^{n}x_{3jk}\lesssim \widetilde{TC}_3;\forall k$$

$$\sum_{j=1}^{n}x_{4jk}\lesssim \widetilde{TC}_4;\forall k$$

$$\Pr\left(\sum_{i=1}^{m}x_{ijk}\gtrsim \tilde{W}_{jk}\right)\gtrsim \beta_{jk};\forall j,k$$

$$\Pr\left(x_{ijk}\gtrsim \widetilde{WD}_{ik}\tilde{W}_{jk}\right)\gtrsim 1-\beta_{jk};\forall j,k,i=2,3,\dots,m$$

$$\sum_{l=1}^{L}y_{ljk}\geq \sum_{i=1}^{m}x_{ijk};\forall j,k$$

$$x_{ijk}\geq 0;\forall i,j,k$$

$$y_{ljk}\geq 0;\forall l,j,k \tag{2}$$

where $\widetilde{LC}$, and $\tilde{W}_{jk},\left(j=1,2,\dots n;k=1,2,\dots,K\right)$, represents requirement vectors and are treated as normally distributed FRVs whose mean and variances are considered as triangular FNs. Also the other requirement vector $\widetilde{TC}_s$, ($s=2,3,4$) are taken as triangular FNs. The coefficients of the objectives

$$\widetilde{WTC}_{ijk}, \widetilde{OC}_{ik}, \widetilde{RTC}_{ik}, \widetilde{TCW}_{ijk}, \widetilde{OS}_{jk}, \widetilde{RE}_{ik}, \widetilde{RS}_{jk} \left(k = 1, 2, ..., K; i = 1, 2, ..., m; j = 1, 2, ..., n \right)$$

are imprecise price parameters represented in terms of triangular FNs. The parameters of the constraints

$$\widetilde{WD}_{ik} \left(i = 1, 2, ..., m; k = 1, 2, ..., K \right)$$

are also taken as triangular FNs. The other parameters

$$L_k, RF_i \left(i = 1, 2, ..., m; k = 1, 2, ..., K \right)$$

of the model represented using real numbers and γ, β_{jk} denote real numbers lying in $[0,1]$. As some parameters of the objectives are triangular FNs, then the objectives $\tilde{Z}_1$ and $\tilde{Z}_2$ are also triangular FNs and the symbols $\lesssim, \gtrsim, \cong$ represents less than or equal, greater than or equal and equal respectively in fuzzy sense.

Now applying CCP technique (discussed elaborately in chapter 3) to all the probabilistic constraints of model (2), the system constraints are modified as follows

$$\sum_{j=1}^{n} \sum_{k=1}^{K} L_k \left(x_{1jk} + \sum_{i=2}^{m} RF_i x_{ijk} \right) \lesssim E\left(\widetilde{LC}\right) + \sqrt{V\left(\widetilde{LC}\right)} \Phi^{-1}\left(\gamma\right);$$
for $i = 1, 2, ..., m; j = 1, 2, ..., n; k = 1, 2, ..., K$

$$\sum_{i=1}^{m} x_{ijk} \gtrsim E\left(\tilde{W}_{jk}\right) + \sqrt{V\left(\tilde{W}_{jk}\right)} \Phi^{-1}\left(\beta_{jk}\right); \text{ for } j = 1, 2, ..., n; k = 1, 2, ..., K$$

$$x_{ijk} \gtrsim \widetilde{WD}_{ik} E\left(\tilde{W}_{jk}\right) + \sqrt{V\left(\tilde{W}_{jk}\right)} \Phi^{-1}\left(1 - \beta_{jk}\right); \text{ for }$$
$$i = 1, 2, ..., m; j = 1, 2, ..., n; k = 1, 2, ..., K$$

Hence the FMOCCP model (2) is converted into the equivalent FP problem using the derived methodology as

Minimize

$$
\tilde{Z}_1 \cong \sum_{i=1}^{m}\sum_{j=1}^{n}\sum_{k=1}^{K} L_k \left(\widetilde{WTC}_{ijk} + \widetilde{OC}_{ik} \right) x_{ijk} + \sum_{i=2}^{m}\sum_{j=1}^{n}\sum_{k=1}^{K} L_k \left(\widetilde{RTC}_{ik} + \widetilde{OC}_{1k} \right) RF_i x_{ijk}
$$

$$
+ \sum_{l=1}^{L}\sum_{j=1}^{n}\sum_{k=1}^{K} L_k \left(\widetilde{TCW}_{ljk} + \widetilde{OS}_{jk} \right) y_{ljk}
$$

Maximize $\tilde{Z}_2 \cong \displaystyle\sum_{i=2}^{m}\sum_{j=1}^{n}\sum_{k=1}^{K} L_k \widetilde{RE}_{ik} x_{ijk} + \sum_{l=1}^{L}\sum_{j=1}^{n}\sum_{k=1}^{K} L_k \widetilde{RS}_{jk} y_{ljk}$

subject to

$$
\sum_{j=1}^{n}\sum_{k=1}^{K} L_k \left(x_{1jk} + \sum_{i=2}^{m} RF_i x_{ijk} \right) \lesssim E\left(\widetilde{LC} \right) + \sqrt{V\left(\widetilde{LC} \right)} \Phi^{-1}\left(\gamma \right)
$$

$$
\sum_{j=1}^{n} x_{2jk} \lesssim \widetilde{TC}_2 ; \forall k
$$

$$
\sum_{j=1}^{n} x_{3jk} \lesssim \widetilde{TC}_3 ; \forall k
$$

$$
\sum_{j=1}^{n} x_{4jk} \lesssim \widetilde{TC}_4 ; \forall k
$$

$$
\sum_{i=1}^{m} x_{ijk} \gtrsim E\left(\tilde{W}_{jk} \right) + \sqrt{V\left(\tilde{W}_{jk} \right)} \Phi^{-1}\left(\beta_{jk} \right) ; \forall j,k
$$

$$x_{ijk} \gtrsim \widetilde{WD}_{ik}\, E\left(\tilde{W}_{jk}\right) + \sqrt{V\left(\tilde{W}_{jk}\right)}\, \Phi^{-1}\left(1 - \beta_{jk}\right); \forall j, k, i = 2, 3, \ldots, m$$

$$\sum_{l=1}^{L} y_{ljk} \geq \sum_{i=1}^{m} x_{ijk}; \forall j, k$$

$$x_{ijk} \geq 0; \forall i, j, k$$

$$y_{ljk} \geq 0; \forall l, j, k \tag{3}$$

The mean and variances of the normally distributed FRVs $\widetilde{LC}$ are

$$E\left(\widetilde{LC}\right) = \left(eLC^1, eLC, eLC^2\right) \text{ and } V\left(\widetilde{LC}\right) = \left(vLC^1, vLC, vLC^2\right).$$

Then the square root of the triangular FN

$$V\left(\widetilde{LC}\right) \text{ is } \sqrt{V\left(\widetilde{LC}\right)} = \left(\sqrt{vLC^1}, \sqrt{vLC}, \sqrt{vLC^2}\right).$$

Similarly the mean and variance of the other FRVs is considered.

Now, considering all the FNs as triangular FNs of the form $\tilde{a} = \left(a^1, a, a^2\right)$, (where the superscript '1' represents left tolerance and '2' represents right tolerance) the fuzzy model is decomposed into the following form as

Minimize

$$Z_1^L = \sum_{i=1}^{m}\sum_{j=1}^{n}\sum_{k=1}^{K} L_k \left(\left(WTC_{ijk}^1 + \left(WTC_{ijk} - WTC_{ijk}^1\right)\alpha\right) + \left(OC_{ik}^1 + \left(OC_{ik} - OC_{ik}^1\right)\alpha\right)\right)x_{ijk} +$$
$$\sum_{i=2}^{m}\sum_{j=1}^{n}\sum_{k=1}^{K} L_k \left(\left(RTC_{ik}^1 + \left(RTC_{ik} - RTC_{ik}^1\right)\alpha\right) + \left(OC_{1k}^1 + \left(OC_{1k} - OC_{1k}^1\right)\alpha\right)\right)RF_i x_{ijk} +$$
$$\sum_{l=1}^{L}\sum_{j=1}^{n}\sum_{k=1}^{K} L_k \left(\left(TCW_{ljk}^1 + \left(TCW_{ljk} - TCW_{ljk}^1\right)\alpha\right) + \left(OS_{jk}^1 + \left(OS_{jk} - OS_{jk}^1\right)\alpha\right)\right)y_{ljk}$$

Minimize

$$Z_1^R = \sum_{i=1}^{m}\sum_{j=1}^{n}\sum_{k=1}^{K} L_k \left(\left(WTC_{ijk}^2 - \left(WTC_{ijk}^2 - WTC_{ijk}\right)\alpha\right) + \left(OC_{ik}^2 - \left(OC_{ik}^2 - OC_{ik}\right)\alpha\right)\right)x_{ijk} +$$

$$\sum_{i=2}^{m}\sum_{j=1}^{n}\sum_{k=1}^{K} L_k \left(\left(RTC_{ik}^2 - \left(RTC_{ik}^2 - RTC_{ik}\right)\alpha\right) + \left(OC_{1k}^2 - \left(OC_{1k}^2 - OC_{1k}\right)\alpha\right)\right)RF_i x_{ijk} +$$

$$\sum_{l=1}^{L}\sum_{j=1}^{n}\sum_{k=1}^{K} L_k \left(\left(TCW_{ljk}^2 + \left(TCW_{ljk}^2 - TCW_{ljk}\right)\alpha\right) + \left(OS_{jk}^2 - \left(OS_{jk}^2 - OS_{jk}\right)\alpha\right)\right)y_{ljk}$$

Maximize

$$Z_2^L = \sum_{i=2}^{m}\sum_{j=1}^{n}\sum_{k=1}^{K} L_k \left(RE_{ik}^1 + \left(RE_{ik} - RE_{ik}^1\right)\alpha\right)x_{ijk} + \sum_{l=1}^{L}\sum_{j=1}^{n}\sum_{k=1}^{K} L_k \left(RS_{jk}^1 + \left(RS_{jk} - RS_{jk}^1\right)\alpha\right)y_{ljk}$$

Maximize

$$Z_2^R = \sum_{i=2}^{m}\sum_{j=1}^{n}\sum_{k=1}^{K} L_k \left(RE_{ik}^2 - \left(RE_{ik}^2 - RE_{ik}\right)\alpha\right)x_{ijk} + \sum_{l=1}^{L}\sum_{j=1}^{n}\sum_{k=1}^{K} L_k \left(RS_{jk}^2 - \left(RS_{jk}^2 - RS_{jk}\right)\alpha\right)y_{ljk}$$

subject to

$$\sum_{j=1}^{n}\sum_{k=1}^{K} L_k \left(x_{1jk} + \sum_{i=2}^{m} RF_i x_{ijk}\right) \le \left(eLC^1 + \left(eLC - eLC^1\right)\alpha\right)$$
$$+ \left(\sqrt{vLC^1} + \left(\sqrt{vLC} - \sqrt{vLC^1}\right)\alpha\right)\Phi^{-1}\left(\gamma\right)$$

$$\sum_{j=1}^{n}\sum_{k=1}^{K} L_k \left(x_{1jk} + \sum_{i=2}^{m} RF_i x_{ijk}\right) \le \left(eLC^2 - \left(eLC^2 - eLC\right)\alpha\right)$$
$$+ \left(\sqrt{vLC^2} - \left(\sqrt{vLC^2} - \sqrt{vLC}\right)\alpha\right)\Phi^{-1}\left(\gamma\right)$$

$$\sum_{j=1}^{n} x_{2jk} \le \left(TC_2^1 + \left(TC_2 - TC_2^1\right)\alpha\right); \forall k$$

$$\sum_{j=1}^{n} x_{2jk} \leq \left(TC_2^2 - \left(TC_2^2 - TC_2 \right) \alpha \right); \forall k$$

$$\sum_{j=1}^{n} x_{3jk} \leq \left(TC_3^1 + \left(TC_3 - TC_3^1 \right) \alpha \right); \forall k$$

$$\sum_{j=1}^{n} x_{3jk} \leq \left(TC_3^2 - \left(TC_3^2 - TC_3 \right) \alpha \right); \forall k$$

$$\sum_{j=1}^{n} x_{4jk} \leq \left(TC_4^1 + \left(TC_4 - TC_4^1 \right) \alpha \right); \forall k$$

$$\sum_{j=1}^{n} x_{4jk} \leq \left(TC_4^2 - \left(TC_4^2 - TC_4 \right) \alpha \right); \forall k$$

$$\sum_{i=1}^{m} x_{ijk} \geq \left(eW_{jk}^1 + \left(eW_{jk} - eW_{jk}^1 \right) \alpha \right) + \left(\sqrt{vW_{jk}^1} + \left(\sqrt{vW_{jk}} - \sqrt{vW_{jk}^1} \right) \alpha \right) \Phi^{-1} \left(\beta_{jk} \right); \forall j,k$$

$$\sum_{i=1}^{m} x_{ijk} \geq \left(eW_{jk}^2 - \left(eW_{jk}^2 - eW_{jk} \right) \alpha \right) + \left(\sqrt{vW_{jk}^2} - \left(\sqrt{vW_{jk}^2} - \sqrt{vW_{jk}} \right) \alpha \right) \Phi^{-1} \left(\beta_{jk} \right); \forall j,k$$

$$x_{ijk} \geq \left(WD_{ik}^1 + \left(WD_{ik} - WD_{ik}^1 \right) \alpha \right) \left(eW_{jk}^1 + \left(eW_{jk} - eW_{jk}^1 \right) \alpha \right)$$
$$+ \left(\sqrt{vW_{jk}^1} + \left(\sqrt{vW_{jk}} - \sqrt{vW_{jk}^1} \right) \alpha \right) \Phi^{-1} \left(1 - \beta_{jk} \right); \forall j,k, i = 2,3,\ldots,m$$

$$x_{ijk} \geq \left(WD_{ik}^2 - \left(WD_{ik}^2 - WD_{ik} \right) \alpha \right) \left(eW_{jk}^2 - \left(eW_{jk}^2 - eW_{jk} \right) \alpha \right)$$
$$+ \left(\sqrt{vW_{jk}^2} - \left(\sqrt{vW_{jk}^2} - \sqrt{vW_{jk}} \right) \alpha \right) \Phi^{-1} \left(1 - \beta_{jk} \right); \forall j,k, i = 2,3,\ldots,m$$

$$\sum_{l=1}^{L} y_{ljk} \geq \sum_{i=1}^{m} x_{ijk}; \forall j,k$$

$x_{ijk} \geq 0; \forall i,j,k$

$y_{ljk} \geq 0; \forall l,j,k$

$0 \leq \alpha \leq 1$ \hfill (4)

where $\tilde{Z}_1[\alpha] = [Z_1^L, Z_1^R]$ and $\tilde{Z}_2[\alpha] = [Z_2^L, Z_2^R]$ denotes the α – cut of $\tilde{Z}_1$ and $\tilde{Z}_2$ respectively. Here α represents the degree of fuzziness involved with parameters of the objectives and the system constraints.

Now, considering the ambiguous nature of the parameters, it is quite natural to assume that the decision makers may have fuzzy goals for each of the objectives. To obtain the aspiration level to the fuzzy goals, each objective is solved individually under the modified set of system constraints defined in model (4).

Let $\left(Z_1^L\right)^b, \left(Z_1^R\right)^b, \left(Z_2^L\right)^b, \left(Z_2^R\right)^b$ be the best values of the objectives and $\left(Z_1^L\right)^w, \left(Z_1^R\right)^w, \left(Z_2^L\right)^w, \left(Z_2^R\right)^w$ be the worst values of the objectives obtained by solving each objective independently. Hence the fuzzy objective goal for each of the objectives is expressed as

$$Z_2^L \gtrsim \left(Z_2^L\right)^b; \ Z_2^R \gtrsim \left(Z_2^R\right)^b; \ Z_1^L \lesssim \left(Z_1^L\right)^b; \ Z_1^R \lesssim \left(Z_1^R\right)^b; \hfill (5)$$

Such fuzzy goals are quantified by eliciting the corresponding membership functions on the basis of the achieved values. Thus the membership function of each of the objectives is written as

$$\mu_{Z_2^L} = \begin{cases} 0 & if \quad Z_2^L \leq \left(Z_2^L\right)^w \\ \dfrac{Z_2^L - \left(Z_2^L\right)^w}{\left(Z_2^L\right)^b - \left(Z_2^L\right)^w} & if \quad \left(Z_2^L\right)^w \leq Z_2^L \leq \left(Z_2^L\right)^b; \\ 1 & if \quad Z_2^L \geq \left(Z_2^L\right)^b \end{cases} \hfill (6)$$

$$
\mu_{Z_1^L} = \begin{cases} 0 & if & Z_1^L \geq \left(Z_1^L\right)^w \\[2mm] \dfrac{\left(Z_1^L\right)^w - Z_1^L}{\left(Z_1^L\right)^w - \left(Z_1^L\right)^b} & if & \left(Z_1^L\right)^b \leq Z_1^L \leq \left(Z_1^L\right)^w \; ; \\[2mm] 1 & if & Z_1^L \leq \left(Z_1^L\right)^b \end{cases}
\tag{7}
$$

Similarly, the membership functions $\mu_{Z_1^R}$ and $\mu_{Z_2^R}$ can also be defined. As described in chapter 3, FGP model is now developed for SWM in the next section to achieve the desired goals as much as possible.

8.2.2 Weighted Fuzzy Goal Programming Model

In weighted FGP model formulation process, the membership functions are first converted into flexible membership goals by introducing under- and over- deviational variables to each of them and thereby assigning the highest membership value (unity) as the aspiration level for each of them. Also, it is evident that the achievement of all the membership goals to its highest degree is not possible in a MODM context. So the under-deviational variables are minimized to achieve the goal values of objectives in the decision making environment.

Thus a weighted FGP model is formulated as

Minimize $D = w_1^L d_{1L}^- + w_1^R d_{1R}^- + w_2^L d_{2L}^- + w_2^R d_{2R}^-$

So as to satisfy

$$
\frac{\left(Z_1^L\right)^w - Z_1^L}{\left(Z_1^L\right)^w - \left(Z_1^L\right)^b} + d_{1L}^- - d_{1L}^+ = 1 \; ; \quad \frac{\left(Z_1^L\right)^w - Z_1^L}{\left(Z_1^L\right)^w - \left(Z_1^L\right)^b} + d_{1R}^- - d_{1R}^+ = 1
$$

$$
\frac{Z_2^L - \left(Z_2^L\right)^w}{\left(Z_2^L\right)^b - \left(Z_2^L\right)^w} + d_{2L}^- - d_{2L}^+ = 1 \; ; \quad \frac{Z_2^L - \left(Z_2^L\right)^w}{\left(Z_2^L\right)^b - \left(Z_2^L\right)^w} + d_{2R}^- - d_{2R}^+ = 1
$$

subject to the system constraints as described in model (4). (8)

Here $w_1^L, w_1^R, w_2^L, w_2^R \geq 0$ represents the numerical weights of the goals which are determined as:

$$w_1^L = \frac{1}{\left(Z_1^L\right)^w - \left(Z_1^L\right)^b} \;, \qquad w_1^R = \frac{1}{\left(Z_1^R\right)^w - \left(Z_1^R\right)^b} \;, \qquad w_2^L = \frac{1}{\left(Z_2^L\right)^b - \left(Z_2^L\right)^w} \;,$$

$$w_2^R = \frac{1}{\left(Z_2^R\right)^b - \left(Z_2^R\right)^w}$$

The developed model (8) is solved to find the most satisfactory solution in the decision making environment.

8.2.3 Solution Algorithm

The methodology for describing the model is presented in the form of an algorithm as follows

Step 1: Using CCP technique, the probabilistic constraints are converted into constraints involving only fuzzy uncertainty.
Step 2: On the basis of FNs, the fuzzy constraints and the fuzzy objectives are defuzzified.
Step 3: The individual optimal value of each of the objectives is found in isolation.
Step 4: Construct the fuzzy membership goals of each of the objectives.
Step 5: FGP approach is used to achieve maximum degree of each of the membership goals.
Step 6: Stop.

8.3 A CASE EXAMPLE OF A MUNICIPAL SOLID WASTE MANAGEMENT SYSTEM

In this treatise a modified version of a case example for an MSW management system, studied previously by Guo and Huang (2011), in the recent past has been considered to demonstrate the proposed methodology.

A hypothetical waste management system is considered wherein a manager is responsible for allocating waste flows from two dumping stations to two sorting stations and then to four treatment facilities over a 10-year planning horizon (with two 5-year periods). One dumping station is situated near one sorting station and the other dumping station is situated near the other. It is assumed that wastes are transported from one dumping station to its nearest sorting station to reduce the transportation costs. In that locality one landfill facility, an incinerator, a composting facility and a recycling facility are available to dispose of the garbage collected from the municipal areas. The capacities of incinerator, composting facility and recycling facility are imprecise in nature which are given by

$$\widetilde{300} = \left(280, 300, 320\right), \widetilde{400} = \left(380, 400, 420\right) \text{ and } \widetilde{350} = \left(330, 350, 370\right)$$

tonnes, respectively. The capacity of the landfill is considered as a random variable following fuzzy normal distribution with mean $\tilde{2} \times 10^6 = \left(1, 2, 3\right) \times 10^6$ and variance $\left(4, 6, 9\right)$ tonnes. The incinerator generates residues of 25% of the incoming waste streams. The composting facility generates residue of 10% of the incoming waste streams and the recycling facility generates residue of 8% of the incoming waste streams. Table 1 presents waste transportation costs, operation costs of the facilities which are taken as triangular FNs. Table 2 represents the data for the revenue from the sorting and treatment facilities. Table 3 presents the waste generation rates of the different cities which are considered as normally distributed FRVs. Table 4 shows the diversion rate under different periods.

In this formulation it is assumed that at least 5%, 8%, 7% of the total wastes are transferred to the waste treatment facilities *viz.*, incinerator, composting and recycling, respectively, due to the paucity of available land and for

Table 1. Cost of waste management facilities

	Period 1(k=1)	Period 2 (k=2)
	Operating Cost (Rs./t)	
Landfill	$\widetilde{2170}$	$\widetilde{2380}$
Incinerator	$\widetilde{4060}$	$\widetilde{4410}$
Composting	$\widetilde{2940}$	$\widetilde{3150}$
Recycling	$\widetilde{4410}$	$\widetilde{4760}$

continued on following page

Table 1. Continued

	Period 1($k=1$)	Period 2 ($k=2$)
Sorting Station 1	$\widetilde{3150}$	$\widetilde{3290}$
Sorting Station 2	$\widetilde{3150}$	$\widetilde{3290}$
Transportation Cost (Rs./t)		
Sorting Station to Landfill Facility		
Sorting station 1	$\widetilde{3010}$	$\widetilde{3360}$
Sorting station 2	$\widetilde{3150}$	$\widetilde{3500}$
Sorting Station to Incinerator Facility		
Sorting station 1	$\widetilde{3290}$	$\widetilde{3500}$
Sorting station 2	$\widetilde{3150}$	$\widetilde{3430}$
Sorting Station to Composting Facility		
Sorting station 1	$\widetilde{4200}$	$\widetilde{4550}$
Sorting station 2	$\widetilde{4410}$	$\widetilde{4760}$
Sorting Station to Recycling Facility		
Sorting station 1	$\widetilde{5740}$	$\widetilde{6160}$
Sorting station 2	$\widetilde{5740}$	$\widetilde{6160}$
Treatment Facilities to Landfill		
Incinerator	$\widetilde{2100}$	$\widetilde{2800}$
Composting	$\widetilde{2450}$	$\widetilde{3150}$
Recycling	$\widetilde{2240}$	$\widetilde{2940}$
Dumping Station 1 to Sorting Station 1		
Sorting Station 1	$\widetilde{2170}$	$\widetilde{2450}$
Dumping Station 2 to Sorting Station 2		
Sorting Station 2	$\widetilde{2100}$	$\widetilde{2380}$

Table 2. Revenue from treatment facilities

Facilities	Period 1($k=1$)	Period 2 ($k=2$)
Incinerator	$\widetilde{1260}$	$\widetilde{1260}$
Composting	$\widetilde{840}$	$\widetilde{840}$
Recycling	$\widetilde{3220}$	$\widetilde{3220}$
Sorting Station 1	$\widetilde{840}$	$\widetilde{840}$
Sorting Station 2	$\widetilde{1260}$	$\widetilde{1260}$

Table 3. Waste generation rates

Waste Generation ($t \, / \, d$)	Period 1 ($k=1$)	Period 2 ($k=2$)
Sorting Station 1	mean = $\widetilde{820}$ variance = $\widetilde{20}$ probability = 0.90	mean = $\widetilde{840}$ variance = $\widetilde{30}$ probability = 0.85
Sorting Station 2	mean = $\widetilde{530}$ variance = $\widetilde{12}$ probability = 0.85	mean = $\widetilde{550}$ variance = $\widetilde{20}$ probability = 0.90

Table 4. Waste diversion rates

Facilities	Period 1 ($k=1$)	Period 2 ($k=2$)
Incinerator	$\tilde{5}$ %	$\tilde{5}$ %
Composting	$\tilde{8}$ %	$\tilde{8}$ %
Recycling	$\tilde{7}$ %	$\tilde{7}$ %

revenue generation. So these numbers are taken as left sided FNs which are presented in the Table 4.

Now, the problem under consideration is how to direct the waste flows effectively from the two cities to suitable waste treatment and disposal facilities so as to minimize the net system costs and maximize the net revenues. Based on the obtained information, MSW management model has been formulated according to the proposed methodology with the same setting and resolved by the proposed algorithm.

8.4 RESULTS AND DISCUSSIONS

The developed model for minimizing the net system costs and maximizing the net revenues is solved using the *software LINGO (Ver 11.0)*. The results obtained for different values of α are presented in the following Table 5 and Table 6. In Table 5 the transportation cost from two sorting stations to four treatment facilities are presented and in Table 6 the transportation cost from two dumping stations to two sorting stations are offered. The revenue from different treatment facilities and two sorting stations are also calculated. Also the operating cost of two sorting stations and different waste management

Table 5. Achieved system cost for different α - cuts

α		Sorting Station	Transportation Cost (Rs. 10^6)	Revenue From Facilities (Rs. 10^6)
0.8	1	Landfill	$\left[844.05, 851.44\right]$	
	1	Incinerator	$\left[1255.52, 1270.94\right]$	$\left[459.03, 479.90\right]$
	1	Composting	$\left[5600.50, 5636.63\right]$	$\left[1064.24, 1100.32\right]$
	1	Recycling	$\left[6665.19, 6728.22\right]$	$\left[3608.51, 3640.03\right]$
0.8	2	Landfill	$\left[3314.27, 3356.64\right]$	
	2	Incinerator	$\left[2321.07, 2340.89\right]$	$\left[872.02, 911.66\right]$
	2	Composting	$\left[716.72, 723.29\right]$	$\left[129.66, 134.05\right]$
	2	Recycling	$\left[813.60, 821.29\right]$	$\left[440.28, 444.13\right]$

continued on following page

Table 5. Continued

α	Sorting Station		Transportation Cost (Rs. 10^6)	Revenue From Facilities (Rs. 10^6)
0.9	1	Landfill	$\left[761.17, 764.48\right]$	
	1	Incinerator	$\left[1303.64, 1311.61\right]$	$\left[480.60, 491.40\right]$
	1	Composting	$\left[5649.02, 5685.29\right]$	$\left[1079.09, 1097.22\right]$
	1	Recycling	$\left[6722.65, 6754.36\right]$	$\left[3638.97, 3654.82\right]$
0.9	2	Landfill	$\left[3307.87, 3328.96\right]$	
	2	Incinerator	$\left[2307.12, 2316.94\right]$	$\left[874.67, 894.33\right]$
	2	Composting	$\left[719.79, 7230.80\right]$	$\left[13101, 133.21\right]$
	2	Recycling	$\left[817.26, 821.11\right]$	$\left[442.18, 444.11\right]$
1	1	Landfill	684.98	
	1	Incinerator	1344.09	499.50
	1	Composting	5697.74	1094.02
	1	Recycling	6780.42	3669.58
1	2	Landfill	3308.72	
	2	Incinerator	2300.67	880.20
	2	Composting	722.85	132.37
	2	Recycling	820.70	443.97

facilities are evaluated. Then the net system cost is calculated as {(transportation cost + operational cost) – revenue}.

From the Table 5 it is seen that for $\alpha = 0.8$ the waste transportation cost varies in the interval

$$\left[21530.92, 21729.34\right] \times 10^6 \left(\text{in Rs.}\right)$$

Table 6. Achieved transportation cost of waste from dumping station to sorting station for different α - cuts

α		Dumping Station	Transportation Cost (Rs. 10^6)	Revenue From Sorting (Rs. 10^6)
0.8	1	Sorting station 1	$\left[7037.05,\ 7122.81\right]$	$\left[3158.53, 3287.64\right]$
0.8	2	Sorting station 2	$\left[4453.15, 4536.77\right]$	$\left[2070.34, 2155.07\right]$
0.9	1	Sorting station 1	$\left[7389.16, 7433.93\right]$	$\left[3190.81, 3255.36\right]$
0.9	2	Sorting station 2	$\left[4451.19, 4492.77\right]$	$\left[2091.52, 2133.89\right]$
1	1	Sorting station 1	7679.98	3223.09
1	2	Sorting station 2	4459.01	112.70

and the revenue falls in

Rs. $\left[6573.74,\ 6710.09\right] \times 10^6.$

Also from the Table 6 it is observed that for $\alpha = 0.8$ the waste transportation cost from dumping stations to sorting stations lies in the interval

$\left[11490.20, 11659.58\right] \times 10^6 \left(\text{in Rs.}\right)$

and the revenue from sorting station varies in the interval

$\left[5228.87,\ 5442.71\right] \times 10^6 \left(\text{in Rs.}\right)$

Again, if the operational cost of sorting and different waste treatment facilities, and the transportation cost of residue be included then the total cost is

$\left[69727.00, 70512.40\right] \times 10^6 \text{Rs.}$

Thus the net system cost for $\alpha = 0.8$ is

$$\left[57924.30, 58359.70\right] \times 10^6 \, \text{Rs.}$$

Similarly the net system cost for $\alpha = 0.9$ and $\alpha = 1$ be

$$\left[58579.50, 5879.50\right] \times 10^6 \, \text{Rs. and } 59164.00 \times 10^6 \, \text{Rs.}$$

respectively.

8.5 CONCLUSION

In this chapter a fuzzy stochastic multi-objective linear programming model has been developed for decision making under multiple uncertainties, and applied to the long term planning of MSW management system. All the random variables in the models are considered as independent FRVs following normal distribution whose mean and variance are known and all the fuzzy coefficients are taken as triangular FNs. Instead of using triangular FNs and FRV following normal distribution, trapezoidal FNs and other fuzzy probability distribution may also be used. Detailed solution steps have been provided for clear demonstration of the proposed methodology. At first wastes are stored at dumping stations and then from dumping stations wastes are shifted to sorting stations and then to different treatment facilities. In the research article developed by Guo and Huang (2011) the transportation cost of wastes from dumping stations to sorting facilities and the operational cost of different sorting facilities are not included, but here transportation cost of wastes from dumping stations to sorting facilities and the operational cost of different sorting facilities are comprised. Hence the methodology discussed in this chapter includes more practical situations. Thus the article for SWM discussed in this book is more acceptable to different municipal authorities than the other techniques in the context of MSW management. The developed methodology can also be applied to other environmental problems that involve uncertainties presented in multiple formats. However, it is hoped that the method outlined in this chapter may open up many new vistas into the way of making decisions in MSW system in the current fuzzy multi-objective decision making arena.

REFERENCES

Angelo, E. S. C., & Park, H. S. (2018). Fuzzy multi-objective optimization case study based on an anaerobic co-digestion process of food waste leachate and piggery wastewater. *Journal of Environmental Management, 223*, 314–323. doi:10.1016/j.jenvman.2018.06.009 PMID:29935446

Bellman, R. E., & Zadeh, L. A. (1970). Decision making in a fuzzy environment. *Management Science, 17*(4), 141–164. doi:10.1287/mnsc.17.4.B141

Biswas, A., & Modak, N. (2011). A fuzzy goal programming method for solving chance constrained programming with fuzzy parameters. *Communications in Computer and Information Science, 140*, 187–196. doi:10.1007/978-3-642-19263-0_23

Biswas, A., & Modak, N. (2012). Using fuzzy goal programming technique to solve multiobjective chance constrained programming problems in a fuzzy environment. *International Journal of Fuzzy System Applications, 2*(1), 71–80. doi:10.4018/ijfsa.2012010105

Chang, N. B., & Wang, S. F. (1994). A location model for the site selection of solid waste management facilities with traffic congestion constraints. *Civil Engineering Systems, 11*(4), 287–306. doi:10.1080/02630259508970151

Charnes, A., & Cooper, W. W. (1962). Chance-constrained programming. *Management Science, 6*(1), 73–79. doi:10.1287/mnsc.6.1.73

Charnes, A., & Cooper, W. W. (1963). Deterministic equivalents for optimizing and satisfying under chance constraints. *Operations Research, 11*(1), 18–39. doi:10.1287/opre.11.1.18

Cheng, G. H., Huang, G. H., Li, Y. P., Cao, M. F., & Fan, Y. R. (2009). Planning of municipal solid waste management systems under dual uncertainties: A hybrid interval stochastic programming approach. *Stochastic Environmental Research and Risk Assessment, 23*(6), 707–720. doi:10.100700477-008-0251-5

Delgado, M., Verdegay, J. L., & Vila, M. A. (1989). A general model for fuzzy linear programming. *Fuzzy Sets and Systems, 29*(1), 21–29. doi:10.1016/0165-0114(89)90133-4

Geoffrion, A. M. (1967). Stochastic programming with aspiration or fractile criteria. *Management Science, 13*(9), 672–679. doi:10.1287/mnsc.13.9.672

Guo, P., & Huang, G. H. (2011). Inexact fuzzy-stochastic quadratic programming approach for waste management under multiple uncertainties. *Engineering Optimization*, *43*(5), 525–539. doi:10.1080/030521 5X.2010.499940

Guo, P., Huang, G. H., & He, L. (2008). An inexact stochastic mixed integer linear semi-infinite programming approach for solid waste management and planning under uncertainty. *Stochastic Environmental Research and Risk Assessment*, *22*(6), 759–775. doi:10.100700477-007-0185-3

Guo, P., Huang, G. H., He, L., & Li, H. L. (2009). Interval-parameter fuzzy-stochastic semi-infinite mixed-integer linear programming for waste management under uncertainty. *Environmental Modeling and Assessment*, *14*(4), 521–537. doi:10.100710666-008-9143-9

Guo, P., Huang, G. H., & Li, Y. P. (2008). Inexact stochastic quadratic programming approach for municipal solid waste management. *Journal of Environmental Engineering and Science*, *7*(6), 569–579. doi:10.1139/S08-029

Hannan, E. L. (1980). Linear programming with multiple fuzzy goals. *Fuzzy Sets and Systems*, *6*(3), 235–248. doi:10.1016/0165-0114(81)90002-6

Howe, B., Maier, D., & Baptista, A. (2003). A language for spatial data manipulation. *Journal of Environmental Informatics*, *2*(2), 23–37. doi:10.3808/jei.200300020

Infanger, G. (1993). *Planning Under Uncertainty: Solving Large-Scale Stochastic Linear Programs*. Boyd and Fraser Publishing Company.

Iskander, M. G. (2006). Exponential membership function in stochastic fuzzy goal programming. *Applied Mathematics and Computation*, *173*(2), 782–791. doi:10.1016/j.amc.2005.04.014

Joshi, R., & Ahmed, S. (2016). Status and challenges of municipal solid waste management in India: A review. *Cogent Environmental Science*, *2*(1), 1–18. doi:10.1080/23311843.2016.1139434

Kataoka S A (1963). Stochastic programming model. *Econometrica, 31*, 181–196.

Kirca, J., & Erkip, N. (1988). Selecting transfer station locations for large solid waste systems. *European Journal of Operational Research*, *38*(3), 339–349. doi:10.1016/0377-2217(88)90224-X

Leimbach, M. (1996). Development of a fuzzy optimization model, supporting global warming decision-making. *Environmental and Resource Economics*, *7*(2), 163–192. doi:10.1007/BF00699290

Li, Y. P., Huang, G. H., Liu, Y. Y., Zhang, Y. M., & Nie, S. L. (2008). An inexact stochastic quadratic programming method for municipal solid waste management. *Civil Engineering and Environmental Systems*, *25*(2), 139–155. doi:10.1080/10286600801908949

Liu, B. (2001). Fuzzy random chance-constrained programming. *IEEE Transactions on Fuzzy Systems*, *9*(5), 713–720. doi:10.1109/91.963757

Maqsood, I., & Huang, G. H. (2003). A two-stage interval-stochastic programming model for waste management under uncertainty. *Journal of the Air & Waste Management Association*, *53*(5), 540–552. doi:10.1080/10473289.2003.10466195 PMID:12774987

Maqsood, I., Huang, G. H., & Zeng, G. M. (2004). An inexact two-stage mixed integer linear programming model for waste management under uncertainty. *Civil Engineering and Environmental Systems*, *21*(3), 187–206. doi:10.1080/10286600410001730698

Mir, M. A., Ghazvinei, P. T., Sulaiman, N. M. N., Basri, N. E. A., Saheri, S., Mahmood, N. Z., ... Aghamohammadi, N. (2016). Application of TOPSIS and VIKOR improved versions in a multi criteria decision analysis to develop an optimized municipal solid waste management model. *Journal of Environmental Management*, *166*, 109–115. doi:10.1016/j.jenvman.2015.09.028 PMID:26496840

Muneeb, S. M., Adhami, A. Y., Jalil, S. A., & Asim, Z. (2018). Decentralized bi-level decision planning model for municipal solid waste recycling and management with cost reliability under uncertain environment. *Sustainable Production and Consumption*, *16*, 33–44. doi:10.1016/j.spc.2018.05.009

Narasimhan, R. (1980). On fuzzy goal programming–Some comments. *Decision Sciences*, *11*, 532–538. doi:10.1111/j.1540-5915.1980.tb01142.x

Nidoni, P. G. (2017). Incineration Process For Solid Waste Management And Effective Utilization Of By Products. *International Research Journal of Engineering and Technology.*, *4*(12), 378–382.

Soltani, A., Hewage, K., Reza, B., & Sadiq, R. (2015). Multiple stakeholders in multi-criteria decision-making in the context of Municipal Solid Waste Management: A review. *Waste Management (New York, N.Y.), 35*, 318–328. doi:10.1016/j.wasman.2014.09.010 PMID:25301545

Tanaka, H., Okuda, T., & Asai, K. (1973). On fuzzy mathematical programming. *Journal of Cybernetics and Systems, 3*(4), 37–46. doi:10.1080/01969727308545912

Tang, J. F., Yang, L. I. U., Fung, R. Y. K., & Luo, X. (2008). Industrial waste recycling strategies optimization problem: Mixed integer programming model and heuristics. *Engineering Optimization, 40*(12), 1085–1100. doi:10.1080/03052150802294573

Tozlu, A., Ozahi, E., & Abusoglu, A. (2016). Waste to energy technologies for municipal solid waste management in Gaziantep. *Renewable & Sustainable Energy Reviews, 54*, 809–815. doi:10.1016/j.rser.2015.10.097

Wang, Z., Ren, J., Goodsite, M. E., & Xu, G. (2018). Waste-to-energy, municipal solid waste treatment, and best available technology: Comprehensive evaluation by an interval-valued fuzzy multi-criteria decision making method. *Journal of Cleaner Production, 172*, 887–899. doi:10.1016/j.jclepro.2017.10.184

Zhu, Z., & Revelle, C. (1993). A cost allocation method for facilities siting with fixed-charge cost functions. *Civil Engineering Systems, 7*(1), 29–35. doi:10.1080/02630259008970567

Chapter 9
On Solving Fuzzy Multi-Objective Multi-Choice Stochastic Transportation Problems

ABSTRACT

This chapter presents solution procedures for solving unbalanced multi-objective multi-choice stochastic transportation problems in a hybrid fuzzy uncertain environment. In this chapter, various types of unbalanced multi-objective fuzzy stochastic transportation models are considered with the assumption that the parameters representing supplies of the products at the origins and demands of the products at the destinations, capacity of the conveyances, associated with the system constraints are either fuzzy numbers (FNs) or fuzzy random variables (FRVs) with some known continuous fuzzy probability distributions. The multi-choice cost parameters are considered as FNs. In this chapter, two objectives are considered: total transportation cost and total transportation time. As the transportation cost mainly depends on fuel prices and since fuel prices are highly fluctuating, the cost parameters are taken as multi-choice cost parameters with possibilistic uncertain nature. The time of transportation mainly depends on vehicle conditions, quality of roads, and road congestion. Due to these uncertain natures, the parameters representing time of transportation are also taken as fuzzy uncertain multi-choice parameters. In this transportation model, these objectives are minimized satisfying the constraints: product availability constraints, requirement of the product constraints, and capacity of the conveyance constraints. Numerical examples are provided for the sake of illustration of the methodology presented in this chapter, and also achieved solutions are compared with the solutions obtained by some existing methodologies to establish its effectiveness.

DOI: 10.4018/978-1-5225-8301-1.ch009

9.1 MULTI-OBJECTIVE MULTI-CHOICE TRANSPORTATION PROBLEM

Each organization always keeps a motivation to find a better process to produce their products and deliver them to the markets in a smooth way. Transportation model is the most powerful frame for fulfilling each goal of the organizations. The transportation problem is a distribution-type linear programming problem (LPP), concerned with transferring goods between various origins and destinations. Generally, in every manufacturing organization two types of transportations are needed. First of all raw materials are transported to the factory and secondly the product produced in the factory are transported from factory to various markets. Therefore, it is the essential part of every organization. Again, the products manufactured in the factory are transferred from factory to various markets in various routes. Therefore, it is an important task for the managers of the organizations to identify exactly one among the various routes in such a manner that the combination of choices should minimize the overall transportation cost.

The basic transportation problem (TP) originally modelled by Hitchcock (1941) and discussed in details by Koopmans (1949). As the coefficient of the objective functions of the TPs could represent the transportation cost, transportation time, loss during transportation, etc. Therefore, in practical life TP is multi-objective in nature. Lee et al. (1973) developed a technique to solve the multi-objective TPs. Diaz (1978) presented an alternative procedure to generate all non-dominated solutions to the multi-objective TPs. Isermann (1979) and Diaz (1979) developed algorithms for identifying all of the non-dominated solutions for a linear multi-objective TP. Ravindran et al., (1987) and Hiller and Leiberman (1990) considered a mathematical model in which an appropriate constraint is to be chosen using binary variables. A method for modeling the multi-choice programming problem, using binary variables was presented by Chang (2007). A methodology for solving a multi-objective TP with nonlinear cost and multi-choice demand was proposed by Maity and Roy (2015).

In classical TPs, it is assumed that the decision maker (DM) is sure about the precise value of availability and demand of the products. In real life, the demand and supply values are not always known precisely due to some uncontrollable factors, insufficient data, fluctuating financial market etc. The probability theory and fuzzy set theory are the two useful techniques to analyze the uncertain situation.

Dantzig (1963) was first to formulate the mathematical model of probabilistic programming where the parameters are random variable with some known probability distribution. The Chance constrained programming (CCP) technique was first introduced by Charnes and Cooper (1959) to solve stochastic programming problems. It was further studied by Vajda (1972), Sengupta (1972) and Luhandjula (1983). Bit et al. (1992) solved the chance constrained multi-objective TP by applying fuzzy programming technique where the parameters are normally distributed random variables. In 2010 Mahapatra et al. (2010) presented a technique to solve multi-objective TP involving log-normal and extreme value distribution, respectively. Mahapatra et al., (2013) proposed a method for solving multi-choice stochastic TP with availability and demand follows extreme value distributed random variables. Quddoos et al., (2014) developed a methodology for solving multi choice stochastic TP with general form of distributions. Recently, Gupta et al. (2018) discussed a solution procedure of a multi-objective capacitated TP in an uncertain environment in which the demand and supply parameters of the problem follows Pareto, Weibull, normal, extreme value, Cauchy and logistic distributed random variables.

Using the concept of fuzzy set theory (Zadeh, 1965), Zimmermann (1976) first introduced fuzzy linear programming (FLP) as an extension of conventional LP. Subsequently, Zimmermann's FLP appeared as an efficient fuzzy optimization method for solving the TPs. Chanas and Kuchta (1996) proposed the concept of the optimal solution for solving TPs with fuzzy cost coefficients expressed as L-R FNs, and developed an algorithm for obtaining the optimal solution. Additionally, Chanas and kuchta (1998) designed an algorithm for solving integer fuzzy TP with fuzzy demand and supply values in the sense of maximizing the joint satisfaction of the fuzzy goal and the constraints. Liu and Kao (2004) described a method for solving fuzzy TP based on extension principle. A two stage cost minimizing fuzzy TP with supply and demand as trapezoidal FNs presented by Gani and Razak (2006). Lie et al. (2008) proposed a new method based on goal programming for solving fuzzy TP with fuzzy costs. Lin (2009) applied genetic algorithm for solving TPs with fuzzy coefficients. In recent years Dutta and Murthy (2010) presented a TP with an objective function involving multi-choice parameters in fuzzy framework. In 2017, Maity and Roy (2017) developed a multi-objective multi-choice TP problem using fuzzy decision variables. Also, Patel and Dhodiya (2017) solved a multi-objective interval TP using grey situation decision making theory based on grey numbers. Recently, a new approach for solving intuitionistic fuzzy multi-objective TP is developed by Roy et al. (2018). In recent years Dutta and Murthy (2010) presented a TP with an objective function involving multi-choice parameters in fuzzy framework.

While research works were moved by considering two specific types of uncertainty, viz., probabilistic uncertainty and possibilistic uncertainty independently, the researchers felt the importance of considering simultaneous occurrence of both the uncertainties under a common frame work for its modeling aspects applicable in different planning problems. To deal with co-occurrence of probabilistic and fuzzy uncertainties, the hybrid approaches of stochastic programming and fuzzy programming was proposed by Hulsurkar et al. (1997). Sakawa et al. (2004) proposed an interactive method for solving multi-objective fuzzy LPPs with random variable coefficients. In 2014 Kundu et al. (201) investigated a methodology for solving multi-objective solid TP in which the cost coefficients follow normal distributed random variables. Ojha et al. (2014) developed a methodology for solving TPs with fuzzy stochastic cost parameters. Dutta et al. (2016) constructed genetic algorithm based fuzzy stochastic TP with continuous random variables.

Again, most of the researchers followed the conventional fuzzy probabilistic programming approach for solving multi-objective TP with two constraints one possibilistic and other probabilistic. But in real life situation the parameters associated with supply and demand of the transportation are not only probabilistic or possibilistic rather a mixture of both. To handle this type of TP, the concept of FRV is presented in this chapter and the parameters associated with supply are considered as Burr-XII distributed and extreme value distributed FRVs, whereas the parameters associated with demand follows power function distributed and Pareto distributed FRVs.

In this chapter an unbalanced multi-objective, multi-choice TP (MOMCTP) are considered in fuzzy stochastic environment. The supplies are taken as fuzzily described Bur XII distributed and extreme value distributed random variables whereas the parameters representing demands of the products at the markets are involved with power function distributed and Pareto distributed FRVs. Like the previous chapters CCP technique is applied to the chance constraints to convert probabilistic fuzzy MOMCTP model to fuzzy MOMCTP model. The hyper parameters of all the FRVs and the multi-choice cost coefficients are considered as FNs with triangular form. Also the capacity of the conveyances is taken as trapezoidal FNs. Then the defuzzification process based on the proportional probability density function corresponding to the membership function of the trapezoidal FN and triangular FNs are used to develop the MOMCTP in crisp environment. Then the individual optimal solution of each decomposed objectives is found to construct the membership goals of the objectives. Finally, a weighted fuzzy goal programming (FGP) model is used for achieving the highest membership degree of each of the defined fuzzy goals to the extent possible. To illustrate the developed model a hypothetical example considered by Kundu et al., (2014) is considered and solved and compared with the existing methodology (Kundu et al., 2014).

9.1.1. Mathematical Model for Multi-Objective Multi-Choice Transportation Problem

Different multi-objective, multi-choice fuzzy stochastic unbalanced transportation models are considered in this chapter in which the products are transported from some sources to some destinations through some conveyances. The main goal is to find optimal transportation plan so that all the objectives relating to the problem are minimized. The objective may be minimization of the total transportation cost, total delivery time, loss during transportation etc. Also, if the profit is considered then that objective may be of maximization type and the objective is converted into minimization type by applying suitable methods. The availability and demands of the products at the sources and destination are taken FRVs following different continuous probability distributions, capacity of the conveyances are considered as trapezoidal FNs and the multi-choice cost parameters are taken as triangular FNs.

In this chapter two different multi-objective unbalanced transportation models are discussed. In both the models it is assumed that some products are shifted from m sources to n destinations via l conveyances. In the first model the coefficients of the objectives i.e. cost parameters are taken as FNs and the right hand coefficients of the constraints i.e. the availability and demands of the products at the sources and destination are considered as FRVs. In the second model the multi-choice cost parameters are taken as triangular FNs and the availability and demands of the products at the sources and destination are taken as FRVs, capacity of the conveyances are considered as trapezoidal FNs and the multi-choice cost parameters are taken as triangular FNs.

Figure 1. Transportation of products from sources to destinations via conveyances

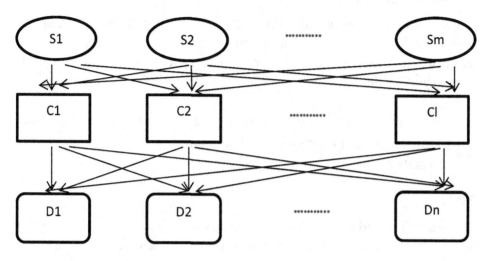

Model I

In this model it is assumed that the products are shifted from m sources to n destinations. Also in this model the availability and demand parameters are assumed as FRVs and all other parameters are considered as FNs. The following notations are used to formulate the proposed model:

Description of the Crisp Terms

$i =$ number of sources; $i = 1, 2, \ldots, m$.

$j =$ number of destinations; $j = 1, 2, \ldots, n$.

$k =$ number of conveyance; $k = 1, 2, \ldots, l$.

$p =$ number of objectives; $p = 1, 2, \ldots, P$.

$x_{ijk} =$ amount of product transferred from i-th source to j-th destination through $k -$ th conveyance.

Fuzzy Parameters

The cost parameters are uncertain in nature due to the insufficient information, fluctuating financial market, fuel price, labour salary etc. Therefore these parameters are taken as triangular FNs. Also capacity of the conveyances is not always definite. Thus the conveyance capacity is taken as trapezoidal FN.

$\tilde{c}^p_{ijk}$ = unit transportation cost for transporting the product from i-th source to j-th destination through k − th conveyance.

$\tilde{e}_k$ = capacity of the k-th conveyance.

FRVs

The availability and demands of the products at the sources and destinations are uncertain in nature. It may depend on the raw material, requirement of the product in various competitive markets. So these are taken as FRVs.

$\tilde{a}_i$ = availability of the products at the i − th source.

$\tilde{b}_j$ = demand of the products at the j − th destination.

On the basis of the above parameters the unbalanced multi-objective TP in fuzzy environment is presented as

$$\text{Min } \tilde{Z}_p \cong \sum_{k=1}^{l}\sum_{i=1}^{m}\sum_{j=1}^{n}\tilde{c}^p_{ijk}x_{ijk}; \; p = 1, 2, ..., P.$$

subject to

$$\sum_{k=1}^{l}\sum_{j=1}^{n}x_{ijk} \lesssim \tilde{a}_i; \; i = 1, 2, ..., m.$$

$$\sum_{k=1}^{l}\sum_{i=1}^{m}x_{ijk} \gtrsim \tilde{b}_j; \; j = 1, 2, .., n.$$

$$\sum_{i=1}^{m}\sum_{j=1}^{n}x_{ijk} \lesssim \tilde{e}_k; \; k = 1, 2, ..., l.$$

$$x_{ijk} \geq 0 \,;\, i = 1,2,...,m; \, j = 1,2,..,n. \tag{1}$$

Here the cost parameters $\tilde{c}_{ijk}^{p}$ are triangular FNs. The availability parameters $\tilde{a}_{i}; \left(i = 1,2,...,u \right)$ and the requirement parameters $\tilde{b}_{j}; \left(j = 1,2,...,v \right)$ are also taken as FRVs with some known probability distributions. The capacity of the conveyance $\tilde{e}_{k}; \left(k = 1,2,...,l \right)$ is considered as trapezoidal FNs.

Model II

As in model I, it is also assumed that the products are shifted from m sources to n destinations. But in this model the cost parameters are multi choice cost parameters. The following notations are used to formulate the proposed model:

Description of the Crisp Terms

$i =$ number of sources; $i = 1,2,...,m.$
$j =$ number of destinations; $j = 1,2,...,n.$
$k =$ number of conveyance; $k = 1,2,...,l.$
$p =$ number of objectives; $p = 1,2,..,P.$
$q =$ number of choices of cost parameters; $q = 1,2,...,Q.$
$x_{ijk} =$ amount of product transferred from i-th source to j-th destination through $k-$th conveyances.

Fuzzy Parameters

As in model I, the multi choice cost parameters, capacity of the conveyances are taken as FNs.

$\tilde{c}_{ijk}^{pq} = q$-th choice unit transportation cost for transporting the product from i-th source to jth destination through k-th conveyance.
$\tilde{e}_{k} =$ capacity of the k-th conveyance.

FRVs

The availability and demands of the products at the sources and destinations are uncertain in nature due to the fluctuating availability of raw materials, requirement of the product in various competitive markets as described in model I. So these are taken as FRVs.

$\tilde{a}_i$ = availability of the products at the i – th source.

$\tilde{b}_j$ = demand of the products at the j – th destination.

Thus an unbalanced multi-objective TP in fuzzy environment is presented using the above defined parameters as

$$\text{Min } \tilde{Z}_p \cong \sum_{k=1}^{l}\sum_{i=1}^{m}\sum_{j=1}^{n}\left\{\tilde{c}_{ij}^{p1},\ \tilde{c}_{ij}^{p2},...,\tilde{c}_{ij}^{pq}\right\}x_{ijk};$$

$$q = 1,2,...,Q; p = 1,2,...,P.$$

subject to

$$\sum_{k=1}^{l}\sum_{j=1}^{n}x_{ij} \leq \tilde{a}_i\ ; i = 1,2,...,m.$$

$$\sum_{k=1}^{l}\sum_{i=1}^{m}x_{ij} \geq \tilde{b}_j\ ; j = 1,2,..,n.$$

$$\sum_{i=1}^{m}\sum_{j=1}^{n}x_{ijk} \lesssim \tilde{e}_k\ ; k = 1,2,...,l.$$

$$x_{ijk} \geq 0\ ; i = 1,2,...,m; j = 1,2,..,n. \tag{2}$$

Here $\tilde{c}_{ijk}^{p1}, \tilde{c}_{ijk}^{p2},...,\tilde{c}_{ijk}^{pq}$ are triangular FNs. As in the previous model the availability parameters $\tilde{a}_i;\left(i = 1,2,...,u\right)$ and the requirement parameters $\tilde{b}_j;\left(j = 1,2,...,v\right)$ are also taken as FRVs following different continuous probability distributions. Also the capacities of the conveyance $\tilde{e}_k;\left(k = 1,2,...,l\right)$ are considered as trapezoidal FNs.

Although two multi-objective transportation models are presented in this chapter, but the only difference of model I and model II are the multi-choice natures of the objective parameters of model II. The authors presented the model I in front of the readers to give an idea that the objective parameters may not be regarded as multi-choice parameters. However, in the methodological development the solution methodology of model II are only described as the model II can be regarded as the generalization of model I.

9.1.2. Fuzzy Programming Model

In this chapter it is assumed that the availabilities of the product at the factories and demands of the product at the markets are FRVs following some continuous probability distribution. Therefore the constraints in model I and model II are expressed as

$$\Pr\left(\sum_{j=1}^{n}\sum_{k=1}^{l} x_{ijk} \leq \tilde{a}_i\right) \geq 1-\gamma_i$$

and

$$\Pr\left(\sum_{i=1}^{m}\sum_{k=1}^{l} x_{ijk} \geq \tilde{b}_j\right) \geq 1-\delta_j.$$

Applying CCP technique, the fuzzy probabilistic constraints

$$\Pr\left(\sum_{j=1}^{n}\sum_{k=1}^{l} x_{ijk} \leq \tilde{a}_i\right) \geq 1-\gamma_i$$

and

$$\Pr\left(\sum_{i=1}^{m}\sum_{k=1}^{l} x_{ijk} \geq \tilde{b}_j\right) \geq 1-\delta_j$$

are converted into fuzzy constraints as follows
The probabilistic constraints

$$\Pr\left(\sum_{j=1}^{n}\sum_{k=1}^{l} x_{ijk} \leq \tilde{a}_i\right) \geq 1-\gamma_i\left(i=1,2,\ldots,u\right)$$

in which the availability parameters $\tilde{a}_i$ follow Bur-XII distributed FRVs are converted as

$$\Pr\left(\sum_{j=1}^{n}\sum_{k=1}^{l}x_{ijk} \le \tilde{a}_i\right) \ge 1 - \gamma_i \, i.e. \int_{\sum_{j=1}^{n}\sum_{k=1}^{l}x_{ijk}}^{\infty} s_i t_i a_i^{t_i-1}\left(1+a_i^{t_i}\right)^{-(s_i+1)} da_i \ge 1 - \gamma_i$$

$$i.e.\, 1 + \left(\sum_{j=1}^{n}\sum_{k=1}^{l}x_{ijk}\right)^{t_i} \le \frac{1}{\left(1-\gamma_i\right)^{\frac{1}{s_i}}} \, (i = 1, 2, ..., u)$$

$$i.e. \sum_{j=1}^{n}\sum_{k=1}^{l}x_{ijk} \le \left[\frac{1}{\left(1-\gamma_i\right)^{\frac{1}{s_i}}} - 1\right]^{\frac{1}{t_i}} \, (i = 1, 2, ..., u)$$

(where $s_i \in \tilde{\beta}_i[\alpha]$, $t_i \in \tilde{\mu}_i[\alpha]$)

This inequality is true for all $\alpha \in (0,1]$. Then the above constraints can be expressed in terms of $\alpha - \text{cut}$ as

$$\sum_{j=1}^{n}\sum_{k=1}^{l}x_{ijk} \le \left[\frac{1}{\left(1-\gamma_i\right)^{\frac{1}{\tilde{\beta}_i[\alpha]}}} - 1\right]^{\frac{1}{\tilde{\mu}_i[\alpha]}} \, (i = 1, 2, ..., u) \tag{3}$$

Now using first decomposition theorem, the above equation is reduced to the following form as

$$\sum_{j=1}^{n}\sum_{k=1}^{l}x_{ijk} \le \left[\frac{1}{\left(1-\gamma_i\right)^{\frac{1}{\tilde{\beta}_i}}} - 1\right]^{\frac{1}{\tilde{\mu}_i}} \, (i = 1, 2, ..., u) \tag{4}$$

Similarly, the other availability constraints

$$\Pr\left(\sum_{j=1}^{n}\sum_{k=1}^{l}x_{ijk} \leq \tilde{a}_{i}\right) \geq 1 - \gamma_{i}\left(i = u+1, u+2, ..., m\right)$$

in which $\tilde{a}_{i}$ follows extreme value distributed FRVs are modified as

$$\Pr\left(\sum_{j=1}^{n}\sum_{k=1}^{l}x_{ijk} \leq \tilde{a}_{i}\right) \geq 1 - \gamma_{i} i.e. \int_{\sum_{j=1}^{n}\sum_{k=1}^{l}x_{ijk}}^{\infty} \frac{1}{s_{i}} e^{-\frac{(a_{i}-t_{i})}{s_{i}}} e^{-e^{-\frac{(a_{i}-t_{i})}{s_{i}}}} da_{i} \geq 1 - \gamma_{i}$$

$$i.e.\, e^{-e^{-\frac{\left[\sum_{j=1}^{n}\sum_{k=1}^{l}x_{ijk}-t_{i}\right]}{s_{i}}}} \leq \gamma_{i} i.e. \sum_{j=1}^{n}\sum_{k=1}^{l}x_{ijk} \leq t_{i} + s_{i}\ln\left(-\ln\left(\gamma_{i}\right)\right)\left(i = u+1, u+2, ..., m\right)$$

(where $s_{i} \in \tilde{\beta}_{i}[\alpha]$, $t_{i} \in \tilde{\mu}_{i}[\alpha]$). First expressing in terms of $\alpha - $cut and then using first decomposition theorem, the above inequality are expressed as

$$\sum_{j=1}^{n}\sum_{k=1}^{l}x_{ijk} \leq \tilde{\mu}_{i} + \tilde{\beta}_{i}\ln\left(-\ln\left(\gamma_{i}\right)\right)\left(i = u+1, u+2, ..., m\right) \tag{5}$$

Again, CCP technique is applied to the fuzzy probabilistic demand constraints

$$\Pr\left(\sum_{i=1}^{m}\sum_{k=1}^{l}x_{ijk} \geq \tilde{b}_{j}\right) \geq 1 - \delta_{j} \ (j = 1, 2, ..., v$$

in which $\tilde{b}_{j}$ are power function distributed FRVs. Thus the fuzzy chance constraints in this situation are transformed as

$$\Pr\left(\sum_{i=1}^{m}\sum_{k=1}^{l}x_{ijk} \geq \tilde{b}_{j}\right) \geq 1 - \delta_{j} i.e. \int_{c_{j}}^{\sum_{i=1}^{m}\sum_{k=1}^{l}x_{ijk}} \frac{r_{j}}{\left(d_{j}-c_{j}\right)^{r_{j}}}\left(b_{j}-c_{j}\right)^{r_{j}-1} db_{j} \geq 1 - \delta_{j}$$

$$i.e. \left(\sum_{i=1}^{m} \sum_{k=1}^{l} x_{ijk} - c_j \right)^{r_j} \geq \left(d_j - c_j \right)^{r_j} \left(1 - \delta_j \right)$$

and

$$\sum_{i=1}^{m} \sum_{k=1}^{l} x_{ijk} \leq d_j$$

$$i.e. \sum_{i=1}^{m} \sum_{k=1}^{l} x_{ijk} \geq c_j + \left(d_j - c_j \right) \left(1 - \delta_j \right)^{\frac{1}{r_j}}, (j = 1, 2, ..., v)$$

(where $c_j \in \tilde{\lambda}_j [\alpha], d_j \in \tilde{\rho}_j [\alpha], r_j \in \tilde{\varphi}_j [\alpha]$) and

$$\sum_{i=1}^{m} \sum_{k=1}^{l} x_{ijk} \leq d_j, (j = 1, 2, ..., v)$$

The above inequalities can be written in terms of $\alpha - $ cut and first decomposition theorem as

$$\sum_{i=1}^{m} \sum_{k=1}^{l} x_{ijk} \geq \tilde{\lambda}_j + \left(\tilde{\rho}_j - \tilde{\lambda}_j \right) \left(1 - \delta_j \right)^{\frac{1}{\tilde{\varphi}_j}}, (j = 1, 2, ..., v) \tag{6}$$

$$\sum_{i=1}^{m} \sum_{k=1}^{l} x_{ijk} \leq \tilde{\rho}_j, (j = 1, 2, ..., v) \tag{7}$$

Finally the remaining fuzzy probabilistic demand constraints

$$\Pr \left(\sum_{i=1}^{m} \sum_{k=1}^{l} x_{ijk} \geq \tilde{b}_j \right) \geq 1 - \delta_j \ (j = v + 1, v + 2, ..., n)$$

following Pareto distribution are renewed as

$$\Pr\left(\sum_{i=1}^{m}\sum_{k=1}^{l}x_{ijk} \geq \tilde{b}_{j}\right) \geq 1 - \delta_{j}, \ (j = v+1, v+2, \ldots, n)$$

$$\text{i.e.} \ \int_{c_j}^{\sum_{i=1}^{m}\sum_{k=1}^{l}x_{ijk}} \frac{r_j c_j^{r_j}}{b_j^{r_j+1}} \, db_j$$

$$\text{i.e.} \sum_{i=1}^{m}\sum_{k=1}^{l}x_{ijk} \geq \frac{c_j}{\delta_j^{\frac{1}{r_j}}}, \ (j = v+1, v+2, \ldots, n)$$

(where $c_j \in \tilde{\lambda}_j[\alpha], r_j \in \tilde{\varphi}_j[\alpha]$)

Expressing the constraint in terms of $\alpha-$cut and then applying first decomposition theorem

$$\sum_{i=1}^{m}\sum_{k=1}^{l}x_{ijk} \geq \frac{\tilde{\lambda}_j}{\delta_j^{\frac{1}{\tilde{\varphi}_j}}}, \ (j = v+1, v+2, \ldots, n). \tag{8}$$

Thus the MOMCTP in fuzzy environment can be developed as

$$\text{Min } \tilde{Z}_p = \sum_{i=1}^{m}\sum_{j=1}^{n}\sum_{k=1}^{l}\left\{\tilde{c}_{ijk}^{p1}, \tilde{c}_{ijk}^{p2}, \ldots, \tilde{c}_{ijk}^{pq}\right\} x_{ijk}$$

$$q = 1, 2, \ldots, Q; p = 1, 2, \ldots, P.$$

Subject to

$$\sum_{j=1}^{n}\sum_{k=1}^{l}x_{ijk} \leq \left[\frac{1}{\left(1-\gamma_i\right)^{\frac{1}{\tilde{\beta}_i}}} - 1\right]^{\frac{1}{\tilde{\mu}_i}} \ (i = 1, 2, \ldots, u)$$

$$\sum_{j=1}^{n}\sum_{k=1}^{l}x_{ijk} \leq \tilde{\mu}_i + \tilde{\beta}_i \ln\left(-\ln\left(\gamma_i\right)\right)\left(i = u+1, u+2, ..., m\right)$$

$$\sum_{i=1}^{m}\sum_{k=1}^{l}x_{ijk} \geq \tilde{\lambda}_j + \left(\tilde{\rho}_j - \tilde{\lambda}_j\right)\left(1 - \delta_j\right)^{\frac{1}{\tilde{\phi}_j}}, (j = 1, 2, ..., v)$$

$$\sum_{i=1}^{m}\sum_{k=1}^{l}x_{ijk} \leq \tilde{\rho}_j, \ (j = 1, 2, ..., v)$$

$$\sum_{i=1}^{m}\sum_{k=1}^{l}x_{ijk} \geq \frac{\tilde{\lambda}_j}{\delta_j^{\frac{1}{\tilde{\phi}_j}}}, \ (j = v+1, v+2, ..., n)$$

$$\sum_{i=1}^{m}\sum_{j=1}^{n}x_{ijk} \leq \tilde{e}_k; \left(k = 1, 2, ..., l\right).$$

$$x_{ijk} \geq 0; i = 1, 2, ..., m; j = 1, 2, .., n; k = 1, 2, ..., l. \tag{9}$$

Here multi-choice cost parameters and the parameters of all the FRVs are considered as triangular FNs. Thus, these parameters are expressed as

$$\tilde{c}_{ijk}^{pq} = \left(\left(c_{ijk}^{pq}\right)_1, c_{ijk}^{pq}, \left(c_{ijk}^{pq}\right)_4\right);$$

$$\left(q = 1, 2, ..., Q\right); \left(p = 1, 2, ..., P\right); \left(i = 1, 2, ..., m\right);$$

$$(j = 1, 2, ... n; \left(k = 1, 2, ..., l\right);)$$

$$\frac{1}{\tilde{\beta}_i} = \left(\left(\frac{1}{\beta_i}\right)_1, \frac{1}{\beta_i}, \left(\frac{1}{\beta_i}\right)_4\right); (i = 1, 2, ..., u);$$

$$\frac{1}{\tilde{\mu}_i} = \left(\left(\frac{1}{\mu_i} \right)_1, \frac{1}{\mu_i}, \left(\frac{1}{\mu_i} \right)_4 \right); (i = 1, 2, \ldots, u);$$

$$\tilde{\beta}_i = \left(\left(\beta_i \right)_1, \beta_i, \left(\beta_i \right)_4 \right); (i = u+1, u+2, \ldots, m);$$

$$\tilde{\mu}_i = \left(\left(\mu_i \right)_1, \mu_i, \left(\mu_i \right)_4 \right); (i = u+1, u+2, \ldots, m);$$

$$\tilde{\lambda}_j = \left(\left(\lambda_j \right)_1, \lambda_j, \left(\lambda_j \right)_4 \right); (j = 1, 2, \ldots, n);$$

$$\tilde{\rho}_j = \left(\left(\rho_j \right)_1, \rho_j, \left(\rho_j \right)_4 \right); (j = 1, 2, \ldots, v)$$

$$\frac{1}{\tilde{\varphi}_j} = \left(\left(\frac{1}{\varphi_j} \right)_1, \frac{1}{\varphi_j}, \left(\frac{1}{\varphi_j} \right)_4 \right); (j = 1, 2, \ldots, n). \tag{10}$$

Also the capacities of the conveyances are considered as trapezoidal FNs. Therefore

$$\tilde{e}_k = \left(\left(e_k \right)_1, \left(e_k \right)_2, \left(e_k \right)_3, \left(e_k \right)_4 \right); (k = 1, 2, \ldots, l). \tag{11}$$

9.1.3 Multi-Objective Multi-Choice Transportation Model in Crisp Environment

The authors already clarify to the readers that defuzzification of FN is needed to find an equivalent crisp value of the FN. Thus defuzzification of FNs is applied in this subsection to form a MOMCTP model. In the proposed model the multi-choice cost parameters and the hyper parameters of the FRVs are considered as triangular FNs and the capacity of the conveyances are taken as trapezoidal FNs. The crisp values associated with the FNs of model (9) are obtained by a defuzzification method (based on proportional probability density function of the corresponding membership functions) presented in chapter 2 as

$$\hat{c}_{ijk}^{pq} = \frac{\left(c_{ijk}^{pq} \right)_1 + c_{ijk}^{pq} + \left(c_{ijk}^{pq} \right)_4}{3}; (q = 1, 2, \ldots, Q); \quad ; (k = 1, 2, \ldots, l);$$
$$(p = 1, 2, \ldots, P); (i = 1, 2, \ldots, m); (j = 1, 2, \ldots, n)$$

$$\frac{1}{\hat{\beta}_i} = \frac{\left(\dfrac{1}{\beta_i}\right)_1 + \dfrac{1}{\beta_i} + \left(\dfrac{1}{\beta_i}\right)_4}{3} \ ; \frac{1}{\hat{\mu}_i} = \frac{\left(\dfrac{1}{\mu_i}\right)_1 + \dfrac{1}{\mu_i} + \left(\dfrac{1}{\mu_i}\right)_4}{3} \ ; \left(i = 1, 2, \ldots, u\right);$$

$$\hat{\beta}_i = \frac{\left(\beta_i\right)_1 + \beta_i + \left(\beta_i\right)_4}{3} \ ; \hat{\mu}_i = \frac{\left(\mu_i\right)_1 + \mu_i + \left(\mu_i\right)_4}{3} \ ; \left(i = u+1, u+2, \ldots, m\right);$$

$$\hat{\lambda}_j = \frac{\left(\lambda_j\right)_1 + \lambda_j + \left(\lambda_j\right)_4}{3} \ ; \left(j = 1, 2, \ldots, n\right)$$

$$\hat{\rho}_j = \frac{\left(\rho_j\right)_1 + \rho_j + \left(\rho_j\right)_4}{3} \ ; \left(j = 1, 2, \ldots, v\right);$$

$$\frac{1}{\hat{\varphi}_j} = \frac{\left(\dfrac{1}{\varphi_j}\right)_1 + \dfrac{1}{\varphi_j} + \left(\dfrac{1}{\varphi_j}\right)_4}{3} \ ; \left(j = 1, 2, \ldots, n\right) \ ;$$

$$\hat{e}_k = \left[\left(e_k\right)_1 + \left(e_k\right)_2 + \left(e_k\right)_3 + \left(e_k\right)_4 - \frac{\left(\left(e_k\right)_1 * \left(e_k\right)_2 - \left(e_k\right)_3 * \left(e_k\right)_4\right)}{\left(\left(e_k\right)_4 + \left(e_k\right)_3 - \left(e_k\right)_1 - \left(e_k\right)_2\right)}\right] \ ;$$

$$\left(k = 1, 2, \ldots, l\right). \tag{12}$$

Thus the MOMCTP in crisp environment can be expressed as

$$\text{Min } \hat{Z}_p = \sum_{i=1}^{m}\sum_{j=1}^{n}\sum_{k=1}^{l} \left\{\hat{c}_{ijk}^{p1}, \ \hat{c}_{ijk}^{p2}, \ldots, \hat{c}_{ijk}^{pq}\right\} x_{ijk} \ ;$$

$$q = 1, 2, \ldots, Q; p = 1, 2, \ldots, P.$$

subject to

$$\sum_{j=1}^{n}\sum_{k=1}^{l} x_{ijk} \leq \left[\frac{1}{\left(1-\gamma_i\right)^{\frac{1}{\hat{\beta}_i}}} - 1\right]^{\frac{1}{\hat{\mu}_i}} \left(i = 1, 2, \ldots, u\right)$$

$$\sum_{j=1}^{n}\sum_{k=1}^{l}x_{ijk} \le \hat{\mu}_{i} + \hat{\beta}_{i}\ln\left(-\ln\left(\gamma_{i}\right)\right)\left(i = u+1, u+2, ..., m\right)$$

$$\sum_{i=1}^{m}\sum_{k=1}^{l}x_{ijk} \ge \hat{\lambda}_{j} + \left(\hat{\rho}_{j} - \hat{\lambda}_{j}\right)\left(1 - \delta_{j}\right)^{\frac{1}{\hat{\phi}_{j}}}, (j = 1, 2, ..., v)$$

$$\sum_{i=1}^{m}\sum_{k=1}^{l}x_{ijk} \le \hat{\rho}_{j}, \ (j = 1, 2, ..., v)$$

$$\sum_{i=1}^{m}\sum_{k=1}^{l}x_{ijk} \ge \frac{\hat{\lambda}_{j}}{\delta_{j}^{\frac{1}{\hat{\phi}_{j}}}}, \ (j = v+1, v+2, ..., n)$$

$$\sum_{i=1}^{m}\sum_{j=1}^{n}x_{ijk} \le \hat{e}_{k}, \ \left(k = 1, 2, ..., l\right).$$

$$x_{ijk} \ge 0 \ ; i = 1, 2, ..., m; j = 1, 2, .., n; k = 1, 2, ..., l. \tag{13}$$

9.1.4 Conversion of Multi-Choice Objective Function to an Equivalent Form

In this chapter, the proposed model is developed for maximum Q choices for any cost coefficients of the objective function. The objective function is transformed by introducing binary variables as developed by Biswal and Acharya (2009). The number of binary variables depends on the number of choices of the cost coefficients. If number of choices be q, then q is either a power of 2 or it lies between two powers of 2. i.e. either $q = 2^b$ or $2^{b-1} \le q \le 2^b$. Now the following two situations are considered to develop the model in the chapter.

Case 1

Let in the $p-$th objective all the cost coefficients have q choices and let they are $\hat{c}_{ijk}^{p1},\ \hat{c}_{ijk}^{p2},...,\hat{c}_{ijk}^{pq}$.

If $q=2^b$, then b binary variables $z_{ijk}^{p1}, z_{ijk}^{p2},..., z_{ijk}^{pb}$ are introduce. With the help of these binary variables the $p-$th objective is modifies as

$$\hat{Z}_p = \sum_{i=1}^{m}\sum_{j=1}^{n}\sum_{k=1}^{l}\left\{\begin{array}{l}\hat{c}_{ijk}^{p1}z_{ijk}^{p1}z_{ijk}^{p2}\cdots z_{ijk}^{pb}+\hat{c}_{ijk}^{p2}\left(1-z_{ijk}^{p1}\right)z_{ijk}^{p2}\cdots z_{ijk}^{pb}+\hat{c}_{ijk}^{p3}\left(1-z_{ijk}^{p2}\right)z_{ijk}^{p1}z_{ijk}^{p3}\cdots z_{ijk}^{pb}+\\ \cdots+\hat{c}_{ijk}^{p(b+2)}\left(1-z_{ijk}^{p1}\right)\left(1-z_{ijk}^{p2}\right)z_{ijk}^{p3}\cdots z_{ijk}^{pb}+\cdots+\\ \hat{c}_{ijk}^{pq}\left(1-z_{ijk}^{p1}\right)\left(1-z_{ijk}^{p2}\right)\left(1-z_{ijk}^{p3}\right)\cdots\left(1-z_{ijk}^{pb}\right)\end{array}\right\}x_{ijk}$$

$$z_{ijk}^{p1}, z_{ijk}^{p2},...z_{ijk}^{pb} = 0\,\text{or}\,1;\ 0 \le z_{ijk}^{p1}+z_{ijk}^{p2}+...+z_{ijk}^{pb} \le b\,;$$

$$i=1,2,...,m;\ j=1,2,..,n;\ k=1,2,...,l. \tag{14}$$

Case 2

Let in the $p-$th objective all the cost coefficients have q choices and let they are $\hat{c}_{ijk}^{p1},\ \hat{c}_{ijk}^{p2},...,\hat{c}_{ijk}^{pq}$.

If $2^{b-1} \le q \le 2^b$, then b binary variables $z_{ijk}^{p1}, z_{ijk}^{p2},...z_{ijk}^{pb}$ are considered. Now expand 2^b as

$$2^b = \binom{b}{0}+\binom{b}{1}+\binom{b}{2}+...+\binom{b}{r_1}+\binom{b}{r_1+1}+...+\binom{b}{r_2}+...+\binom{b}{b}.$$

Now select the smallest number of consecutive terms from the above expansion whose sum is either equal to q or just greater than q. Let the terms be $\binom{b}{r_1},\binom{b}{r_1+1},...,\binom{b}{r_2}$. Then using the binary variables and the above binomial coefficients, assign q binary codes to q number of choices for p-th objective in the following form

Min

$$\hat{Z}_p = \sum_{i=1}^{m} \sum_{j=1}^{n} \sum_{k=1}^{l} \left[\sum_{e=1}^{\binom{b}{r_1}} U_e^{pr_1} V_e^{pr_1} \hat{c}_{ijk}^{pe} + \sum_{e=1}^{\binom{b}{r_1+1}} U_e^{p(r_1+1)} V_e^{p(r_1+1)} \hat{c}_{ijk}^{p\left(\binom{b}{r_1}+e\right)} + \right.$$
$$\left. \cdots + \sum_{e=1}^{\binom{b}{r_2-1}} U_e^{p(r_2-1)} V_e^{p(r_2-1)} \hat{c}_{ijk}^{p\left(\binom{b}{r_1}+\binom{b}{r_1+1}+\cdots+\binom{b}{r_2-2}+e\right)} + \sum_{e=1}^{q-L} U_e^{pr_2} V_e^{pr_2} \hat{c}_{ijk}^{p(L+e)} \right] x_{ijk}$$

(15)

where

$$L = \binom{b}{r_1} + \binom{b}{r_1+1} + \cdots + \binom{b}{r_2-2} + \binom{b}{r_2-1},$$

$$U_e^{pt} = \left\{ z_{ijk}^{ps_1} z_{ijk}^{ps_2} \cdots z_{ijk}^{ps_t} : t = r_1, r_1+1, \ldots, r_2 \text{ and } s_1 < s_2 < \ldots < s_t \right\},$$

$$V_e^{pt} = \left\{ \prod_{e=1}^{b} \left(1 - z_{ijk}^{pe} \right) : e \notin \left\{ s_1, s_2, \ldots, s_t \right\} \right\},$$

$$s_1 = \left\{ 1, 2, \ldots, (b-t) + 1 \right\},$$

$$s_2 = \left\{ 2, 3, \ldots, (b-t) + 2 \right\},$$

$$s_t = \left\{ t, t+1, \ldots, b \right\}.$$

Also $\left(2^b - q \right)$ numbers of binary codes are restricted to overcome the repetitions as follows

$$z_{ijk}^{p1} + z_{ijk}^{p2} + \ldots + z_{ijk}^{pb} \geq r_1 \tag{16}$$

$$z_{ijk}^{p1} + z_{ijk}^{p2} + \ldots + z_{ijk}^{pb} \leq r_2 \tag{17}$$

$$z_{ijk}^{ps_1} + z_{ijk}^{ps_2} + \ldots + z_{ijk}^{ps_{r_2}} \leq r_2 - 1.$$ (18)

Restrictions should be imposed on $z_{ijk}^{ps_1} z_{ijk}^{ps_2} \ldots z_{ijk}^{ps_{r_2}} \in U_e^{pr_2}$, but those binary variables are not included in (17) which are present in the p - th objective as the form of products.

On the basis of the above transformation of objective functions the multi-objective TP is expressed in the following two forms

Model (a)

Min

$$\hat{Z}_p = \sum_{i=1}^{m} \sum_{j=1}^{n} \sum_{k=1}^{l} \left\{ \begin{array}{l} \hat{c}_{ijk}^{p1} z_{ijk}^{p1} z_{ijk}^{p2} \ldots z_{ijk}^{pb} + \hat{c}_{ijk}^{p2}(1 - z_{ijk}^{p1}) z_{ijk}^{p2} \ldots z_{ijk}^{pb} + \hat{c}_{ijk}^{p3}(1 - z_{ijk}^{p2}) z_{ijk}^{p1} z_{ijk}^{p3} \ldots z_{ijk}^{pb} + \\ \ldots + \hat{c}_{ijk}^{p(b+2)}(1 - z_{ijk}^{p1})(1 - z_{ijk}^{p2}) z_{ijk}^{p3} \ldots z_{ijk}^{pb} + \ldots \\ + \hat{c}_{ijk}^{pq}(1 - z_{ijk}^{p1})(1 - z_{ijk}^{p2})(1 - z_{ijk}^{p3}) \ldots (1 - z_{ijk}^{pb}) \end{array} \right\} x_{ijk}$$

Subject to

$$\sum_{j=1}^{n} \sum_{k=1}^{l} x_{ijk} \leq \left[\frac{1}{(1 - \gamma_i)^{\frac{1}{\hat{\beta}_i}}} - 1 \right]^{\frac{1}{\hat{\mu}_i}} \quad (i = 1, 2, \ldots, u)$$

$$\sum_{j=1}^{n} \sum_{k=1}^{l} x_{ijk} \leq \hat{\mu}_i + \hat{\beta}_i \ln\left(-\ln\left(\gamma_i\right)\right) (i = u + 1, u + 2, \ldots, m)$$

$$\sum_{i=1}^{m} \sum_{k=1}^{l} x_{ijk} \geq \hat{\lambda}_j + \left(\hat{\rho}_j - \hat{\lambda}_j\right)\left(1 - \delta_j\right)^{\frac{1}{\hat{\phi}_j}}, (j = 1, 2, \ldots, v)$$

$$\sum_{i=1}^{m} \sum_{k=1}^{l} x_{ijk} \leq \hat{\rho}_j, \quad (j = 1, 2, \ldots, v)$$

$$\sum_{i=1}^{m} \sum_{k=1}^{l} x_{ijk} \geq \frac{\hat{\lambda}_j}{\delta_j^{\frac{1}{\hat{\phi}_j}}}, \quad (j = v + 1, v + 2, \ldots, n)$$

$$\sum_{i=1}^{m}\sum_{j=1}^{n} x_{ijk} \leq \hat{e}_k \, ; \left(k = 1, 2, \ldots, l \right).$$

$$0 \leq z_{ijk}^{p1} + z_{ijk}^{p2} + \ldots + z_{ijk}^{pb} \leq b$$

$$z_{ijk}^{p1}, \, z_{ijk}^{p2}, \ldots, z_{ijk}^{pb} = 0 \text{ or } 1$$

$$x_{ijk} \geq 0 \, ; i = 1, 2, \ldots, m; j = 1, 2, \ldots, n; k = 1, 2, \ldots, l; p = 1, 2, \ldots, P \, . \tag{19}$$

Model (b)

Min

$$\hat{Z}_p = \sum_{i=1}^{m}\sum_{j=1}^{n}\sum_{k=1}^{l} \left[\begin{array}{c} \sum_{e=1}^{\binom{b}{r_1}} U_e^{pr_1} V_e^{pr_1} \hat{c}_{ijk}^{pe} + \sum_{e=1}^{\binom{b}{r_1+1}} U_e^{p(r_1+1)} V_e^{p(r_1+1)} \hat{c}_{ijk}^{p\left(\binom{b}{r_1}+e\right)} + \\ \ldots + \sum_{e=1}^{\binom{b}{r_2-1}} U_e^{p(r_2-1)} V_e^{p(r_2-1)} \hat{c}_{ijk}^{p\left(\binom{b}{r_1}+\binom{b}{r_1+1}+\ldots+\binom{b}{r_2-2}+e\right)} + \sum_{e=1}^{q-L} U_e^{pr_2} V_e^{pr_2} \hat{c}_{ijk}^{p(L+e)} \end{array} \right] x_{ijk}$$

subject to

$$\sum_{j=1}^{n}\sum_{k=1}^{l} x_{ijk} \leq \left[\frac{1}{\left(1-\gamma_i\right)^{\frac{1}{\hat{\beta}_i}}} - 1 \right]^{\frac{1}{\hat{\mu}_i}} \left(i = 1, 2, \ldots, u \right)$$

$$\sum_{j=1}^{n}\sum_{k=1}^{l} x_{ijk} \leq \hat{\mu}_i + \hat{\beta}_i \ln\left(-\ln\left(\gamma_i\right)\right)\left(i = u+1, u+2, \ldots, m \right)$$

$$\sum_{i=1}^{m}\sum_{k=1}^{l} x_{ijk} \geq \hat{\lambda}_j + \left(\hat{\rho}_j - \hat{\lambda}_j\right)\left(1-\delta_j\right)^{\frac{1}{\hat{\varphi}_j}}, \left(j = 1, 2, \ldots, v \right)$$

$$\sum_{i=1}^{m}\sum_{k=1}^{l} x_{ijk} \leq \hat{\rho}_j, \; (j = 1, 2, \ldots, v)$$

$$\sum_{i=1}^{m}\sum_{k=1}^{l} x_{ijk} \geq \frac{\hat{\lambda}_j}{\delta_j^{\frac{1}{\hat{\varphi}_j}}}, \; (j = v+1, v+2, \ldots, n)$$

$$\sum_{i=1}^{m}\sum_{j=1}^{n} x_{ijk} \leq \hat{e}_k; \left(k = 1, 2, \ldots, l\right).$$

$$z_{ijk}^{p1} + z_{ijk}^{p2} + \ldots + z_{ijk}^{pb} \geq r_1$$

$$z_{ijk}^{p1} + z_{ijk}^{p2} + \ldots + z_{ijk}^{pb} \leq r_2$$

$$z_{ijk}^{ps_1} + z_{ijk}^{ps_2} + \ldots + z_{ijk}^{ps_{r_2}} \leq r_2 - 1.$$

$$z_{ijk}^{p1}, \; z_{ijk}^{p2}, \ldots, z_{ijk}^{pb} = 0 \text{ or } 1$$

$$x_{ijk} \geq 0 \; ; i = 1, 2, \ldots, m; j = 1, 2, \ldots, n; k = 1, 2, \ldots, l; p = 1, 2, \ldots, P. \tag{20}$$

where

$$L = \binom{b}{r_1} + \binom{b}{r_1 + 1} + \ldots + \binom{b}{r_2 - 2} + \binom{b}{r_2 - 1},$$

$$U_e^{pt} = \left\{ z_{ijk}^{ps_1} z_{ijk}^{ps_2} \ldots z_{ijk}^{ps_t} : t = r_1, r_1 + 1, \ldots, r_2 \text{ and } s_1 < s_2 < \ldots < s_t \right\},$$

$$V_e^{pt} = \left\{ \prod_{e=1}^{b} \left(1 - z_{ijk}^{pe}\right) : e \notin \left\{s_1, \; s_2, \ldots, s_t\right\} \right\},$$

$$s_1 = \left\{1, 2, \ldots, (b-t)+1\right\},$$

$$s_2 = \left\{2, 3, \ldots, (b-t)+2\right\},$$

$$s_t = \left\{t, t+1, \ldots, b\right\}.$$

9.1.5 Construction of Membership Function

It is a well-known fact that in a minimization type problem, the value of the objective function should be substantially less than or equal to some assigned value. This assigned value is known as the aspiration level of the fuzzy goals of the objectives. In this subsection to obtain such aspiration level to the fuzzy goals, each transformed objective function is solved independently under the modified system constraints to find the best independent solution and worst independent solution of each of the objectives.

At first each objectives of the model (a) is solved independently under the modified system constraints to find the best independent solution and worst independent solution of the objectives. Let $\hat{Z}_p^{\,b}$ and $\hat{Z}_p^{\,w}$ $\left(p = 1, 2, \ldots, P\right)$ be the best and worst values obtained by solving each objective independently. Hence the fuzzy objective goal for each of the transformed objectives can be expressed as:

$$\hat{Z}_p \lesssim \hat{Z}_p^{\,b} ; \left(p = 1, 2, \ldots, P\right) \tag{21}$$

Such a fuzzy goal can be quantified by eliciting the corresponding membership functions on the basis of the achieved values. Thus the membership function for each of the objectives can be written as:

$$\mu_{\hat{Z}_p} = \begin{cases} 0 & \text{if} \quad \hat{Z}_p \geq \hat{Z}_p^{\,w} \\ \dfrac{\hat{Z}_p^{\,w} - \hat{Z}_p}{\hat{Z}_p^{\,w} - \hat{Z}_p^{\,b}} & \text{if} \quad \hat{Z}_p^{\,b} \leq \hat{Z}_p \leq \hat{Z}_p^{\,w} ; \left(p = 1, 2, \ldots, P\right) \\ 1 & \text{if} \quad \hat{Z}_p \leq \hat{Z}_p^{\,b} \end{cases} \tag{22}$$

Similarly the fuzzy objective goals and membership unction of each objective can also be obtained by solving each objective independently under modified system constraints in model (b).

9.1.6 Fuzzy Goal Programming Model

In the preceding chapters the authors already stated that in weighted FGP model the above defined membership functions are converted as flexible goals. For this, it is necessary to introduce under- and over- deviational variables for each of the membership functions and the aspiration levels are assigned as unity. Again, in multiple objectives decision making context the full achievement of all the membership goals is not possible. Therefore, it is essential to minimize the under deviational variables for achieving the goal values of objectives as much as possible in the decision making environment. Thus a weighted FGP model can be formulated for the models, model (a) and model (b).

The weighted FGP model for the model (a) is described as

$$\text{Min } D = \sum_{p=1}^{P} w_p d_p^-$$

satisfying

$$\mu_{\hat{Z}_p} + d_p^- - d_p^+ = 1 \, ; \left(p = 1, 2, \dots, P \right)$$

subject to

$$\sum_{j=1}^{n}\sum_{k=1}^{l} x_{ijk} \le \left[\frac{1}{\left(1 - \gamma_i\right)^{\frac{1}{\hat{\beta}_i}}} - 1 \right]^{\frac{1}{\hat{\mu}_i}} \left(i = 1, 2, \dots, u \right)$$

$$\sum_{j=1}^{n}\sum_{k=1}^{l} x_{ijk} \le \hat{\mu}_i + \hat{\beta}_i \ln\left(-\ln\left(\gamma_i\right)\right)\left(i = u + 1, u + 2, \dots, m\right)$$

$$\sum_{i=1}^{m}\sum_{k=1}^{l}x_{ijk} \geq \hat{\lambda}_j + \left(\hat{\rho}_j - \hat{\lambda}_j\right)\left(1 - \delta_j\right)^{\frac{1}{\hat{\phi}_j}}, (j = 1, 2, \ldots, v)$$

$$\sum_{i=1}^{m}\sum_{k=1}^{l}x_{ijk} \leq \hat{\rho}_j, \ (j = 1, 2, \ldots, v)$$

$$\sum_{i=1}^{m}\sum_{k=1}^{l}x_{ijk} \geq \frac{\hat{\lambda}_j}{\delta_j^{\frac{1}{\hat{\phi}_j}}}, \ (j = v + 1, v + 2, \ldots, n)$$

$$\sum_{i=1}^{m}\sum_{j=1}^{n}x_{ijk} \leq \hat{e}_k; \left(k = 1, 2, \ldots, l\right).$$

$$0 \leq z_{ijk}^{p1} + z_{ijk}^{p2} + \ldots + z_{ijk}^{pb} \leq b$$

$$z_{ijk}^{p1}, z_{ijk}^{p2}, \ldots, z_{ijk}^{pb} = 0 \text{ or } 1$$

$$x_{ijk} \geq 0 \, ; i = 1, 2, \ldots, m; j = 1, 2, \ldots, n; k = 1, 2, \ldots, l; p = 1, 2, \ldots, P \ . \tag{23}$$

where $d_p^-, d_p^+ \geq 0$ with $d_p^-.d_p^+ = 0$ and $w_p = \dfrac{c}{\hat{Z}_p^w - \hat{Z}_p^b}$ denotes the fuzzy weights corresponding to the membership goals of each of the objectives and $c > 0$.

Similarly the FGP model for model (b) can also be developed.

In the following subsection the methodological development for solving MOMCTP are presented in the form of an algorithm.

9.1.7. Solution Algorithm

The weighted FGP model for solving MOMCTP in stochastic fuzzy environment is expressed in the form of an algorithm by the following steps

Step 1: The fuzzy probabilistic constraints are converted into fuzzy constraints by applying CCP technique to all the stochastic fuzzy constraints.

Step 2: Using the defuzzification process of FNs, all the fuzzy parameters associated to the objectives as well as constraints, the problem is reduced to MOMCTP in crisp environment.

Step 3: The multi-choice objective functions are modified by applying the transformation technique to multi-choice cost coefficients.

Step 4: The individual best and worst value of all the objectives are found in isolation.

Step 5: Construct the fuzzy membership goals of the objectives.

Step 6: Fuzzy goal programming approach is used to achieve maximum degree of each of the membership goals.

Step 7: Stop.

In the following section a methodology developed by Kundu et al. (2014) for solving multi-objective solid TP are discussed briefly.

9.2 MULTI-OBJECTIVE SOLID TRANSPORTATION PROGRAMMING MODEL

In 2012, Kundu et al. (2014) presented a solution methodology for solving multi-objective solid TP model. In this context a multi-objective solid TP model with fuzzy parameters is presented as

$$\text{Min } Z_p = \sum_{i=1}^{m}\sum_{j=1}^{n}\sum_{k=1}^{K} \tilde{c}_{ijk}^{p} x_{ijk}, \ p = 1, 2, ..., P$$

subject to

$$\sum_{j=1}^{n}\sum_{k=1}^{K} x_{ijk} \lesssim \tilde{a}_{i}; \ i = 1, 2, ..., m$$

$$\sum_{i=1}^{m}\sum_{k=1}^{K} x_{ijk} \gtrsim \tilde{b}_{j}; \ j = 1, 2, ..., n$$

$$\sum_{i=1}^{m}\sum_{j=1}^{n} x_{ijk} \lesssim \tilde{e}_k \ ; \ k = 1, 2, ..., K$$

$$\sum_{i=1}^{m}\sum_{k=1}^{K} c_{ijk}^{l} x_{ijk} \lesssim \tilde{b}_j^{l} \ ; \ j = 1, 2, ..., n \ , \ l \in \left\{1, 2, ..., P\right\}$$

$$x_{ijk} \geq 0 \ \forall i, j, k \qquad\qquad\qquad (24)$$

where $\tilde{a}_i$; $i = 1, 2, ..., m$ denotes the fuzzy amount of the product available at the $i - $th origin, $\tilde{b}_j$; $j = 1, 2, ..., n$ be the fuzzy demands of the product at the $j - $th destination, $\tilde{e}_k$; $k = 1, 2, ..., K$ be the fuzzy transportation capacity of conveyance k, $c_{ijk}^{\hat{p}}$ be the random unit transportation penalty from the $i - $th origin to $j - $th destination via $k - $th conveyance for the $p - $th objective. For $p = l$ (say), $l \in \left\{1, 2, ..., P\right\}$, c_{ijk}^{l} represent unit transportation cost and $\tilde{b}_j^{l}$ is available fuzzy budget amount for the $j - $th destination for the objective Z_l.

9.2.1. Solution Algorithm

The solution procedure developed by Kundu et al. (2014) for solving multi-objective solid TPs with fuzzy uncertain parameters are presented briefly in the form of an algorithm.

Step1: Solve the multi-objective solid TP as a single objective solid TP using, each time, only one objective Z_p ,$\left(p = 1, 2, ..., P\right)$ (ignore all other objectives) to obtain the optimal solution $X_p^{*} = x_{ijk}^{p}$ of P different single objective solid TP.

Step 2: Calculate the values of all the P objective functions at all these P optimal solutions $X_p^{*} \left(p = 1, 2, ..., P\right)$ and find the upper and lower bound for each objective given by $U_p = \max$

$$\left\{Z_p\left(X_1^{*}\right), \ Z_p\left(X_2^{*}\right), Z_p\left(X_3^{*}\right), ..., Z_p\left(X_p^{*}\right)\right\}$$

and

$$L_p = Z_p\left(X_p^*\right)\left(p = 1, 2, \ldots, P\right)$$

respectively.

Step 3: Then an initial fuzzy model is given by

Find X

    subject to

$$Z_p\left(X\right) \le L_p \left(p = 1, 2, \ldots, P\right)$$

and the corresponding constraints where

$$X = \left\{x_{ijk}\right\}, i = 1, 2, \ldots, m; j = 1, 2, \ldots, n; k = 1, 2, \ldots, K$$

Step 4: Construct the linear membership function $\mu_p\left(Z_p\right)$ corresponding to
       p – th objective as

$$\mu_p\left(Z_p\right) = \begin{cases} 1 & if & Z_p \le L_p \\ \dfrac{U_p - Z_p}{U_p - L_p} & if & L_p \le Z_p \le U_p \; ; \; p = 1, 2, \ldots, P \\ 0 & if & Z_p \ge U_p \end{cases}$$

Step 5: Formulate fuzzy LPP using max-min operator as

Max λ

subject to

$$\lambda \le \frac{U_p - Z_p}{U_p - L_p}$$

and the corresponding constraints

$$\lambda \geq 0 \text{ and } \lambda = \min_p \left\{ \mu_p \left(Z_p \right) \right\}$$

Step 6: Now the reduced problem is solved by a linear optimization technique and the optimum compromise solution is obtained.

In the next section a numerical example is provided to illustrated the developed methodology and to compare the achieved results with the solutions achieved by the methodology developed by Kundu et al.(2014).

9.3 NUMERICAL ILLUSTRATION

To illustrate the proposed approach, the developed model (24) is solved by considering the revised form of numerical example studied by Kundu et al. (2014) and compared the achieved solution to the solution obtained by existing methodology (Kundu et al., 2014).

In this modified version of fuzzy stochastic TP the objective parameters are taken as multi choice transportation penalty parameters due to the fluctuating nature of the parameters. In this example it is assumed that some products are transported from two sources to two destinations via two conveyances. Also two objectives are considered in this example, viz., firstly the cost of transportation and secondly the transportation time from two sources to two destinations via two conveyances.

The cost of transportation and the time of transportation from two factories to two markets via two conveyances are given in Table 1.

The MOMCTP in fuzzy stochastic environment is thus constructed as

$$\text{Min } \tilde{Z}_1 \cong \{ \widetilde{10} \, , \, \widetilde{12} \, \}$$

$$x_{111} + \widetilde{10}x_{121} + \widetilde{13}x_{211} + \widetilde{17}x_{221} + \widetilde{15}x_{112} + \left\{ \widetilde{9}, \widetilde{11} \right\} x_{122} + \widetilde{17}x_{212} + \widetilde{14}x_{222}$$

$$\text{Min } \begin{aligned} \tilde{Z}_2 &\cong \widetilde{15}x_{111} + \widetilde{9}x_{121} + \widetilde{12}x_{211} + \left\{ \widetilde{11}, \widetilde{14} \right\} x_{221} + \\ &\left\{ \widetilde{8}, \widetilde{10}, \widetilde{12}, \widetilde{14} \right\} x_{112} + \widetilde{15}x_{122} + \left\{ \widetilde{12}, \widetilde{13} \right\} x_{212} + \widetilde{12}x_{222} \end{aligned}$$

Figure 2. TP

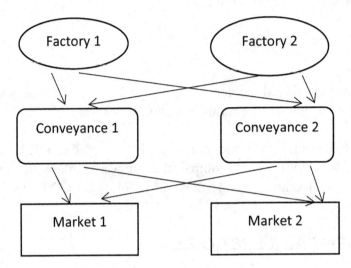

Table 1. Cost and time of transportation

	Factory 1 to Market 1 Via Vehicle 1	Factory 1 to Market 2 Via Vehicle 1	Factory 2 to Market 1 Via Vehicle 1	Factory 2 to Market 2 Via Vehicle 1	Factory 1 to Market 1 Via Vehicle 2	Factory 1 to Market 2 Via Vehicle 2	Factory 2 to Market 1Via Vehicle 2	Factory 2 to Market 2 Via Vehicle 2
Transportation Cost	$\widetilde{10}$, $\widetilde{12}$	$\widetilde{10}$	$\widetilde{13}$	$\widetilde{17}$	$\widetilde{15}$	$\widetilde{9},\widetilde{11}$	$\widetilde{17}$	$\widetilde{14}$
Time of Transportation	$\widetilde{15}$	$\widetilde{9}$	$\widetilde{12}$	$\widetilde{11},\widetilde{14}$	$\widetilde{8},\widetilde{10},\widetilde{12},\widetilde{14}\widetilde{15}$		$\widetilde{12},\widetilde{13}$	$\widetilde{12}$

subject to

$$\Pr\left(\sum_{j=1}^{2}\sum_{k=1}^{2}x_{1jk} \leq \tilde{a}_1\right) \geq 1 - \gamma_1$$

$$\Pr\left(\sum_{j=1}^{2}\sum_{k=1}^{2}x_{2jk} \leq \tilde{a}_2\right) \geq 1 - \gamma_2$$

$$\Pr\left(\sum_{i=1}^{2}\sum_{k=1}^{2}x_{i1k} \geq \tilde{b}_{1}\right) \geq 1-\delta_{1}$$

$$\Pr\left(\sum_{i=1}^{2}\sum_{k=1}^{2}x_{i2k} \geq \tilde{b}_{2}\right) \geq 1-\delta_{2}$$

$$\sum_{i=1}^{2}\sum_{j=1}^{2}x_{ij1} \leq \tilde{e}_{1}$$

$$\sum_{i=1}^{2}\sum_{j=1}^{2}x_{ij2} \leq \tilde{e}_{2}$$

$x_{ijk} \geq 0$ and integers, $\left(i=1,2; j=1,2; k=1,2; p=1,2\right).$ (25)

Here $\tilde{a}_1$ represents Bur-XII distributed FRV, $\tilde{a}_2$ follows extreme value distributed FRV, $\tilde{b}_1$ represents power function distributed FRV and $\tilde{b}_2$ represents FRV following Pareto distribution. Also the capacity of the two conveyances $\tilde{e}_1 = \widetilde{30}$ and $\tilde{e}_2 = \widetilde{42}$ are taken as trapezoidal FNs. The parameters of all the FRV and the multi-choice cost coefficients are considered as triangular FNs. The values of scale, location and shape parameters of different probability distributions are given as follows. Also the first objective $\tilde{Z}_1$ represents the transportation cost and second objective $\tilde{Z}_2$ represents the time of transportation.

- Value of Shape parameters of the Bur-XII distribution (Table 2)
- Value of Scale and location parameter of the Extreme value distribution (Table 3)

Table 2. Parameter of Bur-XII distribution

Shape Parameter	Specific Probability Level
$\dfrac{1}{\tilde{\beta}_1} = \tilde{3}$, $\dfrac{1}{\tilde{\mu}_1} = \tilde{3}$	$\gamma_1 = 0.40$

Table 3. Parameter of extreme value distribution

Scale Parameter	Location Parameter	Specific Probability Level
$\tilde{\beta}_2 = \tilde{8}$	$\tilde{\mu}_2 = \widetilde{29}$	$\gamma_2 = 0.12$

- Value of Scale and Shape parameter of the Power function distribution (Table 4)
- Value of Scale and Shape parameter of the Pareto distribution (Table 5)

The triangular FNs related to the parameters of all the distributions and the multi-choice cost coefficients are taken with the form as

$$\frac{1}{\tilde{\beta}_1} = \tilde{3} = \left(2.95, 3, 3.05\right),$$

$$\frac{1}{\tilde{\mu}_1} = \tilde{3} = \left(2.85, 3, 3.15\right),$$

$$\tilde{\beta}_2 = \tilde{8} = \left(7.5, 8, 8.5\right),$$

Table 4. Parameter of power function distribution

Scale Parameter	Shape Parameter	Specific Probability Level
$\tilde{\lambda}_1 = \widetilde{25}$, $\tilde{\rho}_1 = \widetilde{32}$	$\dfrac{1}{\tilde{\varphi}_1} = \tilde{5}$	$\delta_1 = 0.18$

Table 5. Parameter of Pareto distribution

Scale Parameter	Shape Parameter	Specific Probability Level
$\tilde{\lambda}_2 = \tilde{1}$	$\dfrac{1}{\tilde{\varphi}_2} = \tilde{2}$	$\delta_2 = 0.20$

$$\tilde{\mu}_2 = \widetilde{29} = \left(28, 29, 30\right),$$

$$\tilde{\lambda}_1 = \widetilde{25} = \left(23, 25, 27\right),$$

$$\tilde{\rho}_1 = \widetilde{32} = \left(29.5, 32, 34.5\right),$$

$$\frac{1}{\tilde{\varphi}_1} = \tilde{5} = \left(4.95, 5, 5.05\right),$$

$$\tilde{\lambda}_2 = \tilde{1} = \left(0.6, 1, 2\right),$$

$$\frac{1}{\tilde{\varphi}_2} = \tilde{2} = \left(1, 2, 3\right),$$

$$\widetilde{10} = \left(9.5, 10, 10.5\right),$$

$$\widetilde{12} = \left(11.95, 12, 12.05\right),$$

$$\widetilde{13} = \left(12, 13, 14\right),$$

$$\widetilde{17} = \left(16, 17, 17\right),$$

$$\widetilde{15} = \left(14.2, 15, 15.8\right),$$

$$\tilde{9} = \left(8.8, 9, 9.2\right), \widetilde{11} = \left(10, 11, 12\right),$$

$$\widetilde{14} = \left(13.95, 14, 14.05\right),$$

$$\tilde{8} = \left(7.5, 8, 8.5\right).$$

Also the capacity of the conveyances is taken as trapezoidal FNs. Therefore these parameters are expressed as

$$\tilde{e}_1 = \widetilde{30} = (27,29,32,34) \text{ and } \tilde{e}_1 = \widetilde{42} = (39,41,44,47).$$

As presented in the developed methodology, CCP technique is at first applied to all the fuzzy probabilistic constraints to remove the probabilistic uncertain nature from the constraints and then defuzzification process of FNs is used for finding the crisp value of FNs. Thus the modified form of objectives and constraints of the model (9.25) are presented as

$$\text{Min } \hat{Z}_1 = \{10, 12\}$$

$$x_{111} + 10x_{121} + 13x_{211} + 17x_{221} + 15x_{112} + \{9,11\}x_{122} + 17x_{212} + 14x_{222}$$

$$\text{Min } \begin{array}{l} \hat{Z}_2 = 15x_{111} + 9x_{121} + 12x_{211} + \{11,14\}x_{221} \\ + \{8,10,12,14\}x_{112} + 15x_{122} + \{12,13\}x_{212} + 12x_{222} \end{array}.$$

subject to

$$\sum_{j=1}^{2}\sum_{k=1}^{2} x_{1jk} \leq 44.36$$

$$\sum_{j=1}^{2}\sum_{k=1}^{2} x_{2jk} \leq 35$$

$$\sum_{i=1}^{2}\sum_{k=1}^{2} x_{i1k} \geq 27.59$$

$$\sum_{i=1}^{2}\sum_{k=1}^{2} x_{i1k} \leq 32$$

$$\sum_{i=1}^{2}\sum_{k=1}^{2}x_{i2k} \geq 30$$

$$\sum_{i=1}^{2}\sum_{j=1}^{2}x_{ij1} \leq 30.5$$

$$\sum_{i=1}^{2}\sum_{j=1}^{2}x_{ij2} \leq 42.79$$

$$x_{ijk} \geq 0 \text{ and integers, } \left(i = 1,2; j = 1,2; k = 1,2; p = 1,2\right). \tag{26}$$

In model (26) the readers now seen that probabilistic and possibilistic uncertainties are removed based on the methodology described in this chapter. But still objective parameters are multi choice in nature.

Using the transformation technique as described in this chapter, the MOMCTP in crisp environment is modifies as

$$\text{Min } \begin{aligned}\hat{Z}_1 &= \left\{10Z_{111}^{11} + 12\left(1 - Z_{111}^{11}\right)\right\}x_{111} + 10x_{121} + 13x_{211} \\ &+17x_{221} + 15x_{112} + \left\{9Z_{122}^{11} + 11\left(1 - Z_{122}^{11}\right)\right\}x_{122} + 17x_{212} + 14x_{222}\end{aligned}$$

Min
$$\begin{aligned}\hat{Z}_2 &= 15x_{111} + 9x_{121} + 12x_{211} + \left\{11Z_{221}^{21} + 14\left(1 - Z_{221}^{21}\right)\right\}x_{221} + \\ &\left\{8Z_{112}^{21}Z_{112}^{22} + 10Z_{112}^{21}\left(1 - Z_{112}^{22}\right) + 12Z_{112}^{22}\left(1 - Z_{112}^{21}\right) + 14\left(1 - Z_{112}^{21}\right)\left(1 - Z_{112}^{22}\right)\right\}x_{112} + \\ &15x_{122} + \left\{12Z_{212}^{21} + 13\left(1 - Z_{212}^{21}\right)\right\}x_{212} + 12x_{222}\end{aligned}$$
subject to

$$\sum_{j=1}^{2}\sum_{k=1}^{2}x_{1jk} \leq 44.36$$

$$\sum_{j=1}^{2}\sum_{k=1}^{2}x_{2jk} \leq 35$$

$$\sum_{i=1}^{2}\sum_{k=1}^{2}x_{i1k} \geq 27.59$$

$$\sum_{i=1}^{2}\sum_{k=1}^{2}x_{i1k} \leq 32$$

$$\sum_{i=1}^{2}\sum_{k=1}^{2}x_{i2k} \geq 30$$

$$\sum_{i=1}^{2}\sum_{j=1}^{2}x_{ij1} \leq 30.5$$

$$\sum_{i=1}^{2}\sum_{j=1}^{2}x_{ij2} \leq 42.79$$

$$Z_{111}^{11} \leq 1$$

$$Z_{122}^{11} \leq 1$$

$$Z_{221}^{21} \leq 1$$

$$0 \leq Z_{112}^{21} + Z_{112}^{22} \leq 2$$

$$Z_{112}^{21} \leq 1$$

$$Z_{112}^{22} \leq 1$$

$$Z_{212}^{21} \leq 1$$

$$x_{ijk}, z_{ijk}^{pb} \geq 0 \text{ and integers, } \left(i=1,2; j=1,2; k=1,2; p=1,2\ ; b=1,2\right). \tag{27}$$

Now each nonlinear objective is considered independently and is solved with respect to the system constraints defined in (27) to find the individual optimal values of the objectives. The results are obtained as

$$\hat{Z}_1^b = 592$$

at the point

$$x_{111} = 14, x_{211} = 14, x_{122} = 30$$

and other $x_{ijk} = 0$, and

$$\hat{Z}_2^b = 522$$

at the point

$$x_{121} = 16, x_{221} = 14, x_{112} = 28$$

and other $x_{ijk} = 0$.

The worst value of the objectives are obtained as $\hat{Z}_1^w = 1115$ and $\hat{Z}_1^w = 1039$. Then the fuzzy goals of the objectives are found as

$$\hat{Z}_1 \lesssim 592, \ \hat{Z}_2 \lesssim 522.$$

On the basis of the derived aspiration levels of the fuzzy goals, the following membership functions of each of the objectives are derived as

$$\mu_{\hat{Z}_1} = 2.132 - 0.002 \begin{bmatrix} \left\{ 10Z_{111}^{11} + 12\left(1 - Z_{111}^{11}\right) \right\} x_{111} + 10x_{121} + 13x_{211} + 17x_{221} + 15x_{112} + \\ \left\{ 9Z_{122}^{11} + 11\left(1 - Z_{122}^{11}\right) \right\} x_{122} + 17x_{212} + 14x_{222} \end{bmatrix}$$

(28)

and

$$\mu_{\hat{Z}_2} = 2.001 - 0.002 \begin{bmatrix} 15x_{111} + 9x_{121} + 12x_{211} + \left\{ 11Z_{221}^{21} + 14\left(1 - Z_{221}^{21}\right) \right\} x_{221} + \\ \left\{ 8Z_{112}^{21}Z_{112}^{22} + 10Z_{112}^{21}\left(1 - Z_{112}^{22}\right) + 12Z_{112}^{22}\left(1 - Z_{112}^{21}\right) + 14\left(1 - Z_{112}^{21}\right)\left(1 - Z_{112}^{22}\right) \right\} x_{112} \\ +15x_{122} + \left\{ 12Z_{212}^{21} + 13\left(1 - Z_{212}^{21}\right) \right\} x_{212} + 12x_{222} \end{bmatrix}$$

$$(29)$$

Hence the FGP model is presented by converting the elicited membership functions into membership goals as

Minimize $D = 0.002d_1^- + 0.002d_2^-$

so as to

$$\mu_{\hat{Z}_1} + d_1^- - d_1^+ = 1$$

$$\mu_{\hat{Z}_2} + d_2^- - d_2^+ = 1$$

subject to

$$\sum_{j=1}^{2}\sum_{k=1}^{2} x_{1jk} \leq 44.36$$

$$\sum_{j=1}^{2}\sum_{k=1}^{2} x_{2jk} \leq 35$$

$$\sum_{i=1}^{2}\sum_{k=1}^{2} x_{i1k} \geq 27.59$$

$$\sum_{i=1}^{2}\sum_{k=1}^{2} x_{i1k} \leq 32$$

$$\sum_{i=1}^{2}\sum_{k=1}^{2} x_{i2k} \geq 30$$

$$\sum_{i=1}^{2}\sum_{j=1}^{2} x_{ij1} \leq 30.5$$

$$\sum_{i=1}^{2}\sum_{j=1}^{2} x_{ij2} \leq 42.79$$

$$Z_{111}^{11} \leq 1$$

$$Z_{122}^{11} \leq 1$$

$$Z_{221}^{21} \leq 1$$

$$0 \leq Z_{112}^{21} + Z_{112}^{22} \leq 2$$

$$Z_{112}^{21} \leq 1$$

$$Z_{112}^{22} \leq 1$$

$$Z_{212}^{21} \leq 1$$

$$x_{ijk} \ , z_{ijk}^{pb} \geq 0 \text{ and integers,}$$

$$\left(i = 1,2; j = 1,2; k = 1,2; p = 1,2 \ ; b = 1,2 \right).$$

where

$$d_1^-, d_1^+, d_2^-, d_2^+ \geq 0 \text{ with } d_1^-.d_1^+, \ d_2^-.d_2^+ = 0 \tag{30}$$

The *software* LINGO (*Ver.11.0*) is used to solve the problem.

The optimal solution of the problem is obtained as $\hat{Z}_1 = 722$ and $\hat{Z}_2 = 783$ at the solution point $x_{211} = 29$, $x_{122} = 25$, $x_{222} = 5$ and other $x_{ijk} = 0$. This indicates that the total transportation cost is 722 and the total time of

Table 6. Compromise solution achieved by methodology presented in this chapter

Objective	Solution Point	Crisp Value of the Objective	Membership Value
$\tilde{Z}_1$	$x_{211} = 29$, $x_{122} = 25$, $x_{222} = 5$ and other $x_{ijk} = 0$	$\hat{Z}_1 = 722$	$\mu_{\hat{Z}_1} = 0.75$
$\tilde{Z}_2$		$\hat{Z}_2 = 783$	$\mu_{\hat{Z}_2} = 0.52$

Table 7. Comparison of solutions

Methodology	Solution Point	Objective Value	Membership Value
Method captured by Kundu et al. (2014)	$x_{111} = 2.72$, $x_{121} = 12.22$, $x_{211} = 12.46$, $x_{112} = 11.09$, $x_{122} = 11.56$, $x_{212} = 4.53$, $x_{222} = 10.81$, other $x_{ijk} = 0$	$\hat{Z}_1 = 862.78$ $\hat{Z}_2 = 858.27$	$\mu_{\hat{Z}_1} = 0.59$ $\mu_{\hat{Z}_2} = 0.58$
Proposed method	$x_{211} = 29$, $x_{122} = 25$, $x_{222} = 5$ and other $x_{ijk} = 0$	$\hat{Z}_1 = 722$ $\hat{Z}_2 = 783$	$\mu_{\hat{Z}_1} = 0.75$ $\mu_{\hat{Z}_2} = 0.52$

transportation is 783. From this solution it can be conclude that to achieve the optimal solution, it is not necessary to transport the product from all the sources to all the destinations. Because the transportation of the product between a source and a destination having longer distance may cause the increase the transportation costs.

The solutions achieved through FGP technique are summarized in Table 6.

The achieved objective values obtained by using the technique developed by Kundu et al. (2014) is $\hat{Z}_1 = 862.78$ and $\hat{Z}_2 = 858.27$.

The solutions achieved by the proposed methodology and by the procedure of Kundu et al. (2014) are summarized in Table 7.

From Table 7 and Figure 3 it is observed that the values of both the objectives by the proposed method are less than the corresponding objective values by the method developed by Kundu et al. (2014). So the proposed methodology is more acceptable for solving these types of TPs.

Figure 3a. Comparison of solutions in bar diagram

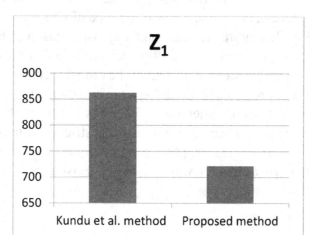

Figure 3b. Comparison of solutions in bar diagram

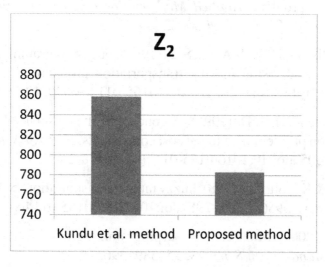

9.4 RESULTS AND DISCUSSIONS

The purpose of this chapter is to present a solution procedure for an unbalanced MOMCTP in which cost/time parameters of the objectives are taken as either FNs or multi-choice parameters with fuzzy uncertain nature. The availability and demands parameters in this chapter are considered as FRVs following Pareto, extreme value, power function and Bur-XII distribution. The hyper parameters of the FRVs are taken triangular FNs and the capacity of the conveyances is considered as trapezoidal FNs. The parameters of the MOMCTP model can also be taken as other type of FNs viz., Gaussian FN, intuitionistic FN, Pythagorean FN etc. and may also be taken as discrete FN in future. Also, other continuous probability distributions and discrete probability distributions may be considered instead of the probability distributions used in this chapter. The proposed methodology can be extended for solving fuzzy stochastic TP with cost coefficients are FRVs. The model can be extended to include breakable items, space constraints, some restriction on the conveyances etc. However it is hoped that the proposed technique for solving MOMCTP may open up new vistas into the way of making decision in the current fuzzy MOMC decision making arena.

REFERENCES

Biswal, M. P., & Acharya, S. (2009). Transformation of a multi-choice linear programming problem. *Applied Mathematics and Computation*, *210*(1), 182–188. doi:10.1016/j.amc.2008.12.080

Bit, A. K., Biswal, M. P., & Alam, S. S. (1992). Fuzzy programming approach to multicriteria decision making transportation problem. *Fuzzy Sets and Systems*, *50*(2), 135–141. doi:10.1016/0165-0114(92)90212-M

Chanas, S., & Kuchta, D. (1996). A concept of the optimal solution of the transportation problem with fuzzy cost coefficients. *Fuzzy Sets and Systems*, *82*(3), 299–305. doi:10.1016/0165-0114(95)00278-2

Chanas, S., & Kuchta, D. (1998). Fuzzy integer transportation problem. *Fuzzy Sets and Systems*, *98*(3), 291–298. doi:10.1016/S0165-0114(96)00380-6

Chang, C. T. (2007). Multi-choice goal programming, *OMEGA*. *International Journal of Management Sciences*, *35*, 389–396.

Charnes, A., & Cooper, W. W. (1959). Chance-constrained programming. *Management Science*, 6(1), 73–79. doi:10.1287/mnsc.6.1.73

Dantzig, G. B. (1963). *Linear programming and extensions*. Princeton University Press.

Diaz, J. A. (1978). Solving multiobjective transportation problem. *Ekonom- Mat. Obzor.*, *14*, 267–274.

Diaz, J. A. (1979). Finding a complete description of all efficient solutions to a multiobjective transportation problem. *Ekonom- Mat. Obzor.*, *15*, 62–73.

Dutta, D., & Murthy, S. (2010). Multi-choice goal programming approach for a fuzzy transportation problem. *IJRRAS*, *2*, 132–139.

Dutta, S., Acharya, S., & Mishra, R. (2016). genetic algorithm based fuzzy stochastic transportation programming problem with continuous random variables. *OPSEARCH*, *53*(4), 835–872. doi:10.100712597-016-0264-7

Gani, A., & Razak, K. A. (2006). Two stage fuzzy transportation problem. *The Journal of Physiological Sciences; JPS*, *10*, 63–69.

Gupta, S., Ali, I., & Chaudhary, S. (2018). *Multi-objective capacitated transportation: a problem of parameters estimation, goodness of fit and optimization*. Granular Computing. doi:10.100741066-018-0129-y

Hiller, F., & Lieberman, G. (1990). *Introduction to Operations Research*. New York: McGraw-Hill.

Hitchcock, F. L. (1941). The Distribution of Product from Several Sources to Numerous Localities. *Journal of Mathematical Physics*, *20*(1-4), 224–230. doi:10.1002apm1941201224

Hulsurkar, S., Biswal, M. P., & Sinha, S. B. (1997). Fuzzy Programming Approach to Multi-objective Stochastic Linear Programming Problems. *Fuzzy Sets and Systems*, *88*(2), 173–181. doi:10.1016/S0165-0114(96)00056-5

Isermann, H. (1979). The enumeration of all efficient solutions for a linear multiobjective transportation problem. *Naval Res. Logist. Quart.*, *2*(1), 123–139. doi:10.1002/nav.3800260112

Koopmans, T. C. (1949). Optimum utilization of the transportation problem. *Econometrica*, *17*, 3–4. doi:10.2307/1907301

Kundu, P., Kar, S., & Maiti, M. (2014). Multiobjective solid transportation problems with budget constraint in uncertain environment. *International Journal of System Science*, *45*(8), 1668–1682. doi:10.1080/00207721.2012.748944

Lee, S. M., & Moore, L. J. (1973). Optimizing transportation problems with multiple objectives. *Transactions of the American Institute of Electrical Engineers*, *5*(4), 333–338. doi:10.1080/05695557308974920

Li, L., Huang, Z., Da, Q., & Hu, J. (2008). A new method based on goal programming for solving transportation with fuzzy cost. In: International Symposiums on Information Processing, 3-8.

Lin, F. T. (2009), Solving the transportation problem with fuzzy coefficients using genetic algorithms. *IEEE International Conference on Fuzzy Systems*, 1468-1473.

Liu, S. T., & Kao, C. (2004). Solving fuzzy transportation problem based on extension principle. *European Journal of Operational Research*, *153*(3), 661–674. doi:10.1016/S0377-2217(02)00731-2

Luhandjula, M. K. (1983). Linear programming under randomness and fuzziness. *Fuzzy Sets and Systems*, *10*(1-3), 45–55. doi:10.1016/S0165-0114(83)80103-1

Mahapatra, D. R., Roy, S. K., & Biswal, M. P. (2010). Stochastic based on multi-objective transportation problems involving normal randomness. *Advanced Modeling and Optimization*, *12*, 205–223.

Mahapatra, D. R., Roy, S. K., & Biswal, M. P. (2013). Multi-choice stochastic transportation problem involving extreme value distribution. *Applied Mathematical Modelling*, *37*(4), 2230–2240. doi:10.1016/j.apm.2012.04.024

Maity, G., & Roy, S. K. (2016). Solving a multi-objective transportation problem with nonlinear cost and multi-choice demand. *International Journal of Management Science and Engineering*, *11*(1), 62–70. doi:10.1080/17509653.2014.988768

Maity, G., & Roy, S. K. (2017). Multiobjective Transportation Problem Using Fuzzy Decision Variable Through Multi-Choice Programming. *International Journal of Operations Research and Information Systems*, *8*(3), 82–96. doi:10.4018/IJORIS.2017070105

Meniconi, M., & Barry, D. M. (1996). The power function distribution: A useful and simple distribution to assess electrical component reliability. *Microelectronics and Reliability*, *36*(9), 1207–1212. doi:10.1016/0026-2714(95)00053-4

Merran, E., Nicholas, H., & Brian, P. (n.d.). *Statistical distributions*. John Wiley & Sons, Inc.

Ojha, A., Das, B., Mondal, S. K., & Maiti, M. (2014). A transportation problem with fuzzy stochastic cost. *Applied Mathematical Modelling*, *38*(4), 1464–1481. doi:10.1016/j.apm.2013.08.022

Patel, J. G., & Dhodiya, J. M. (2017). Solving Multi-Objective Interval Transportation Problem Using Grey Situation Decision-Making Theory Based On Grey Numbers. *International Journal of Pure and Applied Mathematics*, *113*, 219–233.

Quddoos, A., Hasan, G. U., & Khalid, M. M. (2014). Multi-choice stochastic transportation problem involving general form of distributions. *SpringerPlus*, *3*(1), 1–9. doi:10.1186/2193-1801-3-565 PMID:25332865

Rabindran, A., Philips Don, T., & Solberg James, J. (1987). *Operations Research; Principles and Practice* (2nd ed.). New York: John Wiley and Sons.

Roy, S. K., Ebrahimnejad, A., Verdegay, J., & Das, S. (2018). New approach for solving intuitionistic fuzzy multi-objective transportation problem. *Sadhana*, *43*(1), 1–12. doi:10.100712046-017-0777-7

Sakawa, M., Kato, K., & Katagiri, H. (2004). An interactive fuzzy satisfying method for multiobjective linear programming problems with random variable coefficients through a probability maximization model. *Fuzzy Sets and Systems*, *146*(2), 205–220. doi:10.1016/j.fss.2004.04.003

Saneifard, R., & Saneifard, R. (2011). A modified method for defuzzification by probability density function. *Journal of Applied Sciences Research*, *7*(2), 102–110.

Sengupta, J. K. (1972). Stochastic Programming: Methods and Applications. North-Holland Publishing Company.

Vajda, S. (1972). *Probabilistic programming*. New York: Academic press.

Zadeh, L. A. (1965). Fuzzy Sets. *Information and Control*, 8(3), 338–353. doi:10.1016/S0019-9958(65)90241-X

Zimmermann, H. J. (1976). Description and optimization of fuzzy systems. *International Journal of General Systems*, 2(4), 209–215. doi:10.1080/03081077608547470

Chapter 10

A Fuzzy Multi-Objective Stochastic Programming Model for Allocation of Lands in Agricultural Systems

ABSTRACT

In this chapter, a fuzzy stochastic multi-objective programming model is presented for planning proper allocation of agricultural lands in hybrid uncertain environment so that optimal production of several seasonal crops in a planning year can be achieved. In India, demands of various seasonal crops are gradually increasing due to rapid growth of population, whereas agricultural lands are gradually decreasing due to urbanization. Therefore, it is a huge challenge to the planners to balance this situation by proper planning for the utilization of agricultural lands and resources. From that viewpoint, the methodology is developed in this chapter. To make the model more realistic, the resource parameters incorporated with the problem are considered either in the form of fuzzy numbers (FNs) or random variables having fuzzy parameters. The two main objectives of this agricultural land allocation model are considered as maximizing the production of seasonal agricultural crops and minimizing the total expenditure by utilizing total cultivable lands in a planning period. These objectives are optimized based on the constraints: land utilization, machine-hours, man-days, fertilizer requirements, water supply, etc. As the parameters associated with the constraints are imprecise and uncertain in nature, the constraints are represented using either FN or fuzzy random variables (FRVs). The reasons behind the consideration of fuzzy constraints or fuzzy chance constraints (i.e., the reason for considering the parameters associated with the constraints as FNs or FRVs in the model) are clarified in detail. As a study region, the District Nadia, West Bengal, India is taken into account for allocation of land. To illustrate the potential use of the approach, the model solutions are compared with the existing land allocation of the district.

DOI: 10.4018/978-1-5225-8301-1.ch010

10.1 BACKGROUND AND PLANNING
IN AGRICULTURAL SECTOR

In agricultural sector proper utilization of cultivable lands and production planning are two most important tasks for both social and economic perspectives. Agricultural sector is the oldest and most essential sectors in the world. Due to the increasing growth of population, the demand for the agricultural products is rapidly increasing. One way to meet the demand of the society is to increasing the cultivating land areas scientifically. But a developing country, like India, is losing land due to rapid population growth, urbanization and industrialization. Therefore, there is an increasing need for designing appropriate mathematical models for land allocation planning in agricultural systems. Mathematical Programing (MP) models for agricultural planning problems are widely used since Heady (1954) demonstrated the use of linear programming (LP) for land allocation to crop planning problems.

Thereafter, LP models are widely used for maximizing the production of various crops (Arnold and bennet, 1975), allocation of cultivable lands (Glen, 1987), and minimizing the cost of cultivation of the farmers (Barnard and Nix, 1973). Thereafter, several LP models of different farm planning problems are extensively studied (Nix, 1979; Black and Hlubik, 1980). The potential use of LP for agricultural planning was studied further by Tsai *et al.* (1987). Qingzhen *et al.* (1991) developed an optimal production plan for crop and livestock. Some researchers (Wiens, 1976; Adams *et al.*, 1977; Simmons and Pomareda, 1975) used quadratic programming techniques to formulate the relationship between demand and prices and also to incorporate certain risk factors in agricultural problems. Mathematical models for agricultural water management which are essential for crop area planning were developed by Leenhardt *et al.* (2004) and Ding *et al.* (2006).

Generally, several conflicting objectives such as maximizing production of crops, minimizing expenditures, maximizing profit, etc., are involved with agricultural planning. As demonstrated in this book, Goal Programming (GP) appeared as a powerful tool for solving different types of problems with conflicting objectives. GP was first introduced by Charnes and Cooper (1961) and its methodological developments were performed by Ijiri (1965), Ignizio (1976) and several others. A review on GP was made by Romero (1986), Tamiz and Jones (1995) and others. Lee and Clayton (1972) successfully implemented GP methodology in different decision making problems. The use of preemptive priority based GP to land-use planning problem was discussed by Pal and Basu (1996). Saker and Quaddus (2002) formulated a nationwide crop planning model using GP and discussed the importance of three different goals for the case problem. Oliveria *et al.* (2003) presented a GP model for forest farm planning problems. Ghosh *et al.* (2005) suggested a GP formulation for nutrient management for rice production.

However, in actual land use planning contexts, the decision makers are often faced with different inexact parameter values due to imprecision in human judgement. One of the major approaches to deal with such problem is fuzzy programming approach. Bellman and Zadeh (1970) first introduced the concept of decision making in fuzzy environment. In fuzzy programming methodology, an optimization problem can be viewed as the process of finding a satisfying solution by maximizing the membership goals. In agricultural land allocation planning, Sahoo *et al.* (2006) and Zhou *et al.* (2007) formulated fuzzy multi-objective linear programming (FMOLP) model by defining membership functions, which deal with the fuzziness of the decision makers aspirations with respect to the goals. Zeng *et al.* (2010) developed FMOLP model for crop area planning problem using triangular FNs. In 2015 Murmu and Biswas (2015) applied fuzzy logic and neural network in agricultural sector for the classification of various agricultural crops.

In the situation of agricultural planning, assigning of definite aspiration levels to the goals of the problem frequently creates decision trouble in most of the farm planning situations and thus conventional GP is not suitable for solving agricultural planning problems. For successfully handling such problems, fuzzy goal programming (FGP) technique has been introduced by Hannan (1980) and Narasimhan (1980). Pal and Moitra (2003), Biswas and Pal (2005) applied FGP to solve land use planning problems in agricultural systems. Agricultural land allocation problem using FGP studied further by Sharma *et al.* (2007). FGP based genetic algorithm approach to nutrient management has been developed by Sharma and Jana (2009).

In land allocation problems, another kind of uncertainty which is frequently appeared can be handled using stochastic programming to deal with probabilistic uncertain parameters in MP problems. Considering the probabilistic and possibilistic behaviour of agricultural land allocation problems, a multistage fuzzy-stochastic quadratic programming approach was framed by Li *et al.* (2009) by developing a hybrid water-management model for agricultural sustainability. Cui *et al.* (2015) applied a two stage stochastic programming model in agricultural water resource management system. Recently, fuzzy stochastic programming model is applied to determine optimum crop patterns and water balance in a farm (Dutta *et al.*, 2016) and in water resources management (Subagadis *et al.*, 2016). A credibility-based chance constrained optimization model for integrated agricultural and water resources management was developed by Lu et al. (2016). In recent years Jana et al. (2016) and Biswas & Modak (2017) applied FGP to agricultural decision making problem in fuzzy stochastic environment.

In this chapter, an FGP model is adopted for optimal production of seasonal crops by utilizing the cultivable land and the available productive resources and to minimize the total expenditure as much as possible. Due to insufficient and inexact availability of the information some of the resource parameters are taken as FRVs and others as triangular FNs (TFNs). As like in other chapters CCP methodology is employed in hybrid uncertain environment to construct a fuzzy programming model from a fuzzy stochastic programming model. The deterministic equivalent of the model is derived using the defuzzification method of TFNs. After that, individual optimal solution of each objective representing product of several crops and total expenditure in agricultural sector is found in isolation to construct the fuzzy membership goals of each objective. After that membership goals of each objective are converted into membership function to develop the FGP model. Finally, a weighted FGP model is constructed to find the most satisfactory decision for the cropping plan in agricultural decision making environment. A case study based on the collected data from Nadia district of West Bengal (India) is used to demonstrate the proposed methodology.

10.1.1 Mathematical Model for Land Allocation Problem in Agricultural Sector

For the formulation of the mathematical model for increasing the production of various agricultural products by proper land utilization in agricultural sector, the total time period (i.e., one year) is divided into a number of seasons according to the climate conditions. Based on the assumption that C numbers of crops are cultivated during S different seasons, the mathematical model for land allocation is formulated. The decision variables and different types of parameters used to formulate the land allocation model in this chapter are presented as follows:

Index Sets

The following indices are used to develop the land allocation model in agricultural sector.

c=crop; $c = 1, 2, ..., C$;
s=season; $s = 1, 2, ... S$;
t=fertilizer; $t = 1, 2, ..., T$;

Objectives

Out of several objectives in agricultural sector, the authors in this book emphasize on two important objectives, viz., i) to maximize the total production and ii) to minimize the total expenditure for cultivating various seasonal crops during a planning year. The objectives are represented as follows:

$\tilde{Z}_1$ = total production of various crops during a planning year (in '000metric ton ('000mt));

$\tilde{Z}_2$ = total expenditure for cultivating various crops during a planning year (in Indian Rupee) (INR);

Decision Variable

x_{cs} = allocation of the land for cultivating the crop c in the season s (in hectare (ha));

Crisp Parameter

γ_s = specific probability level for the probabilistic constraint s;

Fuzzy Parameters

Since the parameters associated with the land allocation problems are not certain, some vagueness is inevitable with the parameters due to lack of knowledge and information, so some sort of uncertainties are involved with them. For example, production of crops mainly depends on climate conditions, quality of soli, fertilizers, etc. Also production depends on natural calamities. Due to these imprecise natures, production of crops is not exact.

Other parameters are also vague in nature due to various uncontrollable factors. These uncertainties mainly are of possibilistic nature and thus these uncertain parameters are represented by FN.

$\tilde{P}_{cs}$ = estimated production of the crop c per ha during the season s in Kg/ha;

$\tilde{E}_{cs}$ = estimated expenditure for cultivating the crop c during the season s in INR/ha;

$\tilde{A}_s$ = total farming land for cultivating crops in the season s in ('000 ha);

$\tilde{H}_{cs}$ = average machine hours required per ha for the crop c during the season s in (hrs/ha);

$\tilde{H}_s$ = total machine hours required during the season s in ('00hrs);

$\tilde{D}_{cs}$ = average man-days required per ha for the crop c during the season s in (days/ha);

$\tilde{D}_s$ = total man-days required during the season s in ('000days);

$\tilde{F}_{tcs}$ = average amount of fertilizer t required per ha for the crop c in the season s in (Kg/ha);

$\tilde{F}_t$ = total amount of fertilizer t required in the planning year in ('000mt);

$\tilde{W}_{cs}$ = estimated amount of water consumption per ha for the crop c during the season s in (inch/ha);

$\tilde{L}_{cs}$ = estimated minimum land allocation for the crop c during the season s in ('000ha);

Fuzzy Random Variable

The total water supply in a planning year in an agricultural land allocation problem is uncertain in nature. It very much depends mainly on the natural rains at rainy season i.e., it depends on the amount of rain happens in a year. Thus the rainfall is probabilistic in nature. Also, cultivators may have used some alternative sources of water for various crops during a season for increasing the production without solely depending on the rainfall. These sources of water are imprecisely defined. So the total water supply is not only probabilistic in nature, but imprecision involved inherently within it. Therefore this resource parameter is considered as FRV using FNs as hyper parameters.

$\tilde{W}_s$ = total supply of water available during the season s in inch which is normally distributed;

Thus in land allocation model in agricultural sector, considering total water supply as FRVs and all other parameters are expressible using FNs, a mathematical model in hybrid fuzzy stochastic environment is formulated as

$$\text{Max } \tilde{Z}_1 \cong \sum_{c=1}^{C} \sum_{s=1}^{S} \tilde{P}_{cs} x_{cs}$$

$$\text{Min } \tilde{Z}_2 \cong \sum_{c=1}^{C} \sum_{s=1}^{S} \tilde{E}_{cs} x_{cs}$$

subject to

$$\sum_{c=1}^{C} x_{cs} \lesssim \tilde{A}_s \; ; \; \left(s = 1, 2, ..., S\right) \text{[land utilization constraints]}$$

$$\sum_{c=1}^{C} \tilde{H}_{cs} x_{cs} \gtrsim \tilde{H}_s \; ; \; \left(s = 1, 2, ..., S\right) \text{[machine-hour constraints]}$$

$$\sum_{c=1}^{C} \tilde{D}_{cs} x_{cs} \gtrsim \tilde{D}_s \; ; \; \left(s = 1, 2, ..., S\right) \text{[man-days constraints]}$$

$$\sum_{c=1}^{C} \sum_{s=1}^{S} \tilde{F}_{tcs} x_{cs} \lesssim \tilde{F}_t \; ; \; \left(t = 1, 2, ..., T\right) \text{[fertilizer requirement constraints]}$$

$$\text{Pr}\left(\sum_{c=1}^{C} \tilde{W}_{cs} x_{cs} \gtrsim \tilde{W}_s\right) \geq \gamma_s \; ; \; \left(s = 1, 2, ..., S\right) \text{[water supply constraints]}$$

$$x_{cs} \gtrsim \tilde{L}_{cs} \; ; \; \left(c = 1, 2, ..., C; s = 1, 2, ..., S\right) \text{[minimum land allocation constraints]} \tag{1}$$

In this model $\tilde{W}_s \left(s = 1, 2, \ldots, S \right)$ are considered as FRVs whose mean $E\left(\tilde{W}_s\right)$ and variance $Var\left(\tilde{W}_s\right)$ are taken as FNs. All other parameters $\tilde{P}_{cs}$, $\tilde{E}_{cs}$, $\tilde{A}_s$, $\tilde{H}_{cs}$, $\tilde{H}_s$, $\tilde{D}_{cs}$, $\tilde{D}_s$, $\tilde{F}_{tcs}$, $\tilde{F}_t$, $\tilde{W}_{cs}$, $\tilde{L}_{cs}$ are also taken as FNs. From the previous year's data it is observed that a minimum level of land allocation $\tilde{L}_{cs}$ is required for the crop c in the season s.

From the above developed model, it is quite clear to the readers that like SWM model agricultural land allocation model is also represented by a multi-objective linear programming model in fuzzy stochastic environment. The methodological development of fuzzy stochastic multi-objective linear programming (FSMOLP) model representing agricultural land allocation model is identical to methodologies described in chapter 3.

In the next section a FSMOLP model in hybrid uncertain environment is considered and then solved using FGP technique to express the above developed agricultural land allocation model.

10.2 METHODOLOGY FOR SOLVING AGRICULTURAL LAND ALLOCATION MODEL

In this section a weighted FGP model is developed to solve FSMOLP problem in hybrid uncertain fuzzy environment. The coefficients of the objectives and the left sided parameters of all the constraints are taken as FNs. The right sided parameters of the constraints are either FNs or FRVs with FNs as parameters. In the solution process the FSMOLP problem are converted into fuzzy programming model using CCP technique in hybrid fuzzy environment. Then the deterministic model is developed from the fuzzy programming model by applying defuzzification process of FNs. Afterwards each objective is solved independently under the modified system constraints to construct the membership goals of each objective. Finally, weighted FGP model is constructed to achieve the most satisfactory decision in the hybrid uncertain fuzzy decision making arena. Then the developed methodology is applied in the context of land allocation problem in agricultural sector for validating the model.

10.2.1 Development of Agricultural Land Allocation Model

Now, the model representing agricultural land allocation model developed above are solved using the methodology discussed in chapter 3. The FSMOLP model for land allocation in agricultural sector is presented (as in section 10.1) as follows

$$\text{Max } \tilde{Z}_1 \cong \sum_{c=1}^{C}\sum_{s=1}^{S}\tilde{P}_{cs}x_{cs}$$

$$\text{Min } \tilde{Z}_2 \cong \sum_{c=1}^{C}\sum_{s=1}^{S}\tilde{E}_{cs}x_{cs}$$

subject to

$$\sum_{c=1}^{C}x_{cs} \lesssim \tilde{A}_s \, ; \, \left(s = 1, 2, ..., S\right)$$

$$\sum_{c=1}^{C}\tilde{H}_{cs}x_{cs} \gtrsim \tilde{H}_s \, ; \, \left(s = 1, 2, ..., S\right)$$

$$\sum_{c=1}^{C}\tilde{D}_{cs}x_{cs} \gtrsim \tilde{D}_s \, ; \, \left(s = 1, 2, ..., S\right)$$

$$\sum_{c=1}^{C}\sum_{s=1}^{S}\tilde{F}_{tcs}x_{cs} \lesssim \tilde{F}_t \, ; \, \left(t = 1, 2, ..., T\right)$$

$$\text{Pr}\left(\sum_{c=1}^{C}\tilde{W}_{cs}x_{cs} \gtrsim \tilde{W}_s\right) \geq \gamma_s \, ; \, \left(s = 1, 2, ..., S\right)$$

$$x_{cs} \gtrsim \tilde{L}_{cs} \, ; \, \left(c = 1, 2, ..., C; s = 1, 2, ..., S\right) \tag{2}$$

Here the objective parameters $\tilde{P}_{cs}$, representing the production of different crops and $\tilde{E}_{cs}$, expressing the expenditure for cultivation

$$\left(c = 1, 2, ..., C; s = 1, 2, ..., S\right),$$

left side parameters of some constraints

$$\tilde{H}_{cs}, \tilde{D}_{cs}, \tilde{F}_{tcs}, \tilde{W}_{cs}, \left(c = 1, 2, ..., C; s = 1, 2, ..., S; t = 1, 2, ..., T\right)$$

and right sided parameters

$$\tilde{A}_{s}, \tilde{H}_{s}, \tilde{D}_{s}, \tilde{F}_{t}, \tilde{L}_{cs} \left(c = 1, 2, ..., C; s = 1, 2, ..., S; t = 1, 2, ..., T\right)$$

of the non-probabilistic constraints are taken as TFNs. The right sided parameters $\tilde{W}_{s} (s = 1, 2, ..., S)$ of the probabilistic constraints are considered as FRVs following normal distribution. As the parameters of the objectives are TFNs, therefore, the objectives $\tilde{Z}_{1}$, $\tilde{Z}_{2}$ as a whole are also TFNs (as the sum and scalar multiple of FNs is again an FN of same type). Also the symbols $\cong, \underset{\sim}{\leq}$ and $\underset{\sim}{\geq}$ represents equality, less than or equal and greater than or equal respectively in fuzzy sense.

10.2.2 Fuzzy Programming Model Formulation

The readers already understood that throughout this book only CCP methodology is applied to the probabilistic constraints to free from probabilistic uncertainty. So, in this section fuzzy programming model is developed from the fuzzy stochastic programming model using CCP methodology.

As $\tilde{W}_{s} (s = 1, 2, ..., S)$ is a FRV following normal distribution, then the stochastic constraints

$$\Pr\left(\sum_{c=1}^{C} \tilde{W}_{cs} x_{cs} \underset{\sim}{\geq} \tilde{W}_{s}\right) \geq \gamma_{s} ; \left(s = 1, 2, ..., S\right)$$

are modified through CCP methodology as follows

$$\Pr\left(\sum_{c=1}^{C}\tilde{W}_{cs}x_{cs} \gtrsim \tilde{W}_s\right) \geq \gamma_s \; ; \; \left(s = 1, 2, \ldots, S\right)$$

i.e., $\left(\dfrac{\tilde{W}_s - E\left(\tilde{W}_s\right)}{\sqrt{Var\left(\tilde{W}_s\right)}} \lesssim \dfrac{\sum_{c=1}^{C}\tilde{W}_{cs}x_{cs} - E\left(\tilde{W}_s\right)}{\sqrt{Var\left(\tilde{W}_s\right)}}\right) \geq \gamma_s \; ;$

$$\left(s = 1, 2, \ldots, S\right)$$

i.e. $\Phi\left(\dfrac{\sum_{c=1}^{C}\tilde{W}_{cs}x_{cs} - E\left(\tilde{W}_s\right)}{\sqrt{Var\left(\tilde{W}_s\right)}}\right) \geq \gamma_s \; ;$

$$\left(s = 1, 2, \ldots, S\right)$$

i.e. $\displaystyle\sum_{c=1}^{C}\tilde{W}_{cs}x_{cs} \gtrsim E\left(\tilde{W}_s\right) + \Phi^{-1}\left(\gamma_s\right)\sqrt{Var\left(\tilde{W}_s\right)}\left(s = 1, 2, \ldots, S\right)$ \hfill (3)

Therefore the fuzzy programming model of the model (2) is presented as

$$\text{Max } \tilde{Z}_1 \cong \sum_{c=1}^{C}\sum_{s=1}^{S}\tilde{P}_{cs}x_{cs}$$

$$\text{Min } \tilde{Z}_2 \cong \sum_{c=1}^{C}\sum_{s=1}^{S}\tilde{E}_{cs}x_{cs}$$

subject to

$$\sum_{c=1}^{C}x_{cs} \lesssim \tilde{A}_s \; ; \; \left(s = 1, 2, \ldots, S\right)$$

$$\sum_{c=1}^{C} \tilde{H}_{cs} x_{cs} \gtrsim \tilde{H}_s \, ; \, \left(s = 1, 2, ..., S \right)$$

$$\sum_{c=1}^{C} \tilde{D}_{cs} x_{cs} \gtrsim \tilde{D}_s \, ; \, \left(s = 1, 2, ..., S \right)$$

$$\sum_{c=1}^{C} \sum_{s=1}^{S} \tilde{F}_{tcs} x_{cs} \lesssim \tilde{F}_t \, ; \, \left(t = 1, 2, ..., T \right)$$

$$\sum_{c=1}^{C} \tilde{W}_{cs} x_{cs} \gtrsim E\left(\tilde{W}_s \right) + \Phi^{-1} \left(\gamma_s \right) \sqrt{Var\left(\tilde{W}_s \right)} \left(s = 1, 2, ..., S \right)$$

$$x_{cs} \gtrsim \tilde{L}_{cs} \, ; \, \left(c = 1, 2, ..., C; s = 1, 2, ..., S \right) \tag{4}$$

10.2.3 Construction of Deterministic Model

In this section deterministic model of the fuzzy programming model developed above is constructed based on defuzzification methods discussed in chapter 2. For simplicity, all the fuzzy parameters in this chapter are taken as TFNs. Other type of FNs can also be used instead of TFNs. In that case there will be no variation in the methodological development except the change in the nature of the FNs.

As all the fuzzy parameters of the land allocation model are considered as TFNs, therefore these FNs can be presented as

$$\tilde{P}_{cs} = \left(P_{cs}^1, P_{cs}, P_{cs}^2 \right),$$

$$\tilde{E}_{cs} = \left(E_{cs}^1, E_{cs}, E_{cs}^2 \right),$$

$$\tilde{H}_{cs} = \left(H_{cs}^1, H_{cs}, H_{cs}^2 \right),$$

$$\tilde{D}_{cs} = \left(D_{cs}^1, D_{cs}, D_{cs}^2 \right),$$

$$\tilde{F}_{tcs} = \left(F^1_{tcs}, F_{tcs}, F^2_{tcs} \right),$$

$$\tilde{W}_{cs} = \left(W^1_{cs}, W_{cs}, W^2_{cs} \right),$$

$$\tilde{L}_{cs} = \left(L^1_{cs}, L_{cs}, L^2_{cs} \right),$$

$$\tilde{A}_s = \left(A^1_s, A_s, A^2_s \right),$$

$$\tilde{H}_s = \left(H^1_s, H_s, H^2_s \right),$$

$$\tilde{D}_s = \left(D^1_s, D_s, D^2_s \right),$$

$$\tilde{F}_t = \left(F^1_t, F_t, F^2_t \right).$$

Again in the model (4) the mean $E\left(\tilde{W}_s\right)$ and variance $Var\left(\tilde{W}_s\right)$ of the FRVs $\tilde{W}_s$ are regarded as TFNs. Therefore, these fuzzy parameters are expressed as

$$E\left(\tilde{W}_s\right) = \left(eW^1_s, eW_s, eW^2_s \right),$$

$$Var\left(\tilde{W}_s\right) = \left(vW^1_s, vW_s, vW^2_s \right).$$

Since the square root of an FN is again an FN of the same type, therefore $\sqrt{Var\left(\tilde{W}_s\right)}$ is also a TFN of the form

$$\sqrt{Var\left(\tilde{W}_s\right)} = \left(\sqrt{vW^1_s}, \sqrt{vW_s}, \sqrt{vW^2_s} \right).$$

Now the defuzzification process (canonical form of a fuzzy number), which is discussed in Chapter 2, is used to find the defuzzified value of all the fuzzy parameters. Thus the defuzzified value of these FNs are evaluated based on the canonical form of an FN as

$$V\left(\tilde{P}_{cs}\right) = \frac{P^1_{cs} + 4P_{cs} + P^2_{cs}}{6},$$

$$V\left(\tilde{E}_{cs}\right) = \frac{E^1_{cs} + 4E_{cs} + E^2_{cs}}{6},$$

$$V\left(\tilde{H}_{cs}\right) = \frac{H^1_{cs} + 4H_{cs} + H^2_{cs}}{6},$$

$$V\left(\tilde{D}_{cs}\right) = \frac{D^1_{cs} + 4D_{cs} + D^2_{cs}}{6},$$

$$V\left(\tilde{F}_{tcs}\right) = \frac{F^1_{tcs} + 4F_{tcs} + F^2_{tcs}}{6},$$

$$V\left(\tilde{W}_{cs}\right) = \frac{W^1_{cs} + 4W_{cs} + W^2_{cs}}{6},$$

$$V\left(\tilde{L}_{cs}\right) = \frac{L^1_{cs} + 4L_{cs} + L^2_{cs}}{6},$$

$$V\left(\tilde{A}_{s}\right) = \frac{A^1_{s} + 4A_{s} + A^2_{s}}{6},$$

$$V\left(\tilde{H}_{s}\right) = \frac{H^1_{s} + 4H_{s} + H^2_{s}}{6},$$

$$V\left(\tilde{D}_{s}\right) = \frac{D^1_{s} + 4D_{s} + D^2_{s}}{6},$$

$$V\left(\tilde{F}_{t}\right) = \frac{F^1_{t} + 4F_{t} + F^2_{t}}{6},$$

$$V\left(E\left(\tilde{W}_s\right)\right) = \frac{eW_s^1 + 4eW_s + eW_s^2}{6},$$

$$V\left(\sqrt{Var\left(\tilde{W}_s\right)}\right) = \frac{\sqrt{vW_s^1} + 4\sqrt{vW_s} + \sqrt{vW_s^2}}{6} \tag{5}$$

On the basis of the above defuzzified values of the TFNs, the multi-objective linear programming (MOLP) in crisp environment is constructed from the model (2) and model (4) as

$$\text{Max } V\left(\tilde{Z}_1\right) = \sum_{c=1}^{C}\sum_{s=1}^{S} V\left(\tilde{P}_{cs}\right) x_{cs}$$

$$\text{Min } V\left(\tilde{Z}_2\right) = \sum_{c=1}^{C}\sum_{s=1}^{S} V\left(\tilde{E}_{cs}\right) x_{cs}$$

subject to

$$\sum_{c=1}^{C} x_{cs} \leq V(\tilde{A}_s); \left(s = 1, 2, \ldots, S\right)$$

$$\sum_{c=1}^{C} V\left(\tilde{H}_{cs}\right) x_{cs} \geq V\left(\tilde{H}_s\right); \left(s = 1, 2, \ldots, S\right)$$

$$\sum_{c=1}^{C} V\left(\tilde{D}_{cs}\right) x_{cs} \geq V\left(\tilde{D}_s\right); \left(s = 1, 2, \ldots, S\right)$$

$$\sum_{c=1}^{C}\sum_{s=1}^{S} V\left(\tilde{F}_{tcs}\right) x_{cs} \leq V\left(\tilde{F}_t\right); \left(t = 1, 2, \ldots, T\right)$$

$$\sum_{c=1}^{C} V\left(\tilde{W}_{cs}\right) x_{cs} \geq V\left(E\left(\tilde{W}_s\right)\right) + \Phi^{-1}\left(\gamma_s\right) V\left(\sqrt{Var\left(\tilde{W}_s\right)}\right)\left(s = 1, 2, \ldots, S\right)$$

$$x_{cs} \geq V\left(\tilde{L}_{cs}\right);\ \left(c = 1, 2, \ldots, C; s = 1, 2, \ldots, S\right) \tag{6}$$

or,

$$\text{Max } V\left(\tilde{Z}_1\right) = \sum_{c=1}^{C} \sum_{s=1}^{S} \frac{P_{cs}^1 + 4P_{cs} + P_{cs}^2}{6} x_{cs}$$

$$\text{Min } V\left(\tilde{Z}_2\right) = \sum_{c=1}^{C} \sum_{s=1}^{S} \frac{E_{cs}^1 + 4E_{cs} + E_{cs}^2}{6} x_{cs}$$

subject to

$$\sum_{c=1}^{C} x_{cs} \leq \frac{A_s^1 + 4A_s + A_s^2}{6};\ \left(s = 1, 2, \ldots, S\right)$$

$$\sum_{c=1}^{C} \frac{H_{cs}^1 + 4H_{cs} + H_{cs}^2}{6} x_{cs} \geq \frac{H_s^1 + 4H_s + H_s^2}{6};\ \left(s = 1, 2, \ldots, S\right)$$

$$\sum_{c=1}^{C} \frac{D_{cs}^1 + 4D_{cs} + D_{cs}^2}{6} x_{cs} \geq \frac{D_s^1 + 4D_s + D_s^2}{6};\ \left(s = 1, 2, \ldots, S\right)$$

$$\sum_{c=1}^{C} \sum_{s=1}^{S} \frac{F_{tcs}^1 + 4F_{tcs} + F_{tcs}^2}{6} x_{cs} \leq \frac{F_t^1 + 4F_t + F_t^2}{6};\ \left(t = 1, 2, \ldots, T\right)$$

$$\sum_{c=1}^{C} \frac{W_{cs}^1 + 4W_{cs} + W_{cs}^2}{6} x_{cs} \geq \frac{eW_s^1 + 4eW_s + eW_s^2}{6} +$$
$$\Phi^{-1}\left(\gamma_s\right) \frac{\sqrt{vW_s^1} + 4\sqrt{vW_s} + \sqrt{vW_s^2}}{6}\ \left(s = 1, 2, \ldots, S\right)$$

$$x_{cs} \geq \frac{L_{cs}^1 + 4L_{cs} + L_{cs}^2}{6};\ \left(c = 1, 2, \ldots, C; s = 1, 2, \ldots, S\right) \tag{7}$$

10.2.4 Fuzzy Goals and Membership Functions

As explained in the previous chapters the MOLP model is now solved in crisp environment using the *software* LINGO (ver.11) to find best and worst values of two objectives. Let $V\left(\tilde{Z}_1\right)^b$, $V\left(\tilde{Z}_1\right)^w$ be the best and worst value of the objective $V\left(\tilde{Z}_1\right)$ representing the production of the crops and $V\left(\tilde{Z}_2\right)^b$, $V\left(\tilde{Z}_2\right)^w$ be the best and worst value of the objective $V\left(\tilde{Z}_2\right)$ expressing the total expenditure in agricultural sector, respectively.

Then, the fuzzy goal of the objectives is expressed as:

$$\sum_{c=1}^{C}\sum_{s=1}^{S}\frac{P_{cs}^1 + 4P_{cs} + P_{cs}^2}{6} x_{cs} \gtrsim V\left(\tilde{Z}_1\right)^b \tag{8}$$

$$\sum_{c=1}^{C}\sum_{s=1}^{S}V\left(\tilde{E}_{cs}\right)x_{cs} \lesssim V\left(\tilde{Z}_2\right)^b \tag{9}$$

On the basis of the above defined fuzzy goals, the membership function of each objective is formed as

$$\mu_{V(\tilde{Z}_1)} = \begin{cases} 0 & if & \sum_{c=1}^{C}\sum_{s=1}^{S}\frac{P_{cs}^1 + 4P_{cs} + P_{cs}^2}{6}x_{cs} \leq V\left(\tilde{Z}_1\right)^w \\[3mm] \dfrac{\sum_{c=1}^{C}\sum_{s=1}^{S}\frac{P_{cs}^1 + 4P_{cs} + P_{cs}^2}{6}x_{cs} - V\left(\tilde{Z}_1\right)^w}{V\left(\tilde{Z}_1\right)^b - V\left(\tilde{Z}_1\right)^w} & if & V\left(\tilde{Z}_1\right)^w \leq \sum_{c=1}^{C}\sum_{s=1}^{S}\frac{P_{cs}^1 + 4P_{cs} + P_{cs}^2}{6}x_{cs} \leq V\left(\tilde{Z}_1\right)^b \\[3mm] 1 & if & \sum_{c=1}^{C}\sum_{s=1}^{S}\frac{P_{cs}^1 + 4P_{cs} + P_{cs}^2}{6}x_{cs} \geq V\left(\tilde{Z}_1\right)^b \end{cases} \tag{10}$$

$$\mu_{V(\tilde{Z}_2)} = \begin{cases} 0 & \text{if} \quad \sum_{c=1}^{C}\sum_{s=1}^{S} V\left(\tilde{E}_{cs}\right) x_{cs} \geq V\left(\tilde{Z}_2\right)^w \\ \dfrac{V\left(\tilde{Z}_2\right)^w - \sum_{c=1}^{C}\sum_{s=1}^{S} V\left(\tilde{E}_{cs}\right) x_{cs}}{V\left(\tilde{Z}_2\right)^w - V\left(\tilde{Z}_2\right)^b} & \text{if} \quad V\left(\tilde{Z}_2\right)^b \leq \sum_{c=1}^{C}\sum_{s=1}^{S} V\left(\tilde{E}_{cs}\right) x_{cs} \leq V\left(\tilde{Z}_2\right)^w \\ 1 & \text{if} \quad \sum_{c=1}^{C}\sum_{s=1}^{S} V\left(\tilde{E}_{cs}\right) x_{cs} \leq V\left(\tilde{Z}_2\right)^b \end{cases}$$

$$(11)$$

With the above defined membership functions the FGP model is developed in the next section.

10.3 FUZZY GOAL PROGRAMMING MODEL FORMULATION

After the membership function of each objective is constructed, an FGP model is formulated considering above defined membership functions as flexible membership goals by introducing under- and over- deviational variables to each of them and thereby assigning the highest membership value (unity) as the aspiration level to each of them. As explained in the previous chapters, the under-deviational variables are minimized in FGP to achieve the aspired goal values of objectives as much as possible in the decision making environment.

Thus an FGP model for the model (6) and model (7) is formulated as follows.

$$\text{Min D} = w_1 d_1^- + w_2 d_2^-$$

and satisfy $\mu_{V(\tilde{Z}_1)} + d_1^- - d_1^+ = 1$;

$$\mu_{V(\tilde{Z}_2)} + d_2^- - d_2^+ = 1;$$

$$\sum_{c=1}^{C} x_{cs} \leq \frac{A_s^1 + 4A_s + A_s^2}{6}; \quad \left(s = 1, 2, \ldots, S\right)$$

$$\sum_{c=1}^{C} \frac{H_{cs}^1 + 4H_{cs} + H_{cs}^2}{6} x_{cs} \geq \frac{H_s^1 + 4H_s + H_s^2}{6}; \left(s = 1, 2, \ldots, S\right)$$

$$\sum_{c=1}^{C} \frac{D_{cs}^1 + 4D_{cs} + D_{cs}^2}{6} x_{cs} \geq \frac{D_s^1 + 4D_s + D_s^2}{6}; \left(s = 1, 2, \ldots, S\right)$$

$$\sum_{c=1}^{C} \sum_{s=1}^{S} \frac{F_{tcs}^1 + 4F_{tcs} + F_{tcs}^2}{6} x_{cs} \leq \frac{F_t^1 + 4F_t + F_t^2}{6}; \left(t = 1, 2, \ldots, T\right)$$

$$\sum_{c=1}^{C} \frac{W_{cs}^1 + 4W_{cs} + W_{cs}^2}{6} x_{cs} \geq \frac{eW_s^1 + 4eW_s + eW_s^2}{6} +$$

$$\Phi^{-1}\left(\gamma_s\right) \frac{\sqrt{vW_s^1} + 4\sqrt{vW_s} + \sqrt{vW_s^2}}{6} \left(s = 1, 2, \ldots, S\right)$$

$$x_{cs} \geq \frac{L_{cs}^1 + 4L_{cs} + L_{cs}^2}{6}; \left(c = 1, 2, \ldots, C; s = 1, 2, \ldots, S\right) \tag{12}$$

Finally, the developed model (12) is solved to find the most satisfactory optimal solution in the decision making environment.

10.4 SOLUTION ALGORITHM

The methodology for describing the above model is presented in the form of an algorithm as follows

Step 1: CCP methodology in hybrid uncertain environment is applied to the fuzzy stochastic programming model to form a fuzzy programming model.
Step 2: On the basis of Canonical form of FNs, the fuzzy constraints and the fuzzy objectives are defuzzified.
Step 3: The individual optimal value of each of the objective is found in isolation under modified set of system constraints.
Step 4: Construct the fuzzy goals of each of the objectives.
Step 5: Linear membership function of each objective is formed.

Step 6: FGP approach is used to achieve maximum degree of each of the membership goals.

Step 7: Stop.

In the next section, a case example is taken into consideration to demonstrate the methodology discussed in this book.

10.5 A CASE STUDY OF A LAND UTILIZATION PLANNING IN AGRICULTURAL SYSTEM

The land-use planning problem for production of the principal crops of the Nadia district in West Bengal, India is considered to illustrate the proposed methodology. The available data of the previous planning years were collected from different sources of agricultural planning units.

The agricultural crop year in India is from July to June. During this planning year there are mainly three seasonal crop-cycles; viz. Pre-Khariff, Khariff and Rabi successively appear in the state West Bengal. The khariff crops are sown in the period between June/July and harvested in September/October, i.e., within the rainy season of West Bengal. The Rabi season and Pre-Khariff season take place between October/November to March/April and March/April to May/June, respectively. Generally, Aman-Paddy and Sugarcane are the two common crop harvested in Khariff season. Wheat, Mustard, Lentil, Boro-paddy and Potato are mainly cultivated in Rabi season, and Jute, Sugarcane, Aus-Paddy are cultivated in the Pre-Khariff season.

The different types of seasonal crops and the associated decision variables used in the proposed model are given in Table 1.

Here $x_{21} = x_{22} = x_{23}$

As the production of various crops in different seasons depends on mainly climate conditions, soil quality and demands of crops, therefore, these are imprecise in nature. Also, the expenditure in agricultural sector depends on soil conditions, price of different seeds, number of farmers/labours involved, and wage of the farmers. So these resources are considered as TFNs which are represented in Table 2.

Also from the available data it is observed that the total farming land, total machine hours, total man-days required for a particular season varies

Table 1. Seasonal crops and associated decision variables

Season (s)	Crop (c)	Variable $\left(x_{cs}\right)$
Pre-Khariff (1)	Jute (1)	x_{11}
	Sugarcane (2)	x_{21}
	Aus-paddy (3)	x_{31}
Khariff (2)	Sugarcane (2)	x_{22}
	Aman-paddy (4)	x_{42}
Rabi (3)	Sugarcane (2)	x_{23}
	Boro-paddy (5)	x_{53}
	Wheat (6)	x_{63}
	Mustard (7)	x_{73}
	Potato (8)	x_{83}
	Lentil (9)	x_{93}

in different planning years. So these three parameters are also taken as TFNs which are given in Table 3.

Again average machine hours, average man-days are fluctuating in different seasons of various planning years. So these parameters are considered as TFNs which are presented in Table 4.

Since, the production of different crops in agricultural sector is not precise in general as it's depends on quality of soil, therefore the requirement of fertilizers (Basak, 2000) varies in different seasons of a planning year. Also to maintain the soil quality, to increase the production of different crops, there is an increasing demand of using compost by the cultivator in recent

Table 2. Production and expenditure of various seasonal crops

Crop (c)	Production $\tilde{P}_{cs}$ (Kg/ha)	Expenditure $\tilde{E}_{cs}$ (Rs/ha)
Jute $(1)\,x_{11}$	$\widetilde{2717} = \big(2700, 2717, 2750\big)$	$\widetilde{17430} = \big(17000, 17430, 17500\big)$
Sugarcane $(2)\,x_{21}$	$\widetilde{67676} = \big(67100, 67676, 68400\big)$	$\widetilde{30922} = \big(30450, 30922, 30950\big)$
Aus-Paddy $(3)\,x_{31}$	$\widetilde{3979} = \big(3900, 3979, 4000\big)$	$\widetilde{14500} = \big(12500, 14500, 14800\big)$
Aman-Paddy $(4)\,x_{42}$	$\widetilde{4644} = \big(4600, 4644, 4800\big)$	$\widetilde{14000} = \big(13200, 14000, 14200\big)$
Boro-Paddy $(5)\,x_{53}$	$\widetilde{5625} = \big(5615, 5625, 5800\big)$	$\widetilde{25000} = \big(23200, 25000, 25100\big)$
Wheat $(6)\,x_{63}$	$\widetilde{3309} = \big(3300, 3309, 3310\big)$	$\widetilde{12000} = \big(10500, 12000, 12300\big)$
Mustard $(7)\,x_{73}$	$\widetilde{1240} = \big(1220, 1240, 1260\big)$	$\widetilde{8700} = \big(8200, 8700, 8800\big)$
Potato $(8)\,x_{83}$	$\widetilde{25218} = \big(25000, 25218, 25450\big)$	$\widetilde{35932} = \big(35200, 35932, 36000\big)$
Lentil $(9)\,x_{93}$	$\widetilde{1316} = \big(1300, 1316, 1320\big)$	$\widetilde{6500} = \big(5800, 6500, 6600\big)$

Figure 1a. Map of West Bengal

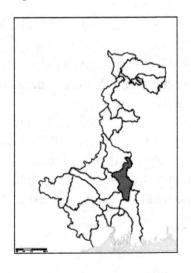

Figure 1b. Agricultural map of West Bengal

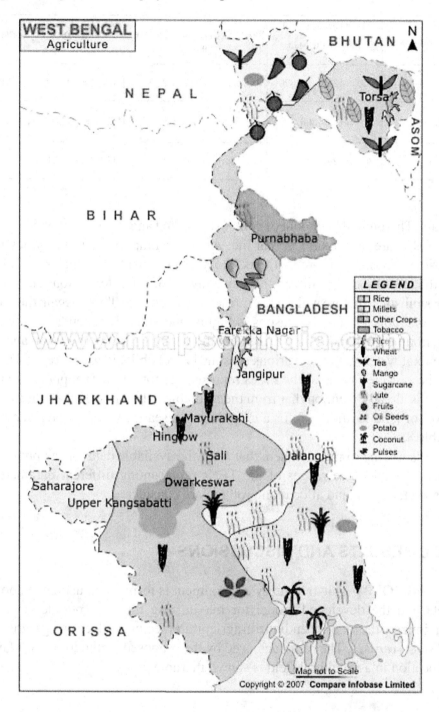

Table 3. Data description for productive resources

Season (s)	Total Farming Land ($\tilde{A}_s$ in ('000 ha)	Total Machine Hours $\tilde{H}_s$ in ('00 hrs)	Total Man-Days $\tilde{D}_s$ in ('000 days)
Pre-Khariff	$\widetilde{300} = (299, 300, 320)$	$\widetilde{145.22} = (145, 145.22, 146)$	$\widetilde{14.27} = (14.25, 14.27, 14.29)$
Khariff	$\widetilde{300} = (299, 300, 320)$	$\widetilde{72.54} = (72, 72.54, 73)$	$\widetilde{6.51} = (6.50, 6.51, 6.52)$
Rabi	$\widetilde{300} = (299, 300, 320)$	$\widetilde{353.73} = (353, 353.73, 354.5)$	$\widetilde{11.31} = (11.3, 11.31, 11.32)$

years. Therefore the amount of compost required and the amount of compost available are not precise in real life. Also consumption of water varies for various crops. Therefore in Table 5, total requirement of fertilizer, in Table 6, the utilization of fertilizer, the consumption of water for various crops are possibilistic in nature which are represented in terms of TFNs. Again the total water supply in various seasons is highly uncertain. It depends largely on environmental conditions i.e. the amount of rain happen in a season and so the total water supply in various seasons is probabilistic in nature. In Table 7, the expected value of the FRVs representing total water supply is given.

It is already mention that from the available data it is seen that minimum level of land is allocated for a crop during a season which is presented in Table 8.

It is worthy to mention here that from the available data for the previous years the tolerance ranges of the TFNs representing different parameters associated with land allocation problem are considered.

10.6 RESULTS AND DISCUSSIONS

The FSMOLP problem in fuzzy environment is formulated using the above data and the developed model for maximizing the total production and minimizing the total expenditure in agricultural sector is solved using *software LINGO (ver. 11)*. The result achieved by the proposed methodology for land allocation in agricultural field is shown in Table 9.

Table 4. Data description for utilization of resources

Season	Crops	Average Machine Hours $\tilde{H}_{cs}$ in (hrs/ha)	Average Man-Days $\tilde{D}_{cs}$ in (days/ha)
Pre-Khariff	Jute $(1)\,x_{11}$	$\widetilde{66} = (64, 66, 68)$	$\widetilde{90} = (88, 90, 92)$
	Sugarcane $(2)\,x_{21}$	$\widetilde{58.2} = (56, 58.2, 60.4)$	$\widetilde{41} = (39, 41, 43)$
	Aus-Paddy $(3)\,x_{31}$	$\widetilde{139} = (136, 139, 142)$	$\widetilde{60} = (57, 60, 63)$
Khariff	Aman-Paddy $(4)\,x_{42}$	$\widetilde{66} = (64, 66, 68)$	$\widetilde{60} = (58, 60, 62)$
	Sugarcane $(2)\,x_{21}$	$\widetilde{58.2} = (56, 58.2, 60.4)$	$\widetilde{41} = (39, 41, 43)$
Rabi	Sugarcane $(2)\,x_{21}$	$\widetilde{58.2} = (56, 58.2, 60.4)$	$\widetilde{41} = (39, 41, 43)$
	Boro-Paddy $(5)\,x_{53}$	$\widetilde{267} = (262, 267, 272)$	$\widetilde{60} = (58, 60, 62)$
	Wheat $(6)\,x_{63}$	$\widetilde{66} = (65.5, 66, 66.5)$	$\widetilde{39} = (38, 39, 40)$
	Mustard $(7)\,x_{73}$	$\widetilde{33.5} = (33, 33.5, 34)$	$\widetilde{30} = (28, 30, 32)$
	Potato $(8)\,x_{83}$	$\widetilde{112} = (111, 112, 115)$	$\widetilde{70} = (67, 70, 73)$
	Lentil $(9)\,x_{93}$	$\widetilde{49} = (48.5, 49, 49.5)$	$\widetilde{15} = (14, 15, 16)$

The existing land allocation and production based on the collected are presented in Table 10.

The comparison of the land allocation between the proposed methodology and existing land allocation is shown in Figure 2.

The comparison of production of various crops in different seasons between the achieved solutions and existing production data are shown in Figure 3.

The existing annual expenditure and expenditure obtained by proposed methodology are INR 6733.40 million, and INR 10976.30 million respectively.

Table 5. Data description for requirement of fertilizer

Fertilizer ($\tilde{F}_t$)	Amount ('000mt)
Nitrogen (N)	$\widetilde{52} = \left(51, 52, 53\right)$
Phosphate (P)	$\widetilde{32} = \left(31, 32, 32.5\right)$
Potash (K)	$\widetilde{24.5} = \left(24, 24.5, 24.8\right)$

Figure 2. Comparison between land allocation

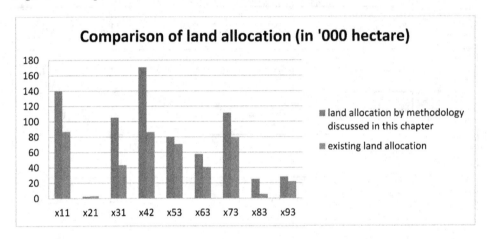

Figure 3. Comparison between production of various crops

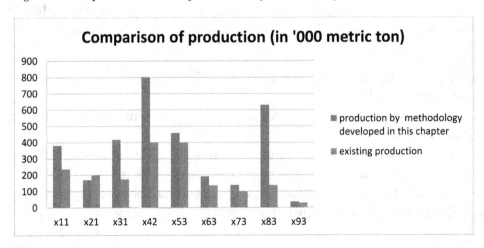

Table 6. Data description for utilization of fertilizer and consumption of water

Crops	Nitrogen N (Kg/ha)	Phosphate P (Kg/ha)	Potash K (Kg/ha)	Water Consumption $\widetilde{W}_{cs}$ (inch/ha)
Jute $(1)\, x_{11}$	$\widetilde{39} = (36,39,41)$	$\widetilde{20} = (18,20,22)$	$\widetilde{19} = (17,19,21)$	$\widetilde{20} = (19.5,20,20.5)$
Sugarcane $(2)\, x_{21}$	$\widetilde{200} = (175,200,225)$	$\widetilde{100} = (96,100,105)$	$\widetilde{100} = (90,100,110)$	$\widetilde{60} = (57.5,60,62.5)$
Aus-Paddy $(3)\, x_{31}$	$\widetilde{41} = (39,41,43)$	$\widetilde{20.5} = (20,20.5,21)$	$\widetilde{21} = (20,21,22)$	$\widetilde{34} = (32.2,34,35.8)$
Aman-Paddy $(4)\, x_{42}$	$\widetilde{36.5} = (36,36.5,37)$	$\widetilde{19} = (18,19,20)$	$\widetilde{21} = (20,21,22)$	$\widetilde{50} = (47.8,50,50.2)$
Boro-Paddy $(5)\, x_{53}$	$\widetilde{110} = (100,110,120)$	$\widetilde{51} = (47,51,55)$	$\widetilde{51} = (47,51,55)$	$\widetilde{70} = (69,70,71)$
Wheat $(6)\, x_{63}$	$\widetilde{110} = (100,110,120)$	$\widetilde{58} = (53,58,60)$	$\widetilde{58} = (55,58,60)$	$\widetilde{15} = (14.8,15,15.2)$
Mustard $(7)\, x_{73}$	$\widetilde{83} = (80,83,86)$	$\widetilde{41} = (40,41,42)$	$\widetilde{41} = (40,41,42)$	$\widetilde{10} = (9.6,10,10.4)$
Potato $(8)\, x_{83}$	$\widetilde{150} = (135,150,165)$	$\widetilde{78} = (70,78,85)$	$\widetilde{78} = (70,78,85)$	$\widetilde{18} = (17.3,18,18.7)$
Lentil $(9)\, x_{93}$	$\widetilde{22.5} = (20,22.5,25)$	$\widetilde{63} = (60,63,65)$	$\widetilde{27} = (25,27,29)$	$\widetilde{10} = (9.5,10,10.5)$

Table 7. Data description of supply of water

Season	$E\left(\tilde{W}_s\right)$ (inch/ha)	$\sqrt{Var\left(\tilde{W}_s\right)}$ (inch/ha)
Pre-Khariff	$\widetilde{5000} = \left(4600, 5000, 5300\right)$	$\widetilde{411} = \left(405, 411, 415\right)$
Khariff	$\widetilde{6200} = \left(6100, 6200, 6300\right)$	$\widetilde{492} = \left(485, 492, 497\right)$
Rabi	$\widetilde{11000} = \left(10750, 11000, 11500\right)$	$\widetilde{1975} = \left(1950, 1975, 1995\right)$

Table 8. Minimum level of land utilization for various crops

Crops	Minimum Land Utilization $\tilde{L}_{cs}$ ('000 ha)
Jute $\left(1\right) x_{11}$	$\widetilde{139} = \left(135, 139, 145\right)$
Sugarcane $\left(2\right) x_{21}$	$\widetilde{1.5} = \left(1.2, 1.5, 2.1\right)$
Aus-Paddy $\left(3\right) x_{31}$	$\widetilde{43} = \left(42, 43, 50\right)$
Aman-Paddy $\left(4\right) x_{42}$	$\widetilde{92} = \left(91, 92, 94\right)$
Boro-Paddy $\left(5\right) x_{53}$	$\widetilde{80} = \left(78, 80, 86\right)$
Wheat $\left(6\right) x_{63}$	$\widetilde{57} = \left(56, 57, 60\right)$
Mustard $\left(7\right) x_{73}$	$\widetilde{110} = \left(109, 110, 115\right)$
Potato $\left(8\right) x_{83}$	$\widetilde{25} = \left(24, 25, 26\right)$
Lentil $\left(9\right) x_{93}$	$\widetilde{30} = \left(27, 30, 33\right)$

Table 9. Achieved solution

Crop	Jute (1)	Sugarcane (2)	Aus Paddy (3)	AmanPaddy (4)	Boro Paddy (5)	Wheat (6)	Mustard (7)	Potato (8)	Lentil (9)
Land allocation in (ha)	140000	2499	105244	170780	80257	57666	111333	25000	28000
Production ('000 mt)	379.13	168.24	415.23	709.80	453.74	189.6	138.05	631.11	36.74

Table 10. Existing land allocation and production

Crop	Jute (1)	Sugarcane (2)	Aus-Paddy (3)	Aman-Paddy (4)	Boro-Paddy (5)	Wheat (6)	Mustard (7)	Potato (8)	Lentil (9)
Land allocation in (ha)	86815	2940	43500	86250	70800	40900	79500	5450	21800
Production ('000mt)	236.11	198.97	173.12	400.55	398.32	135.37	98.63	137.44	28.71

The annual expenditure obtained by solving the mathematical models for cultivating crops in various seasons is compared to the existing annual expenditure in Figure 4.

From this diagram it is seen that the annual expenditure for cultivating various crops obtained by methodology developed in this chapter increases than the existing annual expenditure. Because in this methodology the authors give emphasize to the utilization of the land to increase the production as much as possible not on expenditure. As in the country like India where the population is very high proper land utilization is extremely important.

Again the existing total annual income in previous year is INR 31199.30 million, whereas the total annual income obtained by developed methodology is INR 53117.70 million. The annual income obtained by the suggested methodology from different crops in various seasons is compared to the existing annual income in Figure 5.

This shows that although the expenditure is slightly increased than the existing annual expenditure, but the total annual income is much higher than the existing annual income. Also the production of various crops increases which is realistic as the population also gradually increases. Also from the results obtained by methodology presented in this chapter, it is seen that the

Figure 4. Comparison between expenditure for cultivating crops

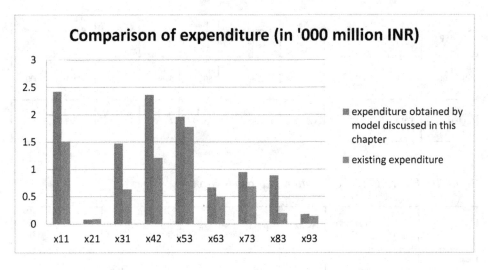

Figure 5. Comparison between annual income

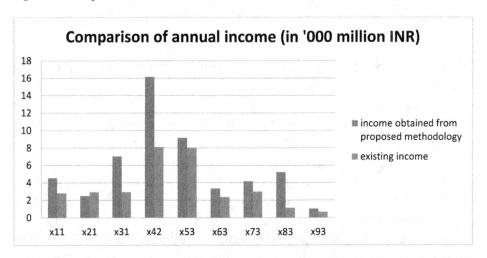

production of Aman-Paddy is much higher than the Aus-Paddy. This result is more acceptable in real life, because the production of Aman-Paddy suits the environmental conditions of West Bengal much more than the Aus-Paddy production. Also the demand of Aman-Paddy and Boro-Paddy in market is much higher than the Aus-Paddy in West Bengal. This indicates that this methodology gives more scientific and better land allocation for a season for the various crops. Thus this suggested methodology is much more acceptable to the agricultural planners.

10.7 CONCLUSION

In this methodology a FGP model for optimal land allocation problem in an agricultural system is demonstrated in fuzzy stochastic environment. This research article provides a new look into the way of analysing the different farm-related activities in an imprecise decision making environment. After analysing the results, the model recommends more land allocation than the existing land allocation for cultivating various crops in different seasons of a planning year and thus this proposed methodology is more acceptable to the agricultural planners. This proposed model can be used for agricultural planning in any part of the country. Again in future different input parameters involved with the agricultural land allocation problems can be represented in the form of intuitionistic FN, as, in insufficient supplied data or information, intuitionistic fuzzy set can be defined more precisely than fuzzy set. Also in this article only the parameter representing water supply is taken as FRV. But the same amounts of probabilistic uncertainties are also involved with the other parameters. Therefore if all parameters of the model are considered as FRVs, then the model becomes more realistic, however very much complicated. For this reason other parameters are considered as fuzzy parameters. In future research work all the parameters may be taken as FRVs whose parameters are FN of various forms. However it is hoped that this solution procedure can contribute to the future studies in farming and may open up new vistas into the way of making decisions in complex agricultural planning problems in hybrid multi-objective decision making (MODM) arena.

REFERENCES

Adams, R. M., King, G. A., & Johnson, W. E. (1977). Effects of energy cost increases and regional allocation policies on agriculture production. *American Journal of Agricultural Economics*, 59(3), 444–455. doi:10.2307/1239646

Arnold, G. W., & Bennet, D. (1975). The problem of finding an optimal solution in: Study of agricultural systems. In G. E. Dalton (Ed.), Applied Science publishers (pp. 129–173). London: Academic Press.

Basak, R. K. (2000). *Soil testing and fertilizer recommendation*. New Delhi: Kalyani Publisher.

Bellman, R. E., & Zadeh, L. A. (1970). Decision making in a fuzzy environment. *Management Science*, *17*(4), 141–164. doi:10.1287/mnsc.17.4.B141

Biswas, A., & Modak, N. (2017). A Multiobjective Fuzzy Chance Constrained Programming Model for Land Allocation Planning in Agricultural Sector: A case study. International Journal of Computational Intelligence Systems, 10(1), 196-211. doi: org/ doi:10.2991/ijcis.2017.10.1.14

Biswas, A., & Pal, B. B. (2005). Application of fuzzy goal programming technique to land use planning in agricultural system. *Omega*, *33*(5), 391–398. doi:10.1016/j.omega.2004.07.003

Black, J. R., & Hlubik, J. (1980). Basics of computerized linear programs for ration formulation. *Journal of Dairy Science*, *63*(8), 1366–1378. doi:10.3168/jds.S0022-0302(80)83090-6

Charnes, A., & Cooper, W. W. (1961). *Management Models and Industrial Application of Linear Programming*. New York: John Wiley & Sons Inc.

Cui, L., Li, Y., & Huang, G. (2015). Planning an Agricultural Water Resources Management System: A Two-Stage Stochastic Fractional Programming Model. *Sustainability*, *7*(8), 9846–9863. doi:10.3390u7089846

Dutta, S., Sahoo, B. C., Mishra, R., & Acharya, S. (2016). Fuzzy Stochastic Genetic Algorithm for Obtaining Optimum Crops Pattern and Water Balance in a Farm. *Water Resources Management*, *30*(12), 4097–4123. doi:10.100711269-016-1406-7

Ghosh, D., Sharma, D. K., & Mattison, D. (2005). Goal programming formulation in nutrient management for rice production. *International Journal of Production Economics*, *95*(1), 1–7. doi:10.1016/j.ijpe.2003.09.018

Glen, J. (1987). Mathematical models in farm planning: A survey. *Operations Research*, *35*(5), 641–666. doi:10.1287/opre.35.5.641

Hannan, E. L. (1980). Linear programming with multiple fuzzy goals. *Fuzzy Sets and Systems*, *6*(3), 235–248. doi:10.1016/0165-0114(81)90002-6

Heady, E. O. (1954). Simplified presentation and logical aspects of linear programming technique. *Journal of Farm Economics*, *36*(5), 1035–1048. doi:10.2307/1234313

Ignizio, J. P. (1976). *Goal Programming and Extensions*. Lexington, MA: Lexington Books.

Ijiri, Y. (1965). *Management Goals and Accounting for Control*. Amsterdam: North Holland.

Jana, R. K., Sharma, D. K., & Chakraborty, B. (2016). A hybrid probabilistic fuzzy goal programming approach for agricultural decision-making. *International Journal of Production Economics*, *173*, 134–141. doi:10.1016/j. ijpe.2015.12.010

Lee, S. M., & Clayton, E. R. (1972). A Goal Programming Model for Academic Resource Allocation. *Management Science*, *18*(8), 395–408. doi:10.1287/ mnsc.18.8.B395

Leenhardt, D., Trouvat, J. L., Gonzalès, G., Pérarnaud, V., Prats, S., & Bergez, J. E. (2004). Estimating irrigation demand for water management on a regional scale. I. ADEAUMIS, a simulation platform based on bio-decisional modelling and spatial information. *Agricultural Water Management*, *68*(3), 207–232. doi:10.1016/j.agwat.2004.04.004

Li, Y. P., Huang, G. H., Wang, G. Q., & Huang, Y. F. (2009). A hybrid fuzzy-stochastic water-management model for agricultural sustainability under uncertainty. *Agricultural Water Management*, *96*(12), 1807–1818. doi:10.1016/j.agwat.2009.07.019

Lu, H., Du, P., Chen, Y., & He, L. (2016). A credibility-based chance constrained optimization model for integrated agricultural and water resources management: A case study in south central china. *Journal of Hydrology (Amsterdam)*, *537*, 408–418. doi:10.1016/j.jhydrol.2016.03.056

Murmu, S., & Biswas, S. (2015). Application of Fuzzy Logic and Nural Network in Crop Classification: A Review. *Aquatic Procedia*, *4*, 1203–1210. doi:10.1016/j.aqpro.2015.02.153

Narasimhan, R. (1980). On fuzzy goal programming–Some comments. *Decision Sciences*, *11*, 532–538. doi:10.1111/j.1540-5915.1980.tb01142.x

Nix, J. (1979). Farm management, The state of the art (or Science). *Journal of Agricultural Economics*, *30*(3), 277–292. doi:10.1111/j.1477-9552.1979. tb02143.x

Oliveria, F., Volpi, N., & Sanquetta, C. (2003). Goal programming in planning problem. *Applied Mathematics and Computation*, *140*(1), 165–178. doi:10.1016/S0096-3003(02)00220-5

Pal, B. B., & Basu, I. (1996). Selection of appropriate priority structure for optimal land allocation in agricultural planning through goal programming. *Indian Journal of Agricultural Economics*, *51*, 342–354.

Pal, B. B., & Moitra, B. N. (2003). Fuzzy goal programming approach to long-term land allocation planning problem in agricultural system: A case study. In *Proceedings of the fifth International Conference on Advances in Pattern Recognition*. Allied Publishers Pvt. Ltd.

Qingzhen, Z., Changyu, W., Zhimin, Z., Yunxiang, Z., & Chuanjiang, W. (1991). The application of operations research in the optimization of agricultural production. *Operations Research*, *39*(2), 194–205. doi:10.1287/opre.39.2.194

Romero, C. (1986). A survey of generalized goal programming (1970–1982). *European Journal of Operational Research*, *25*(2), 183–191. doi:10.1016/0377-2217(86)90084-6

Sahoo, B., Lohani, A. K., & Sahu, R. K. (2006). Fuzzy multi-objective and linear programming based management models for optimal land–water–crop system planning. *Water Resources Management*, *20*(6), 931–948. doi:10.100711269-005-9015-x

Saker, R. A., & Quaddus, M. A. (2002). Modelling a nationwide crop planning problem using a multiple criteria decision making tool. *Computers & Industrial Engineering*, *42*(2-4), 541–553. doi:10.1016/S0360-8352(02)00022-0

Sharma, D. K., & Jana, R. K. (2009). Fuzzy goal programming based genetic algorithm approach to nutrient management for rice crop planning. *International Journal of Production Economics*, *121*(1), 224–232. doi:10.1016/j.ijpe.2009.05.009

Sharma, D. K., Jana, R. K., & Gaur, A. (2007). Fuzzy goal programming for agricultural land allocation problems. *Yugoslav Journal of Operations Research*, *17*(1), 31–42. doi:10.2298/YJOR0701031S

Simmons, R. L., & Pomareda, C. (1975). Equilibrium quantity and timing of Mexican vegetable exports. *American Journal of Agricultural Economics*, *57*(3), 472–479. doi:10.2307/1238410

Subagadis, Y. H., Schütze, N., & Grundmann, J. (2016). A Fuzzy-Stochastic Modeling Approach for Multiple Criteria Decision Analysis of Coupled Groundwater-Agricultural Systems. *Water Resources Management, 30*(6), 2075–2095. doi:10.100711269-016-1270-5

Tamiz, M., Jones, D. F., & El-Darzi, E. (1995). A review of goal programming and its applications. *Annals of Operations Research, 58*(1), 39–53. doi:10.1007/BF02032309

Tanaka, H., Okuda, T., & Asai, K. (1973). On fuzzy mathematical programming. *Journal of Cybernetics and Systems, 3*(4), 37–46. doi:10.1080/01969727308545912

Tsai, Y. J., Mishoe, J. W., & Jones, J. W. (1987). Optimization multiple cropping systems: Simulation studies. *Agricultural Systems, 25*(3), 165–176. doi:10.1016/0308-521X(87)90018-7

Wang, P., Li, J., & Li, J. (2006). The system reform and development trend of irrigation water management in China. *Zhongguo Nongcun Shuili Shuidian, 4*, 18–20.

Wiens, T. B. (1976). Peasant, risk aversion and allocative behaviour: A quadratic programming experiment. *American Journal of Agricultural Economics, 58*(4), 629–635. doi:10.2307/1238805

Zeng, X., Kang, S., Li, F., Zhang, L., & Guo, P. (2010). Fuzzy multi-objective linear programming applying to crop area planning. *Agricultural Water Management, 98*(1), 134–142. doi:10.1016/j.agwat.2010.08.010

Zhou, H., Zhang, H., Zhang, C., & Xiao, J. M. (2007). Optimization and evaluation of multi-objective crop pattern based on irrigation water resources allocation. *Nongye Gongcheng Xuebao (Beijing), 23*, 45–49.

Conclusion

This book in its first part makes an attempt to present various multi-objective linear and non-linear mathematical programming models under fuzzy stochastic uncertain environments in front of the readers and then in its last part these developed models are applied scientifically to solve different real-life decision-making problems.

It is a well-known fact to all the researchers and decision makers that the real-life decision-making problems become more and more complex in nature and involves different types of uncertain parameters due to the presence of uncertain or imprecise data or linguistic information. These uncertainties can generally be expressed in possibilistic and probabilistic manners. In this book the authors have already explained that the existing methodologies on multi-objective decision making in crisp environments fails to handle these types of complex decision-making problems and hence cannot provide satisfactory solution acceptable to the decision makers in imprecise decision making environments. Therefore, it is necessary to develop some methodologies through which these mathematical programming problems under uncertain environment can be solved successfully. Throughout the book, various methodologies on multi-objective decision making under fuzzy stochastic uncertain environment are presented by the authors.

Throughout this book the authors described several mathematical programming models in fuzzy stochastic environments. The authors give emphasis on fractional and quadratic programming problems as a special case of non-linear programming problems in fuzzy stochastic uncertain environments from the view point of their potential use in many real-life decision-making models. The chance constrained programming technique in fuzzy environment is used throughout the book as a tool to develop fuzzy programming models.

To formulate equivalent multi-objective programming models in crisp environment a large number of predefined well known defuzzification methodologies (which are discussed in the first chapter of this book) are taken into consideration throughout the book. It is also clearly explained the superiority of the methodologies developed in this book with the other predefined methodologies. The authors in this book applied the concept of fuzzy goal programming methodology for achieving best compromise solutions of the objectives acceptable to the decision makers.

Finally, in the last part of the book the developed methodologies in fuzzy stochastic uncertain environments are applied to municipal solid waste management problems, agricultural land use planning problems and multi-choice transportation problems to shows the applicability of those methods in real life contexts. Also the authors explained that the methodologies presented in those chapters cannot be restricted to the above mentioned fields in terms of its applicability, but also can be applied to a wide variety of real life decision making problems.

It is worthy to mention here that from the view point of different methodological developments and applications in several real-life decisions-making fields, the book helps the researchers not only who are already familiar with this branch of mathematics but also it would become very helpful to those people who are apparently new in this field. The authors also hope that after going through the book the readers will be interested to extend their research study in this field.

As the methodological development of multi-objective decision making in uncertain environments and applications to different decision problems is still young in compare to conventional mathematical programming, extensive study in this field is essential to make it a powerful tool for solving real world decision making problems.

About the Authors

Animesh Biswas is now serving as an Associate Professor in the Department of Mathematics, University of Kalyani, India. He joined this university as an Assistant Professor in 2006. Formerly, he served Sikkim Manipal University of Health, Medical and Technological Sciences, Sikkim, India and RCC Institute of Information Technology, Kolkata, India as a Lecturer in Mathematics. He is a Senior Member of IEEE, Computational Intelligence Society, International Economics Development Research Center (IEDRC), Life Member of Indian Statistical Institute, Kolkata, Operational Research Society of India, Tripura Mathematical Society, Tripura, India and Member of World Academy of Science, Engineering and Technology (WASET), International Association of Engineers (IAENG), Soft Computing Research Society, India, Multicriteria Decision Making Society, Germany, etc. The area of his research includes Fuzzy Stochastic Programming, Fuzzy Control, Multicriteria Decision Making in different variants of fuzzy environments, Artificial Intelligence and their applications to real life planning problems. Dr. Biswas have published more than fifty research articles in different leading international journals and conferences. He attended more than twenty international conferences, presented papers and chaired several technical sessions in India and abroad. Five research students have received Ph.D. degree under his supervision. He is one of the reviewers of different leading International Journals and Conferences.

Arnab Kumar De received his bachelor degree in Mathematics from The University of Burdwan, Burdwan, India in the year 2005. In 2007 he obtained his post graduate degree in Applied Mathematics from Jadavpur University, Kolkata, India. He received the Ph.D. degree in Mathematics from University of Kalyani, Kalyani, India in the year 2017. Presently, he is an Assistant Professor of Mathematics in Government College of Engineering and Textile Technology, Serampore, under Maulana Abul Kalam

Azad University of Technology, West Bengal, India. He received National merit Scholarship, U. G. C. merit scholarship for securing first position in first class from The University of Burdwan. Also he got Dharanidhar Roy medal in 2005. He is a member of Indian Statistical Institute, Kolkata and Operational Research Society of India. He published research articles in various international journals and presented papers in several international conferences. His current research interest includes stochastic programming, fuzzy programming, fuzzy stochastic multi-objective decision making, fuzzy multiple criteria decision making, type-II fuzzy set theory, Pythagorean fuzzy set theory, transportation problem, solid waste management, etc.

Index

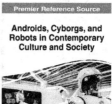

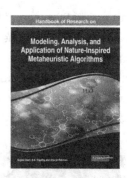

Ensure Quality Research is Introduced to the Academic Community

Become an IGI Global Reviewer for Authored Book Projects

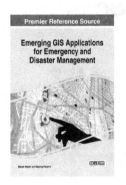

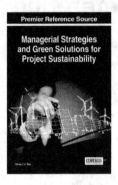

The overall success of an authored book project is dependent on quality and timely reviews.

In this competitive age of scholarly publishing, constructive and timely feedback significantly expedites the turnaround time of manuscripts from submission to acceptance, allowing the publication and discovery of forward-thinking research at a much more expeditious rate. Several IGI Global authored book projects are currently seeking highly qualified experts in the field to fill vacancies on their respective editorial review boards:

Applications may be sent to:
development@igi-global.com

Applicants must have a doctorate (or an equivalent degree) as well as publishing and reviewing experience. Reviewers are asked to write reviews in a timely, collegial, and constructive manner. All reviewers will begin their role on an ad-hoc basis for a period of one year, and upon successful completion of this term can be considered for full editorial review board status, with the potential for a subsequent promotion to Associate Editor.

If you have a colleague that may be interested in this opportunity, we encourage you to share this information with them.